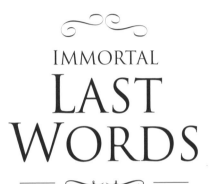

IMMORTAL
LAST
WORDS

'**Don't let it end like this. Tell them I said something.**'

PANCHO VILLA
20 July 1923

Immortal
LAST
WORDS

HISTORY'S MOST MEMORABLE DYING REMARKS, DEATHBED DECLARATIONS AND FINAL FAREWELLS

TERRY BREVERTON

Quercus

INTRODUCTION

Our last words are important – they are a 'keepsake' for future generations, but also our last chance to express how we see ourselves, our lives, the world around us and what really matters when the inevitable happens. Over the millennia, the deathbed has inspired some of history's most memorable, poignant, uplifting and occasionally humorous remarks. The dying words of the great statesmen, poets, scientists, novelists and warriors – the eminent men and women who have shaped world events – are often cited to capture the spirit of the times or inspire great works and deeds. But there are also remarks from individuals who did not have such an impact on history, but whose dying words are equally important as they shed light on the nature of the human condition.

Beginning with '*Living for ever*' – the oldest known epitaph on an Egyptian tomb – this book presents the legendary last words of antiquity, such as the inspiring words of one of the outnumbered and doomed Spartans at Thermopylae: '*If the Persians [Medes] darken the sun with their arrows, we shall have our fight in the shade.*' Ironically, the last words of Socrates, the ancient world's greatest philosopher, were rather more mundane: '*Crito, we owe a cock to Asclepius. Do pay it. Don't forget.*' Most of us know of Julius Caesar's '*Et tu, Brute?*' but around the same time the Roman poet Horace perceptively said of his body of work: '*I have executed a memorial longer lasting than bronze ... I shall not altogether die.*'

Deathbed statements often reflect the character of the speaker or sometimes reveal their deepest thoughts on their worldly deeds. Henry VIII famously uttered: '*Monks! Monks! Monks!*' perhaps hinting at the guilt he felt about the destruction of the monasteries. Nostradamus was uncannily prescient, as he informed his assistant: '*You will not find me alive at sunrise*', whereas Pancho Villa seemed desperate in his last moments, pleading: '*Don't let it end like this. Tell them I said something.*' Oscar Wilde was, as usual, witty as he quipped: '*My wallpaper and I are fighting a duel to the death*', whereas King George V seemed angry as he shouted: '*God damn you!*' to his faithful nurse and housekeeper as he expired.

Other last words are particularly poignant – a line in Kurt Cobain's suicide note reads: '*It's better to burn out than to fade away*' – while others are more humorous, such as the great economist John Maynard Keynes who joked: '*I should have drunk more champagne*', or the celebrity chef Keith Floyd who happily chortled: '*I've not felt this well for ages.*'

The last words in this book have been arranged in chronological order based on the date of the speaker's death. Each dying remark is accompanied by succinct contextual information about the author and a brief explanation of the circumstances that gave rise to the quotation. The 370 entries in this book have been gathered from a wide variety of historical sources such as epitaphs on gravestones and monuments, sayings, speeches, obituaries, pamphlets, newspapers and letters and, of course, the reports of those present when the speaker passed away.

The history of the world is represented in these pages – a voyage through the ages seen through some of history's most memorable final utterances. Some of the sentiments expressed are unbelievably sad while others are optimistic; some final words have become famous while others have remained obscure, but all reflect the follies and greatness of mankind – its heroes and villains, war and peace and the absolute power of language to influence our feelings and challenge our minds. It is written to be informative and entertaining but also, I hope, thought-provoking and inspirational.

Terry Breverton

'Living for ever!'

From the sarcophagus of Menkaura

Menkaura was the pharaoh who built the third and smallest of the pyramids at Giza. His name means 'last long [*men*] the vital forces [*kau*] of the sun god [Ra]'. When he died unexpectedly, work on his sophisticated pyramid complex was abandoned. At the end of the twelfth century, Saladin's son and heir attempted to demolish the pyramids, starting with Menkaura's. He found it almost as expensive to destroy as it had been to build, and gave up. In 1837, the Egyptologist Richard Vyse discovered deep inside the pyramid Menkaura's beautiful basalt sarcophagus. On 13 October, however, it sank with the ship *Beatrice* as she made her way to Britain.

> 'Colonel Vyse says that when he had reached the sarcophagus chamber inside the pyramid, he found there the stone sarcophagus of the king, and the wooden cover of the inside coffin, which was made of cedar. The body of the king had been carried to the upper chamber in the pyramid, and had literally been torn to pieces, most probably when the pyramid was broken open in AD 1196 in search of treasure.
>
> The sarcophagus and cover of the coffin were shipped on board an English vessel; but, alas! the ship was wrecked and the sarcophagus found a resting-place at the bottom of the sea near Gibraltar. Fortunately the wooden cover was cast up by the sea, and the British Museum (third Egyptian Room) possesses this, together with a small fragment of the stone sarcophagus, and some fragments of the mummy. On the cover are two lines of inscription ...
>
> Osiris, king of Upper and Lower Egypt, Menkaura, the ever living, born of Nut [the goddess of the celestial waters, i.e. the sky], substance of Seb [the god of the earth]; thy mother Nut is spread over thee; she renders thee divine by annihilating thy enemies. O king Menkaura, living for ever.'

'All composite things pass away. Strive for your own liberation with diligence.'

Buddha's final words to his attendants

Buddha means Enlightened or Awakened One. The name generally refers to Siddhartha Gautama, the key figure of Buddhism and the Supreme Buddha of the age. According to most traditions, Gautama lived many lives before coming to our present world era. Born a prince in modern Nepal, he was escorted out of his palace at the age of 13 and came across the Four Sights: an old crippled man, a diseased man, a decaying corpse, and finally an ascetic. He realized that age, disease, death and pain were inescapable, and that the poor would always outnumber the rich. However, even if one were wealthy, all humans shared these same afflictions. Neither money nor peace could relieve people of fear and anxiety, nor lead them to ultimate happiness. Departing from the palace wearing rags, Gautama studied meditation, becoming an ascetic in his search for the truth. He found that liberation from worry could be attained only by reaching a state of absolute tranquillity and enlightenment.

According to the Theravada tradition, the oldest Buddhist school, in his last sermon Gautama encouraged his disciples to diligently *'Doubt everything. Find your own light'* and seek the truth, not holding on to that which was impermanent. After 45 years of teaching, the Buddha, aged about 80, passed into Parinirvana, the deathless state of Nirvana. According to the Mahaparinibbana Sutta of the Pali Canon, he announced that he was about to die, and had his last meal, which was an offering from Cunda, a blacksmith. He fell violently ill, but asked an attendant to tell Cunda that he was not the cause. The Mahayana Vimalakirti Sutra states that Gautama pretended to be ill to demonstrate the impermanence and pain of the defiled world, thereby encouraging his followers to strive for Nirvana. His final words are echoed in George Harrison's 1970 song 'All Things Must Pass'.

'Go, stranger, and tell the Lacedaemonians [Spartans] that here we lie, obedient to their commands'

Epitaph by Simonides of Ceos over the Spartan tomb at Thermopylae

In August 480 BCE, Leonidas went to meet Xerxes' army at the pass of Thermopylae, where he was joined by forces from other Greek city-states to form an army between 4,000 and 7,000 strong. He took only his body-guard of 300 hand-picked warriors to lead the army, as the rest of the Spartan army was co-ordinating with the Greek navy against the Persian navy. The Persian army was said to consist of between 80,000 and 290,000 men-at-arms. Xerxes waited to attack for four days, expecting the small Greek army to flee. On the fifth and sixth days, in a frontal attack, perhaps 20,000 Persians died. On the seventh day, a traitor led a Persian force by a mountain track to the rear of the Greeks. Leonidas sent away most of his Greek troops to fight another day, and remained in the pass with his 300 Spartans, as well as 900 helots and 700 Thespians who refused to leave, to cover the retreat. Now attacked from the front and rear, Leonidas was killed, but the Spartans retrieved his body and protected it until their final defeat. The modern Leonidas Monument at Thermopylae reads: *'Come and get them!'*, which was the Spartans' response when the Persians asked them to put down their weapons. Herodotus recorded:

'The men were buried where they fell; and for these, as well as for those who were slain before being sent away by Leonidas, there is an inscription which runs:
> "Here one, facing in fight three hundred myriads of foemen,
> Thousand four did contend, men of the Peloponnese."
This is the inscription for the whole body, and for the Spartans separately there is:
> "Go stranger, and tell the Lacedaemonians [Spartans]
> That here we lie, obedient to their commands."'

'If the Persians [Medes] darken the sun with their arrows, we shall have our fight in the shade'

Defiant words spoken during his last speech

Xerxes, the son of Darius I, led a force of perhaps 100,000 Persians across the Dardanelles, over a bridge of boats, to begin the Second Persian War. His army passed through Thrace and Macedonia and into Thessaly. The Olympic Games were in progress, but all the Greek states began to mobilize. A small army was sent to the Thermopylae Pass, which guarded the entrance to Boeotia and Attica, to hold the advance. It was the only road that connected Thessaly with central Greece and Athens. By the third day of fighting, the Persians had suffered far greater losses, trying to force their way through the pass. However, the Greek traitor Ephialtes showed the Persians a flanking route through another pass, and the defending Phocians were forced to withdraw to save their own city. To give the main force of 5,000 Greek hoplites time to retreat before the whole army was surrounded, King Leonidas I of Sparta remained at the pass with 300 of his bodyguards, 900 helots and 700 Thespians to fight a rearguard action.

All the Greek defenders were killed, but they delayed the Persians for long enough to allow the Greek army to re-form at the Isthmus of Corinth and win at Plataea, and for the Athenian navy to be victorious at the Battle of Salamis, effectively ending the invasion. Dieneces was *'a most virtuous'* Spartan officer, and Herodotus noted:

> 'Thus nobly did the whole body of Lacedaemonians [Spartans] and Thespians behave. One man is said to have distinguished himself above all the rest: Dieneces the Spartan. A speech which he made before the Greeks engaged the Medes [Persians], remains on record. One of the Trachinians told him, "Such was the number of the barbarians, that when they shot forth their arrows the sun would be darkened by their multitude." Dieneces, not at all frightened at these words, but making light of the Median numbers, answered, "Our Trachinian friend brings us excellent tidings. If the Medes darken the sun, we shall have our fight in the shade."'

‘No living Athenian through my instrumentality ever put on mourning’

Dying words

Thucydides called Pericles *'the first citizen of Athens'*, and the period in which he led Athens, from 461 BCE until his death 32 years later, is known as *'the Age of Pericles'*. Under his influence Athens became the cultural centre of the Greek world, and he fostered democracy there. Pericles lived for the first two and a half years of the Peloponnesian War, and according to Thucydides, his death was a disaster for Athens, as his successors were inferior to him. Pericles' last spoken words seem to have been a reference to the claim that he had not put any political opponents to death, for certainly Athens had lost military personnel under his rule. Another unsourced but prevalent version of his last words was *'There is no God.'*

A great plague had broken out in Athens in 430 BCE, and in 429 it returned with fresh virulence. Pericles had already lost two sons to the plague, and shut himself in his house to mourn and stay away from the affairs of state. However, he was himself stricken; he recovered, but was soon after attacked by a fever, which he was too weak to resist.

'Being now near his end, the best of the citizens and those of his friends who survived were sitting around him holding discourse of his excellence and power, how great they had been, and estimating all his achievements and the number of his trophies, – there were nine of these which he had set up as the city's victorious general. This discourse they were holding with one another, supposing that he no longer understood them but had lost consciousness. He had been attending to it all, however, and speaking out among them said he was amazed at their praising and commemorating that in him which was due as much to fortune as to himself, and which had fallen to the lot of many generals besides, instead of mentioning his fairest and greatest title to their admiration; "for," said he, "no living Athenian through my instrumentality ever put on mourning [clothes]".'

SOCRATES
469 BCE–399 BCE

'Crito, we owe a cock to Asclepius. Do pay it. Don't forget.'

Last words, from Plato's dialogue on the death of Socrates

Socrates was tried before a jury of 500 of his fellow Athenians, accused of *'refusing to recognize the gods recognized by the state'* and of *'corrupting the youth'*. His accusers were given three hours to present their case, after which he had three hours to defend himself. Socrates was 70 years old and familiar to most Athenians, but his anti-democratic views had turned many against him. Two of his students, Alcibiades and Critias, had twice briefly overthrown the democratic government of the city, leading to thousands of citizens being deprived of their property and either banished from the city or executed. Socrates was found guilty by a vote of 280 to 220 and was given a death sentence whereby he would have to drink hemlock. He was thus his own executioner, but was allowed to have his friends and pupils present.

Plato, Socrates' most famous student, was ill and therefore did not attend the poisoning, although he knew all those who were present. He describes the scene through the narrative of the fictional character Phaedo. Socrates pleaded with his friends to stop crying, and walked around until his legs became heavy. He then lay on his back, as the attendant instructed. Squeezing a foot hard, the attendant asked Socrates if he felt anything. Socrates said that he did not. The attendant did the same to his calves and, going higher, told him that he was becoming cold and stiff. Then he felt him one last time and warned him that when the poison reached his heart he would be gone.

As the chill sensation approached his waist, Socrates spoke his last words: *'Crito, we owe a cock to Asclepius. Do pay it. Don't forget.' 'Of course,'* said Crito. *'Do you want to say anything else?'* There was no reply to this question, and soon afterwards Socrates died. Crito closed his mouth and eyelids, and the fictional Phaedo said: *'This was the end of our friend, the best, wisest and most upright man of any that I have ever known.'*

ALEXANDER THE GREAT, ALEXANDER III OF MACEDON
356 BCE–10 or 11 June 323 BCE

'To the strongest!'

Last words on his death bed

Numerous causes, including poisoning and a malarial relapse, have been proposed for Alexander's collapse on a June afternoon in the Babylonian palace of King Nebuchadnezzar II. After a banquet and drinking party hosted by his friend Medius of Larissa about a week earlier, Alexander fell seriously ill and took to his bed. He treated himself with hellebore, a plant that could be used as a cure-all and as a poison, but his condition worsened. He lost the ability to move, except for his right arm, and could barely speak. Alexander's wife Roxanne was pregnant, and there was no obvious heir to the empire. When his generals filed in to pay their last respects, they asked him which of them was to succeed him. His voice when he replied may have been indistinct. He may have murmured '*Krater'oi*', '*to Craterus*', one of his favourite generals, but Craterus was not present, and the others may have chosen to hear '*tôi kratistôi*', '*to the strongest*'. Craterus was killed in battle in 321 BCE before he could assume control, and Alexander's great empire was soon split into four kingdoms.

Alexander's body was submerged in honey, which does not disintegrate and is a hermetic seal. It is said that he had asked to be buried at the Ammoneion of the Libyan Oasis in modern-day Siwa. However, during the struggle for succession following his death, one of his generals, Perdikkas, had his mummified remains transported to Macedonia in a golden funeral cart. Another general, Ptolemy, intercepted the procession and rerouted the remains to Memphis in Egypt, where he displayed them as a symbol of the legitimacy of his own rule over that part of Alexander's former empire. Ptolemy's son later moved the remains to the new capital, Alexandria, but by 400 CE both mummy and tomb had vanished. It is said that Alexander's epitaph was '*A tomb now suffices him for whom the world was not enough.*'

⟨Everything will shortly be turned upside down⟩

Attributed last words

We are unsure whether this philosopher left the Greek colony of Sinope on the Black Sea for exile because he was associated with fraud, or because he was captured by pirates and sold into slavery. Xeniades the Corinthian was said by Diogenes Laertius to have purchased Diogenes from the pirates and subsequently supported him. Diogenes of Sinope made a virtue of extreme poverty, living as a beggar but being greatly respected. Diogenes Laertius wrote a life of the philosopher:

> 'He is said to have died when he was nearly ninety years of age, but there are different accounts given of his death. For some say that he ate an ox's foot raw, and was in consequence seized with a bilious attack, of which he died; others ... say that he died of holding his breath for several days ... Others say that he, while intending to distribute a polypus to his dogs, was bitten by them through the tendon of his foot, and so died. But his own greatest friends ... rather sanction the story of his having died from holding his breath ... On this there was a quarrel, as they say, between his friends, as to who should bury him and they even came to blows ... And they placed over him a pillar, and on that a dog in Parian marble. And at a later period his fellow citizens honoured him with brazen statues, and put this inscription on them:
>
> "E'en brass by lapse of time doth old become,
> But there is no such time as shall efface,
> Your lasting glory, wise Diogenes;
> Since you alone did teach to men the art
> Of a contented life: the surest path
> To glory and a lasting happiness."

Xeniades asked, *'How do you want to be buried?'* to which Diogenes answered: *'Face downwards.'* Xeniades asked him why, and Diogenes responded: *'Because everything will shortly be turned upside down.'*

DEMOSTHENES
384 BCE–322 BCE

'Cast out this body of mine unburied'

Part of last speech

After Alexander's death in 323 BCE, the great orator and general Demosthenes again urged the Athenians to seek independence from Macedonia. Antipater, Alexander's successor in the region, demanded that the Athenians turn over Demosthenes and others who were advocating rebellion. Demosthenes fled rather than be handed over. Archias of Thurii, a former tragic actor like Demosthenes had been, was one of Antipater's followers. He found where Demosthenes had hidden, and led Thracian spearmen to the sanctuary of the Temple of Poseidon on Calauria. Archias asked Demosthenes to come to Antipater. However, Demosthenes had dreamt that he would not be safe:

'Archias at this beginning to grow angry and to threaten him, "Now," said Demosthenes, "you speak like the genuine Macedonian oracle; before you were but acting a part. Therefore forbear only a little, while I write a word or two home to my family." Having thus spoken, he withdrew into the temple and taking a scroll as if he meant to write, he put the reed into his mouth, and biting it as he was wont to do when he was thoughtful or writing, he held it there some time. Then he bowed down his head and covered it. The soldiers that stood at the door, supposing all this to proceed from want of courage and fear of death, in derision called him effeminate, and faint-hearted, and coward. And Archias drawing near, desired him to rise up, and repeating the same kind of thing he had spoken before, he once more promised to make his peace with Antipater. But Demosthenes, perceiving that now the poison had pierced, and seized his vitals, uncovered his head, and fixing his eyes upon Archias, "Now," said he, "as soon as you please, you may commence the part of Creon in the tragedy, and cast out this body of mine unburied. But, O gracious Neptune, I, for my part while I am yet alive will rise up and depart out of this sacred place; though Antipater and the Macedonians have not left so much as thy temple unpolluted." After he had thus spoken and desired to be held up, because already he began to tremble and stagger, as he was going forward, and passing by the altar, he fell down, and with a groan gave up the ghost.'

ARCHIMEDES OF SYRACUSE
c.287 BCE–c.212 BCE

'Wait till I've finished my problem' or 'Do not disturb my circles'

Attributed last words, based upon the account of Marcellus sacking Syracuse

Archimedes was an astronomer, mathematician, physicist, engineer and inventor, the ancient world's equivalent of Leonard da Vinci. The fabulous 'Antikythera mechanism', the first known mechanical computer, discovered in 1900, may well have been his invention. He died when the Romans captured Syracuse after a two-year siege, Plutarch recorded that *'although he made many excellent discoveries, he is said to have asked his kinsmen and friends to place over the grave where he should be buried a cylinder enclosing a sphere, with an inscription giving the proportion by which the containing solid exceeds the contained'*. The tomb was found by Cicero (106 BCE–43 BCE) in 75 BCE.

'But nothing afflicted Marcellus so much as the death of Archimedes, who was then, as fate would have it, intent upon working out some problem by a diagram, and having fixed his mind alike and his eyes upon the subject of his speculation, he never noticed the incursion of the Romans, nor that the city was taken. In this transport of study and contemplation, a soldier, unexpectedly coming up to him, commanded him to follow to Marcellus; which he declining to do before he had worked out his problem to a demonstration, the soldier, enraged, drew his sword and ran him through. Others write that a Roman soldier, running upon him with a drawn sword, offered to kill him; and that Archimedes, looking back, earnestly besought him to hold his hand a little while, that he might not leave what he was then at work upon inconclusive and imperfect; but the soldier, nothing moved by his entreaty, instantly killed him. Others again relate that, as Archimedes was carrying to Marcellus mathematical instruments, dials, spheres, and angles, by which the magnitude of the sun might be measured to the sight, some soldiers seeing him, and thinking that he carried gold in a vessel, slew him. Certain it is that his death was very afflicting to Marcellus; and that Marcellus ever after regarded him that killed him as a murderer.'

HANNIBAL, SON OF HANNIBAL BARCA
248 BCE–183 or 182 BCE

'Let us ease the Roman people of their continual care, who think it long to await the death of an old man'

Reputed last words

This Carthaginian general fought against the expansion of Rome in the Mediterranean. In the Second Punic War, he famously marched an army including war elephants from Spain, over the Pyrenees and the Alps, into Italy. There, he won three great victories at Trebia, Trasimene and Cannae, and occupied much of Italy for 15 years. A Roman counter-invasion of North Africa forced his return, and he was defeated at Zama. He was forced to undertake financial reforms to pay the Roman war indemnity, so became unpopular and was forced into exile. He went first to the Seleucid court of Antiochis III, advising on his war with Rome, but had to flee again, to Armenia and then to the court of Prusias in Bithynia.

The Romans still wanted Hannibal dead, and when Prusias agreed to give him up, Hannibal took poison at Nicomedia, aged 64. Polybius remarked:

'How wonderful is it that in the course of sixteen years, during which he maintained the war in Italy, he should never once dismiss his army from the field, and yet be able, like a good governor, to keep in subjection so great a multitude, and to confine them within the bounds of their duty, so that they never mutinied against him nor quarrelled among themselves. Though his army was composed of people of various countries – of Africans, Spaniards, Gauls, Carthaginians, Italians, and Greeks – men who had different laws, different customs, and different languages, and, in a word, nothing among them that was common – yet, so dexterous was his management that, notwithstanding this great diversity, he forced all of them to acknowledge one authority, and to yield obedience to one command. And this, too, he accomplished in the midst of very varied fortune. How high as well as just an opinion must these things convey to us of his ability in war!'

LUCIUS CORNELIUS SULLA FELIX
c.138 BCE –78 BCE

'No friend ever served me, and no enemy ever wronged me, whom I have not repaid in full'

Self-made epitaph

Sulla was a Roman general who became a powerful dictator, ruthlessly eliminating political opposition. Towards the end of his reign, however, he strengthened the constitution that he had previously almost completely ignored, and retired to his estates. From Plutarch's *Parallel Lives* we note:

'Sulla not only foresaw his own death, but may be said to have written about it also. For he stopped writing the twenty-second book of his Memoirs two days before he died, and he there says that the Chaldaeans foretold him that, after an honourable life, he was to end his days at the height of his good fortunes ... and one day before he died, on learning that the magistrate ... Granius, refused to pay a debt he owed the public treasury, in expectation of his death, he summoned him to his room, stationed his servants about him, and ordered them to strangle him; but with the strain which he put upon his voice and body, he ruptured his abscess and lost a great quantity of blood. In consequence of this his strength failed, and after a night of wretchedness, he died, leaving two young children by Metella ...

The day was cloudy in the morning, and the expectation was that it would rain, but at last, at the ninth hour, the corpse was placed upon the funeral pyre. Then a strong wind smote the pyre, and roused a mighty flame, and there was just time to collect the bones for burial, while the pyre was smouldering and the fire was going out, when a heavy rain began to fall, which continued till night. Therefore his good fortune would seem to have lasted to the very end, and taken part in his funeral rites. At any rate, his monument stands in the Campus Martius, and the inscription on it, they say, is one which he wrote for it himself, and the substance of it is, that no friend ever surpassed him in kindness, and no enemy in mischief.'

GAIUS JULIUS CAESAR
100 BCE–15 March 44 BCE

'Et tu, Brute?'
('You too, Brutus?')

Attributed last words

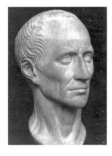

Julius Caesar was murdered by a group of senators led by Marcus Junius Brutus (85–42 BCE), who had been a close friend. In Shakespeare's play, Caesar begins to resist the attack, but resigns himself to death when he sees Brutus:

CAESAR: Doth not Brutus bootless kneel?
CASCA: Speak, hands, for me! (*They stab Caesar.*)
CAESAR: Et tu, Brute? Then fall, Caesar! (*Dies.*)
CINNA: Liberty! Freedom! Tyranny is dead!

Caesar had been warned to '*Beware the Ides of March*', and it was on that day that he was assassinated by the group, who believed that he had become over-powerful. Shakespeare drew inspiration from the Roman historian Gaius Suetonius Tranquillus' *Lives of the Twelve Caesars*:

'As he took his seat, the conspirators gathered about him as if to pay their respects ... Cimber caught his toga by both shoulders. As Caesar cried, "Why, this is violence!" one of the Cascas stabbed him from one side just below the throat. Caesar caught Casca's arm and ran it through with his stylus, but as he tried to leap to his feet, he was stopped by another wound. When he saw that he was beset on every side by drawn daggers, he muffled his head in his robe, and at the same time drew down its lap to his feet with his left hand, in order to fall more decently, with the lower part of his body also covered. And in this wise he was stabbed with three and twenty wounds, uttering not a word, but merely a groan at the first stroke, though some have written that when Marcus Brutus rushed at him, he said in Greek, "You too, my child?"'

Caesar had previously spared Brutus' life when Brutus fought for Pompey in the Civil Wars. After Caesar's death, Brutus was allowed to leave Rome, but Octavian (Augustus) declared the group of senators to be murderers, and Brutus committed suicide after the second Battle of Philippi.

'She was a woman of surpassing beauty'

Words of Cassius Dio, c.210–230 CE

'For she was a woman of surpassing beauty, and at that time, when she was in the prime of her youth, she was most striking; she also possessed a most charming voice and knowledge of how to make herself agreeable to every one. Being brilliant to look upon and to listen to, with the power to subjugate every one, even a love-sated man already past his prime, she thought that it would be in keeping with her role to meet Caesar, and she reposed in her beauty all her claims to the throne ...'

As the last real pharaoh of the Ptolemaic dynasty, Cleopatra had a liaison with Julius Caesar that helped her keep the throne, and they had a son, Caesarion. After Caesar's assassination in 44 BCE, she aligned with Mark Antony in opposition to Caesar's heir Octavian (later known as Emperor Augustus). With Antony she had twins and another son. After losing the sea battle of Actium to Octavian, Antony committed suicide, and Cleopatra did likewise, traditionally by the bite of two asps. According to Plutarch's *Life of Antony*:

'Cleopatra sent to Caesar [Octavian] a letter which she had written and sealed; and, putting everybody out of the monument but her two women, she shut the doors. Caesar, opening her letter, and finding pathetic prayers and entreaties that she might be buried in the same tomb with Antony, soon guessed what she was doing. At first he was going himself in all haste, but, changing his mind, he sent others to see. The thing had been quickly done. The messengers came at full speed, and found the guards apprehensive of nothing; but on opening the doors, they saw her stone-dead, lying upon a bed of gold, set out in all her royal ornaments. Iras, one of her women, lay dying at her feet, and Charmion, just ready to fall, scarce able to hold up her head, was adjusting her mistress's diadem. And when one that came in said angrily, "Was this well done of your lady, Charmion?" "Extremely well," she answered, "and as became the descendant of so many kings"; and as she said this, she fell down dead by the bedside.'

Cleopatra's son Caesarion was declared pharaoh, but Octavian had him killed.

'I have executed a memorial longer lasting than bronze ... I shall not altogether die.'

Lines from his *Odes*

The leading lyric poet and satirist of the Augustan Age sensed his immortality. In 38 BCE he was introduced to Gaius Maecenas, a man of letters who was also one of Octavian's main political advisers, and who became an influential patron. In 35 BCE Horace published Book I of the *Satires*, poems stating his firm rejection of public life, the evil of ambition and aiming at wisdom through serenity. After Octavian had defeated Antony and Cleopatra, Horace produced his *Epodes*, which mocked social abuses, and a second book of *Satires*. After 27 BCE he published three books of *Odes*, representing himself as heir to the Greek lyric poets in verses celebrating love, wine, nature, friends and moderation. After 23 BCE he wrote three *Epistles*, the third known as the *Ars Poetica*, and in 17 BCE composed the *Secular Hymn*.

In 8 BCE Horace's influential patron Maecenas died, one of his last requests to his friend Octavian (now the Emperor Augustus) being: *'Remember Horace as you would remember me.'* Just 59 days later, Horace too died after a short illness. Upon his deathbed and unable to write, he dictated his will, requesting that his farm in the Sabine Hills be left to Augustus, and that he himself be buried next to Maecenas' tomb on the Esquiline Hill. Already at the time of Horace's death his *Odes* had become a school textbook, their excellence being so great that they had few ancient lyrical successors. They fell out of favour in the piety of medieval times, but the *Satires* and the *Epistles* continued to be read because of their moralistic tones. The *Odes* became popular again with the Renaissance and, along with the *Ars Poetica*, exerted influence on Western poetry through the nineteenth century. Thus Horace's works have lasted and inspired for over two millennia.

'My God, my God, why hast thou forsaken me?'

Matthew 27:46

'Father, forgive them, for they know not what they are doing.' Luke 23:34

'I tell you the truth, today you will be with me in paradise.' Luke 23:42

'When Jesus saw his mother there, and the disciple whom he loved standing nearby, he said to his mother, "Dear woman, here is your son," and to the disciple, "Here is your mother." From that time on, this disciple took her into his home.' John 19:26–27

'I am thirsty.' John 19:28

'Father, into thy hands I commend my spirit.' Luke 23:46

'It is finished.' John 19:30

Jesus of Nazareth is believed by Christians to be the son of God and Saviour of mankind through whom God revealed himself to the world, and whose crucifixion reconciles the world with God. The above statements – known as *The Seven Last Words of Christ* – were the inspiration for the 1787 composition by Joseph Haydn, *The Seven Last Words of Our Saviour on the Cross*. The first exclamation is a repetition of the first line of Psalm 22, a psalm of David, and is thus a prophetic fulfilment. Jesus felt alone for the first time in his life, before regaining his faith in God. In the second statement he forgives his persecutors. In the third, he assures one of the criminals alongside him that he will go to heaven, as he has expressed his faith in Jesus. In the fourth statement, Jesus ensures that his mother will be cared for after his death, by the apostle John. In the fifth, he fulfils the Messianic prophecy of Psalm 69, in which line 21 reads: *'They put gall in my food and gave me vinegar for my thirst.'* The Roman guards did indeed give him vinegar to drink. Jesus' final two statements show that his evangelizing mission had been accomplished.

NERO CLAUDIUS CAESAR AUGUSTUS GERMANICUS
(BORN LUCIUS DOMITIUS AHENOBARBUS)
15 December 37 CE–9 June 68 CE

'Too late! This is fidelity!'

Dying words

Nero was adopted by his great-uncle Claudius to become heir to the throne, and was proclaimed Emperor of Rome on 13 October 54 CE. He is remembered as the emperor who *'fiddled while Rome burned'* during the great fire of 64 CE. It is claimed that in 55 CE he poisoned Britannicus, his 15-year-old stepbrother and the real heir to the Roman Empire, and in 59 CE he ordered the murder of his own mother. He executed his former wife Octavia after allowing her back to Rome from exile, and gave her head to his new wife Poppeia; and he is said to have kicked Poppeia to death when she was pregnant. In 62–63 CE he executed several rivals. When his legions began to rise in revolt, the Senate refused to back Nero and he fled into hiding.

'... he wept and said again and again: "What an artist the world is losing!"... [he] read that he had been pronounced a public enemy by the senate, and that they were seeking him to punish in the ancient fashion; and he asked what manner of punishment that was. When he learned that the criminal was stripped, fastened by the neck in a fork and then beaten to death with rods, in mortal terror he seized two daggers which he had brought with him, and then, after trying the point of each, put them up again, pleading that the fatal hour had not yet come ... anon he reproached himself for his cowardice in such words as these: "To live is a scandal and a shame – this does not become Nero, does not become him – one should be resolute at such times – come, rouse thyself." And now the horsemen were at hand who had orders to take him off alive. When he heard them, he quavered: "Hark, now strikes on my ear the trampling of swift-footed coursers!" and drove a dagger into his throat ... He was all but dead when a centurion rushed in, and as he placed a cloak to the wound, pretending that he had come to aid him, Nero merely gasped: "Too late!" and "This is fidelity!" With these words he was gone, with eyes so set and starting from their sockets that all who saw him shuddered with horror.'

'Dear me, I believe I am becoming a god'

Reputed last words

The founder of the line of Flavian emperors of Rome, Vespasian stabilized the Roman Empire after Nero's excesses. He commanded the Second Legion during the invasion of Britain in 43 CE, and became a Roman consul and then Governor of Africa. Trusted by Nero, he suppressed the Jewish Revolt of 66–70 CE. During the rapid turnover of emperors following the death of Nero in 68 CE, Vespasian prepared his bid for power. The legions of Egypt, Judaea, Syria and the Danube all declared for him, and he sent his commander Primus ahead to secure Italy on his behalf. A bloody, victory was achieved at Cremona, and Primus took Rome in December 69 CE.

The senate passed a law conferring the powers of emperor on Vespasian and he arrived in Rome in the late summer of 70 CE, having left his elder son Titus in charge in Judaea. Titus completed Vespasian's suppression of Judaea, Jerusalem being taken in August of that year, and the Temple destroyed. The spoils were used to finance the building of the Colosseum. Vespasian's objectives were to repair Rome's finances after Nero's reign, to restore discipline in the army following the Civil Wars and to ensure the succession of his son Titus, all of which he achieved.

Suetonius tells us: *'Titus complained of the tax which Vespasian had imposed on the contents of the city urinals. Vespasian handed him a coin which had been part of the first day's proceeds: "Does it smell bad?" he asked. And when Titus said "No" he went on: "Yet it comes from urine."'* This is often misquoted as *'Money has no smell.'* Vespasian set an example by living a simple life, leading to Tacitus observing that he was the first man to improve after becoming emperor. He met his approaching death with equanimity, and was indeed deified. His last words were: *'Dear me, I believe I am becoming a god. An emperor ought at least to die on his feet.'*

'I deserve not death, but I repent nothing else in my life except for one thing'

Dying words

Titus, the elder son of Emperor Vespasian, was the second in the Flavian dynasty. Vespasian is reported to have said: *'Either my son shall be my successor, or no one at all.'* Titus became commander of one of his father's three legions in Judaea in 67 CE, and played a leading role in Vespasian being proclaimed emperor by the eastern provinces. In 70 CE Jerusalem fell to his troops, and he had the Great Temple there destroyed, with only the 'Wailing Wall' surviving. The massive Arch of Titus, which celebrates his triumph over the Jews, still stands in Rome. On 24 June 79 CE Titus succeeded his father as emperor, despite being deeply disliked in the Senate and among the people as he continued his father's unpopular economic policies. One month later, when the eruption of Mount Vesuvius overwhelmed towns including Pompeii and Herculaneum, it was said to be the revenge of Israel.

Titus finished his father's Flavian Amphitheatre, better known today as the Colosseum, and inaugurated it with a series of lavish games and spectacles. At the closing of the games he officially dedicated the amphitheatre and the baths, his final recorded act as emperor. He is said to then have broken down in tears. After this, he set out for the Sabine territories, but fell ill at the first posting station, dying of fever. Suetonius and Cassius Dio both accuse his younger brother Domitian of having left the ailing Titus for dead. Some believe that the he killed the heirless emperor with poisoned sea-slug. Cassius Dio believed that Titus, in his dying words, alluded to his failure to have his brother executed when he was found to be openly plotting against him. However, Domitian's first act as Emperor of Rome was to deify Titus.

AKIBA BEN JOSEPH
c.50 CE–135 CE

'The paper burns, but the words fly free'
Reputed last words

An illiterate, poverty-stricken shepherd from Lydda in Palestine, Akiba was married late in life to Rachel, the daughter of a wealthy man. She accepted him on condition that he devoted himself to learning, but was disowned by her father for doing so. When their child started school, Akiba accompanied him and so learned to read. At the age of 40 he was admitted to the rabbinical academy of a Pharisaic teacher, and found himself championing the poor against the rich. In 96 CE he went to Rome with other rabbis to petition the Emperor Domitian to revoke anti-Jewish laws. Fortunately he received a bequest from a Jewish convert in Rome that allowed him to set up an academy near Jaffa, which attracted thousands of students. He developed a new method of textual interpretation that attached significance to every word of the Hebrew Scriptures, and this allowed him to adjust the law to the needs of the times. Regarded as one of the founders of rabbinic Judaism, he also rearranged the haphazard organization of Oral Law.

Akiba played an important role in the Bar Kokhba revolt against Rome (132–135), during which he insisted on continuing to teach the Law, though it was a capital offence. Presiding over the Sanhedrin, the rabbinical court, he believed that the Judaean commander Simon Bar Kokhba could be the new Messiah. This was the third major rebellion by the Jews of Judaea against Rome, and the last of the Jewish–Roman Wars. The revolt was crushed after three bitter years, with General Severus being recalled from Britain. He was Emperor Hadrian's finest general, and according to Cassius Dio, 580,000 Jews were killed, with hundreds of towns and villages razed. Hadrian attempted to exterminate Judaism altogether, prohibiting Torah Law and killing clerics and scholars. Akiba was tortured and executed by the Romans, being burnt at the stake. He had been flayed while repeating the *'Shema Yisrael Adonai Eloheinu Adonai Echad'* ('Hear, O Israel! The Lord is our God! The Lord is One!'). Because of Akiba, it is customary for Jews to recite the *'Shema'* as their last words.

MARCUS AURELIUS ANTONINUS AUGUSTUS, EMPEROR OF ROME
26 April 121–17 March 180

'Go to the rising sun, for I sink to my setting'

Historical account of Marcus Aurelius' death

'... the Emperor Marcus Aurelius disembarked upon the unknown shore. It is said that on the last day but one of his life, knowing that his end was near, for he had refused food and drink, he sent for his friends, and with a smile for the vanities of the world [*ridens res humanas*], and such indifference for death that it appeared contempt, he asked: "Why do you weep for me? Why don't you rather consider the pestilence and the common death?" And as they were about to go, he said: "Since you now let me depart, I bid you farewell and I go on before you." Then they asked to whose care he commended Commodus, and he answered, "To you, if he be worthy, and to the immortal gods." Finally, when the officer of the guard asked for the watchword, he said, "Go to the rising sun, for I sink to my setting." On the last day he saw Commodus only, and but a moment, for fear lest he take the disease. Then he covered up his head as if for sleep, and that night gave up the ghost.'

Roman emperor from 161, Marcus Aurelius wrote his *Meditations* during 170–180 while campaigning away from Rome. The work is still revered today as a paean to serving one's country without personal gain (and should be compulsory reading for today's politicians). It was written in Greek, as that language had the complexities lacking in Latin to express philosophical thought. An important Stoic philosopher, Marcus Aurelius is regarded as the last of the 'Five Good Emperors'. He fought the Parthian Empire in Asia and the Germanic tribes across Europe, and ensured that his son Commodus succeeded him as emperor. Cassius Dio noted that he *'was involved in a multitude of troubles throughout practically his entire reign. But for my part, I admire him all the more for this very reason, that amid unusual and extraordinary difficulties he both survived himself and preserved the empire.'*

'Twenty-two acknowledged concubines, and a library of sixty-two thousand volumes attested the variety of his inclinations'

Character sketch by Edward Gibbon

Edward Gibbon (1737–1794), the English historian and Member of Parliament, describes Gordian the Younger as a *'venerable proconsul'* who accompanied his father Gordian I into Africa as his lieutenant. Gordian I was 80 when he became emperor, so he quickly co-opted his 46-year-old son to rule with him. They reigned jointly for only 22 days. Of Gordian II, Gibbon declares:

'Twenty-two acknowledged concubines, and a library of sixty-two thousand volumes, attested the variety of his inclinations; and from the productions which he left behind him, it appears that the former as well as the latter were designed for use rather than for ostentation. The Roman people ... rested the public hope on those latent virtues which had hitherto, as they fondly imagined, lain concealed in the luxurious indolence of private life ... As soon as the Gordians had appeased the first tumult of a popular election, they removed their court to Carthage. ... The feeble court of Carthage was alarmed by the rapid approach of Capelianus, governor of Mauritania, who, with a small band of veterans, and a fierce host of barbarians, attacked a faithful, but unwarlike province.

The younger Gordian sallied out to meet the enemy at the head of a few guards, and a numerous undisciplined multitude, educated in the peaceful luxury of Carthage. His useless valour served only to procure him an honourable death on the field of battle. His aged father, whose reign had not exceeded thirty-six days, put an end to his life on the first news of the defeat. Carthage, destitute of defence, opened her gates to the conqueror, and Africa was exposed to the rapacious cruelty of a slave, obliged to satisfy his unrelenting master with a large account of blood and treasure. The fate of the Gordians filled Rome with just but unexpected terror.'

‘From the lands where the sun rises to western shores,
people are crying and wailing ... the Franks, the Romans,
all Christians, are stung with mourning and great worry ...
the young and old, glorious nobles, all lament the loss of
their Caesar ... the world laments the death of Charles ...
O Christ, you who govern the heavenly host, grant
a peaceful place to Charles in your kingdom.
Alas for miserable me.’

Anonymous monk of Bobbio, in Emilia Romagna, Italy,
lamenting the death of Charlemagne

Charlemagne, son of Pepin the Short, was King of the Franks from 768.
In 53 military campaigns he expanded the kingdom to cover most of Western and
central Europe. After conquering Italy, he was crowned Holy Roman Emperor
Charles I by Pope Leo III in 800, becoming a temporary rival to the Byzantine
emperor in Constantinople. He is also recognized as Charles I in the king lists of
France and Germany. His reign saw a flourishing of art, culture and Christianity.

In 806 Charlemagne divided his empire among his three sons: Pepin, Charles
and Louis. However, Pepin died in 810 and Charles in 811. Only Louis remained,
so absorbed in piety that he seemed unfit to govern. Nevertheless, in 813, at a
solemn ceremony, Louis the Pious was elevated from the rank of King of
Aquitaine to that of co-emperor, and the 71-year-old Charlemagne uttered his
Nunc Dimittis: *'Blessed be Thou, O Lord God, Who hast granted me the grace to see
with my own eyes my son seated on my throne!'*

In January 814 Charlemagne fell ill with pleurisy. He died seven days later,
aged 72, having reigned for 47 years, and was buried immediately in Aachen
Cathedral. In 1165, Frederick I opened the tomb and re-interred his remains in a
magnificent gold and silver casket that can still be seen today. Charlemagne was
succeeded by his son Louis, who inherited the massive Carolingian Empire. Its
later division between Louis' sons laid the foundations for the modern states of
France and Germany.

POPE ST GREGORY VII, HILDEBRAND, ILDEBRANDO BRONIZI DE SOANA
c.1015–25 May 1085

‹I have loved justice and hated iniquity; therefore I die in exile›

Reputed last words

Born in Tuscany, Hildebrand served as a chaplain to Pope Gregory VI, and was himself pope from 22 April 1073 until his death, being beatified in 1584 and canonized in 1728. Upon becoming pope, he began an extensive programme of reform in the Church, enforcing celibacy and opposing simony, clerical marriage and lay investiture, which enabled kings to appoint Church officials. He issued the *Dictatus Papae*, which proclaimed papal supremacy, stating that the Pope inherited the personal sanctity of St Peter. While these reforms vastly increased Church powers, Gregory remained unconcerned about the political consequences. In particular, he earned the enmity of the Holy Roman Emperor, Henry IV, who attempted to undermine his powers.

On Christmas Day 1075, Gregory was kidnapped by a Roman nobleman, Cencio i Frangipane, while he was celebrating mass in the great church of Santa Maria Maggiore. He was soon released by the Roman people, but he blamed Henry IV for the affair. Henry carried on attacking the Pope in letters and speeches, and announced his deposition at the Synod of Worms in 1076. In despair, Gregory excommunicated Henry, thus becoming the first pope to stand up to, and excommunicate, a king. The two were reconciled at Canossa in 1077, as Henry sought absolution. In 1080, Gregory sided with rebellious German nobles against Henry, and excommunicated the Holy Roman Emperor again. In response, Henry oversaw the crowning of one of his own men, Guibert of Ravenna, as Pope Clement III. Henry besieged Rome between 1081 and 1083, taking the city in 1084. Gregory escaped to Castel Sant'Angelo on the banks of the Tiber, and his ally, the Norman Robert Guiscard of Salerno ('Robert the Weasel') soon entered Rome and rescued him. However, much of Rome was sacked in the fighting and the Roman populace turned against Guiscard in dismay. Gregory was forced to flee Rome for refuge in Monte Cassino, and then to Salerno, where he died the following year.

'King Henry being in Normandy, after some writers, fell from or with his horse, whereof he caught his death; but Ranulphe says he took a surfeit by eating of a lamprey, and thereof died'

Historical account of Henry I's death

Before he died in 1087, William the Conqueror (known at the time as William the Bastard) divided his possessions amongst his three surviving sons. William II took England, the eldest son Robert had Normandy, and the youngest son Henry received money. However, William II was killed in 1100 while hunting in the New Forest, by an arrow shot by Walter Tyrell, and the throne passed to his elder brother. Robert, however, was returning from four years of fighting on the First Crusade, and within days Henry had seized the royal treasury at Westminster and proclaimed himself King of England. He later defeated Robert at Tinchebray to take Normandy as well. Duke Robert, the rightful King of England, spent the rest of his life in prison, dying in Cardiff Castle in 1134.

Henry was not one of the more compassionate kings, throwing a treacherous burgher named Conan Pilatus from a tower in Rouen. In 1119, Henry's son-in-law, Eustace de Pacy, and Ralph Harnec, the constable of Ivry, exchanged their children as hostages. When Eustace blinded Harnec's son, Harnec demanded vengeance and Henry allowed him to blind and mutilate Eustace's two daughters, who were also Henry's own grandchildren. Eustace and his wife Juliane, Henry's daughter, were outraged and threatened to rebel. Henry arranged to meet his daughter at a parley at Breteuil, only for Juliane to draw a crossbow and attempt to assassinate her father.

Henry holds the record for the largest number of acknowledged illegitimate children born to any English king, with 22 offspring for whom there is documentation, plus at least another three daughters. He probably died of food-poisoning in Normandy from lampreys (eel-like fish). His remains were sewn into the hide of a bull to preserve them, and taken back to Reading Abbey, which was destroyed during the Reformation.

'For the Name of Jesus and the protection of the Church I am ready to embrace death'

Last words, according to Edward Grim, an eyewitness

As Lord Chancellor, Becket controlled all state affairs for the benefit of Henry II. However, Henry wanted absolute control of the Church as well, so appointed his friend Becket to be Archbishop of Canterbury from 1162. A rift grew between the men, Becket taking the side of the Pope, who almost excommunicated Henry. When Becket returned from exile, he was assassinated by four of Henry II's knights in Canterbury Cathedral, after they had tried to drag him outside. Knowing he was about to die, he knelt and began to pray to God, Our Lady and the martyr St Denys:

'Scarce had he said the words than the wicked knight, fearing lest he should be rescued by the people and escape alive, leapt upon him suddenly ... wounded this lamb who was sacrificed to God on the head, cutting off the top of the crown ...; and by the same blow he wounded the arm of him who tells this. For he, when the ... monks and clerks fled, stuck close to the sainted Archbishop and held him in his arms till the one he interposed was almost severed.

Then he received a second blow on the head but still stood firm. At the third blow he fell on his knees and elbows, offering himself a living victim, and saying in a low voice, "For the Name of Jesus and the pro-tection of the Church I am ready to embrace death." Then the third knight inflicted a terrible wound as he lay, by which the sword was broken against the pavement, and the crown which was large was separated from the head. The fourth knight prevented any from inter-fering so that the others might freely perpetrate the murder. As to the fifth, no knight but that clerk who had entered with the knights, that a fifth blow might not be wanting to the martyr who was in other things like to Christ, he put his foot on the neck of the holy priest and precious martyr, and, horrible to say, scattered his brain and blood over the pavement, calling out to the others, "Let us away, knights; he will rise no more."'

'It is clear to me that I must leave everything and go hence from thee'

Last words to his son Tuli

'He ordered couriers to ride swiftly to his nearest son, Tuli, who was camped not far away. When the Master of War, now a man grown, dismounted at the yurt of the Khan, he found his father lying upon a carpet near the fire, wrapped in felt and sable robes. "It is clear to me," the old Mongol greeted the prince, "that I must leave everything and go hence from thee." He had been sick for some time, and this sickness, he knew now, was draining away his life. He ordered to his side the general officers of the horde, and while they knelt with Tuli, listening intently to his words, he gave them clear directions how to carry on the war against the Sung that he had begun but could not finish. Tuli, especially, was to take over all lands in the east, as Chatagai was to do in the west, while Ogotai must be supreme over them, the Kha Khan at Karakorum. Like the nomad he was, he died uncomplaining, leaving to his sons the greatest of empires and the most destructive of armies, as if his possessions had been no more than tents and herds. This was in the year 1227, the Year of the Mouse in the Cycle of the Twelve Beasts.'

Born Temujin, Genghis was the khan (ruler) and khagan (emperor) of the Mongol Empire, the largest continuous empire in history. He united the north-east Asian nomadic tribes, and his domain spread across Asia and China. He overcame at least 20 kingdoms, with the policy of *'All who surrender will be spared; whoever does not surrender, but opposes with struggle and dissension, shall be annihilated.'* His last words in legend were: *'Hero! A real hero!'* and to his commanders, *'I wish to die at home. Let not my end disarm you, and on no account weep for me, lest the enemy be warned of my death.'* His final words to his sons were: *'With heaven's aid I have conquered for you a huge empire. But my life was too short to achieve the conquest of the World. The task is left to you.'*

'Traitor was I never'

Part of last speech

'Sir William Wallace was instantly transferred to London, where he was brought to trial in Westminster Hall, with as much apparatus of infamy as the ingenuity of his enemies could devise. He was crowned with a garland of oak, to intimate that he had been king of outlaws. The arraignment charged him with high treason, in respect that he had stormed and taken towns and castles, and shed much blood. "Traitor," said Wallace, "was I never." The rest of the charges he confessed and proceeded to justify them. He was condemned, and executed by decapitation, 1305. His head was placed on a pinnacle on London Bridge, and his quarters were distributed over the kingdom.'

William Wallace, the leader in the fight for Scottish independence, was captured on 3 August near Glasgow and transported for a show trial in Westminster Hall. He had no lawyers and no jury, and was not allowed to speak. However, when accused of being a traitor, he shouted, *'I could not be a traitor to Edward, for I was never his subject,'* also quoted as *'Traitor was I never!'* He then asserted that his king was John Balliol. Balliol had been King of Scotland from 1292 to 1296, but had been forced by Edward I to abdicate and go into exile. Wallace was taken from the hall, stripped naked and dragged through the city for four miles at the heels of a horse to the Elms at Smithfield, wrapped in the hide of an ox to stop him being ripped apart and to prolong the agony. He was hanged, drawn and quartered – strangled by hanging but released while still alive, emasculated, eviscerated and his bowels burnt before him, then beheaded and his body cut into four parts. His tarred head was placed on a pike above London Bridge, along with the heads of other patriots, and his preserved limbs were displayed in Newcastle, Berwick, Stirling, and Aberdeen. *'A cruel yet fully deserved death,'* wrote an observer. On the National Wallace Monument in Stirling is inscribed Wallace's uncle's proverb, from Bower's *Scotichronicon* of 1444: *'This is the truth I tell you: of all things freedom's most fine. / Never submit to live, my son, in the bonds of slavery entwined.'*

JACQUES DE MOLAY
c.1244–18 March 1314

'Let evil swiftly befall those who have wrongly condemned us – God will avenge us'

Last words at the stake, according to Godfrey de Paris, an eyewitness

Jacques de Molay joined the Knights Templar in 1265, aged just 21. He later became Grand Preceptor of all England. He was elected twenty-third and last Grand Master of the Knights Templar shortly after they had been defeated by the Muslims and expelled from the Holy Land. The order's headquarters was temporarily established in Cyprus, and many Templars returned to Europe, while de Molay sought support for a new crusade to recapture Jerusalem. In 1307 he was summoned to France by Pope Clement V, the French puppet pope whom Philippe IV had installed at Avignon. The call was ostensibly to discuss combining with the Knights Hospitaller for a new crusade. Philippe IV and other French nobles were jealous of the wealth and lands of the Templars, and Clement informed de Molay that Philippe had laid charges against the Templars of homosexuality, heresy and blasphemy. De Molay challenged the king to make the charges public, and after weeks of secret plotting, Philippe suddenly arrested almost 5,000 Templars. Pope Clement initially chose not to intervene, but eventually sided with the king.

Over the following seven years, the imprisoned Templars endured continuous torture, confessions and executions until Phillipe felt he had enough power to kill de Molay. Despite the torture, de Molay had continued to be loyal to his order, refusing to disclose the location of its funds. In 1314, he disavowed a forged confession, such a disavowal being punishable by death. With Geoffroy de Charney, Preceptor of Normandy, he was slowly roasted to death over a hot, smokeless fire. All Templar lands and known wealth was confiscated. Henry Hart Milman's *History of Latin Christianity* (1855) states that de Molay's last words were: *"'Clement, iniquitous and cruel judge, I summon thee within forty days to meet me before the throne of the Most High." According to some accounts this fearful sentence included the King.'* A month later, Pope Clement V died of cancer, and within seven months Phillipe IV died in a hunting accident. De Molay's dying words had come true. In 2002, a document of 1308 confirming Clement's absolution for de Molay and other Templars was found in the Vatican's secret archives.

AGNOLO DI TURA DEL GRASSO
*c.*1300–post 1350

'There was no one wept for the dead,
for all awaited death'

From Agnolo di Tura, *The Plague in Siena: An Italian Chronicle*

Di Tura was a shoemaker and tax-collector who chronicled the Black Death in Siena. The bubonic plague wiped out between 30 and 60 per cent of the population of Europe at this time.

'The mortality began in Siena in May [1348]. It was a cruel and horrible thing; and I do not know where to begin to tell of the cruelty and the pitiless ways. It seemed to almost everyone that one became stupefied by seeing the pain. And it is impossible for the human tongue to recount the awful thing. Indeed one who did not see such horribleness can be called blessed. And the victims died almost immediately. They would swell beneath their armpits and in their groins, and fall over dead while talking. Father abandoned child, wife husband, one brother another; for this illness seemed to strike through the breath and sight. And so they died. And none could be found to bury the dead for money or friendship. Members of a household brought their dead to a ditch as best they could, without priest, without divine offices. Nor did the death bell sound. And in many places in Siena great pits were dug and piled deep with the multitude of dead. And they died by the hundreds both day and night, and all were thrown in those ditches and covered over with earth. And as soon as those ditches were filled more were dug.

And I, Agnolo di Tura, called the Fat, buried my five children with my own hands. And there were also those who were so sparsely covered with earth that the dogs dragged them forth and devoured many bodies throughout the city. There was no one who wept for any death, for all awaited death. And so many died that all believed that it was the end of the world. And no medicine or any other defence availed. And the lords selected three citizens who received a thousand gold florins from the commune of Siena that they were to spend on the poor sick and to bury the poor dead. And it was all so horrible that I, the writer, cannot think of it and so will not continue ...'

PETRARCH (FRANCESCO PETRARCA)
20 July 1304–19 July 1374

'We are continually dying; I while I am writing these words, you while you are reading them, others when they hear them or fail to hear them'

Letter to Philippe de Cabassoles, *c.*1360

On the morning before his seventieth birthday, Petrarch was found by his daughter Francesca slumped over his desk having died sometime during the night with a pen in his hand. He was buried in the parish church, but six years later, his remains were transferred to a sarcophagus built by his son-in-law. The red marble tomb can still be seen in the main square in Arquà Petrarca, Padua. Petrarch lived through the harshest times of the plague and lost nearly everyone he knew to it. His son, grandson, numerous friends, and of course Laura, his writings for whom will live for ever. In 1327, his first sight of a woman called Laura triggered an outpouring of passion in sonnets that lasted for over 20 years. Laura was a married woman whose identity is obscure. Petrarch's 'Letter to Prosperity' reflects on his unrequited love for her and her early death from plague: *'In my younger days I struggled constantly with an overwhelming but pure love affair – my only one, and I would have struggled with it longer had not premature death, bitter but salutary for me, extinguished the cooling flames. I certainly wish I could say that I have always been entirely free from desires of the flesh, but I would be lying if I did.'* His Church career did not allow him to marry, but he had two illegitimate children. His son, Giovanni, was born in 1337 but died of the plague in 1361, and a daughter, Francesca, was born in 1343.

Petrarch was one of the first people to refer to the Dark Ages. His writings and his development of the sonnet form influenced countless others, such as Boccaccio and Shakespeare. He revived recognition that a poet and intellectual was an important member of society, and royalty and nobles sought his company. In a letter to a friend, he even claimed that he had caused his own plague to spread over Europe.

JOHN HUSS (JAN HUS, JAN HUSS, JOHN HUS)
c.1372–6 July 1415

‘You are now going to burn a goose, but in a century you will have a swan which you can neither roast nor boil’

Last words at the stake

This Bohemian priest, philosopher, reformer, and professor at Prague's Charles University was tried as a heretic for preaching that following the Bible was more important than adherence to Church dogma. He was extremely important in the growing reformist movement in Europe, and his ideas were to influence Martin Luther a century later:

‘When the chain was put about him at the stake, he said, with a smiling countenance, "My Lord Jesus Christ was bound with a harder chain than this for my sake, and why then should I be ashamed of this rusty one?" When the faggots were piled up to his very neck, the duke of Bavaria was so officious as to desire him to abjure. "No, (said Huss) I never preached any doctrine of an evil tendency; and what I taught with my lips I now seal with my blood." He then said to the executioner, "You are now going to burn a goose (Huss signifying goose in the Bohemian language), but in a century you will have a swan which you can neither roast nor boil." If he were prophetic, he must have meant Martin Luther, who shone about a hundred years after, and who had a swan for his arms. The flames were now applied to the faggots, when our martyr sung a hymn with so loud and cheerful a voice that he was heard through all the cracklings of the combustibles, and the noise of the multitude. At length his voice was interrupted by the severity of the flames, which soon closed his existence. Then, with great diligence, gathering the ashes together, they cast them into the river Rhine, that the least remnant of that man should not be left upon the earth, whose memory, notwithstanding, cannot be abolished out of the minds of the godly, neither by fire, neither by water, neither by any kind of torment.'

JEROME OF PRAGUE (JERONÝM PRAŽSKÝ)
1379–30 May 1416

'This soul in flames I offer Christ, to Thee'

Last words at the stake

After visiting universities across Europe, Jerome returned to Prague and professed his admiration for the teachings of the reformer John Wycliffe. He became friendly with John Huss and an adherent of the Hussite movement in Bohemia, which favoured Wycliffe's doctrines of the fallibility of the established Church. Huss was imprisoned, but Jerome continued disseminating his friend's teachings until he himself was arrested. He was kept in such poor conditions that he fell ill and was induced to recant, and to renounce Wycliffe and Huss in 1415. He was also forced to write letters that agreed with Huss being burned for heresy. On 26 May 1416 Jerome was tried but on the second day recanted his recantation and was burned at the stake two days later.

'Jerome exclaimed, "What barbarity is this! For three hundred and forty days have I been confined in a variety of prisons. There is not a misery, there is not a want, that I have not experienced ..." Jerome received the same sentence that had been passed upon his martyred countryman. In consequence of this, he was, in the usual style of popish affectation, delivered over to the civil power: but as he was a layman, he had not to undergo the ceremony of degradation. They had prepared a cap of paper painted with red devils, which being put upon his head, he said, "Our Lord Jesus Christ, when He suffered death for me a most miserable sinner, did wear a crown of thorns upon His head, and for His sake will I wear this cap" ... Jerome was resolved to seal the doctrine with his blood; and he suffered death with the most distinguished magnanimity. In going to the place of execution he sang several hymns, and when he came to the spot, which was the same where Huss had been burnt, he knelt down, and prayed fervently. He embraced the stake with great cheerfulness, and when they went behind him to set fire to the faggots, he said, "Come here, and kindle it before my eyes; for if I had been afraid of it, I had not come to this place." The fire being kindled, he sang a hymn, but was soon interrupted by the flames; and the last words he was heard to say these, "This soul in flames I offer Christ, to Thee."'

JOAN OF ARC, JEANNE D'ARC
c.1412–30 May 1431

'Hold the cross high so I may see it through the flames!'

Attributed last words at the stake

At her trial in 1431, Joan of Arc said, *'I was in my thirteenth year when God sent a voice to guide me. At first, I was very much frightened. The voice came towards the hour of noon, in summer, in my father's garden ... If I said that God did not send me, I should condemn myself; truly God did send me.'* The voice told her to serve France against the English, instructing her to cut her hair, dress in men's uniform and take up arms. By 1429, the English and their Burgundian allies were occupying Paris and all of France north of the River Loire. Henry VI of England was claiming the French crown and resistance was minimal. Joan convinced a board of theologians, and then the Dauphin, to allow her to become a captain of troops. In 1429, she led the forces to lift the Siege of Orleans and then won at Troyes and Patay.

Her victories allowed the Dauphin to be crowned Charles VII on 17 July 1429, with Joan at his side at Rheims Cathedral. She was captured in 1430 by Burgundians, possibly through Charles's treachery, and sold to the English. The English in turn handed her over to the ecclesiastical court at Rouen led by Pierre Cauchon, the pro-English Bishop of Beauvais. 'The Maid of Orleans' was interrogated for over a year, tried for heresy and witchcraft, and forced to promise never to wear a man's clothes again. However, she was still in prison, with not enough evidence to condemn her, when she donned male clothing again, probably being tricked into doing so as there was nothing else to wear. Declared a heretic, after 14 months of interrogation she was tried and burned at the stake in Rouen market-place, with her ashes being thrown into the Seine. Charles VII did not attempt to come to her assistance. Her last words were also said to be *'Jesus! Jesus! Jesus!'* In 1456, a second trial was held and she was pronounced innocent. She was canonized in 1920.

RICHARD III, RICHARD PLANTAGENET, KING OF ENGLAND
2 October 1452–22 August 1485

'Treason! Treason! Treason! Treason! Treason!'

Traditional last words

The Yorkist king Richard III had usurped the throne, killing the rightful heirs, when the Lancastrian claimant, Henry Tudor, invaded Wales and began raising an army. Henry's army was badly outnumbered at Bosworth Field, and Richard III had taken hostage the son of Thomas Stanley, Henry's stepfather, to ensure Stanley's support. However, Stanley threw his forces into battle on the side of his kinsman, who became Henry VII when Richard was killed. Polydore Vergil wrote around 1512–13:

> 'Henry abode the brunt longer than ever his own soldiers would have wanted, who were now almost out of hope of victory, when William Stanley [Thomas's brother] with three thousand men came to the rescue: then truly in a very moment the residue all fled, and king Richard alone was killed fighting manfully in the thickest press of his enemies ... The report is that king Richard might have sought to save himself by flight; ... and some of them ... suspected treason, and exhorted him to fly, yea and when the matter began manifestly to quail, they brought him swift horses; but he, who was not ignorant that the people hated him ... is said to have answered, that that very day he would make end either of war or life, such great fierceness and such huge force of mind he had ... he came to the field with the crown upon his head, that thereby he might either make a beginning or end of his reign ...

> After that, commanding to pack up all bag and baggage, Henry with his victorious army proceeded in the evening to Leycester, where, for refreshing of his soldiers from their travail and pains, and to prepare for going to London, he tarried two days. In the meantime the body of king Richard naked of all clothing, and laid upon horse back with the arms and legs hanging down on both sides, was brought to the abbey of monks Franciscan at Leycester, a miserable spectacle in good sooth, but not unworthy for the mans life, and there was buried two days after without any pomp or solemn funeral.

'As a dying man always does'

Response on deathbed when asked how he enjoyed his food

Ruler of the Florentine Republic during the Italian Renaissance, Lorenzo the Magnificent was a diplomat, statesman and great patron of scholars, poets and artists.

'Savonarola [the celebrated Dominican priest who became leader of Florence in 1494] accordingly came, but, before he would consent to receive him as a penitent, required that he should declare his adherence to the true faith; to which Lorenzo assented. He then insisted on a promise from Lorenzo, that if he had unjustly obtained the property of others, he would return it. Lorenzo, after a short hesitation, replied, "Doubtless, father, I shall do this, or, if it be not in my power, I shall enjoin it as a duty upon my heirs." Thirdly, Savonarola required that he should restore the republic to liberty, and establish it in its former state of independence: to which Lorenzo not choosing to make any reply, the priest left him without giving him his absolution ...

No species of reputation is so cheaply acquired as that derived from death-bed fortitude. When it is fruitless to contend, and impossible to fly, little applause is due to that resignation which patiently awaits its doom. It is not therefore to be considered as enhancing that dignity of character which Lorenzo had so frequently displayed, that he sustained the last conflict with equanimity. "To judge from his conduct, and that of his servants," says Politiano [the poet Angelo Poliziano], "you would have thought that it was they who momentarily expected that fate, from which he alone appeared to be exempt." Even to the last the scintillations of his former vivacity were perceptible. Being asked, on taking a morsel of food, how he relished it, "As a dying man always does" was his reply. Having affectionately embraced his surrounding friends, and submitted to the last ceremonies of the church, he became absorbed in meditation, occasionally repeating portions of scripture, and accompanying his ejaculations with elevated eyes and solemn gestures of his hands, till the energies of life gradually declining, and pressing to his lips a magnificent crucifix, he calmly expired.'

POPE ALEXANDER VI, RODERIC LLANÇOL, later RODERIC DE BORJA I BORJA
1 January 1431–18 August 1503

'Wait a minute'

Dying words uttered after last confession

Basically a syphilitic, greedy sex maniac, a poisoner and a murderer, Alexander became a byword for the debased standards of the Church of his time. The Spaniard had bribed his way to the papacy, and as early as 1460, when he was a cardinal, he had been reported to Pius II for holding obscene dances with naked women in a garden at Siena. From the official diary of German chaplain Johann Burchard, Alexander's master of ceremonies, we learn that 'the pope's Christianity was a pretence'. Alexander had at least 12 bastard children, including Cesare, Giovanni, Lucrezia and Jofre, and his numerous mistresses ensured that the 'Vatican was again a brothel'.

> 'On Sunday evening, 30 October [1501], Don Cesare Borja gave his father a supper in the apostolic palace, with 50 decent prostitutes or courtesans in bright garb in attendance, who after the meal danced with the servants and others there, first fully dressed and then naked ... Following the supper, lampstands holding lighted candles were placed on the floor and chestnuts strewn about, which the prostitutes, naked and on their hands and knees, had to pick up with their mouths as they crawled in and out among the lampstands ... The Pope watched and admired their noble parts. The evening ended with an obscene contest of these women, coupled with male servants of the Vatican, for prizes which the Pope presented. Don Cesare, Donna Lucrezia and the Pope later each took a partner of their liking for further dalliances.'

Burchard recorded that in 1503, Cesare and Alexander were both taken ill with fever. Cesare recovered, but Alexander VI's stomach became swollen and turned to liquid, while his face became wine-coloured and his skin began to peel off. Finally his stomach and bowels bled profusely. After more than a week of intestinal bleeding and convulsive fevers, and after accepting the last rites and making a confession, he died at the age of 72. He is said to have uttered the words *'Wait a minute'* before expiring. His successor refused to hold a mass for Alexander, saying, *'It is blasphemous to pray for the damned.'*

CESARE BORGIA
13 September 1475–12 March 1507

'Here lies in little earth one who was feared by all, who held peace and war in his hand'

Inscription on his tomb beneath the altar of Santa Maria, Viana, Navarre, Spain

'Aut Caesar aut nihil' (*'Either Caesar or nothing'*) was the motto inscribed on Cesare Borgia's sword, while *'Aut Caesar aut nihil et nihil fuit'* (*'Either Caesar or nothing and nothing came of it'*) was the title of a requiem mass that was celebrated in the Santa Maria Church in his remembrance. In 1537, the Bishop of Calahorra visited the church and was horrified that so great a sinner was buried there, so Borgia's tomb was destroyed and his remains were transferred to an unconsecrated site outside the church so that his body would be *'trampled on by men and beasts'*. They stayed there until 1945, when they were accidentally exhumed by some workmen. In 2007, the Archbishop of Pamplona finally allowed the remains to be moved back inside the church, on the day before the 500th anniversary of Borgia's death.

Cesare was an illegitimate son of Cardinal Roderic Llançol y Borja, later Pope Alexander VI, and the brother of Lucrezia Borgia. He was made Bishop of Pamplona at the age of 15, and Cardinal of Valencia at 18. After his brother Giovanni Borgia's assassination in 1497, possibly on Cesare's own orders, he resigned his ecclesiastical offices and took command of the papal armies. In 1498 he married the sister of the King of Navarre, to win French support for a campaign to regain control of the Papal States. He had a series of military successes in the Papal States (1499–1503), gaining a reputation for ruthlessness, and by both treachery and bravery acquired lands across Italy. His political astuteness led Machiavelli to cite him as an example of the new 'Prince'. Borgia's gains proved fruitless, however, when Pope Alexander died in 1503 and the new pope, Julius II, demanded that he give up the lands. He escaped from prison in Spain and died fighting for Navarre at the Siege of Viana. His last words were said to have been: *'I have provided in the course of my life for everything except death, and now, alas, I am to die unprepared.'*

'While I thought I was learning to live, I have been learning how to die'

From his *Notebooks* of 1508–1518

Leonardo da Vinci, the illegitimate son of a notary and a peasant woman, is often regarded as a genius. He was a polymath, breaking new frontiers in science, mathematics, anatomy, engineering, sculpture, architecture, botany, invention, music and painting. Possibly the greatest painter ever, his few remaining works include *The Mona Lisa* and *The Last Supper*. The art historian Helen Gardner wrote that *'his mind and personality seem to us superhuman, the man himself mysterious and remote'*. Georgio Vasari's 1568 *Lives of the Artists* notes:

'In the normal course of events many men and women are born with remarkable talents; but occasionally, in a way that transcends nature, a single person is marvellously endowed by Heaven with beauty, grace and talent in such abundance that he leaves other men far behind, all his actions seem inspired and indeed everything he does clearly comes from God rather than from human skill. Everyone acknowledged that this was true of Leonardo da Vinci, an artist of outstanding physical beauty, who displayed infinite grace in everything that he did and who cultivated his genius so brilliantly that all problems he studied he solved with ease.'

In October 1515, Francis I of France recaptured Milan, and in 1516, Leonardo entered the king's service. Vasari recorded that Francis held Leonardo's head in his arms as da Vinci died three years later. Twenty years after this, the goldsmith Cellini reported that Francis had said: *'There had never been another man born in the world who knew as much as Leonardo, not so much about painting, sculpture and architecture, as that he was a very great philosopher.'* Remarkably for the time, Leonardo wrote: *'The earth is not in the centre of the Sun's orbit nor at the centre of the universe, but in the centre of its companion elements, and united with them. And any one standing on the moon, when it and the sun are both beneath us, would see this our earth and the element of water upon it just as we see the moon, and the earth would light it as it lights us.'*

BAYARD, CHEVALIER DE (PIERRE TERRAIL LE VIEUX, SEIGNEUR DE BAYARD)

1473–30 April 1524

'I have no regret in dying'

Last words and message for the king

'They carried him within the shadow of a great tree, and laid him, as he asked, facing the enemy. It was the moment of farewell, and many of them were in tears. Alègre [the Provost of Paris] bent down. "Tell the king," said Bayard, "that I die happy in his service and with sword in hand, as I have always wished. And I have no regret in dying, except that I lose the means of serving him any more."'

Known after his death as '*le chevalier sans peur et sans reproche*' ('*the knight without fear and beyond reproach*'), Bayard was called by his contemporaries '*le bon chevalier*' ('*the good knight*'). During military service, he was knighted after the Battle of Fornovo, where he had captured a standard. In 1502 he was taken prisoner at Milan, and was later wounded at Canossa. He distinguished himself at the Siege of Genoa and in 1512 fought in the Battle of Ravenna. When war again broke out between Francis I and the Holy Roman Emperor Charles V, Bayard, with 1,000 men, held Mézières for France against an army of 35,000, compelling Charles' generals to raise the siege. His resistance saved central France from invasion, and he was celebrated in the parlement in Paris. Francis I thus gained the time to drive out Charles V's forces from France in 1521. Bayard was next sent into Italy with Admiral Bonnivet, who was defeated at Robecco and severely wounded during his retreat. Bonnivet implored Bayard to save the army. Bayard repulsed the foremost pursuers, but was mortally wounded by the stone ball of an arquebus, which fractured his spine.

His first exclamation was '"*Jesus, mon Dieu, je suis mort!*" ... *At his own insistence, he was placed with his back to a tree, and his face turned in the path of the approaching enemy. His friends would have borne him away from the melee, but he would not suffer it. "Let me die in peace. It is all over with me. I am mortally hurt. I know it, and I would not, in my last moments, turn my back upon the enemy for the first time in my life."'* Propped up against the tree, for want of a crucifix he was confessed with the cruciform hilt of his own sword acting as a cross. Even the Spanish commander Pescara and Charles, Duc de Bourbon, attended him at his death. Other last words are said to be '*Pity me not. I die as a man of honour ought, in discharge of my duty. They indeed are objects of pity who fight against their king, their country, and their oath.*'

NICCOLÒ DE BERNARDO DI MACHIAVELLI
3 May 1469–21 June 1527

'Tanto nomini nullum par elogium'
('No eulogy would be adequate to praise so great a name')

Inscribed on a cenotaph at the Church of Santa Croce, Florence

The site of Machiavelli's grave is unknown, and attributed to him is the saying: *'I desire to go to Hell and not to Heaven. In the former place I shall enjoy the company of popes, kings and princes, while in the latter are only beggars, monks and apostles.'* Called the founder of modern political science, he was a writer, philosopher, and civil servant in Florence. Appointed Secretary to the Chancery after the execution of Savonarola, he wrote *The Art of War* and other books, but his most famous work, *The Prince*, was not published until five years after his death, and thirteen years after he completed it. Much of it is based upon the successful state-building strategies of Cesare Borgia. From 1503 to 1506, Machiavelli was in charge of the Florentine militia, training the citizenry and distrusting mercenaries, and he led his army to victory against Pisa in 1509. However, when the Pope and the Medici used Spanish mercenaries to overrun Florence in 1512, he was deposed from all posts.

In 1513 he was tried for conspiracy and tortured using the strappado technique. The victim's hands are first tied behind his back, and then he is suspended by means of a rope attached to his wrists, which most likely dislocates both arms. Weights may be added to the body to intensify the effect and increase the pain. The torture, known also as 'reverse hanging', was used by the Inquisition and is still in use today (in 1996, the European Court of Human Rights found Turkey guilty of strappado and other medieval tortures). Machiavelli denied all charges and was released to return to his estate, where he wrote the treatises for which he is famous. He tells us that *'no prince is ever benefited by making himself hated'* and *'Let not princes complain of the faults committed by the people subjected to their authority, for they result entirely from their own negligence or bad example.'* Francis Bacon noted his importance: *'We are much beholden to Machiavelli and others, that write what men do, and not what they ought to do.'*

'Pluck up thy spirits, man, and be not afraid to do thine office, my neck is very short'

Last words to his executioner, according to his son-in-law, William Roper

A statesman, lawyer, scholar and author, known throughout Europe as a Renaissance humanist, More was Henry VIII's Lord Chancellor from 1529. A friend of the king, he also acted as his secretary, interpreter, speech-writer, chief diplomat, adviser and confidant. The previous Chancellor, Cardinal Wolsey, had failed to obtain Henry's divorce from Catherine of Aragon so that he could marry Anne Boleyn. Wolsey was on his way to London to be tried for treason when he died. Henry broke with the Church of Rome, and declared himself Supreme Head of the Church in England, triggering the Reformation, establishing the Anglican Church and allowing him to divorce and remarry. More resigned the chancellorship, arguing continually against the divorce and the split with Rome. In 1534 he was arrested for refusing to swear an oath of succession, repudiating the Pope and accepting the annulment of Henry's marriage. He was tried for treason at Westminster and on 6 July 1535 was executed on Tower Hill.

'... from thence led towards the place of execution, where going up the scaffold, which was so weak that it was ready to fall, he said to Mr Lieutenant, "I pray you, I pray you, Mr Lieutenant, see me safe up, and for my coming down let me shift for myself." Then desired he all the people thereabouts to pray for him, and to bear witness with him, that he should then suffer death in and for the faith of the holy Catholic Church, which done he kneeled down, and after his prayers said, he turned to the executioner, and with a cheerful countenance spake unto him. "Pluck up thy spirits, man, and be not afraid to do thine office, my neck is very short. Take heed therefore thou shoot not awry for saving thine honesty." So passed Sir Thomas More out of this world to God upon the very same day in which himself had most desired.'

'Lastly, I make this vow, that mine eyes desire thou above all things'

Last letter to Henry VIII

In late December 1535, probably suffering from cancer and sensing that she was dying, the former queen made her will and wrote one final letter, to Henry VIII:

> 'My Lord and Dear Husband, The hour of my death draweth fast on, the tender love I owe thou forceth me, my case being such, to commend myself to thou, and to put thou in remembrance with a few words of the health and safeguard of thine soul which thou ought to prefer before all worldly matters, and before the care and pampering of thy body, for the which thou has cast me into many calamities and thineself into many troubles. For my part, I pardon thou everything, and I desire to devoutly pray God that He will pardon thou also. For the rest, I commend unto thou our daughter Mary, beseeching thou to be a good father unto her, as I have heretofore desired. I entreat thou also, on behalf of my maids, to give them marriage portions, which is not much, they being but three. For all mine other servants I solicit the wages due them, and a year more, lest they be unprovided for. Lastly, I make this vow, that mine eyes desire thou above all things. Katharine the Queen.'

In Catherine's 24-year marriage, of six births, only one child survived, the future Queen Mary I. Henry VIII wanted a male heir, and his desire to marry Anne Boleyn set in motion the events leading to the breaking away of the English Church from Rome. In 1533, Archbishop Cranmer declared the secret marriage of Henry and Anne to be valid, and the king's marriage with Catherine was dissolved. Catherine refused to accept Henry as Supreme Head of the Church of England and continued to consider herself his rightful wife and queen until her death. In 1535 she was transferred to the decaying Kimbolton Castle. She wore a hair shirt and stayed in one small room, leaving only to attend mass. She was forbidden to see or write to her daughter. Henry offered both Catherine and Mary better quarters and each other's company if they would acknowledge Anne Boleyn as his new queen. Neither did.

ANNE BOLEYN
Between 1500 and 1509–19 May 1536

'I heard say the executioner was very good, and I have a little neck'

Conversation with the Constable of the Tower of London
on the morning of her execution

Anne Boleyn was the second wife of Henry VIII and the mother of Elizabeth I. On 2 May 1536, she was arrested and taken to the Tower of London. On 12 May, four men, including her own brother, were put on trial, falsely accused of having sexual relations with her. On 15 May, Anne was accused of adultery, incest and high treason, and two days later her brother and the other men were executed. Henry commuted Anne's sentence from burning to beheading and brought a swordsman from France, rather than use a common axe.

On the morning of her execution, Anne sent for the Constable of the Tower, who wrote: *'And in the writing of this she sent for me, and at my coming she said, "Mr Kingston, I hear I shall not die afore noon, and I am very sorry therefore, for I thought to be dead by this time and past my pain." I told her it should be no pain, it was so little. And then she said, "I heard say the executioner was very good, and I have a little neck", and then put her hands about it, laughing heartily.'* She then climbed the scaffold and made a short speech to the crowd:

'Good Christian people, I am come hither to die, for according to the law, and by the law I am judged to die, and therefore I will speak nothing against it. I am come hither to accuse no man, nor to speak anything of that, whereof I am accused and condemned to die, but I pray God save the king and send him long to reign over you, for a gentler nor a more merciful prince was there never: and to me he was ever a good, a gentle and sovereign lord. And if any person will meddle of my cause, I require them to judge the best. And thus I take my leave of the world and of you all, and I heartily desire you all to pray for me. O Lord have mercy on me, to God I commend my soul.'

JANE SEYMOUR, QUEEN CONSORT OF HENRY VIII
1508–24 October 1537

> **'Here lies Jane, a phoenix**
> **Who died in giving another phoenix birth.**
> **Let her be mourned, for birds like these**
> **Are rare indeed.'**

Jane Seymour's epitaph in St George's Chapel, Windsor Palace

Jane was the third wife of Henry VIII, but she never gave up her Roman Catholic faith. Because of this she tried to have Henry's eldest child, Mary Tudor, brought to court and made heir to the throne behind any children that Jane might have with Henry. She also sought clemency for the ringleaders of the Pilgrimage of Grace, thus earning the king's anger. Jane was the mother of Henry VIII's longed-for heir, Prince Edward, and after his birth she immediately sent the following letter to the Privy Council:

'Right trusty and well beloved, we greet you well, and for as much as by the inestimable goodness and grace of Almighty God, we be delivered and brought in childbed of a prince, conceived in most lawful matrimony between my lord the king's majesty and us, doubting not but that for the love and affection which you bear unto us and to the commonwealth of this realm, the knowledge thereof should be joyous and glad tidings unto you, we have thought good to certify you of the same. To the intent you might not only render unto God condign thanks and prayers for so great a benefit but also continually pray for the long continuance and preservation of the same here in this life to the honour of God, joy and pleasure of my lord the king and us, and the universal weal, quiet and tranquillity of this whole realm. Given under our signet at my lord's manor of Hampton Court the 12th day of October. Jane the Quene.'

Jane died of puerperal fever twelve days after the birth. Henry wore black for a year and was buried alongside her.

CATHERINE HOWARD, QUEEN CONSORT OF ENGLAND
1520 or 1521–13 February 1542

'Yours as long as life endures'

Letter to Thomas Culpeper, dated spring 1541

Henry VIII referred to his fifth wife as *'the rose without a thorn'*. In 1540, Thomas Cranmer's secretary, Ralph Morice, wrote to his master: *'The King's affection was so marvellously set upon that gentlewoman , as it was never known that he had the like to any woman.'* Catherine married Henry almost immediately after his annulment from Anne of Cleves was arranged. However, she found her new husband repulsive, as he weighed over 20 stone and had foul-smelling ulcers on his thighs and lower legs. Early in 1541, she embarked upon a romance with Henry's favourite courtier, Thomas Culpeper, whom she had desired since she came to court two years before. As the liaison progressed, she employed people in her household to prevent them informing on her relationship, one of them being her former lover Francis Dereham.

Dereham and Culpeper were tortured and executed. Katherine admitted to her premarital indiscretions, but maintained that she had always been faithful to Henry. She was accused of high treason and executed, being laid to rest next to her cousin, Anne Boleyn, in the Tower of London. At her trial, an incriminating letter written by her to Culpeper was produced. It read:

'Master Culpeper, I heartily recommend me unto you, praying you to send me word how that you do. It was showed me that you was sick, the which thing troubled me very much till such time that I hear from you, praying you to send me word how that you do, for I never longed so much for a thing as I do to see you and to speak with you, the which I trust shall be shortly now ... I pray you to give me a horse for my man for I had much ado to get one and therefore I pray send me one by him and in so doing I am as I said before, and thus I take my leave of you, trusting to see you shortly again and I would you was with me now that you might see what pain I take in writing to you. Yours as long as life endures, Katheryn.'

JAMES V, KING OF SCOTLAND
c.10 April 1512–14 December 1542

'It came with a lass, it will pass with a lass'

Dying words

'James was dying in his thirty-first year, of the sorrow of this world, for which human physicians could of course devise no remedy. Disease of the mind, in temperaments ardent and excitable as that of James V, quickly generates bodily malady, and "he became" we are told, "so heavy and dolorous that he neither eat nor drank any thing that had good digestion, and became so vehement sick that no man had hope of his life". But still the one painful remembrance which had swallowed up all others was present with him; forever he harped on his old strain, "Oh, fled is Oliver! Is Oliver taken?" and these words he was heard to murmur to himself at intervals as long as he retained the power of articulation. In one of his moments of self-recollection, however, "he sent for certain of his lords, both spiritual and temporal, to give him counsel; but ere they came he was well nigh strangled with extreme melancholy. By this time the post came out of Linlithgow, showing the King good tidings that the Queen was delivered." The King briefly inquired "whether it were man or woman that had been born to him". The messenger replied that it was "a fair daughter". "Farewell," exclaimed the King, with prophetic reference, "to the crown of Scotland: it came with a lass, and it will pass with a lass." ... pronouncing which he twice repeats the sorrowful ejaculation alas! to express the disappointment of his last earthly hope. "And so," continues the chronicler, "he commended himself to Almighty God, and turned his back to his lords, and his face to the wall."'

It seems that the young king died after a nervous collapse following the battle against the English at Solway Moss, where his favourite, Sir Oliver Sinclair de Pitcairns, had led the Scots forces to their heaviest defeat in history. James' only surviving legitimate child, Mary I, Queen of Scots, was just six days old. His comment reveals that he believed the Stuart line, which began with Robert the Bruce's daughter, would cease with his own.

HENRY VIII, KING OF ENGLAND
28 June 1491–28 January 1547

'Monks! Monks! Monks!'

Last utterances

Henry came to the throne in 1509, and in attempting to get a male heir was responsible for the Reformation and the Dissolution of the Monasteries. Probably suffering from Type II diabetes, he became obese, with a waist measurement of 54 inches (137 cm) and ulcerated legs, hastening his death at the age of only 55. He was buried in St George's Chapel in Windsor Castle, alongside Jane Seymour. With six wives, he eventually produced three legitimate heirs, Edward VI, Mary I and Elizabeth I, none of whom left descendants, so his dream of a Tudor dynasty died out with Elizabeth's death in 1603. Of his wives, Anne of Cleves and Catherine Parr survived him; Catherine of Aragon, the mother of the future Mary I, died in 1535; Jane Seymour died two weeks after giving birth to the future Edward VI in 1537; Anne Boleyn was executed in 1536, when her daughter, the future Elizabeth I, was only two years old; Catherine Howard was executed in 1542. These last two marriages were annulled after the executions.

During the Dissolution, monasteries, cathedrals, abbeys and churches were stripped of all their wealth, and destroyed, and many monks and nuns became beggars across the land. Perhaps Henry was hallucinating, therefore, when he spoke his last words. In his final speech to Parliament, on 24 December 1545, as Supreme Head of the Church of England, he railed against its members:

'Be not judges yourselves of your own fantastical opinions and vain expositions; and although you be permitted to read Holy Scriptures and to have the Word of God in your mother tongue, you must understand it is licensed so to do only to inform your conscience and inform your children and families, not to make Scripture a railing and taunting stock against priests and preachers. I am very sorry to know and hear how irreverently that precious jewel, the Word of God, is disputed, rhymed, sung, and jangled in every alehouse and tavern, contrary to the true meaning and doctrine of the same.'

FRANÇOIS RABELAIS
c.1494–9 April 1553

'I have nothing, owe a great deal, and the rest I leave to the poor'
Single statement in his last will and testament, 1533

There are various versions of Rabelais' last words. Peter Motteux, in his *Life of Rabelais* (2005), states that they were: '*I am going to seek a great perhaps; draw the curtain, the farce is played.*' Rabelais was in turn a Franciscan friar, Benedictine monk, humanist, curate and doctor, whose series of four comic novels *Gargantua and Pantagruel* are classics of literature. From him we get the adjective Rabelaisian, meaning something coarsely humorous. His obscene wit and ecclesiastical satire led to his condemnation by the Sorbonne. His protagonists are giants travelling in a world full of greed and stupidity. With his outrageous anecdotes he concentrated upon the physical joys of life – food, drink, sex, and the bodily functions connected to them – and mocked asceticism and oppressive religious and political forces. His precept was '*Drink always and you shall never die.*' In Book One he also tells us, when requiring a drink of wine to cure thirst: '*Nature abhors a vacuum.*' '*Speak the truth and shame the Devil*' from the author's prologue shows his distaste for the attitudes of the Church of his day. Other sayings from Rabelais are: '*Plain as the nose in a man's face*' and '*Looking as like ... as one pea does like another.*'

Using the pseudonym of Alcofribas Nasier, an anagram of his name, Rabelais saw his works banned by the Church, and later placed on the Vatican's Index of Forbidden Books. Symptomatic of his relationship with the Church is the following anti-Inquisition passage in Book Four:

> 'Yet these devilish heretics refuse to learn and know it. Burn 'em, tear 'em, nip 'em with hot pincers, drown 'em, hang 'em, spit 'em at the bunghole, pelt 'em, paut 'em, bruise 'em, beat 'em, cripple 'em, dismember 'em, cut 'em, gut 'em, bowel 'em, paunch 'em, thrash 'em, slash 'em, gash 'em, chop 'em, slice 'em, slit 'em, carve 'em, saw 'em ... and carbonnade 'em on gridirons, these wicked heretics!'

'I see Heaven open and Jesus on the right hand of God'

Last words at the stake

Cranmer was involved in Henry VIII's negotiations with the Pope over divorcing Catherine of Aragon, and in 1533 Henry appointed him Archbishop of Canterbury in an effort to overthrow papal supremacy in England. Cranmer annulled Henry's marriage to Catherine, supported his marriage to Anne Boleyn, and later helped him divorce her. After the king's death in 1547, he became an influential adviser to the young Edward VI, moving England in a Protestant direction. He wrote the Forty-two Articles, from which the Thirty-nine Articles of Anglican belief are derived. When the Catholic Mary I became queen, Cranmer (the author of the original English Book of Common Prayer), Nicholas Ridley (the Bishop of London) and Hugh Latimer (the Bishop of Worcester) stood trial as Protestant heretics. Cranmer's case was appealed to the Pope, but while he awaited a response, Ridley and Latimer were executed and Cranmer was forced to watch their burning. Before he died, Latimer was alleged to have said: *'Be of good comfort, Master Ridley; we shall this day light such a candle, by God's grace, in England as I trust shall never be put out.'*

While waiting for a decision on his appeal, Cranmer recanted six times, to no avail. On 21 March 1556, he was taken to St Mary's Church in Oxford and, following a sermon, ordered to recant publicly. However, he repudiated his recantations, *'And forasmuch as my hand offended in writing contrary to my heart, therefore my hand shall first be punished; for if I may come to the fire it shall be first burned ... And as for the pope, I refuse him, as Christ's enemy, and Antichrist with all his false doctrine.'* After he was taken to the stake and the fire started, Cranmer held his right hand directly into the flame and cried out his last words for everyone to hear. His final words at the stake have also been recorded as *'This is the hand that wrote it, and therefore shall it suffer first punishment'*, and *'I have sinned, in that I signed with my hand what I did not believe with my heart. When the flames are lit, this hand shall be the first to burn.'*

'Now I'm oiled. Keep me from the rats.'

Attributed last words

This Italian satirist is considered the father of pornographic writing, and known as the 'Scourge of Princes' for his sarcastic attacks on the aristocracy and the Church. His great friend, the artist Titian, painted him at least three times, and on another occasion came to him with a problem. The Duke of Urbino had commissioned Titian to paint a nude portrait of his old and ugly wife. Titian feared the consequences, so Aretino hired a beautifully proportioned prostitute to pose for the body, telling Titian to add a flattering portrait of the duchess for the head. Titian named the painting *The Venus of Urbino*, which pleased the duchess immensely. When Aretino and Titian presented the finished painting to the duke, he sighed and said, '*If I could have had that girl's body, even with my wife's head, I would have been a happier man.*' Aretino collapsed in a fit of laughter that provoked a stroke. He was unconscious by the time a priest was brought to administer the last rites. No sooner had the priest finished than Aretino opened his eyes, spoke his final words and died. Another source states that he died of suffocation from laughing too much.

Born illegitimate, Aretino was exiled from his native city of Arezzo, and in Rome came under the patronage of a rich banker, who was also a patron of the great painter Raphael. When Pope Leo X's pet elephant Hanno died, Aretino wrote a last will and testament for the animal, satirizing the leading figures in Rome, including the Pope. Later, some of his ribald sonnets caused such outrage that he had temporarily to flee from Rome. A bishop tried to have him assassinated, and he went to Venice, which he described as *'the seat of all vices'*. From the relative security of independent Venice, Aretino was said to have '*kept all that was famous in Italy in a kind of state of siege*', as leading figures were afraid of his scornful observations of their characters. Cultural historian Jacob Burckhardt wrote that he was '*the father of modern journalism*' and that '*to the coarsest as well as the most refined malice he added a grotesque wit so brilliant that in some cases it does not fall short of that of Rabelais*'.

'When I am dead and opened, you shall find "Calais" lying in my heart'

Attributed last words

Despite the above being given in the 1808 edition of Raphael Holinshed's *Chronicles of England, Scotland and Ireland* as Mary's last words, the original account is:

> 'As touching the manner of whose death, some say that she died of a timpanie [abdominal illness], some by her much sighing before her death supposed she died of thought and sorrow. Whereupon her council seeing her sighing, and desirous to know the cause, to the end they might minister more ready consolation unto her, feared (as they said) that she took some thought for the king's majesty her husband, who was gone from her. To whom she answered again; Indeed (said she) that may be one cause, but that is not the greatest wound that pierces my oppressed mind: but what was she would not express to them. Albeit afterward she opened the matter more plainly to mistress Rice and mistress Clarence (if it be true that they told me, who himself heard it off mistress Rice) who then being most familiar with her, and most bold about her, told her that they feared she took thought for king Philip's departing from her. Not that only (said she) but when I am dead and opened, you shall find Calais lying in my heart ... And here an end of Queen Marie ...'

Having inherited the Spanish throne upon his father's abdication, Philip II of Spain returned to England in 1557 to persuade his wife Queen Mary to support Spain in the war against France. The English forces fared badly, and as a result lost Calais, England's sole remaining continental possession, on 13 January 1558. Mary died at the end of the year, allegedly saying that her husband's name and Calais would be engraved on her heart. She had returned England to Catholicism on her accession, burning over 300 Protestant 'heretics' in the Marian Persecution, but her successor, her half-sister Elizabeth, took the country back to the Protestant faith with the Act of Settlement, which introduced a greater degree of toleration.

NOSTRADAMUS (MICHEL DE NOSTREDAME)
21 December 1503–2 July 1566

'You will not find me alive at sunrise'
Last words and final prediction

Nostradamus was by profession an apothecary, but despite his claim that he had discovered a cure for the plague, it was his predictions that brought him real recognition. One of his prophecies reached Catherine de Medici, the wife of Henry II, who believed it was about her husband: *'The young lion will surpass the old one in national field by a single duel. He will pierce his eyes in a golden cage two blows at once, to die a grievous death.'* In 1555, after reading his almanacs, she summoned Nostradamus to Paris to explain them and to draw up almanacs for her children. After Henry was killed when a lance pierced his eye during a tournament in 1559, Nostradamus became famous, and Catherine made him counsellor and physician to the new king.

By 1566, Nostradamus' painful gout had turned into dropsy (oedema), and in late June he summoned his lawyer to draw up an extensive will. On the evening of 1 July, his assistant Jean de Chavigny found him writing at his bench and said, *'Tomorrow, master?'* Nostradamus replied that he would be dead by dawn, and de Chavigny left the room. When he returned the next day, he found Nostradamus dead and a note on the desk: *'Upon the return of the Embassy, the King's gift put in place, Nothing more will be done. He will have gone to God's nearest relatives, friends, blood brothers, Found quite dead near bed and bench.'* Nostradamus began to write his prophetic verses in 1554, divided into ten sections called *Centuries*, which refers to the number of verses in each section.

The *Prophecies* of Nostradamus, the first edition of which appeared in 1555, have rarely been out of print since his death. Stanza 51 from Century 2 seems to refer to the Great Fire of London: *'The blood of the just will be demanded of London burnt by fire in three times twenty plus six. The ancient lady will fall from her high position, and many of the same denomination will be killed.'* The 'ancient lady' is said to be St Paul's Cathedral.

JOHN KNOX
1505/1515–24 November 1572

'Here lies one who neither feared nor flattered any flesh'

Epitaph on tomb, by James Douglas, Earl of Morton, 26 November 1572

The Earl of Morton, Regent of Scotland, in the presence of an immense funeral procession that had followed Knox's body to its last resting place, declared: '*Here lyeth a man who in his life never feared the face of man, who hath been often threatened with dagger, but yet hath ended his days in peace and honour.*' Knox had refused the English bishopric of Rochester because he believed that he would be affected by pride, and left virtually nothing in his will, which reads:

'None have I corrupted. None have I defrauded. Merchandise have I not made – to God's glory I write – of the glorious Evangel of Jesus Christ; but, according to the measure of the grace granted unto me, I have divided the Sermon of Truth in just parts, beating down the rebellion of the proud against God, and raising up the consciences troubled with the knowledge of their sins, by declaring Jesus Christ, the strength of His Death, and the mighty operation of His Resurrection, in the hearts of the Faithful. Of this, I say, I have a testimony this day in my conscience, before God, however the world rage.'

He became a committed Protestant after his friend George Wishart was burned for heresy, joining the Protestants being besieged in St Andrews Castle. Captured by the French, he was forced to row in French galleys for 19 months, and was also exiled in England for years. Knox hated the Catholic Mary of Guise, wife of King James of Scotland and mother of Mary, Queen of Scots, and his *First Blast of the Trumpet Against the Monstrous Regiment of Women* was aimed at Mary Tudor, Mary of Guise and Mary, Queen of Scots. In response to Knox's imprecatory prayers, the Catholic Queen of Scots is reputed to have said: '*I fear the prayers of John Knox more than all the assembled armies of Europe.*' As leader of the Reformation in Scotland, Knox supervised the preparation of the constitution and liturgy of the Reformed Church.

SIR PHILIP SIDNEY
30 November 1554–17 October 1586

'Thy necessity is yet greater than mine'

Words spoken after the poet-courtier received his
death wound at the Battle of Zutphen

An Elizabethan soldier, poet and courtier, Sidney was Governor of Flushing
in the Netherlands. In 1586 he joined Sir John Norris in the Dutch War of Independence against Catholic Spain. He was shot in the thigh, taking 26 days to die.

'The 22nd of September opened gloomily. So thick a mist covered the
Flemish lowlands that a man could not see farther than ten paces.
Sidney, leading a troop of two-hundred horsemen, pushed his way
up to the walls of Zutphen. Chivalrous punctilio caused him to be ill-
defended, for meeting Sir William Pelham in light armour, he threw off
his cuisses, and thus exposed himself to unnecessary danger. The
autumn fog, which covered every object, suddenly dispersed; and the
English now found themselves confronted by a thousand horsemen of
the enemy, and exposed to the guns of the town. They charged, and
Sidney's horse was killed under him. He mounted another, and joined
in the second charge. Reinforcements came up, and a third charge was
made, during which he received a wound in the left leg. The bullet,
which some supposed to have been poisoned, entered above the knee,
broke the bone, and lodged itself high up in the thigh. His horse took
fright, and carried him at a gallop from the field. He kept his seat,
however; and when the animal was brought to order, had himself
carried to Leicester's station.

On the way occurred the incident so well-known to every one who is
acquainted with his name. "Being thirsty with excess of bleeding, he
called for drink, which was presently brought him; but as he was
putting the bottle to his mouth, he saw a poor soldier carried along,
who had eaten his last at the same feast, ghastly casting up his eyes at
the bottle, which Sir Philip perceiving, took it from his head before
he drank, and delivered it to the poor man, with these words, Thy
necessity is yet greater than mine.'

MARY, QUEEN OF SCOTS
8 December 1542–8 February 1587

'Tonight, after dinner, I have been advised of my sentence. I will be executed like a criminal at eight in the morning.'

Her last letter, to her brother-in-law Henry III of France, from Fotheringhay Castle

Mary was only six days old when her father James V died and she became Queen of Scots. In 1558 she married Francis, Dauphin of France, becoming Queen of France the following year. She was widowed the year after that and returned to Scotland, marrying her cousin Lord Darnley, who was killed following an explosion. She then married the man believed to have murdered Darnley, the Earl of Bothwell, but there was an uprising and she fled to England with her one-year-old son, the future James VI. Mary sought protection from her cousin, Elizabeth I, and hoped to inherit the crown of England. However, she was imprisoned for almost twenty years, resented because she was a Catholic. Eventually there was a show trial for treason, where she had no legal counsel, and claimed that as she was not an English subject she could not be convicted of treason. She reminded the jury: '*Remember Gentlemen the Theatre of history is wider than the Realm of England.*' Found guilty, she was sentenced to beheading and forgave her executioners, though it took two blows of the axe to kill her, the first smashing the back of her head. Her son, James VI of Scotland, became James I of England, and ordered Fotheringhay Castle to be obliterated.

Her letter reads in part:

> 'I have not had time to give you a full account of everything that has happened, but if you listen to my doctor and my other unfortunate servants, you will learn the truth, and how, thanks to God, I scorn death and vow that I meet it innocent of any crime, even if I were their subject. The Catholic faith and the assertion of my God-given right to the English crown are the two issues on which I am condemned, and yet I am not allowed to say that it is for the Catholic religion that I die, but for fear of interference with theirs ... The bearer of this letter and his companions, most of them your subjects, will testify to my conduct at my last hour ...'

ROBERT DUDLEY, FIRST EARL OF LEICESTER
24 June 1532–4 September 1588

'Here lies a valiant warrior / Who never drew a sword'

Ben Jonson's epitaph 'Of the Earle of Leister'

'Here lies a valiant warrior,
Who never drew a sword;
Here lies a noble courtier,
Who never kept his word;
Here lies the Earle of Leister,
Who govern'd the Estates;
Whom the Earth could never living love,
And the just Heaven now hates.'

At Christmas 1618, Ben Jonson went to stay with William Drummond of Hawthornden, a Scottish poet well known in literary circles. The account of their conversations was rediscovered and printed in 1842. In it Jonson recounted: '*The Earle of Leister gave a botel of liquor to his Lady, which he willed her to use in any faintness; which she, after his return from Court, not knowing it was poison, gave him, and so he died.*' Thus Jonson believed that Leicester was poisoned. He was one of many who disliked the earl for his powerful influence over Elizabeth I. It was widely believed that the pair were lovers, and they were close for 30 years. Elizabeth had known Leicester from childhood, and from her first year on the throne until his death he was a favourite courtier. For many years he was a suitor for the queen's hand, and although she gave him reason to hope, she believed that marriage to him would bring civil war.

Historians believe that Leicester died of stomach cancer, malaria or a heart condition. He had been unwell for some time, and a week before his death dined with Elizabeth and said his last farewell. On hearing of his death, she locked herself in her apartment for several days, until Lord Burghley had the door broken down. She kept Leicester's final letter, sent six days before his death, in her bedside treasure box. She wrote on it: '*his last letter*' and it was still there when she died 15 years later.

'I have only done my duty as a man is bound to do'

Alfred, Lord Tennyson, *The Revenge*, 1878

A cousin of Sir Walter Raleigh and Sir Francis Drake, Grenville was captaining HMS *Revenge* at Flores when the English fleet was surprised by a larger Spanish squadron. The English fled to sea, but Grenville refused to leave his sick men ashore, and faced the 53 enemy ships with only half a crew. For 12 hours he fought off the Spanish, causing heavy damage to 15 of their galleons. Battle ceased as darkness fell, but next morning the *Revenge* was still afloat, though its mast and sails were gone and its holds were flooded. Grenville ordered his chief gunner to sink the ship to stop it falling into enemy hands, but the survivors wanted him to surrender, and he agreed provided the Spanish granted them full honours of war and returned them to England immediately. The Spanish commander consented and the battle ended. The *Revenge* was captured, and Grenville, mortally wounded, was taken on board the Spanish admiral's ship *San Pablo*, where he died ten days later. Shortly afterwards an enormous storm sank the *Revenge* and 14 Spanish ships.

'"Sink me the ship, Master Gunner
    – sink her, split her in twain!
Fall into the hands of God, not into
    the hands of Spain!"
And the gunner said "Ay ay," but
    the seamen made reply:
"We have children, we have wives,
And the Lord hath spared our lives.
We will make the Spaniard promise,
    if we yield, to let us go;
We shall live to fight again and to
    strike another blow."
And the lion there lay dying, and
    they yielded to the foe.

And the stately Spanish men to their
    flagship bore him then,
Where they laid him by the mast, old
    Sir Richard caught at last,
And they praised him to his face
    with their courtly foreign grace.
But he rose upon their decks and he cried:
"I have fought for Queen and Faith like
    a valiant man and true.
I have only done my duty as a man is
    bound to do.
With a joyful spirit I, Sir Richard
    Grenville, die!"
And he fell upon their decks and he died.'

'Let me not seem to have lived in vain!'

Last words, to his assistant Johannes Kepler

This Danish nobleman was a famous astronomer and alchemist. While a student at Rostock, Germany, he lost part of his nose in a duel and for the rest of his life wore a replacement made from silver and gold. He was said to own one per cent of the entire wealth of Denmark in the 1580s, and he often held large social gatherings in his castle on an island off Copenhagen given to him by Frederick II for finding a new star in the Cassiopeia constellation. Here he entertained guests with a clairvoyant dwarf and a tame elk. During one dinner, however, the elk drank too much beer, fell down the stairs and died. Brahe catalogued 777 stars and studied planetary motions and the origin of comets until Frederick's heir cut off his funds and he moved to Prague as a guest of Emperor Rudolf II. Here he hired the great Johannes Kepler as his assistant in a new laboratory.

In Prague, Brahe became very ill during a banquet. Leaving the banquet before it ended would have been the height of bad manners, and so he remained, despite desperately needing to urinate. His bladder, stretched to its limit, developed an infection, according to Kepler's first-hand account, and by the time he returned home, he could not urinate any more. Later, excruciatingly, he passed a little urine. However, his urinary passage was blocked, leading to insomnia, intestinal fever and delirium. During his last night, he repeated over and over again: '*Let me not seem to have lived in vain!*' Eleven days after the banquet, his delirium subsided for a few hours, and he passed away peacefully. It may be that Brahe did not die from a urinary infection but instead from mercury poisoning, which can cause digestive tract problems, as extremely toxic levels of it were found in his hair and hair roots.

'Here lieth Elizabeth, who reigned a virgin and died a virgin'

Said on 6 February 1659 *'to the Speaker, Knights and Burgeses of the Lower House before her in the great gallery of Whitehall Palace urging her to marry'*

This was Queen Elizabeth's reply to a 1659 petition from the House of Commons: *'To me it shall be a full satisfaction both for the memorial of my name, and for the glory also, if when I shall let my last breath, it be engraven upon my marble tomb, "Here lieth Elizabeth, who reigned a virgin and died a virgin."'* However, an Italian observer wrote in that year: *'My Lord Robert Dudley is ... very intimate with her majesty'*, and the Spanish ambassador related to Philip II that *'Lord Robert has come so much into favour that he does whatever he likes with affairs and it is even said that her majesty visits him in his chamber day and night ...'* There were also rumours of plots to kill Dudley, and that Elizabeth had secret children by him. Amy Dudley died unexpectedly in 1560, breaking her neck in a fall, and Dudley was suspected of his wife's murder.

Pope Pius IV wrote that the queen could never marry without provoking civil war: *'the greater part of the nobility of that island take ill the marriage which the said queen designs to enter with the Lord Robert Dudley ... they fear that if he becomes king, he will want to avenge the death of his father, and extirpate the nobility of that kingdom'* (his father, the Duke of Northumberland, had been executed for treason after attempting to place the Protestant Lady Jane Grey on the throne before the Catholic Queen Mary). In 1562, Elizabeth fell ill and asked the Privy Council to make Dudley Lord Protector of the Realm, creating him Earl of Leicester in 1564. Philip II of Spain wrote in 1565: *'she will either not marry or else marry Robert, to whom she has always been so much attached ... the Queen is in love with Robert'*. In 1566, Dudley claimed that Elizabeth would never marry, recalling that she had said so since she was eight years old; but that he was still hopeful. The 'Virgin Queen' declared to Parliament in 1601: *'It is not my desire to live or to reign longer than my life and my reign shall be for your good.'*

GUY FAWKES
13 April 1570–31 January 1606

'A desperate disease requires a desperate remedy'
Justifying the Gunpowder Plot to the king, 6 November 1606

A soldier with experience of fighting in the Low Countries, and thus used to laying charges for gunpowder, Fawkes belonged to a group of Catholics who wished to get rid of Protestant rule by blowing up Parliament on its State Opening, when they knew that King James I and almost the entire nobility of the country would be inside. They rented a cellar beneath the House of Lords, and managed to hide 36 barrels of gunpowder (about 1,800 lb/800 kg). Some of the conspirators warned the Catholic Lord Monteagle, who informed the king. James I ordered a search of Parliament, and shortly after midnight on 5 November, Fawkes was found leaving the cellar and was arrested. When questioned that day by the king as to how he could contemplate such hideous treason, Fawkes replied that a dangerous disease required a desperate remedy, and that his intentions were to blow the Scotsmen present back into Scotland. Inside the cellar, the barrels of gunpowder were discovered hidden under piles of firewood and coal.

For three or four days Fawkes resisted torture, giving only the names of those conspirators who were already dead or implicated. On 31 January, he and others were tried, found guilty and taken immediately to be hanged, drawn and quartered. The *Weekly News* of 31 January 1606 related that:

'Last of all came the great devil of all, Guy Fawkes, alias Johnson, who should have put fire to the powder. His body being weak with the torture and sickness he was scarce able to go up the ladder, yet with much ado, by the help of the hangman, went high enough to break his neck by the fall. He made no speech, but with his crosses and idle ceremonies made his end upon the gallows and the block, to the great joy of all the beholders that the land was ended of so wicked a villainy.'

MIGUEL DE CERVANTES SAAVEDRA
29 September 1547–23 April 1616

'With one foot already in the stirrup'

Preface to *Los Trabajos de Persiles y Sigismunda*, foreshadowing his own death, written on his deathbed and published posthumously in 1617

In honour of the date on which both Miguel de Cervantes and Shakespeare died, UNESCO established 23 April as the International Day of the Book. However, the *Encyclopedia Hispanica* claims that 23 April would have been the date of Cervantes' burial rather than his death. A novelist, poet and playwright, Cervantes fought heroically and was badly injured at Lepanto. He carried on soldiering until 1575, when he was captured by corsairs. He attempted to escape four times, but was a slave for five years before being ransomed. Later he worked as a tax collector and was several times imprisoned for financial irregularities before the first part of his magnum opus, *Don Quixote (Don Quijote de la Mancha)* was published. He was 58 years old.

A burlesque of sixteenth-century Spanish society, *Don Quixote* tells us: '*Every man is as Heaven made him, and sometimes a great deal worse.*' The work had a profound influence on European literature, often being referred to as the first modern novel and one of the greatest books in history. It opens: '*In some village in La Mancha, whose name I do not care to recall, there dwelt not so long ago a gentleman of the type wont to keep an unused lance, an old shield, a skinny old horse, and a greyhound for racing.*' Don Quixote's epitaph was: '*For if he like a madman lived, / At least he like a wise one died.*' Cultural historian Arnold Hauser wrote in 1951: '*Before Cervantes there had only been good and bad characters, deliverers and traitors, saints and blasphemers, in literature; here the hero is saint and fool in one and the same person.*' The influence of the book can be seen in phrases such as: '*no limits but the sky*', '*give the devil his due*', '*wild goose chase*', '*smell a rat*', '*the proof of the pudding is in the eating*', '*the fair sex*', '*faint heart ne'er won fair lady*', '*forewarned is forearmed*', '*turn over a new leaf*', '*the pot calls the kettle black*', '*Mum's the word*' and '*I shall be as secret as the grave*'.

WILLIAM SHAKESPEARE
c.26 April 1564–23 April 1616

'Good friend for Jesus sake forbeare
To digg the dust encloased heare.
Blest be ye man yt spares thes stones
And curst be he yt moves my bones.'

Epitaph on his tombstone in Holy Trinity Church, Stratford-upon-Avon

Shakespeare was buried on 25 April 1616, just a month after he had made his last will and testament. A contemporary source claimed that *'Shakespeare, Drayton, and Ben Jonson had a merry meeting and it seems drank too hard for Shakespeare died of a fever there contracted.'* His epitaph, said to be self-written, is a plea for his grave to remain undisturbed, as overcrowding in graveyards was a common problem. There is also a bust of Shakespeare in the church, which reads:

'Stay Passenger, why goest thou by so fast?
Read if thou canst, whom envious death hath plast,
With in this monument Shakespeare: with whome,
quick nature dide: Whose name doth deck ys Tombe,
Far more than cost: Sieh all, yt He hath writt,
Leaves living art, but page, to serve his witt.'

His memorial in Poets' Corner, Westminster Abbey, is adapted from a speech by Prospero in *The Tempest*, and reads:

'The Cloud capt Tow'rs,
The Gorgeous Palaces,
The Solemn Templess,
The Great Globe itself,
Yea all which it Inherit,
Shall Dissolve;
And like the baseless Fabrick of a Vision
Leave not a wreck behind.'

'This is a sharp medicine but it is a sure cure for all diseases'

Attributed last words

Raleigh was a courtier and a great favourite of Elizabeth I. He was a Renaissance man, at various times an explorer, historian, philosopher, soldier and poet. As Governor of Virginia he had forbidden the injuring of Indians upon pain of death (Giles Milton, *Big Chief Elizabeth*, 2001). However, his constant privateering missions against the Spanish angered the pro-Catholic James I, and in 1603 he was charged with treason. He was held in the Tower of London under sentence of death until 1616, when he was granted a reprieve to find the fabled city of El Dorado, promising vast wealth for the king. Under Spanish influence, his reprieve was revoked in 1618 after he attacked a Spanish camp near the River Orinoco. One of the judges at his trial later said: *'the justice of England has never been so degraded and injured as by the condemnation of the honorable Sir Walter Raleigh'.*

Before his execution, Raleigh refused to be blindfolded and touched the axe, saying *'Dost thou think that I am afraid of it? This is that that will cure all sorrows.'* *'Let us dispatch (make haste)', he asked the executioner, 'At this hour my ague comes upon me. I would not have my enemies think I quaked from fear.'* Raleigh was asked which way he preferred to lay his head on the executioner's block: *'So the heart be right, it is no matter which way the head lieth.'* William Stebbings records that he spoke in his defence, and concluded with the words, *"'I have a long journey to take and must bid the company farewell." As his fingers felt the edge of the axe, he smilingly said to the sheriffs: "This is a sharp medicine but it is a sure cure for all diseases." Then he bade the reluctant executioner strike, and at two blows his head fell from his body.'* Another account is that Raleigh placed his head on the block and asked his nervous executioner *'What dost thou fear? Strike, man, strike!'* It took two blows to sever his head. *'The Lords,'* his wife wrote, *'have given me his dead body, though they have denied me his life. God hold me in my wits.'* Raleigh's head was embalmed and presented to his wife, who kept it in a red leather bag for the remaining 29 years of her life.

'What then remains, but that we should still cry, / Not to be born, or being born, to die?'

Published posthumously in *The World*, 1629

The statesman, lawyer, jurist, philosopher, author and scientist served as both Attorney-General and Lord Chancellor before having to resign because of financial improprieties. His scientific works established the inductive method, sometimes called the Baconian method, and now generally named the scientific method. In it, one uses facts to form conclusions leading to theories. A leading practitioner of the scientific revolution, he was killed by one of his own experiments. In his *Brief Lives*, John Aubrey describes how Bacon was inspired by the possibility of using snow to preserve meat:

'They were resolved they would try the experiment presently. They alighted out of the coach and went into a poor woman's house at the bottom of Highgate hill, and bought a fowl, and made the woman exenterate it [remove the entrails] ... The Snow so chilled him that he immediately fell so extremely ill, that he could not return to his Lodging ... but went to the Earle of Arundel's house at Highgate, where they put him into ... a damp bed that had not been lain in ... which gave him such a cold that in 2 or 3 days as I remember Mr Hobbes told me, he died of Suffocation.'

On his deathbed, Bacon wrote his last letter to his absent friend Lord Arundel:

'I was also desirous to try an experiment or two touching the conservation and induration [endurance] of bodies. As for the experiment itself, it succeeded excellently well; but in the journey between London and Highgate, I was taken with such a fit of casting as I know not whether it were the Stone, or some surfeit or cold, or indeed a touch of them all three. But when I came to your Lordship's House, I was not able to go back, and therefore was forced to take up my lodging here, where your housekeeper is very careful and diligent about me, which I assure myself your Lordship will not only pardon towards him, but think the better of him for it.'

JOHN DONNE
21 January 1572–31 March 1631

'Death, be not proud, though some have called thee Mighty and dreadful, for thou art not so'

Opening lines from his 'Holy Sonnet X', published two years after his death

> 'Death, be not proud, though some have called thee
> Mighty and dreadful, for thou art not so:
> For those whom thou think'st thou dost overthrow,
> Die not, poor Death; nor yet canst thou kill me ...
> Thou'rt slave to fate, chance, kings, and desperate men,
> And dost with poison, war, and sickness dwell;
> And poppy or charms can make us sleep as well
> And better than thy stroke. Why swell'st thou then?
> One short sleep past, we wake eternally,
> And Death shall be no more: Death, thou shalt die!'

Donne was a superb metaphysical poet who in 1621 was appointed Dean of St Paul's Cathedral. Ten years later he wrote his will, and rose from his sickbed to deliver what is known as the Death's Duel Sermon, portraying life as a steady descent to suffering and death, with salvation and immortality available through embracing Christ's teachings. King Charles I attended, having been told that Donne was delivering one last sermon. Donne preached:

> 'We have a winding sheet in our mother's womb, which grows with us from our conception, and we come into the world, wound up in that winding sheet; for we come to seek a grave ... This whole world is but an universal churchyard, but our common grave ... That which we call life is but Hebdomada mortium, a week of deaths, seven days, seven periods of our life spent in dying, a dying seven times over, and there is an end ... There we leave you in that blessed dependency, to hang upon him that hangs upon the cross, there bathe in his tears, there suck at his wounds, and lie down in peace in his grave, till he vouchsafe you a resurrection, and an ascension into that kingdom which He hath prepared for you with the inestimable price of his incorruptible blood. Amen.'

The huge crowd knew that Donne was preaching his own funeral oration. He died, probably from stomach cancer, two weeks later.

GUSTAVUS ADOLPHUS II, GUSTAF ADOLF
THE GREAT, KING OF SWEDEN
19 December 1594–6 November 1632

'I am the King of Sweden!'

Last words, on the battlefield of Lützen

Engaged in constant warfare during the Thirty Years War, Gustavus led Sweden to victory after victory against the Danes, Poles and Russians, making Sweden the third biggest nation in Europe after Russia and Spain. Gustavus died at Lützen, near Leipzig, but his Swedish army won the grim battle.

'When the king knew that the first battery was taken, he uncovered his head and thanked God, but soon after, learning that the centre had been repulsed, he put himself in charge of the Småland cavalry and charged the Imperial cuirassiers, the "black lads" with whom he had previously told Stålhanské to grapple. Piccolimini hasted to support the cuirassiers; and the Swedes, being overmatched, retreated without perceiving – the fog once again having come over – that they had left the king in the midst of the enemy. A pistol-ball now broke his arm; and as the Duke of Saxe Lauenburg was supporting him out of battle, an Imperial cuirassier came up behind him and shot him in the back. He then fell from his horse, and other cuirassiers now coming up, one of them completed the work of death ... a young gentleman named Leubelfing ... being near when the king fell, and seeing that his charger, wounded in the neck, had galloped away, he dismounted and offered him his own horse. Gustavus stretched out his hand to accept the offer, but was unable. In the meantime, the cuirassiers, attracted to the spot, demanded who the wounded man was. Leubelfing evaded the question, or refused to answer; but the king himself exclaimed "I am the King of Sweden", when he received four gunshot wounds and two stabs, which quickly released him from the agony of his broken arm, the bone of which had pierced the flesh and protruded. The Imperial soldiers about the king, each anxious to possess some trophy, had stripped the body to the shirt, and were about to carry it off, when a party of Swedish cavalry, charging to the spot, dispersed them.'

BENJAMIN 'BEN' JONSON
c.11 June 1572–6 August 1637

'O Rare Ben Jonson'

Jack Young's epitaph, inscribed on Jonson's tomb in Westminster Abbey

A contemporary of Shakespeare and Marlowe, Jonson was a Renaissance dramatist, poet and actor, best remembered for his lyric poems and his satirical plays *The Alchemist, Every Man in His Humour, Poetaster* and *Volpone.* He influenced generations of poets and play-wrights, and in 1616 he became the first (unofficial) Poet Laureate, being granted a pension by James I. His poetry embraced classical ideals but dealt uncompromisingly with the life and characters of James I's court. After an argument in 1625 with James' successor Charles I, he virtually stopped writing court masques. They had cemented his standing as the foremost writer of masques in the Jacobean era, but his collaboration in them with Inigo Jones was destroyed by intense personal rivalry.

Despite the strokes he suffered from 1628, Jonson continued to write until his death. He is buried upright in the north aisle of the nave of Westminster Abbey after telling the Dean: '*Six feet long by two feet wide is too much for me. Two feet by two is all I want.*' The size of his grave could be an indication of his reduced circumstances at the time of his death. It has also been claimed that he asked Charles I for a grave exactly 18 inches square and received an upright grave to fit in the requested space. It has been suggested that the epitaph on his tomb is a play on words: '*Orare Ben Jonson*' is Latin for '*Pray for Ben Jonson*' and could mean that he had converted to Catholicism on his deathbed.

Jonson was honoured within a year of his death by a volume of elegies from his friends (*Jonsonus Viribus*). James Drummond of Hawthornden wrote of him: '*He is a great lover and praiser of himself; a contemner and scorner of others; given rather to lose a friend than a jest ... he is passionately kind and angry; careless either to gain or keep.*' Jonson's own 1616 Epigram XXXIV, *Of Death*, is: '*He that fears death, or mourns it, in the just, / Shows of the resurrection little trust.*'

GALILEO GALILEI
15 February 1564–8 January 1642

'Eppur si muove'
('Nevertheless it moves')

Private recantation after his trial in 1633 by the Inquisition,
stating that the Earth moved around the Sun

The 'father of modern astronomy', Galileo pioneered the 'experimental scientific method'. Observations
with his new telescope convinced him that Copernicus'
sun-centred (heliocentric) theory was correct, and he confirmed it in his *Dialogue Concerning the Two Chief World
Systems* in 1632. The Church responded quickly to this
threat to Christian doctrine that the Earth was the centre of
God's universe. In 1633, aged 69, Galileo was subjected to
a 'show trial' by the Inquisition, after being threatened with
torture and the stake. He was ordered to Rome to stand trial on suspicion of
heresy *'for holding as true the false doctrine taught by some that the sun is the centre
of the world'* since *'it was decided at the Holy Congregation ... on 25 February 1616 that
... the Holy Office would give you an injunction to abandon this doctrine, not to teach
it to others, not to defend it, and not to treat of it; and that if you did not acquiesce in
this injunction, you should be imprisoned'*.

The Inquisition found Galileo *'vehemently suspect of heresy'*, having held the
opinions that the Sun lies motionless at the centre of the universe, that the Earth
is not at its centre and moves, and that one may hold and defend an opinion as
probable after it has been declared contrary to Holy Scripture. He was sentenced
to *'abjure, curse and detest'* those opinions and was ordered to be imprisoned, later
commuted to house arrest for the rest of his life. The *Dialogue* was banned, and
publication of any other of his works was forbidden, including those he might
write in the future. He allegedly recanted in private after the trial. After all, in the
Dialogue he had written: *'I do not feel obliged to believe that same God who endowed
us with sense, reason, and intellect had intended for us to forgo their use.'* In 1992,
Pope John Paul II finally lifted the Edict of the Inquisition from Galileo.

'Stay for the sign'

Last words to his executioner

In the First Civil War (1642–45), Charles' Royalist army was defeated by Parliamentarian and Puritan forces. The king escaped from prison, but was recaptured after the Second Civil War (1648–49). After a show trial, he was beheaded for high treason, and at his execution wore two cotton shirts, so as to prevent the cold weather causing any shivers that the crowd might mistake for fear.

'Charles' last words to his daughter Elizabeth were, "He bid her tell her mother, that his thoughts had never strayed from her, and that love should be the same to the last." The king asked the executioner "Is my hair well?" And taking off his cloak and [Order of St] George, he delivered his George to the bishop saying "Remember." Then putting off his doublet, and being in his waistcoat, he put on his cloak again, and looking upon the block, said to the executioner "You must set it fast." Being told by him it could be now no higher, the king said "When I put out my hands, then." And saying a few words to himself as he stood, with hands and eyes lift up, immediately stooping down, he laid his head upon the block, and the executioner again putting his hair under his cap, his majesty think he had been going to strike, bad him "Stay for the sign"; to which the executioner said, "Yes I will and it please your Majesty." So, after a short pause, his majesty stretching forth his hands, the executioner at one blow severed his head from his body, which being held up and showed to the astonished people, was with his body put in a coffin covered with black velvet, and carried into the Lodging Chamber in Whitehall. It must be dreadfully remembered, that the cruel powers did suspect that the king would not submit his head to the block, and therefore to bring him down to violence to it, they had prepared hooks and staples to haul him as a victim to the slaughter. By the example of his Saviour, he resisted not, he disappointed their wit, and yielded to their malice.'

JAMES GRAHAM, FIRST MARQUESS OF MONTROSE
25 October 1612–21 May 1650

'Open all my veins, that I may swim
To thee, my Maker! in that crimson lake'

Lines Written on the Window of his Jail the Night before his Execution, 1650

An alternative version of Montrose's last writing is called *On Himself, upon Hearing What was his Sentence*:

> 'Let them bestow on ev'ry airth a limb;
> Open all my veins, that I may swim
> To Thee, my Saviour, in that crimson lake;
> Then place my parboil'd head upon a stake,
> Scatter my ashes, throw them in the air:
> Lord (since Thou know'st where all these atoms are)
> I'm hopeful once Thou'lt recollect my dust,
> And confident thou'lt raise me with the just.'

Montrose joined the Covenanters in the Wars of the Three Kingdoms, then from 1644 commanded the Royalist forces of Charles I in Scotland during the Civil War. After several brilliant successes, when he became known as 'the Great Montrose', he was defeated at Philiphaugh in September 1645 and fled to Norway. In March 1650 he landed in Orkney but was unable to raise followers on the mainland. He was surprised and defeated at the Battle of Carbisdale, but managed to escape. He thought he was safe with Neil MacLeod at Ardreyk Castle, but MacLeod betrayed him, and he was taken to Edinburgh and sentenced to be hanged. A gibbet 30 feet in height was mounted on a 6-foot-high platform completely covered in black. Montrose asked: '*How long shall I hang here?*' and his last words were: '*God have mercy on this afflicted land.*' His head was placed on a spike on the Tolbooth and his limbs were put on public display in the other four major cities of Scotland. Eleven years later his body was exhumed and laid to rest with great ceremony by the nobility of Scotland.

'It is not my design to drink or to sleep, but my design is to make what haste I can to be gone'

Words when he was offered a drink on the day of his death, according to the 1659 account of Major Butler, Groom of the Bedchamber to Cromwell

The Civil War broke out in 1642, when Cromwell was 43. The MP soon showed he possessed unexpected abilities. Although having had no previous military experience, he created and led a superb force of cavalry, the 'Ironsides', rising from the rank of captain to that of lieutenant-general in three years. He refused to compromise with the Royalists, and in 1647 he took the side of the New Model Army in the face of attempts to disband it. He was instrumental in the trial and execution of King Charles I in 1649, and after the Commonwealth (1649–53) was established, he became Lord Lieutenant of Ireland, where he presided over the massacres of the garrisons of Drogheda and Wexford. In 1653, after his expulsion of the Rump Parliament, he became Lord Protector of the Commonwealth. His Protectorate (1653–58) was characterized by religious toleration, several successful wars, and profitable commercial treaties with foreign powers.

Cromwell died in great pain, of malaria-related septicaemia. On his deathbed, the devout Puritan said: '*I would be willing to live and be farther serviceable to God and his people; but my work is done. Yet God will be with his people.*' The Protectorate collapsed after his son Richard alienated both the army and Parliament in his attempt to succeed him. After the Restoration of the Monarchy, Cromwell's body was exhumed from Westminster Abbey and symbolically executed on 30 January 1661, the same date that Charles I had been executed. His remains were then hung in chains at Tyburn. Finally they were thrown into a pit, while his severed head was displayed on a pole outside Westminster Hall until 1685.

MAJOR-GENERAL THOMAS HARRISON
1606–13 October 1660

'I do forgive thee with all my heart ... Alas poor man, thou doith it ignorantly, the Lord grant that this sin may be laid to thy charge.'

Last words to his hangman

Harrison fought for Parliament in the Civil War, and became leader of the Fifth Monarchists in the Interregnum. In the First Civil War he led cavalry at Marston Moor, Newbury and Naseby. At the Battle of Langport in 1645, he was seen to break into a rapturous psalm of praise when the Royalists began to fall back. He was involved in the slaughter of the Catholic defenders of Basing House and emerged as one of the most radical of officers, opposing further negotiations with Charles I and denouncing him as the 'Man of Blood' when he heard of his escape from Hampton Court in 1647. In the Second Civil War Harrison saw action at Appleby and commanded the escort of Charles I to Windsor and London in 1649. Charles thought that Harrison would assassinate him.

In the Interregnum Harrison was imprisoned four times for disagreeing with Cromwell. Parliament ordered him to be imprisoned in the Tower of London in May 1660, before Charles II had even landed at Dover. Harrison made no attempt to escape, believing in the righteousness of his actions. At his trial for regicide, he asserted that he had acted in the name of the Parliament of England and entered no plea. Samuel Pepys reported him to be *'looking as cheerful as any man could do in that condition'*.

In Harrison's final moments, the hangman asked for his forgiveness and Harrison replied, *'I do forgive thee with all my heart ...'* giving all the money that remained in his pockets to his executioner. He went bravely to his gruesome death, his religious zeal undiminished to the end, saying: *'God hath covered my head many times in the day of Battle. By God I have leaped over a wall, by God I have runneth through a Troop, and by my God I will go through this death.'*

BLAISE PASCAL
19 June 1623–19 August 1662

'We shall die alone'

Pensées, 1670

A ground-breaking mathematician and physicist, Pascal was also a religious philosopher. In great suffering, his last words were said to be *'May God never abandon me.'* In his posthumous *Pensées* we read the proposition known as Pascal's Wager: *'God is or He is not. But to which side shall we incline? Let us weigh the gain and loss in wagering that God is. Let us estimate the two chances. If you gain, you gain all; if you lose, you lose nothing. Wager then without hesitation that He is.'* His epitaph in St Etienne-du-Mont reads:

'Illustrious for his great knowledge which was recognized by the scholars of all Europe; more illustrious still for the great probity which he exercised in the offices and employments with which he was honoured; but much more illustrious for his exemplary piety. He tasted good and bad fortune, that he might be known in every thing for what he was. He was seen temperate in prosperity and patient in adversity. He sought the aid of God in misfortune, and rendered him thanks in happiness. His heart was devoted to his God, his king, his family, and his friends. He had respect for the great and love for the small; it pleased God to crown all the graces of nature that he had bestowed on him with a divine grace which made his great love for God the foundation, the stay, and the consummation of all his other virtues. Thou, who seest in this epitome the only thing that remains to us of so beautiful a life, admire the fragility of all present things, weep the loss that we have suffered; render thanks to God for having left for a time to earth the enjoyment of such a treasure; and pray his goodness to crown with his eternal glory him whom he crowned here below with more graces and virtues than the limits of an epitaph permit us to relate. His grief-stricken children have placed this epitaph on this spot, which they have composed from the fullness of their hearts, in order to render homage to the truth and not to appear ingrates in the sight of God.'

THOMAS HOBBES
5 April 1588–4 December 1679

'I am about to take my last voyage, a great leap in the dark'

Reputed last words

Hobbes was a political philosopher who believed that nations, like people, were selfishly motivated. Each country was in a constant battle for power and wealth, and to prove his point he wrote: '*If men are not naturally in a state of war, why do they always carry arms and why do they have keys to lock their doors?*' Governments were created to protect people from their own selfishness and evil. Because the people were only interested in promoting their own interests, Hobbes believed in an enlightened kingship and that democracy could never work: '*All mankind [is in] a perpetual and restless desire for power ... that [stops] only in death.*' Thus giving power to the individual would create a dangerous situation that would start a '*war of every man against every man*' and make life '*solitary, poor, nasty, brutish, and short*'.

On 16 January 1679 the diarist John Aubrey wrote to James Wheldon describing Hobbes' final illness and his death:

> 'He fell sick about the middle of October last. His disease was the strangury [painful urination, probably prostate cancer], and the physicians judged it incurable by reason of his great age and natural decay. About the 20th of November, my lord being about to remove from Chatsworth to Hardwick, Mr Hobbes would not be left behind; and therefore with a feather bed laid into the coach; upon which he lay warm clad, he was conveyed safely, and was in appearance as well after that little journey as before it. But seven or eight days after, his whole right side was taken with the dead palsy [a stroke], and at the same time he was made speechless. He lived after this seven days, taking very little nourishment, slept well, and by intervals endeavoured to speak, but could not. In the whole time of his sickness he was free from fever. He seemed therefore to die rather for want of the fuel of life (which was spent in him) and mere weakness and decay, than by power of his disease, which was thought to be only an effect of his age and weakness ...'

'You must pardon me, gentlemen, for being a most unconscionable time a-dying'

Last words on his deathbed

After his father Charles I's execution, and defeat at the Battle of Worcester in 1651, Charles Stuart returned from exile to regain the throne in 1660. He punished the men who had signed his father's death warrant, and exhumed, hanged and beheaded Cromwell's body. The early years of Charles' reign saw the Great Plague (1665) and the Great Fire of London (1666) as well as defeat by the Dutch (1667). In a recent film, *The Libertine*, Johnny Depp played the rakish courtier John Wilmot, 2nd Earl of Rochester, who wrote of the new king:

'God bless our good and gracious king,
Whose promise none relies on;
Who never said a foolish thing,
Nor ever did a wise one.'

Charles is reputed to have replied: *'That is true; for my words are my own, but my actions are those of my ministers.'* The public resented paying taxes that were spent on maintaining Charles' mistresses and illegitimate children, and Rochester also wrote:

'Restless he rolls from whore to whore
A merry monarch, scandalous and poor.'

During his lengthy death from kidney dysfunction, Charles II was surrounded by courtiers. On his deathbed he is also said to have asked his brother, the future King James, to look after his mistresses: *'be well to Portsmouth, and let not poor Nelly starve'* (quoted by Charles Burnett, *History of My Own Time*, 1724 and 1734). This referred to Louise de Kerouaille and Nell Gwynn. Charles seemingly left no legitimate heir, but he had actually married his mistress Lucy Walter (see next entry). Other mistresses included the Countess of Castlemaine, Catherine Pegge, Lucy Walter and Elizabeth Killigrew. Many of their children were created dukes; the dukedoms of Cleveland, Buccleuch and Queensbury, Richmond and Gordon, Monmouth, Grafton and St Albans all stem from the king's affairs. On the last evening of his life, Charles was received into the Roman Catholic Church.

'Do not hack me as you did my Lord Russell'

Last words on Tower Hill to his executioner

James Scott, the Duke of Monmouth, was believed to be an illegitimate son of Charles II, but recent evidence proves that Charles married the duke's mother, Lucy Walter, before Catherine of Braganza, and that Monmouth was therefore the real King of England. He led an unsuccessful rebellion against Charles' Roman Catholic brother and successor, James II, and was executed after defeat at the Battle of Sedgemoor.

'"I will make no speeches," he [Monmouth] exclaimed. "Only ten words, my Lord." He turned away, called his servant, and put into the man's hand a toothpick case, the last token of ill-starred love. "Give it," he said, "to that person." He then accosted John Ketch the executioner, a wretch who had butchered many brave and noble victims, and whose name has, during a century and a half, been vulgarly given to all who have succeeded him in his odious office. "Here," said the Duke, "are six guineas for you. Do not hack me as you did my Lord Russell [William, Lord Russell, had been a friend of Monmouth, inexpertly beheaded by the same executioner John 'Jack' Ketch in 1683 following the Rye House Plot]. I have heard that you struck him three or four times. My servant will give you some more gold if you do the work well." He then undressed, felt the edge of the axe, expressed some fear that it was not sharp enough, and laid his head on the block. The divines in the meantime continued to ejaculate with great energy; "God accept your repentance! God accept your imperfect repentance!" ... The first blow inflicted only a slight wound. The Duke struggled, rose from the block, and looked reproachfully at the executioner. The head sank down once more. The stroke was repeated again and again; but still the neck was not severed, and the body continued to move. Yells of rage and horror rose from the crowd. Ketch flung down the axe with a curse. "I cannot do it," he said; "my heart fails me." "Take up the axe, man," cried the sheriff ... At length the axe was taken up. Two more blows extinguished the last remains of life; but a knife was used to separate the head from the shoulders.'

GILES COREY
c.1611–19 September 1692

'More weight!'

Anonymous verse (early eighteenth century)

'Giles Corey was a wizard strong, a stubborn wretch was he;
And fit was he to hang on high upon the locust tree.
So, when before the Magistrates for trial he did come,
He would no true confession make, but was completely dumb.
"Giles Corey," said the Magistrate, "what hast thou here to plead
To those who now accuse thy soul of crime and horrid deed?"
Giles Corey he said not a word, no single word spoke he.
"Giles Corey," said the Magistrate, "we'll press it out of thee."
They got them then a heavy beam, then laid it on his breast;
They loaded it with heavy stones, and hard upon him pressed.
"More weight," now said this wretched man. "More weight!" again he cried;
And he did no confession make, but wickedly he died.'

Corey was a prosperous farmer and a full member of the Church. He died under the judicial torture of 'peine forte et dure' ('strong and hard punishment') during the Salem Witch Trials. His wife had been arrested, and in April 1692 three women accused him of witchcraft too. After five months in prison he was due to be tried. He knew he faced conviction and execution, so he refused to plead. The penalty for refusing to stand for trial was death by pressing under heavy stones.

Corey was stripped naked, a board placed upon his chest, and rocks piled on the board. He begged to have more weight added, so that his death might come quickly. Massachusetts judge Samuel Sewall reported: '*About noon, at Salem, Giles Corey was press'd to death for standing mute.*' Robert Calef, a critic of the role of the clergy during the trials, wrote that Corey's '*tongue being prest out of his mouth, the Sheriff with his cane forced it in again, when he was dying*'. Corey was buried in an unmarked grave on Gallows Hill. Two days later his wife and six others were taken from jail, brought to Gallows Hill and hanged.

SAMUEL PEPYS
23 February 1633–26 May 1703

'And thus ends all that I doubt I shall ever be able to do with my own eyes in the keeping of my journal'

Last diary entry, 31 May 1669

In January 1664, Pepys' sight failed him for the first time. He consulted as to which glass would best suit his eyes at night, but his eyesight became weaker, and eventually he was forced to stop writing his diary. He believed, erroneously, that reading and writing by candle-light had affected his eyesight, but he did not become blind, and he lived for over 33 years after the closing of the diary. Pepys had a successful career as an MP and naval administrator, but it is tragic that he kept his diaries, with their wonderful descriptions of the Great Plague and the Great Fire of London, for only nine years. They were written in code, and were not rediscovered until 1819, after which they were decoded and published from 1825 onwards. Pepys' diary is a very important document of the Restoration era.

'And thus ends all that I doubt I shall ever be able to do with my own eyes in the keeping of my journal, I being not able to do it any longer, having done now so long as to undo my eyes almost every time that I take a pen in my hand; and, therefore, whatever comes of it, I must forbear: and, therefore, resolve, from this time forward, to have it kept by my people in long-hand, and must therefore be contented to set down no more than is fit for them and all the world to know; or, if there be any thing, which cannot be much, now my amours to Deb [Deborah Willett, a maid with whom Pepys had an affair] are past, and my eyes hindering me in almost all other pleasures, I must endeavour to keep a margin in my book open, to add, here and there, a note in short-hand with my own hand. And so I betake myself to that course, which is almost as much as to see myself go into my grave; for which, and all the discomforts that will accompany my being blind, the good God prepare me! S. P.'

JOHN LOCKE
29 August 1632–28 October 1704

'Stop Traveller! Near this place lieth John Locke.'

Epitaph (in Latin) on his tombstone in High Laver, Essex

An Enlightenment philosopher, Locke developed the theory of the 'Social Contract', influencing Rousseau and Voltaire, and his belief that political sovereignty is based on the consent of the governed forms the basis of the United States Constitution. Liberalism and republicanism owe much of their theoretical underpinnings to Locke, who argued that *'Reason must be our last judge and guide in everything.'* According to Marxist historian Christopher Hill: *'In* The Reasonableness of Christianity *Locke wrote that "the day labourers and tradesmen, the spinsters and dairy maids" must be told what to think. "The greatest part cannot know, and therefore they must believe." But at least Locke did not intend that priests should do the telling; that was for God himself.'*

Locke's epitaph reads in full:

> 'Stop Traveller! Near this place lieth John Locke. If you ask what kind of man he was, he answers that he was contented with his own modest lot. Bred a scholar, he made his learning subservient only to the cause of truth. You will learn this from his writings, which will show you everything about him, with greater truth than the suspect praises of an epitaph. His virtues, if indeed he had any, were too slight to be lauded by him or to be an example to you. Let his vices be buried with him. Of virtue you have an example in the gospels, should you desire it; of vice would there were none for you; of mortality surely you have one here and everywhere, and may thou learn from it. That he was born on the 29th of August in the year of our Lord 1632 and that he died on the 28th of October in the year of our Lord 1704 – this tablet, which itself will soon perish, is a record.'

There is also a memorial at Christ Church Cathedral, Oxford, which reads: *'John Locke 1632–1704 Westminster Scholar and Censor of Moral Philosophy – I know there is truth opposite to falsehood – that it may be found if people will and it is worth the seeking.'*

'I am going away, but the State will always remain'

Words spoken on his deathbed

After a reign of over 72 years, the longest documented reign of any European monarch, Louis died of gangrene four days before his seventy-seventh birthday. Another version of his dying words to his assembled courtiers and servants is: *'Why weep you? Did you think I would live forever? I thought dying would have been harder.'* Ian Dunlop in *Louis XIV* (2001) tells us: *'Reciting the psalm Domine, ad adjuvandum me festina (O Lord, make haste to help me), Louis "yielded up his soul without any effort, like a candle going out".'*

For 54 years of his kingship, Louis personally controlled French government. On Cardinal Mazarin's death in 1661, he astounded the court by becoming his own chief minister, ending the long 'reign of the cardinal-ministers' and sending the powerful and corrupt finance minister, Nicolas Fouquet, to prison for life after a sensational three-year trial (1661–64). The seventeenth century is labelled as the Age of Louis XIV, with his rule being hailed as the supreme example of absolutist government. He epitomized the ideal of kingship, and during his reign France stabilized and became one of the strongest powers in Europe. On the death of his wife Maria Theresa in 1683, the 'Sun King' recalled that she had caused him unease on no other occasion. Only one of their six children survived to adulthood, but Louis had dozens of illegitimate children with his many mistresses. Soon after the queen died, he secretly married Madame de Maintenon, but it was never publicly acknowledged. Dangeau tells us that on his deathbed, the king said to the future Louis XV: *'Do not follow the bad example which I have set you; I have often undertaken war too lightly and have sustained it for vanity. Do not imitate me, but be a peaceful prince, and may you apply yourself principally to the alleviation of the burdens of your subjects.'*

SIR CHRISTOPHER WREN
20 October 1632–25 February 1723

'Reader, if you seek his monument, look around you'
('Lector, si monumentum requiris, circumspice')

Epitaph on Wren's tomb in St Paul's Cathedral, written by his son,
Christopher Wren Jr

Wren was the first person to be buried in the cathedral that he designed
and built, along with another 51 churches, after the Great Fire of London. This
scientist, mathematician and inventor became one of Europe's finest architects.
By the age of 17 he had invented an instrument that wrote in the dark, a pneu-
matic engine, a weather clock and a new deaf-and-dumb language. At the age
of 25 he was Professor of Astronomy at Gresham College, and aged 29 he held
the same post at Oxford University. In his inaugural lecture at Gresham he said:
'*A time will come when men will stretch out their eyes. They should see planets like our
Earth.*' At Gresham he carried out experiments on the laws of motion, and Isaac
Newton pointed out that Wren was his precursor in the development of the law
of gravity. At Oxford, Wren showed that it was possible to send people to sleep for
operations by injecting them with opium. He pioneered blood transfusion, using
a syringe to transfer blood between dogs.

A founding member of the Royal Society in 1662, Wren designed the Sheldonian
Theatre in Oxford. His other works included the Royal Observatory at Greenwich,
the Royal Exchange, Drury Lane Theatre, Chelsea Hospital and the façade of
Hampton Court Palace. St Paul's took 35 years to build, and its dome was the
largest in the world after St Peter's Basilica in Rome. According to tradition, Wren
would often go to London to pay unofficial visits to St Paul's, to check on
the progress of 'my greatest work'. On one of these trips he caught a chill. His
condition worsened, and he died in his ninety-first year, being, as he said, '*worn
out (by God's mercy) a long life in the Royal Service, and having made some figure in
the world*'.

PETER I, PETER THE GREAT
(PYOTR ALEXEYEVICH ROMANOV)
9 June 1672–8 February 1725

'Leave all to ...'

Last note

Crowned tsar in 1682, Peter opened up Russia to the West, bringing in craftsmen and engineers, and sending Russians to Europe to be educated. He reformed the political and economic systems, and formed an efficient army and navy. His programme of modernization and expansion would transform the small tsardom of Russia into a huge empire and a major European power. One of his main goals was to regain access to the Baltic Sea and Baltic trade. In 1700 he started the Northern War with Sweden, in the course of which he founded St Petersburg. At the end of the war Russia was victorious, having conquered the vast lands on the Baltic coast, and in 1721 Peter proclaimed himself emperor. Russia gained access to European trade and St Petersburg became the major sea port. In 1712, Peter had moved the Russian capital to St Petersburg, and he continued paying special attention to the swift construction of the city – his European 'paradise'. The first house built in St Petersburg is still there, a small wooden cottage constructed for Peter himself, the study still filled with his original belongings. Peter had 11 children, and in 1718 his eldest son, 28-year-old Alexei, was tortured until he 'confessed' to a plot to overthrow the tsar. A reign of terror ensued, during which all who had in any way befriended Alexei were impaled, broken on the wheel or slowly tortured to death. Peter watched his own son being whipped with a knout, dying from his injuries.

In early January 1725, Peter had a last attack of uraemia, and before lapsing into unconsciousness scrawled an unfinished note that read: '*Leave all to ...*' Exhausted by the effort, he asked for his daughter Anna Petrovna to be summoned, but by the time she arrived he was in a coma. The Russian historian E.V. Anisimov believes that Count Bassewitz, the Holstein envoy to Peter's court, wanted to convince people that Grand Duchess Anna, rather than Peter's wife, Empress Catherine I, was his intended heir. An autopsy revealed Peter's bladder to be infected with gangrene.

SIR JOHN VANBRUGH
24 January 1664–26 March 1726

**'Under this stone, Reader, survey
Dead Sir John Vanbrugh's house of clay.
Lie heavy on him, Earth! For he
Laid many heavy loads on thee!'**

Epitaph written in 1726 by the clergyman Abel Evans

From 1686 Vanbrugh worked undercover to bring William of Orange to England and depose James II. He was charged with espionage in France and imprisoned for four and a half years, some of that time in the Bastille, before a prisoner exchange took place. He then fought in the landing at Camaret to try to destroy the French fleet at Brest in 1694. In 1696 and 1697 he wrote two controversial Restoration comedies, *The Relapse* and *The Provoked Wife*. They were not only sexually explicit, but championed the rights of women in marriage. Not content with this, he became a superb architect, collaborating with the great Nicholas Hawksmoor on many London churches. Three of Vanbrugh's designs act as milestones in English architecture. Castle Howard, commissioned in 1699, is often described as England's first truly baroque building. The enormous Blenheim Palace, commissioned in 1704, is the largest non-royal domestic building in England, while Seaton Delaval Hall, begun in 1718, is considered his finest architectural masterpiece.

Vanbrugh was said to have died suddenly of an asthma attack, but Laurence Whistler's *Sir John Vanbrugh: Architect and Dramatist* (1809) tells us that he had been forced 'many times' to take the waters at Scarborough:

> 'What he suffered from is not clear, but in September, 1725, it was an attack of asthma, a complaint that was then almost impossible to treat ... On the 12th of March he attended his last meeting at Greenwich Hospital, and a few days later in London developed quinsy. One could have wished the "sweet-natured gentleman" who had done so little evil in the world a more comfortable journey out if it, than by way of that acute tonsillitis in which the temperature rises quickly and the voice becomes blurred and strange, until it is unendurable to swallow, and at last, it may be if one is attended by an eighteenth-century doctor impossible to breathe ...'

SIR ISAAC NEWTON
25 December 1643–20 March 1727

'Nature, and Nature's laws lay hid in night / God said "Let Newton be!" and all was light.'

Alexander Pope, *Epitaph: Intended for Sir Isaac Newton*, 1730

The Latin inscription on the base of Newton's monument in Westminster Abbey translates as:

'Here is buried Isaac Newton, Knight, who by a strength of mind almost divine, and mathematical principles peculiarly his own, explored the course and figures of the planets, the paths of comets, the tides of the sea, the dissimilarities in rays of light, and, what no other scholar has previously imagined, the properties of the colours thus produced. Diligent, sagacious and faithful, in his expositions of nature, antiquity and the holy Scriptures, he vindicated by his philosophy the majesty of God mighty and good, and expressed the simplicity of the Gospel in his manners. Mortals rejoice that there has existed such and so great an ornament of the human race!'

Newton was probably the most influential scientist who ever lived. In mathematics, optics and physics he laid the foundations for modern science and revolutionized the world. He found science a hotchpotch of isolated facts and laws, capable of describing some phenomena but predicting only a few. He left it with a unified system of laws that can be applied to an enormous range of physical phenomena, and used to make exact predications. As mathematician, Newton invented integral calculus, and jointly with Leibniz, differential calculus. He also had a huge impact on theoretical astronomy, defining the laws of motion and universal gravitation, which he used to predict precisely the motions of stars, and the planets around the Sun. Using his discoveries in optics, he constructed the first reflecting telescope. Newton said: '*I do not know what I may appear to the world, but to myself I seem to have been only like a boy playing on the sea-shore, and diverting myself in now and then finding a smoother pebble or a prettier shell than ordinary, whilst the great ocean of truth lay all undiscovered before me*' and '*If I have seen further it is by standing on the shoulders of Giants.*'

GEORGE I, KING OF GREAT BRITAIN AND IRELAND, HIS MOST SERENE HIGHNESS GEORG LUDWIG, ARCHBANNERBEARER OF THE HOLY ROMAN EMPIRE AND PRINCE-ELECTOR, DUKE OF BRUNSWICK LÜNEBURG
28 May 1660–11 June 1727

'George the First was always reckoned / Vile ...'
Epigram by Walter Savage Landor

The succeeding 'German Georges' are also mentioned in the poem by Walter Savage Landor (1775–1864):

> 'George the First was always reckoned
> Vile, but viler George the Second;
> And what mortal ever heard
> Any good of George the Third?
> When from earth the Fourth descended,
> God be praised, the Georges ended.'

The death of Queen Anne in 1714 left no direct heir. The rightful heir, James Edward Stuart, refused to renounce his Catholic faith, and by the Act of Settlement (1701) this meant he could never ascend the throne. No fewer than 50 Catholics were next in line to the crown of the greatest empire the world had ever seen, but the next Protestant was from the tiny German state of Hanover. Georg Ludwig arrived in England aged 54, with a very limited knowledge of his new kingdom, and even less of the English language. He did not like his new country and spent as little time there as possible, dying and being buried in his birthplace of Saxony. In 1721 the minister Robert Walpole was given the role of speaking for the king in all meetings, becoming his representative in Parliament and thus creating the role of the 'prime' minister. As a result of George's lack of interest in governing, the balance of power swung permanently to Parliament.

George was generally disliked, Lord Chesterfield commenting: *'No woman came amiss to him, if they were very willing and very fat. The standard of His Majesty's taste made all those ladies who aspired to his favour, and who were near the statutable size, strain and swell themselves like the frogs in the fable, to rival the bulk and dignity of the ox. Some succeeded, and others burst.'*

LA CONTESSA THÉRÈSE DI VERCELLIS
(*née* DE CHABOD)
1670–December 1728

'Well! A woman that can fart is not yet dead!'

Dying words

The contessa had married Count Hippolyte Vercellis, a Sardinian army officer, in 1690, but he died in 1696. Childless, in 1728 she employed the young Jean-Jacques Rousseau at her house in the Palazzo Cavour in Turin as a footman. She was dying of breast cancer, which made it difficult for her to write, so the 16-year-old Rousseau became responsible for taking down her dictation and attending to her correspondence. The pair became friendly, and he was hoping for substantial benefits from her will, but she had written it in August 1728, only a few weeks after he joined her household. Although he was with her at her death, he was left just 30 livres and the suit he was wearing when the household was broken up. Disappointed, he stole a useless pink ribbon, revealing in his *Confessions* that he had falsely accused a servant girl named Marion of giving it to him in order to escape punishment from the new master of the household, Count Octavian della Rocca. This is Rousseau's account of the contessa's death:

'My principal employ, which was by no means displeasing to me, was to write from her dictating; a cancer in the breast, from which she suffered extremely, not permitting her to write herself ... Afterwards I went in as usual, and was even more assiduous than any one, being afflicted at the sufferings of the unhappy lady, whom I truly respected and beloved for the calmness and fortitude with which she bore her illness, and often did I shed tears of real sorrow without being perceived by any one. At length I saw her expire. She had lived like a woman of sense and virtue, her death was that of a philosopher. She was naturally serious, but towards the end of her illness she possessed a kind of gayety, too regular to be assumed, which served as a counterpoise to the melancholy of her situation. She only kept her bed two days, continuing to discourse cheerfully with those about her to the very last. At last, when she could hardly speak, and in her death agony, she let a big wind escape. "Well!" said she, turning around, "a woman that can fart is not yet dead!" These were her last words.'

'Here continueth to rot the body of Francis Chartres'

Epitaph written by Dr John Arbuthnot, 1732

'HERE continueth to rot
The Body of FRANCIS CHARTRES,
Who with an INFLEXIBLE CONSTANCY,
And INIMITABLE UNIFORMITY of Life
PERSISTED
In spite of AGE and INFIRMITIES,
In the Practice of EVERY HUMAN VICE;
Excepting PRODIGALITY and HYPOCRISY:
His insatiable AVARICE exempted him from
the first,
His matchless IMPUDENCE from the second.
Nor was he more singular
In the undeviating [De]pravity of his Manners
Than successful
In Accumulating WEALTH.
For without TRADE or PROFESSION,
Without TRUST of PUBLIC MONEY,
And without BRIBE-WORTHY Service
He acquired, or more properly created
A MINISTERIAL ESTATE.
He was the only Person of his Time
Who could cheat without the Mask of
HONESTY,
Retain his Primeval MEANNESS
When possess'd of TEN THOUSAND a Year.
And having daily deserved the GIBBETT for
what he did,
Was at last condemn'd to it for what he could
not do.
Oh Indignant Reader!
Think not his Life useless to Mankind!
PROVIDENCE conniv'd at his execrable Designs,
To give to After-ages
A conspicuous PROOF and EXAMPLE,
Of how small Estimation is EXORBITANT
WEALTH
In the sight of GOD,
By his bestowing it on the most Unworthy
of ALL MORTALS.'

Colonel Chartres was an English rake, gambler, brothel-keeper and money-lender, detested by society. The Earl of Chesterfield noted: '*By-gones are by-gones, as Chartres, when he was dying, said of his sins: let us look forwards.*' William Hogarth depicted him in *The Harlot's Progress* as a lecherous old man, behind the procuress, looking libidinously at the unsuspecting country girl new to London. Pope called him '*a man infamous for all manner of vices*' and he was nicknamed 'the Rape-Master General of Great Britain'. In 1730, sensational newspaper reports told of his being sentenced to death for '*a rape on the body of one Anne Bond, his servant maid*'. He paid her £800 to petition for his pardon; she used the money to marry, and bought a tavern with the sign of Colonel Chartres' head. The author of the epitaph, Dr John Arbuthnot, was a well-known satirist, mathematician and physician who created the cartoon figure of John Bull.

ALEXANDER POPE
21 May 1688–30 May 1744

'Here am I, dying of a hundred good symptoms'
Letter to George, Lord Lyttelton, 15 May 1744

Pope is the third most frequently quoted writer in *The Oxford Dictionary of Quotations*, after Shakespeare and Tennyson, famous for his use of the heroic couplet and his satirical poem *The Rape of the Lock*. From the age of 12, he suffered numerous health problems, and was a hunchback, only four foot six inches tall. Pope's tuberculosis caused other complications, including respiratory difficulties, high fevers, inflamed eyes and abdominal pain.

Henry G. Bohn, in *The Life of Alexander Pope* (1857), writes:

'About three weeks before his death, Pope sent copies of his Ethic Epistles ... as present to his friends. "Here I am like Socrates," he said, "dispensing my morality among my friends just as I am dying." Spence [Joseph Spence, Pope's friend] rejoined, "I really had that thought several times when I was last at Twickenham with you, and was apt now and then to look upon myself as Phaedo." "That might be," said Pope, "but you must not expect me now to say anything like Socrates." ... On Sunday 6th of May, Pope appears to have been delirious, and four days later he said to Spence (in what we may call the old vein), "One of the things that I have almost most wondered at is, that there should be any such thing as human vanity. If I had any, I had enough to mortify it a few days ago, for I lost my mind for a whole day." ... A short time before his death, Pope said, "I am so certain of the soul's being immortal, that I seem to feel it within me as it were intuition." ... The day before his death, Hooke, the Roman historian, a zealous Catholic ... now approached the poet ... asking him whether or not he should send for a priest? Pope said, "I do not suppose that is essential, but it will look right; and I heartily thank you for putting me in mind of it." ... Pope died on the evening of Wednesday, the 30th of May, 1744, so easily and imperceptibly, that his attendants did not know the exact time of his departure.'

'Go, traveller, and imitate if you can this earnest and dedicated champion of liberty'

Translation of his self-written Latin epitaph, on his
tomb in St Patrick's Cathedral, Dublin

'Here is laid the body of Jonathan Swift, Doctor of Divinity, Dean of this Cathedral Church, where fierce indignation can no longer rend the heart. Go, traveller, and imitate if you can this earnest and dedicated champion of liberty. He died on the 19th day of October 1745 AD. Aged 78 years.'

An Anglo-Irish essayist, political pamphleteer, poet and satirist, Swift became Dean of St Patrick's Cathedral, Dublin, where he is buried at his own wish next to his friend Esther Johnson. W.B. Yeats considered his epitaph to be *'the greatest ... in history'* and translated it as follows:

'Swift has sailed into his rest;
Savage indignation there
Cannot lacerate his breast.
Imitate him if you dare,
World-besotted traveller; he
Served human liberty.'

In January 1728 Swift had prayed at Johnson's deathbed, after which his mental health began to break down. He had always feared mental illness, once remarking about a tree whose crown had withered, '*I shall be like that tree, I shall die from the top.*' He suffered a stroke in 1742 that left him unable to speak, and his friends, fearful that he would be cheated out of his savings, had him declared '*unsound in mind and memory*', in order to protect his fortune. He is now known to have suffered from Menière's disease. When he died several years later, most of his money went to charity in Dublin. Some was used to establish St Patrick's Hospital for Imbeciles (opened in 1757), which still exists as a psychiatric hospital. He also built an almshouse for old women who were no longer able to maintain themselves. The greatest prose satirist in the English language, Swift is best remembered for *A Tale of a Tub* and *Gulliver's Travels*.

FREDERICK LOUIS OF HANOVER, PRINCE OF WALES
1 February 1707–31 March 1751

'Here lies Fred,
Who was alive and is dead.
Had it been his father,
I had much rather ...'

Horace Walpole's epitaph for the eldest son of George II

Caroline of Ansbach, the wife of George II, said of Frederick: '*My first Dear-born is the greatest ass, and the greatest liar, and the greatest canaille, and the greatest beast in the whole world, and I heartily wish he was out of it.*' George II considered a scheme for excluding Frederick from the English throne so that his second son, William, could succeed him as king. He had arranged Frederick's marriage to Princess Augusta of Saxe-Gotha in 1736, but would not pay him a realistic allowance. Accumulating large debts, Frederick relied for an income on his wealthy friend, George Bubb Dodington. Parliament was obliged to intervene, and the queen was furious. When she saw Frederick from her dressing-room window, she shouted: '*Look! There he goes! That wretch! That villain! I wish the ground would open at this moment and sink the monster to the lowest hole in Hell!*'

Frederick took his pregnant wife from Hampton Court to St James' Palace, to prevent the baby from being delivered under his parents' roof. He was then banished from court. On 20 November 1737, Queen Caroline on her deathbed declared: '*At least I shall have one comfort in having my eyes eternally closed – I shall never see that monster again.*' The king refused to allow Frederick to see his mother before she died, saying to Lord Hervey: '*Bid him go about his business for his poor mother is not in a condition to see him act his false, whining, cringing tricks now, nor am I in a humour to bear his impertinence; and bid him trouble me with no more messages, but get out of my house.*' It is believed that Frederick's own death was caused by septicaemia after being hit on the head by a cricket ball – a case of 'play stopped reign'. His son was George III.

ADMIRAL JOHN BYNG
29 October 1704–14 March 1757

'While he felt like a victim, he acted like a hero'

Horace Walpole, on the day of Byng's execution

Admiral Byng was made a scapegoat, court-martialled and shot for failing *'to do his utmost'* to prevent Minorca falling to the French in the Seven Years' War. His execution was immortalized by Voltaire, who in his novel *Candide* depicts the execution of an officer by firing-squad in Portsmouth. He is told that *'Dans ce pays-ci, il est bon de tuer de temps en temps un amiral pour encourager les autres'* (*'In this country, it is wise to kill an admiral from time to time to encourage the others.'*) Byng was the last of his rank to be executed in this fashion, but even as recently as 2007 the Ministry of Defence refused a posthumous pardon. Byng's execution has been called *'the worst legalistic crime in the nation's annals'*, but his judicial murder ensured that future officers chose to risk battle, even if there was a strong chance of failure. His epitaph at the family vault in All Saints Church, Southill, Bedfordshire, reads:

'To the perpetual Disgrace
of PUBLICK JUSTICE
The Honble. JOHN BYNG Esqr
Admiral of the Blue
Fell a MARTYR to
POLITICAL PERSECUTION
March 14th in the year 1757 when
BRAVERY and LOYALTY
were Insufficient Securities
For the
Life and Honour
of a
NAVAL OFFICER'

GENERAL JAMES WOLFE
2 January 1727–13 September 1759

'Now God be praised. I will die contented.'
Dying words

Having fought valiantly against the French at Louisburg, Wolfe was chosen by Pitt the Elder to lead an assault on Quebec City the following year. After an inconclusive bombardment and a failed attack north of Quebec, he took 200 ships with 9,000 soldiers and 18,000 sailors along the St Lawrence River to the cliffs west of Quebec. At dead of night, in silence, his forces scaled the cliffs to surprise the Marquis de Montcalm's forces. The battle, on the Plains of Abraham, was over in 15 minutes. Both generals were mortally wounded, Wolfe being shot in the arm, shoulder and chest, but French rule in North America was ended for ever.

'They asked him (Wolfe) if he would have a surgeon; but he shook his head, and answered that all was over with him. His eyes closed with the torpor of approaching death, and those around sustained his fainting form. Yet they could not withhold their gaze from the wild turmoil before them, and the charging ranks of their companions rushing though the line of fire and smoke. "See how they run," one of the officers exclaimed, as the French fled in confusion before the levelled bayonets. "Who run?" demanded Wolfe, opening his eyes like a man aroused from sleep. "The enemy, sir," was the reply; "they give way everywhere." "Then," said the dying general, "tell Colonel River, to cut off their retreat from the bridge. Now, God be praised, I die contented," he murmured; and, turning on his side, he calmly breathed his last breath.'

Fighting at Bastia, Captain Horatio Nelson was heard to say to himself: '*What would the immortal Wolfe have done?*' and answer his own question: '*As he did, beat the enemy, or die in the attempt.*' At a dinner in London in the year of Trafalgar, Nelson told the artist Benjamin West that he knew nothing of art except that he always stopped to look at prints of West's painting of Wolfe's death. West replied that he feared Nelson's bravery in battle might provide him with similar subject material, and Nelson responded: '*Then I hope I shall die in the next battle.*'

'... but viler George the Second'

Epigram by Walter Savage Landor

Born in Hanover and raised in Germany, George II spoke extremely poor English and was not the most cultured of individuals, summed up when he said: *'I hate bainting, and boetry too! Neither the one nor the other ever did any good'* (John Ireland, *Hogarth Illustrated*, 1791). Horace Walpole, in his 1847 biography of George, stated: *'He had the haughtiness of Henry the Eighth, without his spirit; the avarice of Henry the Seventh, without his exactions; the indignities of Charles the First, without his bigotry for his prerogative; the vexations of King William, with as little skill in the management of parties; and the gross gallantry of his father, without his good nature or his honesty:– he might, perhaps, have been honest, if he had never hated his father, or had ever loved his son.'*

George had argued constantly with his father George I, and his relationship with Frederick, Prince of Wales, worsened during the 1730s. In 1737 he banished the prince and his family from the royal court. In the same year, he also lost his wife, Queen Caroline. It is claimed (in William M. White, *Emmanuel Swedenborg*, 1856) that when she asked her husband to remarry after her death, he replied, *'Non, j'aurai des maîtresses!' ('No, I will have mistresses!')* She responded, *'Ah, mon Dieu, cela n'empêche pas.' ('My God, that doesn't prevent it.')*

George already had at least one illegitimate child, and his most famous mistress was Henrietta Howard, Countess of Suffolk, who was one of Caroline's ladies of the bedchamber. Against Prime Minister Walpole's advice, George initiated the War of Jenkins' Ear, which evolved into the ruinous War of the Austrian Succession, involving all of Europe. He died of a heart attack in his water closet. His son Frederick predeceased him, so the throne went to George's grandson, George III.

'Après nous, le déluge'

Words of comfort to the king after Rossbach

The favourite mistress of Louis XV presciently said: '*After us, the deluge. I care not what happens when I am dead and gone*' following an assassination attempt on the king, and the disastrous Battle of Rossbach in 1757. At Rossbach, part of the Seven Years' War of 1756–63, Frederick the Great's Prussians hammered the forces of France and the Holy Roman Empire. The financial disaster of the war, coupled with the king's sexual predilection for young girls, orgies and mistresses, made him extremely unpopular, and Madame de Pompadour was in turn blamed for French involvement. France emerged from the war having lost possessions and virtually bankrupt.

According to Robertson Davies in his *Madame de Pompadour* (1954):

'The King had every privilege except that of being at ease. Pompadour provided the atmosphere in which that final luxury was possible. She did not do this, as anyone who thinks about the matter for twenty seconds will know, by twenty years of rapt contemplation of the ceilings of Versailles. Indeed, Pompadour was not a physically ardent woman, and love-making tired her. After about eight years of their association Louis XV did not sleep with her ... But it was to Pompadour that he talked, and it was to Pompadour that he listened.'

However, Louis showed no grief at her passing away from tuberculosis, aged only 42, commenting, '*The marquise has bad weather for her last journey.*' When her body was borne away from Versailles, he was thought to have behaved badly because he watched the sad procession from a balcony. Voltaire wrote: '*I am very sad at the death of Madame de Pompadour. I was indebted to her and I mourn her out of gratitude. It seems absurd that while an ancient pen-pusher, hardly able to walk, should still be alive, a beautiful woman, in the midst of a splendid career, should die at the age of forty.*'

HENRY FOX, FIRST BARON HOLLAND
28 September 1705–1 July 1774

'If Mr Selwyn calls, shew him up: if I am alive I would be glad to see him; if I am dead he would like to see me'

Said in 1774 during his last illness; George Selwyn
had a morbid fascination with corpses

This Whig politician was the father of Charles James Fox and was Secretary for War and Paymaster-General of the Forces, where he reaped a massive fortune before being dismissed as the most hated politician in Britain. He was said to have amassed £50,000 a year for eight years from the position. Professor Riker's 1911 study of Fox tells us that he became a chronic invalid, with few friends except Selwyn to visit him.

> 'One fact which militated against the happiness of Holland's later years was his steadily failing health ... he was taken so ill in Paris during the summer that his death was actually reported. After 1763 he never knew what it was to be free from pain or weakness ... Once or twice, it is true, we detect some allusion to the hate which the public bore him; but never can this be said to have clouded his moments of comfort or happiness ...

> It was now, when Holland was old and suffering, that certain results of his misspent career were beginning to tinge his thoughts with bitterness. In the few remaining years of his life he grew rapidly feebler, frequently longing for death, and latterly given additional pain by witnessing the suffering of his wife, who was slowly dying of cancer. Finally, on July 1, 1774, death came to release him, and he expired at the age of sixty-nine, "quite worn out in mind and body". Fox talked much of (and certainly believed in) his own "honesty" and "good nature" . But his "honesty" took merely the accepted form of loyalty (in general) to political engagements and the interests of his friends; it was an "honesty" which permitted the accumulation of wealth by the aid of government funds; and few great politicians have more significantly reaped the harvest of their misdeeds than Henry Fox.'

'I only regret that I have but one life to lose for my country'

Dying words

Hale fought for the Continental Army during the American Revolutionary War, and is considered to be America's first spy. During the Battle of Long Island, the British were trying to capture the city of New York. Captain Hale volunteered to go behind enemy lines to report on British troop movements. He disguised himself as a Dutch schoolteacher, carrying his Yale diploma to prove his credentials, and knowing that he would be immediately executed if caught. He was ferried across on the night of 12 September, but on the 15th, New York fell and Washington was forced to retreat to the northern tip of Manhattan Island. Major Robert Rogers of the Queens Rangers met Hale in a tavern and saw through his disguise. He lured Hale into betraying himself by pretending to be a patriot too, and apprehended him on 21 September. General William Howe cross-examined Hale, and he was hanged without trial the following day. British Captain John Montresor was present at Hale's execution, and took the news to Washington under a flag of truce:

'He said that Captain Hale had passed through their army, both of Long Island and York Island. That he had procured sketches of the fortifications, and made memoranda of their number and different positions. When apprehended, he was taken before Sir William Howe, and these papers, found concealed about his person, betrayed his intentions. He at once declared his name, rank in the American army, and his object in coming within the British lines ... "On the morning of his execution," continued the officer, "my station was near the fatal spot, and I requested the Provost Marshal to permit the prisoner to sit in my marquee, while he was making the necessary preparations. Captain Hale entered: he was calm, and bore himself with gentle dignity, in the consciousness of rectitude and high intentions. He asked for writing materials, which I furnished him: he wrote two letters ... He was shortly after summoned to the gallows. But a few persons were around him, yet his characteristic dying words were remembered. He said, 'I only regret, that I have but one life to lose for my country.'"'

'Leave your dying father, and go to the defence of your country'

Last words, spoken to his son, Pitt the Younger

Pitt was a supremely capable politician who led Britain during the Seven Years' War against France. He was also known as 'the Great Commoner', because of his long-standing refusal to accept a title. Being disliked by the new king, George III, he became sidelined from power, with the nation refusing to accept his warnings that Britain would lose its American colony unless it altered its policies. Unlike the Hanoverian king, Pitt wanted to give the colonists fundamental liberties – no taxation without consent, independent judges, trial by jury, along with the recognition of the American Continental Congress. In January 1775, the House of Lords rejected his bill for reconciliation, and when war broke out he warned that the Americans could not be conquered. However, due to his failure to ally with Lord Rockingham's party, and because of his support for democratic rights (for the British people as well as the American colonists), he had little personal support.

Pitt's last appearance in the House of Lords was on 7 April 1778, working for a motion urging the king to conclude peace with America on any terms. He said: *'My Lords, any state is better than despair; if we must fall, let us fall like men'*, had a fit and collapsed, the scene being later recorded in a famous painting by Copley. These were the last words he spoke in public. He was taken to his country seat at Hayes, where his son William read to him from Homer about the killing of Hector by Achilles. He died a month later and was buried at Hayes, but the country now realized its enormous loss. The Commons asked the king for Pitt to be buried with the honours of a public funeral, and a sum was voted for a monument to be erected over a new grave in Westminster Abbey. According to Edmund Burke's inscription in the Guildhall, Pitt was *'the minister by whom commerce was united with and made to flourish by war'*. His son William also became an illustrious statesman.

VOLTAIRE
20 February 1694–30 May 1778

'This is no time to make new enemies'
Response on his deathbed, when asked to forswear Satan

François Marie Arouet took the pen name Voltaire, and became one of France's greatest writers and philosophers. He was briefly imprisoned in the Bastille in 1717 for writing a satire on the government, and while there wrote *Oedipe*. In 1726 he was forced into exile in England for three years. Back in Paris he wrote a book praising English institutions, and was forced to leave Paris for his estate at Ferney. Here he produced a constant flow of books, such as *Candide*, plays and letters. He was a critic of religious intolerance and persecution, and the Bishop of Anneci forbade any priest to confess him. Voltaire wagered his friend Wagnière that he would overcome the ban. He faked a mortal illness, and a priest was summoned and very reluctantly gave the last rites. As soon as he left, Voltaire leapt out of bed and said, *'I told you I would be confessed and commune in my bed'*.

At the age of 83 Voltaire at last returned to a hero's welcome in Paris, but soon died there. It seems he arranged to cheat the Church again, as according to Condorcet's *Vie de Voltaire*, he accepted the sacrament on his deathbed. However, in Carlyle's *Essays*, Vol. II, we read: *'The sick man pushed one of his hands against the Cure's calotte [coif], shoving him back, and cried, turning abruptly to the other side, "Let me die in peace."'* In one of Voltaire's works he wrote: *'If God did not exist, it would be necessary to invent Him.'* Another statement attributed to him on his deathbed is: *'I am abandoned by God and man! I will give you half of what I am worth if you will give me six months' life. Then I shall go to hell; and you will go with me. O Christ! O Jesus Christ!'* In 1791 Voltaire's remains were moved to a resting place at the Pantheon in Paris. In 1814, it was claimed that religious fanatics stole the remains and threw them on a rubbish dump.

MAJOR JOHN ANDRÉ
2 May 1750–2 October 1780

'I am reconciled to my death, but I detest the mode'

Words spoken before his execution

André was placed in charge of British secret intelligence and in 1780 began intriguing with American General Benedict Arnold, who commanded the fort at West Point, New York. Arnold agreed to surrender it for £20,000, enabling the British to cut off New England from the rest of the colonies. André was captured in civilian clothes behind American lines. The Americans knew that a high-ranking officer was about to defect to the British, and André's refusal to inform on him gave Arnold time to escape and join the British army. Because Nathan Hale had been hanged as a spy in 1776 by the British, André was condemned to the same fate. Normally officers had the more honourable death of being shot. Alexander Hamilton wrote: '*Never perhaps did any man suffer death with more justice, or deserve it less.*'

'It was his earnest desire to be shot, as being the mode of death most conformable to the feelings of a military man, and he had indulged the hope that his request would be granted. At the moment, therefore, when suddenly he came in view of the gallows, he involuntarily started backward, and made a pause. "Why this emotion, sir?" said an officer by his side. Instantly recovering his composure, he said, "I am reconciled to my death, but I detest the mode." ... The rope being appended to the gallows, he slipped the noose over his head and adjusted it to his neck, without the assistance of the awkward executioner. Colonel Scammel now informed him that he had an opportunity to speak, if he desired it; he raised the handkerchief from his eyes, and said, "I pray you to bear me witness that I meet my fate like a brave man." The wagon being now removed from under him, he was suspended, and instantly expired; it proved indeed "but a momentary pang". He was dressed in his royal regimentals and boots, and his remains, in the same dress, were placed in an ordinary coffin, and interred at the foot of the gallows; and the spot was consecrated by the tears of thousands.'

'The first step toward philosophy is incredulity'

Last words to his daughter

This French philosopher, playwright, and novelist constantly questioned the nature of existence and Christianity to his dying breath. In *Sceptics Walk* (1747) and *Letters on the Blind* (1749), he slowly turned from theism to atheism. In 1749 he was imprisoned for three months for the opinions he had expressed in *Philosophical Thoughts*. He had stated, '*If you impose silence on me about religion and government, I shall have nothing to talk about*', but after his release he reduced the controversial character of his published works. Thus most of his materialistic and anti-religious works and several of his novels were not published during his lifetime. This is how he described the enigma of our existence:

'To be born in imbecility, in the midst of pain and crisis to be the plaything of ignorance, error, need, sickness, wickedness, and passions; to return step by step to imbecility, from the time of lisping to that of doting; to live among knaves and charlatans of all kinds; to die between one man who takes your pulse and another who troubles your head; never to know where you come from, why you come and where you are going! That is what is called the most important gift of our parents and nature. Life.'

Diderot is best known as the editor of the 17-volume *Encyclopédie* (1772), which served to diffuse the views of the French Enlightenment. For him, the aim of the work was '*to assemble the knowledge scattered over the face of the earth; to explain its general plan to the men with whom we live ... so that we may not die without having deserved well of the human race*'. He was fortunate that Catherine the Great had given him a lifelong pension, but towards the end of his life, almost his entire close circle of friends had died. The death of his mistress and intellectual companion Sophie Volland in February 1784 left him grief-stricken, and he died of coronary thrombosis in the house in Paris's Rue de Richelieu that Catherine the Great had given him.

'I who am about to die'

Last utterances

Dr Johnson is cited by *The Oxford Dictionary of National Biography* as *'arguably the most distinguished man of letters in English history'*, and Boswell's biography of the lexicographer as *'the most famous single work of biographical art in the whole of literature'*. John Hawkins' 1787 biography tells us:

'December 13th. At noon, I called at his house, but went not into his room, being told that he was dozing. I was further informed by the servants, that his appetite was totally gone, and that he could take no sustenance. At eight in the evening, of the same day, word was brought me by Mr Sastres, to whom, in his last moments, he uttered these words "Iam moriturus" ("I who am about to die"), that, at a quarter past seven, he had, without a groan, or the least sign of pain or uneasiness, yielded his last breath. At eleven, the same evening, Mr Langton came to me, and, in an agony of mind, gave me to understand, that our friend had wounded himself in several parts of the body ... The fact was, that conceiving himself to be full of water, he had done that, which he had often solicited his medical assistants to do, made two or three incisions in his lower limbs, vainly hoping for some relief from the flux that might follow ...

That, at eight in the morning of the preceding day, upon going into the bedchamber, his master, being in bed ... his master took a case of lancets, and choosing one of them ... drawing his hand under the bed-clothes, they saw his arm move. Upon this they turned down the clothes, and saw a great effusion of blood ... That soon after, he got at a pair of scissors ... and plunged them deep in the calf of each leg ... That he then fell into that dozing which carried him off. That it was conjectured he lost eight or ten ounces of blood; and that this effusion brought on the dozing, though his pulse continued firm till three o'clock. That this act was not done to hasten his end, but to discharge the water that he conceived to be in him, I have not the least doubt. A dropsy was his disease; he looked upon himself as a bloated carcase; and, to attain the power of easy respiration, would have undergone any degree of temporary pain ...'

'Throw a quilt over it'

Last words, referring to his shivering dog

Frederick earned his epithet through lands taken during the War of the Austrian Succession, when Prussia doubled its population and became a power in Europe. He was then involved against France and Russia in the Seven Years' War (1756–63). The finest soldier of his age and the founder of modern Germany was dying when he noticed one of his favourite greyhounds shivering.

'... the rattle of death beginning soon after, which lasted at intervals all day. Selle [the king's chief physician], in Berlin, was sent for by express; he arrived about 3 of the afternoon: the King seemed a little more conscious, knew those about him, "his face red rather than pale, in his eyes still something of their old fire". Towards evening the feverishness abated; the King fell into a soft sleep, with warm perspiration; but, on awakening, complained of cold, repeatedly of cold, demanding wrappage after wrappage (soft quilt); – and on examining feet and legs, one of the Doctors made signs that they were in fact cold, up nearly to the knee. "What said he of the feet?" murmured the King some time afterwards, the Doctor having now stepped out of sight. "Much the same as before," answered some attendant. The King shook his head, incredulous. He drank once, grasping the goblet with both hands, a draught of fennel-water, his customary drink; and seemed relieved by it – his last reflection in this world.

Towards nine in the evening, there had come on a continual short cough, and a rattling in the breast, breath more and more difficult ... For the most part he was unconscious, never more than half-conscious. As the wall-clock above his head struck 11, he asked, "What o'clock?" "Eleven," answered they. "At 4," murmured he, "I will rise." One of his dogs sat on its stool near him; about midnight he noticed it shivering for cold: "Throw a quilt over it," said or beckoned he; that, I think, was his last completely conscious utterance.'

'Permit me to point out you have made three mistakes in spelling'

On reading his death-warrant

'In 1790, shortly after Louis XVI and his family had been conveyed to Versailles, and before the guillotine had been invented, the Marquis de Favras was accused by the Assembly of plotting to murder Lafayette and Necker, carry off the King, place him at the head of the army, and march on Paris. Favras was tried and sentenced to be hanged. Having read his own death-warrant at the request of his accusers, he quietly remarked, "Permit me to point out that you have made three mistakes in spelling."'

The Marquis de Favras was convicted of treason after a two-month show trial. In 1789, he had been involved with the Comte de Provence, the younger brother of Louis XVI, in a plot to rescue the king and the royal family from the Tuileries Palace and take them out of the country. The Comte would become Regent of France, and 30,000 troops would encircle Paris. In the confusion, the city's leaders would be assassinated and the city starved of food, thereby ending the French Revolution. Favras was betrayed and imprisoned, but refused to give any information on the plot's participants. Gouverneur Morris believed that he was hanged as a scapegoat to shield the king's brother. The Comte managed to flee France in 1791, later becoming Louis XVIII. On 1 December 1789, the Assembly passed a law that nobles would face the same fate as commoners, and Favras was sentenced to be hanged, rather than beheaded, the first aristocrat to face this sentence. (The guillotine was not introduced until 1792.) Campan's *Memoirs of Marie Antoinette* record:

'His death was obviously inevitable. During the whole time of the proceedings the populace never ceased threatening the judges and shouting, "A la lanterne!" ['To the lamppost', meaning 'Hang him!'] ... He heard this sentence with wonderful calmness, and said to his judges, "I pity you much if the testimony of two men is sufficient to induce you to condemn ... My greatest consolation is that which I derive from my innocence."'

'The body of Benjamin Franklin, printer
(like the cover of an old book, its contents worn out,
and stript of its lettering and gilding)
Lies here, food for worms.
Yet the work itself shall not be lost,
for it will, as he believed, appear once more
In a new and more beautiful edition, corrected and
amended by its Author Benjamin Franklin RIP.'

Epitaph written by Franklin in 1728, now in the Library of Congress

Ben Franklin became famous as a scientist, inventor, printer, musician, economist and philosopher. His funeral was attended by around 20,000 people, and he was interred in Christ Church Burial Ground, Philadelphia. He had written the above epitaph at the age of 22, before his extraordinary career really started. However, his actual grave reads, as specified in his will, simply *'Benjamin and Deborah Franklin'*. In 1773, he corresponded with a French scientist on the subject of preserving the dead for later revival by more advanced scientific methods, writing: *'I should prefer to an ordinary death, being immersed with a few friends in a cask of Madeira, until that time, then to be recalled to life by the solar warmth of my dear country! But in all probability, we live in a century too little advanced, and too near the infancy of science, to see such an art brought in our time to its perfection.'* At the age of 84, as he lay on his deathbed, his daughter Sarah, who was attending to him, thought he was lying in an awkward position. Aware of his coming demise, he replied in typical fashion: *'A dying man can do nothing easy.'*

This polymath's inventions and achievements are too vast to be recounted here. In the War of Independence, he was ambassador to Europe for the colonies, negotiating French help for America. When he signed the Constitution of the United States of America in 1787, he was the only 'Founding Father' to have signed all five of the documents that established American independence.

WOLFGANG AMADEUS MOZART
(JOHANNES CHRYSOSTOMUS WOLFGANGUS THEOPHILUS MOZART)
27 January 1756–5 December 1791

> **'Stay with me tonight; you must see me die. I have long had the taste of death on my tongue, I smell death, and who will stand by my Constanze, if you do not stay?'**
>
> Words spoken on the day of his death to his sister-in-law,
> Sophie Weber; Constanze was his wife

A child prodigy, Mozart began composing at the age of 5, performing in courts across Europe. George Szell writes of him: '*21 piano sonatas, 27 piano concertos, 41 symphonies, 18 masses, 13 operas, 9 oratorios and cantata, 2 ballets, 40 plus concertos for various instruments, string quartets, trios and quintets, violin and piano duets, piano quartets, and the songs. This astounding output includes hardly one work less than a masterpiece ... Lengthy immersion in the works of other composers can tire. The music of Mozart does not tire, and this is one of its miracles.*' Albert Einstein also recognized his contribution: '*Mozart is the greatest composer of all. Beethoven created his music, but the music of Mozart is of such purity and beauty that one feels he merely found it – that it has always existed as part of the inner beauty of the universe waiting to be revealed ... Listening to Mozart, we cannot think of any possible improvement.*'

Mozart died aged only 35, probably of rheumatic fever, and working until the end. Four years earlier he had written to his father, Leopold:

'As death, when we come to consider it closely, is the true goal of our existence, I have formed during the last few years such close relationships with this best and truest friend of mankind that death's image is not only no longer terrifying to me, but is indeed very soothing and consoling, and I thank my God for graciously granting me the opportunity ... of learning that death is the key which unlocks the door to our true happiness. I never lie down at night without reflecting that – young as I am – I may not live to see another day. Yet no one of all my acquaintances could say that in company I am morose or disgruntled.'

'I die innocent of all the crimes laid to my charge'

Last words spoken moments before his beheading

Louis had been on the throne since 1774, and taxes in France were extremely high, primarily to pay for the wars with England in America and India. There was widespread unrest in the country, and on 5 October 1789, revolutionaries incited a mob of poor Parisian women to march on Versailles and bring the royal family to the Tuileries Palace in Paris to see what conditions were really like in the capital. In 1791 the king tried to flee the country, and his support deteriorated. The following year the National Assembly abolished the monarchy and declared a republic. On 20 January 1793, the National Convention condemned Louis XVI to death. Accompanying Louis at his execution was a priest, Henry Essex Edgeworth, who recorded:

'They surrounded him again, and would have seized his hands. "What are you attempting?" said the King, drawing back his hands. "To bind you," answered the wretches. "To bind me," said the King, with an indignant air. "No! I shall never consent to that: do what you have been ordered, but you shall never bind me ..."

... and in a voice so loud, that it must have been heard at the Pont Tournant, I heard him pronounce distinctly these memorable words: "I die innocent of all the crimes laid to my charge; I pardon those who have occasioned my death; and I pray to God that the blood you are going to shed may never be visited on France." He was proceeding, when a man on horseback, in the national uniform, and with a ferocious cry, ordered the drums to beat ... they dragged him under the axe of the guillotine, which with one stroke severed his head from his body. All this passed in a moment. The youngest of the guards, who seemed about eighteen, immediately seized the head, and showed it to the people as he walked round the scaffold; he accompanied this monstrous ceremony with the most atrocious and indecent gestures. At first an awful silence prevailed; at length some cries of "Vive la République!" were heard.'

'They shall all be guillotined'

Last words spoken before his murder

A Swiss-born physician, political theorist, scientist and journalist, Marat was the leading revolutionary in France along with Robespierre and Danton. In Parliament he argued in favour of mass executions, being mainly responsible for the 'Reign of Terror', but he also believed that Louis XVI should not be executed, on the basis that he could not be held guilty for crimes committed before the ratification of the new French constitution. The king went to the guillotine on 21 January 1793, but Marat had become hated by many fellow revolutionaries for this opinion. In public, however, he was seen as a hero who stood up for the working classes. Marat's Jacobins fought bitterly with the more moderate Girondins, whom he believed to be secret enemies of the new republican state. They tried to have him imprisoned, which led his followers into violent confrontations with them. The fall of the Girondins on 31 May was one of his last achievements.

Marat's debilitating skin infection was causing him great pain, so he spent much of his time in a hot bath to alleviate the discomfort. He was in his bathtub when a 24-year-old woman, Charlotte Corday, arrived, claiming to be a messenger from Caen and begging to be admitted to his quarters. The Girondins were trying to form a breakaway faction in Normandy, and she carried a list of conspirators. Marat ordered her in, and she sat in a chair next to his tub. After reading her list, Marat remarked, '*They shall all be guillotined.*' Corday then drew a knife from her dress and stabbed him in the chest. He called out to his common-law wife, '*Aidez-moi, ma chère amie!*' ('*Help me, my dear friend!*'), and died. Corday was a Girondin with Royalist connections, and her action provoked reprisals in which thousands of the Jacobins' adversaries, both Royalists and Girondins, were executed for treason. She was guillotined four days after his death. During her trial, she testified that she had carried out the assassination alone, saying, '*I killed one man to save 100,000.*' After her death, she was autopsied by the Jacobins to see if she was a virgin, as they suspected her lover would also have been implicated in Marat's death. She was indeed a virgin working alone, believing that her actions would stop the bloodshed across her country.

MARIE ANTOINETTE, QUEEN OF FRANCE
(MARIA ANTONIA JOSEPHA JOHANNA VON HABSBURG-LOTHRINGEN)
2 November 1755–16 October 1793

'Pardon me, monsieur. It was not on purpose.'

Last words, said to her executioner after accidentally stepping upon his foot

The fifteenth child of the Holy Roman Emperor Francis I and the Empress Maria Theresa, Maria Antonia was 14 when she married the Dauphin de France, who became King Louis XVI in 1774. She was disliked at court because she was Austrian, and the starving populace came to resent her gambling and extravagances. She had four children before the French Revolution and the 'Reign of Terror', when her husband was deposed and guillotined. During her trial for treason, her son was forced into accusing her of improper sexual relations with him. According to historian and journalist Jean Charles Lacretelle:

'Responding to the priest who had accompanied her to the foot of the guillotine, who had whispered, "This is the moment, Madame, to arm yourself with courage," she said, "I was a queen, and you took away my crown; a wife, and you killed my husband; a mother, and you deprived me of my children. My blood alone remains: take it, but do not make me suffer long. Courage! I have shown it for years; think you I shall lose it at the moment when my sufferings are to end?"'

Lamartine recorded: *'On reaching the scaffold she inadvertently trod on the executioner's foot. "Pardon me," she said, courteously. She knelt for an instant and uttered a half-audible prayer; then rising and glancing towards the towers of the Temple, "Adieu, once again, my children," she said; "I go to rejoin your father." The infamous wretch exhibited her head to the people, as he was accustomed to do when he had sacrificed an illustrious victim.'*

MADAME ROLAND, JEANNE-MARIE PHILIPON
17 March 1754–8 November 1793

'O Liberty! Liberty! What crimes are committed in your name!'

Last utterance before her beheading

Madame Roland was a political writer and the wife of Jean-Marie Roland de la Platière, a leader of the Girondist party. When the moderate Girondists lost popularity following their protests over the killing of the aristocracy, her husband was forced to flee from Paris to Rouen for safety. Madame Roland was arrested and sent to prison, being tried on false charges of harbouring royalist sympathies. Robespierre had decided that she was to be killed as part of the purge of the Girondist opposition.

Many people were guillotined before it was her turn, and the executioner's block ran red with blood. She shouted to the crowds: '*My friends, I am going to the guillotine. In a few moments I shall be there. They who send me thither will ere long follow me. I go innocent. They will come stained with blood. You who now applaud our execution will then applaud theirs with equal zeal.*' She then bowed before the statue of Liberty in the Place de la Révolution, and uttered her last words. She was bound to the plank, which then fell to its horizontal position, bringing her head under the axe. The steel slid through the groove, and the head of Madame Roland dropped into a basket with the other heads.

Two days after her execution, her husband committed suicide on a country lane outside Rouen. Drawing a long stiletto from the inside of his walking-stick, he placed the head of it against the trunk of a tree, and threw himself upon the sharp weapon, piercing his heart. A piece of paper was pinned to the breast of his coat, upon which was written: '*Whoever finds these remains, respect them as those of a virtuous man. After hearing of my wife's death, I would not stay another day in a world so stained with crime.*'

'One moment more, executioner, one little moment!'

Last words to her executioner

Born Jeanne Bécu, Madame du Barry was the successor to Madame de Pompadour as maîtresse-en-titre of Louis XV. A commoner like Pompadour, she became a courtesan, a high-class prostitute in one of Paris's many salon-brothels, with the Maréchal de Richelieu being one of her main customers. The king noticed her at Versailles, but she could not qualify as a royal mistress without a title. He married her to Comte Guillaume du Barry, and had her birth certificate altered to give her the necessary noble descent. She was presented to the court at Versailles in 1769, and became increasingly unpopular because of the king's financial extravagance towards her. During a stay with her at the Petit Trianon, Louis fell ill with smallpox. At his request, she was sent away from the court, as her continued presence would have prevented him from receiving the last sacrament. After the king's death, she had a liaison with the Duke of Brissac. He was captured by a mob while visiting Paris. Late at night, Madame du Barry heard the sound of a drunken crowd approaching her chateau; they had come to show her Brissac's head.

In 1792, Madame du Barry was suspected of financially assisting émigrés who had fled the Revolution, and was arrested and condemned to death. She tried to save herself by revealing the hiding-places of the jewels and pearls she had hidden around her property, but to no avail. On her way to the guillotine, she continually collapsed in the tumbrel, crying, '*You are going to hurt me! Why?*' and screaming in fear. Her last words to the executioner were '*One moment more, executioner, one little moment.*' She implored the crowd to save her life so frantically that the executioners hurried to kill her lest the mob should turn against them. The guillotine was invented to speed up the beheading of up to 40,000 people during the French Revolution; around three-quarters of these are thought to have been innocent of any crime.

'Thou wilt shew my head to the people; it is worth shewing'

Last words to his executioner

Danton was the acknowledged leader of the French Revolution following the storming of the Bastille in 1789. A moderating influence on the Jacobins, he became marginalized by Robespierre's enforcement of the Reign of Terror. Jacobin extremists wished to arrest him, but Robespierre resisted the proposal for some time. Faced with more pressure, and enticed *'by the motives of selfish policy'*, he eventually relented, and on 30 March 1794, Danton, Camille Desmoulins and others were seized and brought before a revolutionary tribunal. Danton boldly spoke his mind, and to silence him and his co-defendants, it was decreed that any suspect on trial who insulted national justice would not be allowed to speak. *'I will no longer defend myself,'* Danton cried. *'Let me be led to death, I shall go to sleep in glory.'* Almost his last words were inspired by the treachery of Robespierre: *'I could have saved him ... I leave it all in a frightful welter; not a man of them has any idea of government. Robespierre will follow me; he is dragged down by me. Ah, better be a poor fisherman than meddle with the government of men!'* Three months after Danton's execution, Robespierre was himself guillotined. Carlyle wrote of Danton's execution:

'Danton carried a high look in the Death-cart. Not so Camille: it is but one week, and all is so topsy-turvied; angel Wife left weeping; love, riches, Revolutionary fame, left all at the Prison-gate; carnivorous Rabble now howling round. Palpable, and yet incredible; like a madman's dream! Camille struggles and writhes; his shoulders shuffle the loose coat off them, which hangs knotted, the hands tied: "Calm my friend," said Danton; "heed not that vile canaille (*laissez là cette vile canaille*)." At the foot of the Scaffold, Danton was heard to ejaculate: "O my Wife, my well-beloved, I shall never see thee more then!" – but, interrupting himself: "Danton, no weakness!" He said to Herault-Sechelles stepping forward to embrace him: "Our heads will meet there," in the Headsman's sack. His last words were to Samson the Headsman himself: "Thou wilt shew my head to the people; it is worth shewing." So passes, like a gigantic mass, of valour, ostentation, fury, affection and wild revolutionary manhood, this Danton, to his unknown home.'

ANTOINE-LAURENT DE LAVOISIER
26 August 1743–8 May 1794

'It took them only an instant to cut off his head, but France may not produce another like it in a century'

Words of Joseph Louis Lagrange

A chemist, biologist, economist and public servant, Lavoisier is noted for his discovery of the role oxygen plays in combustion, and has been called the 'Father of Modern Chemistry'. He stated the first version of the law of conservation of mass, recognized and named oxygen, helped construct the metric system and wrote the first extensive list of elements. He also discovered that diamond is a crystalline form of carbon. He made many fundamental contributions to chemistry. The revolution in the science that he brought about was a result of a conscious effort to fit all experiments into the framework of a single theory. He established the consistent use of chemical balance, used oxygen to overthrow the phlogiston theory, and developed a new system of chemical nomenclature.

Lavoisier was a friend of Benjamin Franklin, and was one of the French Academicians who rejected Jean-Paul Marat's scientific proposals, after which Marat turned to revolutionary politics. He also intervened on behalf of a number of foreign-born scientists, including the mathematician Joseph Louis Lagrange, granting them exemption from a mandate stripping all foreigners of possessions and freedom. At the height of the French Revolution, Lavoisier was accused by Marat of selling diluted tobacco. As one of 28 French tax collectors, he was branded a traitor and guillotined. An appeal to spare his life so that he could continue his experiments was cut short by the judge: *'The Republic needs neither scientists nor chemists; the course of justice cannot be delayed.'* When his private belongings were delivered to his widow, a brief note was included reading: *'To the widow of Lavoisier, who was falsely convicted.'* Eighteen months after his death, Lavoisier was exonerated by the French government.

ANDRÉ MARIE CHÉNIER
30 October 1762–25 July 1794

'The sleep of death will press upon my lids'

Uncompleted Iamb X of last verses written before his execution

The young poet, famous for his eulogy to Marie-Anne-Charlotte Corday when she assassinated the despised Marat, had been arrested in Paris by two agents seeking someone else. During his 140 days in prison he wrote a series of verses denouncing the Convention that 'hiss and stab like poisoned bullets'. They were smuggled out to his family concealed in a basket of soiled linen. Robespierre remembered Chénier as the author of earlier venomous verses in the *Journal de Paris*, and wanted him dead. Chénier was summarily convicted on a bogus charge of conspiracy on 24 July, and guillotined along with a Princess of Monaco and 36 others the following day. Robespierre himself was executed three days later. The 'poet-martyr' was discovered only in 1819, when his complete poems were published.

In prison, daily expecting death, Chénier wrote several iambs of verse:

VII
'When the sombre slaughterhouse lets the
    bleating sheep
Into its dark and deadly gate,
Shepherds, dogs, and sheep, all of them keep
    Their thoughts on any but their fate ...

VIII
Who will be the prey
On whom the axe will fall today?
Everybody shivers, listens, and is relieved
    to see
That the one called out is not yet he.
It will be you tomorrow, unfeeling fool.

IX
As the sun's last flashing ray,
As the last cool breeze from the shore,
Cheer the close of a dying day,
Thus I strike my lyre once more.
As now by the scaffold I wait,
Each moment of time seems the last,
For the clock, like a finger of fate,
Points onward and onward fast.

X
The sleep of death will press upon my'
    lids.'

MAXIMILIEN FRANÇOIS MARIE ISIDORE DE ROBESPIERRE
6 May 1758–28 July 1794

'Death is the commencement of immortality!'

From the speech delivered in the Convention on 26 July 1794,
the day before his arrest and two days before his execution

'The enemies of the Republic call me tyrant! Were I such they would grovel at my feet ... My life? Oh, my life I abandon without a regret! I have seen the Past; and I foresee the Future ... Death is the commencement of immortality! I leave to the oppressors of the people a terrible testament, which I proclaim with the independence befitting one whose career is so nearly ended; it is the awful truth: "Thou shalt die!"'

Robespierre dominated the Committee of Public Safety, and with Danton and Marat was responsible for the 'Reign of Terror', which killed thousands during the French Revolution. His supporters called him 'the Incorruptible', while his adversaries referred to him as 'the Tyrant' or 'the Bloodthirsty Dictator'. The above speech was given the day he was attacked in Parliament by successive deputies asking for his arrest. Seeing him seemingly struck dumb by the accusations, one deputy shouted: *'The blood of Danton chokes him!'* The Convention ordered the arrest of Robespierre and his supporters, who gathered at the Hôtel de Ville. At 2 a.m. on 27 July 1794, troops approached them, and it seems that Robespierre's jaw was shattered by a gunshot. The next day he was guillotined without trial in the Place de la Révolution, along with 12 followers. Only Robespierre was guillotined face up. When baring Robespierre's neck, the executioner tore off the bandage that was holding his shattered jaw in place, producing an agonizing scream that lasted until the fall of the blade. Earlier that year Robespierre had told the National Convention: *'Terror is nought but prompt, severe, inflexible justice; it is therefore an emanation of virtue; it is less a particular principle than a consequence of the general principle of democracy applied to the most pressing needs of the fatherland.'*

'Don't let the awkward squad fire over me!'

Words spoken shortly before his death, alluding to a body of the Dumfries militia
of which he was a member, and of which he entertained a very poor opinion

Recently voted 'the Greatest Scot', and known as 'the Bard', the poet
and lyricist suffered months of bad health from a heart condition, before dying
(possibly from a blood infection), aged only 37.

'Though Burns now knew he was dying, his good humour was
unruffled, and his wit never forsook him. When he looked up and saw
Dr Maxwell at his bed-side, – "Alas!" he said, "what has brought you
here? I am but a poor crow and not worth plucking." He pointed to
his pistols, those already mentioned the gift of their maker, Blair of
Birmingham, and desired that Maxwell would accept of them, saying
they could not be in worthier keeping, and he should have no more
need of them. This relieved his proud heart from a sense of obligation.
Soon afterwards he saw Gibson, one of his brother-volunteers by the
bed-side with tears in his eyes. He smiled and said, – "John, don't let
the awkward squad fire over me!"

His household presented a melancholy spectacle: the Poet dying; his
wife in hourly expectation of being confined: four helpless children
wandering from room to room, gazing on their miserable parents and
but too little of food or cordial kind to pacify the whole or soothe the
sick. To Jessie Lewars, all who are charmed with the poet's works are
much indebted: she acted with the prudence of a sister and the tenderness of a daughter, and kept desolation away, though she could not keep
disease. – "A tremor," says Maxwell, "pervaded his frame; his tongue,
though often refreshed, became parched; and his mind, when not
roused by conversation, sunk into delirium." On the second and third
day after his return from the Brow [a healing well], the fever increased
and his strength diminished. On the fourth day, when his attendant,
James Maclure; held a cordial to his lips, he swallowed it eagerly – rose
almost wholly up – spread out his hands – sprang forward nigh the
whole length of the bed – fell on his face and expired.'

CATHERINE II OF RUSSIA, CATHERINE THE GREAT (SOPHIE FRIEDERIKE AUGUSTE VON ANHALT-ZERBST-DOMBURG)
2 May 1729–17 November 1796

> **'I shall be an autocrat: that's my trade. And the good Lord will forgive me: that's his.'**
>
> Attributed last words

Other last words are said to be to her physician, who told her: '*Majesty, you must get well! The people need you!*' to which she responded: '*You do not say "must" to a princess.*' However, it seems that she may have said nothing at all: '*Sometime after nine chamberlain Zakhar Zotov, not having been summoned as anticipated, peeked in her bedroom and found nobody. In a closet adjacent he discovered the Empress on the floor. With two comrades Zotov tried to help her up, but she barely opened her eyes once before emitting a faint groan as she exhaled and lapsed into unconscious from which she never recovered.*' She was laid in her bed as doctors and priests gathered around. Aged 67, Catherine had lost all her teeth and was plagued by debilitating varicose veins. A few weeks before her death, she had suffered a minor stroke. Although ill and confused, she still met her current lover, a young officer in the Horse Guards. On 16 November she had her morning coffee and read the newspapers. Within the half-hour she had a second stroke, dying the following day of a cerebral haemorrhage, which was then called apoplexy.

Peter III had been crowned tsar on Christmas Day 1761, but his more capable wife Catherine was planning a coup. On 28 June 1762, she arrived in St Petersburg to be greeted by cheers from her supporters and the crowds. The next morning Peter was forced to abdicate, and a week later he was dead. Catherine went on to become the most powerful sovereign in Europe. She continued Peter the Great's reforms of the Russian state, further increasing central control over the provinces. However, later in life she became more reactionary, leading to widespread repression.

GIOCANTE DE CASABIANCA
c.1788–1 August 1798

'The boy stood on the burning deck / Whence all but he had fled'

Poem by Felicia Dorothea Hemans, first published in the
Monthly Magazine, August 1826

The boy stood on the burning deck
Whence all but he had fled;
The flame that lit the battle's wreck
Shone round him o'er the dead.
Yet beautiful and bright he stood,
As born to rule the storm;
A creature of heroic blood,
A proud, though childlike form.
The flames rolled on ... he would not go
Without his father's word;
That father, faint in death below,
His voice no longer heard.
He called aloud ... "Say, father, say
If yet my task is done!"
He knew not that the chieftain lay
Unconscious of his son.
"Speak, father!" once again he cried
"If I may yet be gone!"
And but the booming shots replied,
And fast the flames rolled on.

Upon his brow he felt their breath,
And in his waving hair,
And looked from that lone post of death,
In still yet brave despair;
And shouted but once more aloud,
"My father, must I stay?"
While o'er him fast, through sail and shroud
The wreathing fires made way,
They wrapped the ship in splendour wild,
They caught the flag on high,
And streamed above the gallant child,
Like banners in the sky.
There came a burst of thunder sound ...
The boy! Oh! Where was he?
Ask of the winds that far around
With fragments strewed the sea.
With mast, and helm, and pennon fair,
That well had borne their part;
But the noblest thing which perished there
Was that young faithful heart.'

During the Battle of the Nile (Aboukir Bay), the young Giocante was serving with his father, Captain Luc-Julien-Joseph Casabianca, aboard the French flagship *L'Orient* when it came under attack from Nelson's fleet. The ship caught fire and the gunpowder magazine exploded, killing father, son and over 1,000 of the 1,100 crew. The battle gave the English effective control of the Mediterranean.

GEORGE WASHINGTON
22 February 1732–14 December 1799

⁶'Tis well⁹

Dying words to his secretary and friend, Tobias Lear

 **Washington was the successful** Commander-in-Chief of the Continental Army in the American Revolutionary War of 1775–83, and was twice unanimously elected the first President of the United States (1789–97). In his Farewell Address to Congress, 17 September 1796, he asked the House to forgive him any unintentional errors, the closing sentence being: *'I shall also carry with me the hope, that my Country will never cease to view them with indulgence; and that, after forty-five years of my life dedicated to its service with an upright zeal, the faults of incompetent abilities will be consigned to oblivion, as myself must soon be to the mansions of rest.'*

Washington had a morbid fear of being buried alive. Every morning he inspected his Virginia plantation on horseback, and on the morning of 12 December 1799, a snowstorm was raging. He arrived home as dinner was beginning and chose not to change his clothes because his guests were waiting. Not long afterwards, the local physician had to be sent for, as Washington's illness developed. Tobias Lear, his private secretary and friend for 15 years, was at his bedside, and wrote:

'About 5 o'clock Dr Craik came again into the room & upon going to the bed side the Genl. said to him, "Doctor, I die hard; but I am not afraid to go; I believed from my first attack that I should not survive it; my breath can not last long." The Doctor pressed his hand, but could not utter a word. He retired from the bed side, & sat by the fire absorbed in grief ... He held out his hand & I raised him up. He then said to the Physicians, "I feel myself going, I thank you for your attentions; but I pray you to take no more trouble about me, let me go off quietly, I can not last long" ... About ten o'clk he made several attempts to speak to me before he could effect it, at length he said, – "I am just going. Have me decently buried; and do not let my body be put into the Vault in less than three days after I am dead." I bowed assent, for I could not speak. He then looked at me again and said, "Do you understand me?" I replied, "Yes." "'Tis well," said he.'

ALEKSANDR VASILIYEVICH SUVOROV, PRINCE OF ITALY, COUNT OF RIMNIKSKI, COUNT OF THE HOLY ROMAN EMPIRE, PRINCE OF SARDINIA, GENERALISSIMO OF RUSSIA'S GROUND AND NAVAL FORCES, FIELD MARSHAL OF THE AUSTRIAN AND SARDINIAN ARMIES

24 November 1729–18 May 1800

'Here lies Suvorov'

Simple inscription on his grave at the Church of the Annunciation in the Alexander Nevski Monastery in St Petersburg; a year later, Tsar Alexander I erected a statue in his memory

Suvorov was surely the general who achieved most but received the least remembrance. He became the 'Generalissimo' of the Russian Empire, and never lost a battle in a lifetime of fighting 52 campaigns for his country. His manual *The Science of Victory* is noted for the sayings '*What is difficult in training will become easy in a battle*' and '*Perish yourself but rescue your comrade!*' He taught his soldiers to attack instantly and decisively to achieve a psychological advantage: '*Attack with the cold steel – Push hard with the bayonet ... The ball may lose its way, the bayonet never. The ball is a fool; the bayonet is a hero.*' Joining the army in 1742 as a private, Suvorov saw action for most of the following 58 years, rising to the most senior rank in Russia. Seriously wounded six times, he called the common soldiers 'brother', and they followed him everywhere.

Early in 1800, Suvorov was recalled to St Petersburg. He had rescued the Russian army from destruction by the French and earned himself the nickname 'the Russian Hannibal', but on his arrival, the newly promoted Generalissimo found his hero's welcome cancelled. His command, rank and titles were stripped from him and he was placed under surveillance. He died heartbroken four months later. In effect the Tsar wanted to remodel his armies and empire on the Prussian model, emphasizing parade-ground discipline, whereas Suvorov's manual required realistic speed and mobility, accuracy of fire and the bayonet. The generals he had trained later forced Napoleon out of Russia, and almost 150 years later, Josef Stalin would revive the memory of the last Russian before him to bear the title Generalissimo, creating the Order of Suvorov in an effort to restore Russian morale in the face of the Nazi invasion.

'Here lies in the horizontal position …'

Epitaph on the grave of a Launceston watchmaker buried in
St Petroc's Church, Lydford, Devon

'Here lies in the horizontal position
The outside *case* of
GEORGE ROUTLEIGH, Watchmaker,
Whose abilities in that line were an honour
To his profession:
Integrity was the *main-spring,*
And prudence the *regulator*
Of all the *actions* of his life:
Humane, generous and liberal,
His *hand* never stopped
Till he had relieved distress;
So nicely regulated were all his *movements*
That he never went wrong
Except when *set-a-going*
By people
Who did not know his *key;*
Even then, he was easily
Set right again:
He had the art of disposing of his *time*
So well
That his *hours* glided away
In one continual round
Of pleasure and delight,
Till an unlucky *moment* put a period to
His existence;
He departured this life
November 14, 1802
Wound up,
In hopes of being taken in *hand*
By his Maker,
And of being
Thoroughly *cleaned, repaired* and *set-a-going*
In the World to come.'

TOUSSAINT L'OUVERTURE, FRANÇOIS-DOMINIQUE TOUSSANT, TOUSSAINT BRÉDA
20 May 1743–8 April 1803

'In overthrowing me you have cut down in Saint-Domingue only the trunk of the tree of liberty, it will spring up again from the roots, for they are many and they are deep'

Speech given when captive on a warship being sent to France

In 1791, a great slave revolt broke out in western Hispaniola (Saint-Domingue, now Haiti), and Toussaint L'Ouverture, a self-educated former domestic slave, crossed the border to eastern Hispaniola (Santo Domingo, now the Dominican Republic) with 600 black slaves. He formed them into a unit to fight with the Spanish colonial army against the French of Saint-Domingue. Becoming hugely successful, Toussaint next decided to fight for the French, if they would agree to free all the slaves. From May 1794 he led forces made up mostly of former slaves, winning concessions from the English and expelling the Spanish. In 1798 he defeated a British invasion of Saint-Domingue, and led an invasion of neighbouring Santo Domingo, freeing the slaves there. In 1801, he issued a constitution for Saint-Domingue that provided for autonomy and decreed that he would be governor for life.

Napoleon retaliated by sending an army, with secret instructions to later restore slavery. There was constant warfare, but Napoleon needed his troops back, so he offered L'Ouverture his freedom and Haiti full independence if he agreed to retire and to integrate his remaining troops into the French army. L'Ouverture agreed to this. In May 1802 he signed a treaty that pledged there would be no return to slavery, and retired to his farm. Three weeks later, he and his family were seized by French troops and deported to France. Napoleon ordered that Toussaint be placed in a dungeon in the mountains, and he was murdered by means of cold, starvation and neglect, dying of pneumonia after months of constant interrogation. Six months later, preoccupied with Europe, Napoleon gave up his possessions in the New World, abandoning Haiti to independence and selling French territory in North America to the United States (the Louisiana Purchase). In exile on St Helena, when asked about his treatment of Toussaint, Napoleon answered, '*What could the death of one wretched Negro mean to me?*'

'Let no man write my epitaph'

Closing words of Emmet's oration from the dock, 19 September 1803

Emmet led an Irish Nationalist rising against the British, in which around 20 military personnel and 50 rebels died. He fled but later returned to Dublin to be near his fiancée, and was captured and tried for high treason. His housekeeper Anne Devlin was tortured and her family imprisoned, with her nine-year-old brother dying, but she would not betray Emmet. The Crown's case was weak, so it secretly bought the assistance of his defence attorney for £200 (worth £160,000 today) and a pension. Emmet knew he would be found guilty, so his speech at his trial was made to posterity, and he became a hero of the Republican cause.

'I do not fear to approach the omnipotent Judge, to answer for the conduct of my whole life; and am I to be appalled and falsified by a mere remnant of mortality here? By you, too, who, if it were possible to collect all the innocent blood that you have shed in your unhallowed ministry, in one great reservoir, Your Lordship might swim in it ... My lords, you are impatient for the sacrifice – the blood which you seek is not congealed by the artificial terrors which surround your victim; it circulates warmly and unruffled, through the channels which God created for noble purposes, but which you are bent to destroy, for purposes so grievous that they cry to heaven. Be yet patient! I have but a few words more to say. I am going to my cold and silent grave: my lamp of life is nearly extinguished: my race is run: the grave opens to receive me, and I sink into its bosom! I have but one request to ask at my departure from this world – it is the charity of its silence! Let no man write my epitaph: for as no man who knows my motives dare now vindicate them. Let not prejudice or ignorance asperse them. Let them and me repose in obscurity and peace, and my tomb remain uninscribed, until other times, and other men, can do justice to my character; when my country takes her place among the nations of the earth, then, and not till then, let my epitaph be written. I have done.'

The day after this speech, Emmet became the last man to be hanged, drawn and quartered in the British Isles. His remains were buried secretly, to prevent his grave being a centre for dissidence, and have never been discovered.

ALEXANDER HAMILTON
11 January 1755–12 July 1804

‘I forgive all that happened’

Dying words to a priest

The powerful Federalist politician Alexander Hamilton was one of the Founding Fathers, and as Washington's first Secretary of the Treasury had laid the economic foundation of the new nation. In 1804, Hamilton assisted Morgan Lewis in winning the governorship of New York against Vice-President Aaron Burr. Hamilton mocked Burr at a dinner party, and the affair was published in the *Albany Register*. Burr demanded an apology, but Hamilton refused as he said he could not recall the incident and a duel was scheduled for 11 July at Weehawken, New Jersey, a common duelling site at which Hamilton's eldest son, Philip, had been killed three years earlier.

A letter Hamilton wrote the night before the duel states that he intended not to shoot at Burr: '*I have resolved, if our interview [duel] is conducted in the usual manner, and it pleases God to give me the opportunity, to reserve and throw away my first fire, and I have thoughts even of reserving my second fire.*' His shot broke a tree branch directly above Burr's head. Burr then fired, hitting Hamilton and the bullet deflecting off a rib to damage his liver and internal organs. His friend Nathaniel Pendleton sat him against a boulder and a doctor named David Hosack examined him. Hamilton whispered: '*This is a mortal wound, Doctor.*'

They carried him into a rowing boat, to take him across New York harbour to get medical attention. He regained consciousness in the bottom of the boat to say: '*My vision is indistinct ... Take care of that pistol. It is undischarged and still cocked. It may go off and do harm. Pendleton knows that I did not intend to fire at him.*' Reaching Manhattan, he supposedly told a doctor: '*Let Mrs Hamilton be immediately sent for. Let the event be gradually broken to her, but give her hopes.*' He continued speaking, and told a priest: '*I have no ill will against Colonel Burr. I met him with a fixed resolution to do him no harm. I forgive all that happened.*' He lasted in great pain until dying the next day.

'Drink, drink, fan, fan, rub, rub'

Nelson's dying words, spoken to his Flag Captain, Thomas Masterman Hardy,
who kissed his cheek and then his forehead, Battle of Trafalgar, 1805

Nelson was revered nationally for his patriotism
and courage. Before the Battle of the Nile in 1797 he told
his officers: *'Before this time to-morrow I shall have gained
a peerage, or Westminster Abbey.'* He was badly wounded
during the failed attack on Santa Cruz de Tenerife in 1797,
and said: *'Let me alone: I have yet my legs and one arm. Tell the
surgeon to make haste and [bring] his instruments. I know I
must lose my right arm, so the sooner it's off the better.'* In 1801,
he refused to see the signal from his admiral to call off his
attack at the Battle of Copenhagen, putting the telescope to his blind eye and
saying: *'I have only one eye – I have a right to be blind sometimes ... I really do not see
the signal!'*

At Trafalgar, Nelson's signal to the fleet before attacking the French and Spanish
was: *'England expects every officer and man to do his duty this day.'* Two friends were
killed next to him, the *Victory*'s wheel was shot away and a wood splinter dented
Captain Hardy's shoe buckle. Nelson commented to Hardy: *'This is too warm work
to last long'* and soon after fell to the deck, saying: *'Hardy, I do believe they have done
it at last ... my backbone is shot through.'* Hardy later came below deck to see Nelson,
and informed him that a number of enemy ships had surrendered. Nelson told
him that he was sure to die, and begged him to pass his possessions to Emma
Hamilton. After reminding him to *'take care of poor Lady Hamilton'*, he added:
'Kiss me, Hardy.' At the last he murmured: *'Thank God I have done my duty ...
Drink, drink, fan, fan, rub, rub.'* He was given a mixture of lemonade and watered
wine, while being fanned to keep him cool and his chest massaged to ease
his pain. His faint final words were: *'God and my country.'* In 1795, Nelson had
prophesied the death he wished: *'My character and good name are in my own
keeping. Life with disgrace is dreadful. A glorious death is to be envied.'*

'I think I could eat one of Bellamy's veal pies'

Alternative attributed last words

Pitt is known as William Pitt the Younger to distinguish him from his father, William Pitt the Elder, who also served as prime minister. He had a career like a shooting star. In January 1781, at the age of 21, he took his seat in the House of Commons. Edmund Burke reacted to his maiden speech in Parliament by calling him *'Not merely a chip off the old block, but the old block itself.'* He was appointed Chancellor of the Exchequer at the age of only 24 in 1783, and became Prime Minister later in the year. A friend of William Wilberforce, he brought forward the anti-slavery bill in 1788. In 1805, after the Battle of Trafalgar, he was toasted at the Lord Mayor of London's banquet as *'the Saviour of Europe'*. He answered that Europe was not to be saved by any one man, and that *'England has saved herself by her exertions; and will, as I trust, save Europe by her example.'*

Always in debt, Pitt refused all offers of financial assistance. A heavy drinker, he probably died of kidney failure and cirrhosis of the liver on 23 January 1806. His debts amounted to a massive £40,000. They were paid by the grateful nation, a public funeral was voted, and Pitt was buried in Westminster Abbey, aged just 46.

John Bellamy had started the first dining room in the House of Commons in 1773, which lasted until it was burnt down in 1834. The ingredients for his veal pie included bones, a pig's trotter, a shoulder of veal and lard. Other last words attributed to Pitt were: *'Oh, my country! How I leave [or love] my country!'* (Stanhope's 1862 *Life of the Rt. Hon. William Pitt,* Vol. IV); and *'My country! Oh, my country!'* (George Rose's diary, 23 January 1806, in *Diaries and Correspondence of George Rose,* ed. Revd L.V. Harcourt, 1860). George Rose (1744–1818) was a political colleague of Pitt's, who resigned from office shortly after his friend's death. His diary entry is for the day of Pitt's death, but some believe that it was hagiographic, replacing the reality of the Bellamy's pie quote.

CHARLES JAMES FOX
24 January 1749–13 September 1806

'I die happy'

Attributed last words

Just as his father's path to being prime minister was blocked by the persona of Pitt the Elder, so Fox's hopes were dashed by his arch-rival Pitt the Younger. A radical and a sympathizer with the Irish nationalists, Fox became a bitter opponent of George III. He regarded the king as a tyrant and supported the American revolutionaries, dressing in the colours of their army. In 1775 he denounced the government of Lord North for losing the American colonies, saying that '*Alexander the Great never gained more in one campaign than the noble lord has lost – he has lost a whole continent.*' He was briefly Britain's first Foreign Secretary in Rockingham's cabinet of 1782, and then in the coalition government of Lord North. However, George III forced Fox and North out of government before the end of the year, replacing them with Pitt the Younger, and Fox spent the following 22 years facing Pitt from the opposition benches.

Fox was an abolitionist and a supporter of the French Revolution, who advocated individual liberty and religious tolerance. After Pitt's death in January 1806, he became Foreign Secretary again in the 'Ministry of all the Talents' but died in office a few months later. The government could not achieve his objectives of peace with France or Catholic emancipation, but the Foreign Slave Trade Bill that he introduced became law posthumously, eliminating two thirds of the slave trade passing through British ports. Introducing the bill, Fox had said that if he '*had been so fortunate as to accomplish that, and that only, I should think I had done enough, and could retire from public life with comfort, and the conscious satisfaction, that I had done my duty*'.

An inveterate gambler, bankrupted twice, a womanizer and a fierce drinker, Fox left £10,000 worth of debts. An autopsy revealed a shrivelled liver, 35 gallstones, and seven pints of transparent fluid in his abdomen. In the last year of his life he was offered a peerage and responded: '*I will not close my politics in that foolish way.*'

'Near this spot
Are deposited the Remains of one
Who possessed Beauty without Vanity'

Byron's epitaph on his dog's memorial at Newstead Abbey,
written 30 November 1808

Whilst a student at Cambridge, Byron was annoyed that university rules banned keeping a dog, so he installed a tame bear. After graduation, he took the bear with him to his ancestral home at Newstead Abbey. Among his other pets there was a cross between a dog and his father's wolf, a 'wolf-dog' named Lyon. His favourite pet however was Boatswain, a black and white dog whose portrait can still be seen at Newstead Abbey.

Boatswain was bitten by a rabid dog in Mansfield town and fell ill. Thomas Moore, Byron's biographer, writes how, as the dog foamed at the mouth, the grief-stricken poet gently wiped away the slaver with his own hands. Despite his debts, Byron commissioned a marble monument for Boatswain and said he wished to be buried next to his best friend.

'Near this spot
Are deposited the Remains of one
Who possessed Beauty without Vanity,
Strength without Insolence,
Courage without Ferocity,
And all the Virtues of Man without his Vices.
This Praise, which would be unmeaning Flattery
If inscribed over human ashes,
Is but a just tribute to the Memory of
BOATSWAIN, a DOG
Who was born at Newfoundland, May, 1803,
And died at Newstead, Nov 18th, 1808 ...
To mark a friend's remains these stones arise;
I never knew but one, – and here he lies.'

'Now, why on earth did I do that?'

Said after jumping off a balcony in Lisbon on 10 February 1813

Erskine was sent home from the Peninsular War in 1809, suspected of insanity, but in 1810, according to Michael Barthop and Richard Hook in *Wellington's Generals: 1810*:

> 'Wellington found himself saddled with the short-sighted and drunken Sir William Erskine. When Wellington remonstrated against Erskine's appointment on the grounds that "he was generally considered to be a madman", [Colonel] Torrens replied: "No doubt sometimes he is a little mad, but in his lucid moments he is an uncommonly clever fellow: and I trust he will have no fit during the campaign, although he looked a little wild when he embarked." It is small wonder that Wellington felt constrained to write: "Really when I reflect on some of the character and attainments of some of the General officers of this army, I tremble."

A fellow officer had called Erskine *'blind as a beetle'*. He took over the command of the Light Division of cavalry, and Wellington wrote: *'It is impossible to trust to his judgment in any critical case.'* While pursuing Marshal Massena's retreating French army, he advanced his men in heavy fog with no scouts and was badly defeated at Casal Bovo in March 1811. At the Battle of Sabugal, three major errors by Erskine saved General Reynier's isolated French corps from destruction. In the Battle of Fuentes de Onoro, he allowed the blockaded French garrison at Almedia to escape. He had forgotten an important order from Wellington, which he kept in his pocket. Colonel Charles Bevan was wrongfully blamed and heroically took his own life rather than slander a superior officer. In 1812, Erskine was declared insane and cashiered.

All sources except one state that in February 1813 Erskine jumped from a window balcony in Lisbon. The exception is *Burke's Peerage* (4th edn, 1833), which states that Erskine, *'being actively engaged in the peninsular war, fell a victim to the fatigues of the campaign, a violent fever, terminating his gallant career, at Brozas'*. He died from his injuries three days later.

CAPTAIN JAMES LAWRENCE
1 October 1781–4 June 1813

'Don't give up the ship!'
Dying command

Joining the United States Navy as a midshipman in 1798, Lawrence served on the *Ganges* and the *Adams* in the war with France, then on the *Enterprise* as a lieutenant in the war against Tripoli in 1803. Later he captained the *Enterprise* in battle, and served constantly until he commanded the *Hornet*, capturing HMS *Peacock* in 1813. Two months after his return to the United States, he took command of the frigate *Chesapeake*, then preparing for sea at Boston, Massachusetts.

She left port on 1 June 1813 and immediately engaged the frigate HMS *Shannon*. Accurate gunfire from the British ship disabled *Chesapeake* within the first few minutes, but Captain Lawrence, mortally wounded by small-arms fire, ordered his officers: '*Don't give up the ship. Fight her till she sinks*' as he was carried below. His crew was overwhelmed by a British boarding party shortly afterwards, and Lawrence died of his wounds as *Chesapeake* was being taken to Halifax, Nova Scotia, by her Royal Navy captors. A contemporary newspaper report reads: 'Our griefs were renewed by the capture of the *Chesapeake* & death of Lawrence; a pride of the navy ... The body of Lawrence was prostrate; but his spirit remained erect. He saw & felt the fortune of war was against him – yet cried out, "Don't Give Up The Ship", though the enemy was carrying everything before him ... May the expiring words of the illustrious Lawrence, "Don't give up the ship", be the eternal motto of every American.'

Captain Lawrence's death was reported to his friend Commodore Oliver Hazard Perry, who ordered a large blue battle ensign stitched with the phrase 'DONT GIVE UP THE SHIP' in bold white letters. 'The Perry Flag' flew from his flagship when he beat the British on Lake Erie in September 1813 and is now displayed in Memorial Hall at the United States Naval Academy in Annapolis.

'Soldiers, when I give the command to fire, fire straight at my heart. Wait for the order. It will be my last to you. I protest against my condemnation. I have fought a hundred battles for France, and not one against her ... Soldiers, Fire!'

Last words, refusing to wear a blindfold

Ney was a general in the French Revolutionary War and the Napoleonic Wars, nicknamed by Napoleon *'le Brave des Braves'* ('the Bravest of the Brave'). His victory at Elchingen led to the surrender of the Austrian army at Ulm and opened the road to Vienna. In the 1812 invasion of Russia, he was given command of the centre at Borodino and entered Moscow with the victorious army. He then commanded the rear guard, being the last to leave Russian soil. He fought at Dresden and Leipzig, and played an important role at Waterloo in 1815, where he led the last desperate charge against the English line. In the summer of 1815, Napoleon was exiled for the second time. Ney was arrested and tried for treason by the Chamber of Peers. On 6 December he was condemned, and was executed the next day. C.A. Fyffe explains in his 1880 *History of Modern Europe* that his speedy execution was an example intended for Napoleon's other marshals and generals:

'On the 7th of December the sentence was executed. Ney was shot in the early morning in an unfrequented spot (near the Observatory in the Jardin du Luxembourg), and the Government congratulated itself that it had escaped the dangers of a popular demonstration and heard the last of a disagreeable business. Never was there a greater mistake. No crime committed in the Reign of Terror attached a deeper popular opprobrium to its authors than the execution of Ney did to the Bourbon family. The victim, a brave but rough half-German soldier, rose in popular legend almost to the height of the Emperor himself. His heroism in the retreat from Moscow became, and with justice, a more glorious memory than Davout's victory at Jena or Moreau's at Hohenlinden. Side by side with the thought that the Bourbons had been brought back by foreign arms, the remembrance sank deep into the heart of the French people that this family had put to death "the bravest of the brave".'

JANE AUSTEN
16 December 1775–18 July 1817

'Nothing but death'

Cassandra Austen's letter to Fanny Knight about Jane's last illness, July 1817

An historically important novelist, Jane Austen lived all her life in the bosom of her close-knit family, writing *Sense and Sensibility, Pride and Prejudice, Mansfield Park, Emma, Persuasion* and *Northanger Abbey.* She was educated by her father and brothers at home, and was hardly known during her lifetime. She published anonymously, and her books did not sell well until the mid nineteenth century. She was ill for over a year before she died, possibly from tubercu-losis, Addison's disease or Hodgkin's lymphoma. Austen's nephew James wrote of her last days:

'Throughout her illness she was nursed by her sister [Cassandra Austen], often assisted by her sister-in-law, my mother [Mary Lloyd, wife of the Revd James Austen]. Both were with her when she died ... While she used the language of hope to her correspondents, she was fully aware of her danger, though not appalled by it. It is true that there was much to attach her to life. She was happy in her family; she was just beginning to feel confidence in her own success; and, no doubt, the exercise of her great talents was an enjoyment in itself. We may well believe that she would gladly have lived longer; but she was enabled without dismay or complaint to prepare for death. She was a humble, believing Christian. Her life had been passed in the performance of home duties, and the cultivation of domestic affections, without any self-seeking or craving after applause ... Her sweetness of temper never failed. She was ever considerate and grateful to those who attended on her. At times, when she felt rather better, her playfulness of spirit revived, and she amused them even in their sadness. Once, when she thought herself near her end, she said what she imagined might be her last words to those around her, and particularly thanked her sister-in-law for being with her, saying: "You have always been a kind sister to me, Mary." When the end at last came, she sank rapidly, and on being asked by her attendants whether there was anything that she wanted, her reply was, "Nothing but death." These were her last words. In quiet-ness and peace she breathed her last on the morning of 18 July, 1817.'

'And what mortal ever heard /
Any good of George the Third?'

Epigram by Walter Savage Landor

This king has had an extremely poor rating in history, but was generally liked by the populace and possessed qualities not seen in the preceding and succeeding Georges. In general, though, Edmund Clerihew Bentley's opinion of him still stands:

> 'George the Third
> Ought never to have occurred
> One can only wonder
> At so grotesque a blunder.'

Walter Bagehot, in his immense *The English Constitution* (1867), stated that *'throughout the greater part of his life George III was a king of "consecrated obstruction"'*. Shelley, in his 1819 sonnet, called him *'an old, mad, blind, despised and dying king'*. Under George III, England lost its American colonies, and on 28 September 1789 Thomas Jefferson wrote to John Adams, then ambassador to Great Britain: *'We I hope shall be left free to avail ourselves of the advantages of neutrality: and yet much I fear the English, or rather their stupid king, will force us out of it.'* Despite the loss of America, England emerged during George's reign as a leading power in Europe.

George III was the son of Frederick, Prince of Wales, and Augusta of Saxe-Coburg-Gotha. The first two Georges had married repectively Sophia Dorothea of Celle and Margravine Caroline of Brandenburg-Ansbach, so George III maintained the German tradition, taking Charlotte of Mecklenburg-Strelitz as his bride. (The wives of Georges IV and V were Caroline of Brunswick and Princess Victoria Mary of Teck, while another son of George III, William IV, married Adelaide of Saxe-Meiningen. Even Queen Victoria's first language was German.

'Here lies One Whose Name was writ in Water'

Keats' self-penned epitaph

'This Grave
contains all that was Mortal
of a
Young English Poet
Who
on his Death Bed
in the Bitterness of his Heart
at the Malicious Power of his Enemies
Desired
these words to be engraven on his Tomb Stone
"Here lies One Whose Name was writ in Water."'

After studying at Guy's Hospital, Keats qualified as an apothecary and was allowed to practise surgery. He became one of the best of the lyrical Romantic poets, but suffered from harsh criticism of his poems right up until his death. Too poor to marry the love of his life, Fanny Brawne, he contracted tuberculosis while caring for his brother and eventually succumbed to the disease in Rome. His last request was to be buried in an unnamed grave in Rome's Protestant Cemetery, with the tombstone reading '*Here lies One Whose Name was writ in Water.*' Two friends, Joseph Severn and Charles Armitage Brown, added the rest of the epitaph.

Keats' great friends Percy Bysshe Shelley and Lord Byron believed that the final straw had been an incredibly cruel review of his epic poem *Endymion* in *Blackwood's Edinburgh Magazine,* which advised him that '*It is a better and a wiser thing to be a starved apothecary than a starved poet; so back to the shop Mr John, back to "plasters, pills and ointment boxes".*' Byron referred to his friend's demise in *Don Juan: 'Tis strange the mind, that very fiery particle, Should let itself be snuffed out by an article.'*

'France, army, head of the army, Joséphine'

Dying words

Exiled on the island of St Helena, in February 1821 Napoleon found that his health had begun to fail rapidly. On 3 May, two British doctors who had recently arrived attended him and could only recommend palliatives, and two days later the former Emperor died. In his will, he had asked to be buried on the banks of the Seine, but the British governor insisted that he should be interred on St Helena. Napoleon wanted the inscription on his tomb to read 'Napoleon Bonaparte', but his fellow exiles the Marquis de Montholon and General Bertrand preferred simply 'Napoleon', because royalty were signed by their first names only. As a result, the tomb was left nameless. In 1840, Louis-Philippe of France had Napoleon's remains returned to France, and they now rest in Les Invalides.

Napoleon's physician carried out an autopsy, which found the cause of death to be stomach cancer, of which his father and sister had also died. However, his valet's diaries led to the theory that Napoleon had been poisoned by arsenic over a period of time. On 23 November 2009, though, *National Geographic* magazine reported:

'Researchers found nothing to indicate arsenic poisoning, such as haemorrhaging inside the heart, in the historical data. What they did find was strong evidence of gastric cancer: rapid weight loss, a stomach filled with a grainy substance indicative of gastrointestinal bleeding – and something of a smoking gun ... "It was a huge mass from the entrance of his stomach to the exit ... It was at least ten centimetres (four inches) long. Size alone suggests the lesion was cancer." ... Napoleon's lesion points to chronic infection by *Helicobacter pylori*, a bacteria that can cause stomach inflammation and increase the likelihood of gastric cancer ... "Even if treated today, he'd have been dead within a year."'

VISCOUNT CASTLEREAGH, ROBERT STEWART, SECOND MARQUESS OF LONDONDERRY
18 June 1769–12 August 1822

'I have done for myself; I have opened my neck'
Dying words

A former Foreign Secretary, Castlereagh was Leader of the House of Commons when he began suffering a nervous breakdown in 1822, possibly brought on by constant criticism and overwork. Indicative of the hostility to him is Byron's epitaph:

> 'Posterity will ne'er survey
> A nobler grave than this:
> Here lie the bones of Castlereagh:
> Stop, traveller, and piss.'

On the advice of his doctor, he returned to his country home. His wife had succeeded in removing pistols and razors from his possession, but Castlereagh managed to lay his hands on a sharp letter-opener. Lord Clanwilliam wrote:

'He said ... that he thought there were plots against him. Four days ago he said to Seymour that he felt himself overworked, and felt it here, putting his hand to his forehead. The same evening he said also to Seymour [Sir George Hamilton Seymour, Castlereagh's private secretary], putting his hand to his head, "My mind, my mind is, as it were, gone." On the 9th he saw the King, and then went home. The King was so alarmed at his manner ... On the morning of the 12th he got up, and went towards his dressing-room, where he met Mr Robinson [Frederick Robinson, Castlereagh's personal assistant], who, I believe, was going to follow him, and said to him very sternly, "Mr Robinson, I will not be watched; go and send Dr Bankhead to me instantly." Three or four minutes elapsed before Dr Bankhead arrived. When he came to the door of the dressing-room, he saw Lord Londonderry standing with his back to him in an upright posture, and both arms in the air. Dr Bankhead said, "For God's sake, my Lord, what are you doing? What is the matter?" He answered, "I have done for myself; I have opened my neck." Bankhead rushed forward and caught him in his arms, as he was in the act of falling. It was but too true.'

'Come, come, no weakness; let's be a man to the last!'

Words spoken just before his death

A short time before his death, Byron was heard to say, '*Shall I sue for mercy?*' After a long pause he added: '*Come, come, no weakness; let's be a man to the last!*' Two young and inexperienced doctors attended the poet on his deathbed in the fever-infected town of Missolonghi. One was Francesco Bruno, Byron's personal physician, and the other Dr Julius Michael Millingen.

'Thus it came about that Francesco Bruno, "an intelligent, but timid student of the art of medicine", and this newly fledged surgeon found themselves faced with the appalling problem of treating a world-famous figure in an illness which neither knew anything about. Both doctors fell back on the usual treatment of the time – bleed the patient and so reduce his fever. For some time Byron resisted them, saying that there had been "more deaths by lancet than by the lance"; he gave in eventually when Millingen warned him that "the disease might operate such a disorganisation in his cerebral and nervous system as entirely to deprive him of reason". The "damned set of butchers", as the poet called his doctors, accordingly bled their patient several times, on one occasion finding it difficult to stop the flow of blood they had started. One pound of blood was taken on April 16 and more at two sessions the next day. "The relief obtained did not correspond to the hopes we had anticipated," said Millingen. The weakened poet sank into unconsciousness and died under his terrified doctors' hands.'

After the autopsy, the two doctors blamed each other for the death: '*Bruno asserted that Millingen was responsible for the death of their patient by delaying the phlebotomy that might have saved him. Millingen claimed for work at the autopsy, putting in a bill of £100, a sum larger by several times than his annual salary from the Greek committee. He refuted Bruno's charges in the press, giving the cause of the poet's death as an attack of "purulent meningitis".*'

‘But there is that within me which shall tire Torture and Time, and breathe when I expire’

Epitaph on marble tablet outside St Mary Magdalene Church,
Hucknall, Nottinghamshire

Byron's first poems were published in 1807. In 1812 he made his maiden speech in the House of Lords, defending the Nottinghamshire lace industry's 'frame breakers'. It was in that year that he said 'he awoke and found himself famous' as the first part of *Childe Harold* was published. He had several affairs, including one with his half-sister Augusta Leigh, who gave birth to his daughter, and one with Lady Caroline Lamb, who famously referred to him as *'mad, bad and dangerous to know'*. In 1816, he was forced to leave England for good. After seven years of writing prodigiously, in 1823 he went to Greece to help in the struggle for independence against Ottoman Turkey. Arriving in Missolonghi on the Adriatic coast in December, he set about building up the revolutionary forces but contracted a fever after going for a ride in a rainstorm. Among his last recorded words were: '*I have given her [Greece] my time, my means, my health – and now I give her my life! – what could I do more?*'

The Greek nation was overwhelmed by grief at Byron's death. In England, the *Morning Chronicle* newspaper reported: '*Thus has perished, in the flower of his age, one of the greatest poets England has produced.*' He is buried in the family vault at Hucknall under a marble plaque donated by the King of Greece. The words inscribed on his tombstone are from his poem *Childe Harold's Pilgrimage*, Canto IV, Stanza 137:

'But I have lived, and have not lived in vain;
My mind may lose its force, my blood its fire;
And my frame perish even in conquering pain;
But there is that within me which shall tire
Torture and Time, and breathe when I expire;
Something unearthly, which they deem not of,
Like the remember'd tone of a mute lyre,
Shall on their soften'd spirits sink, and move
In hearts all rocky now the late remorse of love.'

THOMAS JEFFERSON
13 April 1743–4 July 1826

'Is it the Fourth?'

Dying words

Jefferson's last question on his deathbed was addressed to Dr Robley Dunglison, who replied, *'It soon will be.'* Jefferson answered, *'I resign my spirit to God, my daughter to my country,'* and died on the morning of Independence Day, the fiftieth anniversary of the signing of the Declaration of Independence. The Welsh-American Jefferson was quite possibly the most incorrupt and intelligent statesman in history. Despite the fact that he was the second vice-president and third president of the United States, these achievements are not mentioned on his tombstone. He had said that he wanted to be remembered for what he gave to America, and not what America had given to him. Thus he chose the following words for his tombstone on his Monticello estate in Virginia, with the strict instructions that nothing else should be added.

'HERE WAS BURIED THOMAS JEFFERSON AUTHOR OF THE DECLARATION OF AMERICAN INDEPENDENCE OF THE STATUTE OF VIRGINIA FOR RELIGIOUS FREEDOM AND FATHER OF THE UNIVERSITY OF VIRGINIA.'

His great political rival John Adams, later a correspondent and friend, died a few hours later on that same day, after asking if Jefferson was still alive.

Jefferson lived by the creed of his 23 September 1800 letter to Dr Benjamin Rush, where he defended the constitutional refusal to recognize a state religion – *'I have sworn upon the altar of God eternal hostility against every form of tyranny over the mind of man.'* A Virginian, he was only 33 when he drafted the Declaration of Independence, and he later wrote a bill establishing religious freedom in Virginia. A reluctant candidate for presidency in 1796, he came within three votes of election. When eventually he did assume the presidency, he reduced the national debt by a third. He also sent a naval squadron to fight the Barbary pirates, and acquired the massive Louisiana Territory from Napoleon in 1803. Jefferson was a noted polymath, and at a gathering of 49 Nobel Prize recipients at the White House on 29 April 1962, John F. Kennedy noted that never before had such talent been assembled in one room, except perhaps when Thomas Jefferson had dined alone.

'Thomas Jefferson ...'

Last dying whisper

Following his presidency, Adams retired to his farm in Quincy and began a lengthy correspondence with Thomas Jefferson that lasted over 25 years. Although in his nineties and gravely ill, he resolved to live until the fiftieth anniversary of the Declaration of Independence. On that morning he was woken and asked by his servant Mrs Clark if he knew what day it was. He replied: '*Oh, yes; it is the glorious Fourth of July. It is a great day. It is a good day. God bless it. God bless you all.*' He then lapsed into unconsciousness. Later he awakened and whispered, '*Thomas Jefferson ...*' He is often quoted as having said, '*Thomas Jefferson still survives.*' He was not to know that his great political rival, and later friend and correspondent, had died a few hours earlier that same day.

John Adams represented Massachusetts as a delegate at both the first and second Constitutional Conventions and played a major role gaining European support for the American Revolution. Learned and thoughtful, he was also a trained lawyer and political philosopher. He said that '*People and nations are forged in the fires of adversity*', recollecting his own as well as the American experience. He represented the United States during peace negotiations with Britain, served as George Washington's vice-president, and was elected as the second United States President.

On 1 November 1800, he arrived in the new Capital City to take up his residence in the White House. On his second evening in its damp, unfinished rooms, he wrote to his wife: '*Before I end my letter, I pray Heaven to bestow the best of Blessings on this House and all that shall hereafter inhabit it. May none but honest and wise Men ever rule under this roof.*'

LUDWIG VAN BEETHOVEN
Baptised 17 December 1770–26 March 1827

'Pity, pity – too late!'

Last words according to Anselm Hüttenbrenner, 1860

Born in Bonn, Germany, Beethoven moved to Vienna in his early twenties, studying with Haydn and gaining a reputation as a virtuoso pianist. His hearing began to deteriorate badly from 1798, but he continued to compose, conduct and perform, even after becoming completely deaf. To many he remains simply the greatest musician and composer the world has seen. In *Unfinished Journey* (1976), Yehudi Menuhin called him '*A colossus beyond the grasp of most mortals, with his totally uncom-promising power, his unsensual and uningratiating way with music as with people.*' The Russian political philosopher and noted atheist Mikhail Bakunin said of Beethoven's work: '*Everything will pass, and the world will perish but the Ninth Symphony will remain.*'

Beethoven was ill for some years, being given the last rites two days before his death, which was witnessed by his sister and his friend Anselm Hüttenbrenner. He spoke his last words from his deathbed, when told of a recent gift of 12 bottles of wine. His biographer wrote of his death that at the sound of a crash of thunder, '*the dying man suddenly raised his head from Hüttenbrenner's arm, stretched out his own right arm majestically – like a general giving orders to an army. This was but for an instant; the arm sunk back; he fell back; Beethoven was dead.*' Another version of his last words is '*Plaudite, amici, comedia finita est.*' This is the formula traditionally used to end a performance of commedia dell'arte, and it means '*Applaud, my friends, the comedy is finished.*' Alternative versions include '*I shall hear in Heaven*'; '*I feel as if up to now I had written no more than a few notes*'; and '*There, do you hear the bell? Don't you hear it ringing? The curtain must drop. Yes! My curtain is falling.*' He did probably say to his friend, the Austrian composer and pianist Johann Hummel (1778–1837), who was for some time at his bedside, '*Is it not true, Hummel, that I have some talent after all?*'

'I have been at the death, not of a man, but of a blessed angel'

Eyewitness account of his death

The wonderful English artist, printmaker and poet, unrecognized in his lifetime, was said to have died singing.

'On the day of his death, writes Smith, who had his account from the widow, he composed and uttered songs to his Maker, so sweetly to the ear of his Catherine, that when she stood to hear him, he, looking upon her most affectionately, said, "My beloved! They are not mine. No! they are not mine!" He told her they would not be parted; he should always be about her to take care of her. A little before his death, Mrs Blake asked where he would be buried, and whether a dissenting minister or a clergyman of the Church of England should read the service. To which he answered, that as far as his own feelings were concerned, she might bury him where she pleased. But that as father, mother, aunt and brother were buried in Bunhill Row, perhaps it would be better to lie there. As for service, he should wish for that of the Church of England. In that plain, back room, so dear to the memory of his friends, and to them beautiful from association with him – with his serene cheerful converse, his high personal influence, so spiritual and rare – he lay chanting Songs to Melodies, both the inspiration of the moment, but no longer as of old to be noted down. To the pious songs followed, about six in the summer evening, a calm and painless withdrawal of breath; the exact moment almost unperceived by his wife, who sat by his side. A humble female neighbour, her only other companion, said afterwards: "I have been at the death, not of a man, but of a blessed angel."'

A letter written at the time of Blake's death states: '*He said he was going to that country he had all his life wished to see, and expressed himself happy, hoping for salvation through Jesus Christ. Just before he died his countenance became fair, his eyes brightened, and he burst out into singing of the things he saw in heaven. In truth he died like a saint, as a person who was standing by him observed.*'

'When from earth the Fourth descended / God be praised the Georges ended!'

Epigram by Walter Savage Landor

Famous for his dissolute lifestyle and his Royal Pavilion in Brighton, George became Prince Regent because of George III's madness in 1811, and king in 1820. In 1785, he secretly and illegally married a twice-widowed Roman Catholic, Maria Fitzherbert. In 1795, he was officially married to Princess Caroline of Brunswick, in exchange for Parliament paying over £630,000 to cover his debts. Mrs Fitzherbert, however, still believed that she was the Prince of Wales' true wife, holding the law of the Church to be superior to the law of the State, and the king remained with her for the rest of his life. The marriage to Caroline was a disaster. The first time George saw her, he fled, after famously saying, '*Harris, I am not well; pray get me a glass of brandy.*' He tried unsuccessfully to divorce her after his accession, and they finally separated in 1796 after the birth of their only child, Princess Charlotte. Before meeting Mrs Fitzherbert, the Prince of Wales may have fathered several illegitimate children, with known mistresses including the actress Mary Robinson, the divorcee Grace Elliott, Frances Villiers, Isabella Seymour-Conway and Elizabeth Conyngham. His 1820 coronation was a magnificent affair, costing about £243,000, compared to his father's coronation, which cost around £10,000.

George's alcoholism led to a 50-inch waistline in the 1820s, with people jeering him if he appeared in public. He suffered from breathlessness, cataracts, arteriosclerosis, gout and possibly porphyria, the madness that seemed to have affected his father. Dying, he called out, '*Good God, what is this?*' then clasped his page's hand and said, '*My boy, this is death.*' The *Times* reported: '*There never was an individual less regretted by his fellow-creatures than this deceased king. What eye has wept for him? What heart has heaved one throb of unmercenary sorrow? ... If he ever had a friend – a devoted friend in any rank of life – we protest that the name of him or her never reached us.*'

'All who have served the Revolution have ploughed the sea'

Statement written in his final days, and repeated many times while he was dying

Simón Bolívar was a South American political leader and general. His victories over the Spanish won independence for Bolivia, Panama, Colombia, Ecuador, Peru and Venezuela. He is known as *El Liberator* and 'the George Washington of South America' after he received a letter from the Marquis de Lafayette on behalf of the family of George Washington, along with a gold medallion coined after the capitulation at Yorktown. The medal was inscribed: *'The second Washington of the New World.'* With others, he seized Caracas in his native Venezuela in 1810, proclaiming independence from Spain. In 1814, in command of a small army, he took Bogota, before fleeing to Jamaica. Returning, he retook Venezuela and organized the original republic of Colombia (now Ecuador, Colombia, Panama and Venezuela), becoming its first president on 17 December 1819. He then took Peru, the northern part being named Bolivia in his honour.

Resigning his presidency to leave Colombia and retire in Europe, Bolívar made a final proclamation to the people on 8 December, nine days before he died: *'Colombians! My last wish is for the happiness of the patria. If my death contributes to the end of partisanship and the consolidation of the Union, I shall lowered in peace into my grave'* (Thomas Rourke, *Man of Glory: Simón Bolívar*, 1939). Suffering from tuberculosis, he was taken to hospital in Santa Marta, Colombia, and in his final days said to his physician: *'The three greatest fools (majaderos) of history have been Jesus Christ, Don Quixote – and I!* (John J. Johnson and Doris M. Ladd, *Simón Bolívar and Spanish American Independence*, 1968). Gabriel García Márquez, in *The General in His Labyrinth* (1990 translation), believed that Bolivar's last words were: *'Damn it, how will I ever get out of this labyrinth?'*

JOHANN WOLFGANG VON GOETHE
28 August 1749–22 March 1832

'Do open the shutter in the bedroom, in order that more light may enter'

Dying words

This German polymath wrote the world-renowned drama *Faust*, and his works influenced literature, music, drama, poetry and philosophy across Europe. He was also a noted scientist, writing on animals, plants and the theory of colours, and even on his deathbed was discussing optical phenomena. P. Hume Brown describes Goethe's last hours in his 1920 *Life*:

'On the night of the 19th grave symptoms appeared; shivering, accompanied by pain which gradually ascended from the limbs to the chest, and great difficulty in breathing. The following morning Vogel found an alarming change; his features were distorted, his colour ashen-grey, and the pain in the chest was such that he cried aloud. Towards evening his condition improved, and he was able to rise and even to attempt to read a book in which he had been interested. At seven in the morning of his last day (the 22nd) he requested Ottilie to bring him a portfolio of drawings and spoke to her for some time on optical phenomena. All through his illness he talked confidently of his recovery – and he looked forward to the approach of more genial weather which had hitherto never failed to benefit him. In previous illnesses he had been an irritable patient, but in this last illness those in attendance on him were moved by his sweetness and composure, and his anxiety regarding their comfort. Later in the morning he rose and seated himself in an armchair by his bedside.

During a short sleep he was heard to mutter words indicating that a beautiful female head was floating before him in his dreams. As the forenoon wore on, his mind began to wander, and his thoughts seemed to run on his memories of Schiller. Seeing a scrap of paper on the floor, he asked why Schiller's letters were allowed to lie there. With his forefinger he appeared to trace lines of words in the air – an old habit with him – and he inscribed on the coverlet on his knee what those present took to be the figure of a large W. Shortly after noon the end came. Settling himself in the corner of his chair, he passed imperceptibly away without a struggle.'

ÉVARISTE GALOIS
25 October 1811–31 May 1832

'Don't cry, Alfred. I need all my courage to die at 20.'
Last words to his brother

'The Father of Modern Algebra' was born near Paris, and died of gunshot wounds before he was 21. He failed the École Polytechnique's mathematics entry examination twice because his answers were 'odd'. He was then expelled from the École Normale for attacking the director in a letter to the press. He was arrested for making a threatening speech against the king, acquitted and then imprisoned for illegally wearing a uniform and carrying weapons. Released after six months, he had a disastrous love affair, before being challenged to a duel by a political enemy.

He could not refuse 'an affair of honour' and knew he had little chance of winning at dawn the next day. He therefore spent the night writing down all the mathematics he did not want to die with him, often scrawling in the margin: '*I have not time*' to prove some of his equations. He sent the pages to his friend Auguste Chevalier, before duelling with pistols at 25 paces. He was shot in the intestines, and was taken to hospital, telling his brother: '*Don't cry, I need all my courage to die at twenty.*' He died the day after the duel, possibly of peritonitis. He refused the offices of a priest and was buried in a common grave.

E.T. Bell commented: '*In all the history of science there is no completer example of the triumph of crass stupidity over untameable genius than is afforded by the all too brief life of Évariste Galois.*' Twenty-four years after Galois' death the mathematician Joseph Liouville discovered '*the complete correctness*' of his advanced algebraic theorems. The great German mathematician Herman Weyl (1885–1985) said of Galois' last writings: '*This letter, if judged by the novelty and profundity of ideas it contains, is perhaps the most substantial piece of writing in the whole literature of mankind.*'

'The name of Lafayette shall stand enrolled upon the annals of our race'

Eulogy by President John Quincy Adams to Congress, 31 December 1834

'He devoted himself, his life, his fortune, his hereditary honours, his towering ambition, his splendid hopes, all to the cause of liberty. He came to another hemisphere to defend her. He became one of the most effective champions of our Independence; but, that once achieved, he returned to his own country, and thenceforward took no part in the controversies which have divided us ... Till the hour when the trump of the Archangel shall sound to announce that Time shall be no more, the name of Lafayette shall stand enrolled upon the annals of our race, high on the list of the pure and disinterested benefactors of mankind.'

Lafayette, a French aristocrat and military officer, served under George Washington in the American Revolutionary War, and was wounded at the Battle of Brandywine, but managed to organize a successful retreat. In the middle of the war he returned to France to negotiate an increased French commitment. On his return, he blocked troops led by Cornwallis at Yorktown. He later became commander-in-chief of the National Guard in the French Revolution. In 1824, President Monroe invited him to the United States as part of the fiftieth anniversary of the nation. At the end of his visit, John Quincy Adams, standing beside Jefferson, Madison and Monroe at the White House, bade Lafayette farewell:

'You are ours, sir, by that unshaken sentiment of gratitude for your services which is a precious portion of our inheritance; ours by that tie of love, stronger than death, which has linked your name for the endless ages of time with the name of Washington. At the painful moment of parting with you we take comfort in the thought that, wherever you may be, to the last pulsation of your heart, our country will ever be present to your affections.'

WILLIAM BARRET TRAVIS
9 August 1809–6 March 1836

'God and Texas – Victory or Death!'

Last letter from the Alamo, 3 March 1836

Travis had practised as a lawyer in Mexican Texas, and became a prominent member of the 'War Party', a group of militants opposed to Mexican rule. A pivotal figure in the Anahuac Disturbances, he was promoted to lieutenant colonel of the Legion of Cavalry after the Siege of Bexar, and became the chief recruiting officer for the Texan army. He led the defenders in the Siege and Battle of the Alamo, at which between 182 and 257 Texans, including Travis himself, Jim Bowie and Davy Crockett, gave their lives on 6 March 1836.

On 24 February, Travis had sent an appeal for help that read in part: '*To the People of Texas and All Americans in the World ... I am besieged with a thousand or more of the Mexicans under Santa Anna. I have sustained a continual Bombardment and cannonade for 24 hours and have not lost a man. The enemy has demanded surrender at discretion, otherwise, the garrison is to be put to the sword, if the fort is taken. I have answered the demand with a cannon shot, and our flag still waves proudly over the wall. I shall never surrender or retreat.*' On 3 March, he sent out a courier with his last report, which closed:

'I will, however, do the best I can under the circumstances; and I feel confident that the determined valour and desperate courage heretofore exhibited by my men will not fail them in the last struggle; and although they may be sacrificed to the vengeance of a Gothic enemy, the victory will cost the enemy so dear, that it will be worse to him than a defeat. I hope your honourable body will hasten on reinforcements ammunition, and provisions to our aid as soon as possible ... The power of Santa Anna is to be met here, or in the colonies; we had better meet them here than to suffer a war of devastation to rage in our settlements. A blood red banner waves from the church of Bexar, and in the camp above us, in token that the war is one of vengeance against rebels; they have declared us as such; demanded, that we should surrender at discretion, or that this garrison should be put to the sword ... God and Texas – Victory or Death!
P.S. The enemy's troops are still arriving, and the reinforcements will probably amount to two or three thousand.'

DAVID 'DAVY' CROCKETT
17 August 1786–6 March 1836

'I leave this rule for others when I'm dead, Be always sure you're right, then go ahead'

His motto, dating from the war of 1812

A folk hero, politician and soldier, Crockett came to be known as the 'King of the Wild Frontier'. A superb marksman from Tennessee, he was commander of a battalion in the Creek Indian War in 1813–14. He was a member of the Tennessee legislature twice between 1821 and 1824, and ran for Congress in 1824, before becoming a Congressman in 1827–29, 1829–31 and 1833–35. As a member of the House of Representatives, he supported the rights of squatters, who were barred from buying land in the West unless they already owned property. He opposed Andrew Jackson's Indian Removal Act, causing the President's 1831 re-election defeat. The frontiersman explained, *'I bark at no man's bid. I will never come and go, and fetch and carry, at the whistle of the great man in the White House no matter who he is.'* In 1834, his autobiography *A Narrative of the Life of David Crockett, Written by Himself,* was published. He went east to promote the book and was narrowly defeated for re-election. After another defeat in 1835, he said: *'I told the people of my district that I would serve them as faithfully as I had done; but if not ... you may all go to hell, and I will go to Texas.'* For many years he had been nationally known as a political representative of the frontier.

When he was 49 years old, Crockett died a hero's death at the Alamo, helping Texas to win independence from Mexico. For 11 days of ceaseless fighting and bombardment, around 200 men withstood the Mexican army of Santa Anna. When the battle was over, all the Americans had died, but with them also lay over 2,000 Mexicans. Crockett's body was never found, but at his birthplace a rough limestone slab reads: *'Davy Crockett, Pioneer, Patriot, Soldier, Trapper, Explorer, State Legislator, Congressman, Martyred at The Alamo. 1786–1836.'*

JAMES MADISON
16 March 1751–28 June 1836

'I always talk better lying down'

Reputed last words

James Madison was one of the youngest of the Founding Fathers, and as he lay dying at the age of 85, he was the last living signatory of the US constitution. In late June 1836, some of his companions at his plantation in Virginia suggested giving him stimulants to artificially prolong his life until 4 July, the sixtieth anniversary of the Declaration of Independence. He refused. His niece asked him: *'What is the matter, uncle James?'* He replied: *'Nothing more than a change of mind, my dear. I always talk better lying down.'* These are reputedly his last words, and he passed away in his sleep.

As Jefferson's Secretary of State (1801–09), Madison had supervised the Louisiana Purchase, doubling the nation's size. From his leadership in opposition to Hamilton's financial proposals, which he felt would give undue wealth and power to northern financiers, came the development of the Republican, or Jeffersonian, Party. As president (1809–17), he led the nation into the War of 1812 against Great Britain. During and after the war, he reversed many of his positions, something that may be reflected in his last thoughts.

The first president to have served in the Congress, Madison is considered to be the 'Father of the Constitution'. In 1788, he wrote over a third of the Federalist Papers, still the most influential commentary on the Constitution. He also drafted many basic laws and was responsible for the first ten amendments to the Constitution. A noted political theorist, his most distinctive belief was that the new republic needed checks and balances to protect individual rights from the tyranny of the majority. In a 1788 letter to Thomas Jefferson he wrote: *'Wherever the real power in a Government lies, there is the danger of oppression.'*

ALECSANDR SERGEEVICH POUSHKIN
6 June 1799–29 January 1837

‘I can hardly breathe; I am suffocating’
Alexandre Dumas' essay on Pushkin

‘Alexander Pushkin’ is known as Russia's greatest poet. At a time when most great literature was being written in French and English, Pushkin revolutionized Russian literature with narrative poems, love poems, political poems, short stories, novels, plays, histories and fairy tales. Most of us will have heard of his greatest works *Eugene Onegin* and *Boris Godunov.*

Pushkin challenged his brother-in-law Georges d'Anthès to a duel over an affair with Pushkin's wife and was mortally wounded, lingering two days in great pain. His friend and collaborator, the lexicographer, author and naval doctor Vladimir Dahl, was summoned to his deathbed to look after him. Pushkin died slowly in his apartment, surrounded by his books. According to the Institute of Russian Literature of the Russian Academy of Sciences: *'These books had surrounded Pushkin in his study on 12 Moika, to them he addressed his last words "Farewell, friends."'*

'... the death agony had begun ... Once pressing Dahl's hand he begged, "Lift me up; let us go higher, still higher." Was this the beginning of delirium, or was it a reaching out after God? Coming to himself once more, he pointed to his bookcases, and said to Dahl, "It seemed to me that you and I were climbing up those shelves so high that my head turned." Shortly after, with closed eyes, he felt for Dahl's hand, and said, "Come, come; Let us set off together." On this Dahl, at the risk of hurting him, half raised him, when suddenly, as if aroused by the movement, he opened his eyes, and with transfigured face he said, "It is finished. I am going; I am going." Then falling back on his pillow: "I can hardly breathe; I am suffocating." These were his last words. His breathing, which till now had been regular, grew slower, then ceased. One sigh passed his lips, but so softly and easily that almost no one remarked it; but it was the last. Jukoffsky [a noted poet who became Pushkins' literary executor] looked at Dahl after a moment's silence. "All is over," said Dahl.'

'I trust to God that my life may be spared for nine months longer'

Words spoken at his final birthday banquet, August 1836

The third son of George III, William succeeded his brothers as king as they had no legitimate heirs, and was nicknamed 'the Sailor King' and 'Silly Billy'. He came to the throne when he was 64 years old, and his reign saw several notable reforms.

From 1791, as the Duke of Clarence, William had lived for 20 years with an Irish actress, Dorothea Bland, known by her stage name, Mrs Jordan. They had ten illegitimate children together, all given the surname Fitzclarence. William told a friend: *'Mrs Jordan is a very good creature, very domestic and careful of her children. To be sure she is absurd sometimes and has her humours. But there are such things more or less in all families.'* The affair ended in 1811, Mrs Jordan blaming his debts: *'Money, money, my good friend, has, I am convinced made HIM at this moment the most wretched of men ...'* With her acting career ended, she fled to France to escape her creditors, and died in poverty near Paris in 1816.

Deep in debt, the Duke made many attempts at marrying a wealthy heiress. Finally, in 1818, aged 50, he married the 25-year-old Princess Adelaide of Saxe-Meiningen, who managed to control his debts. The couple had no heir, so his niece Victoria would be the next monarch. William, however, hated Victoria's mother, the Duchess of Kent. At his final birthday banquet in August 1836 he declared that he would survive until Victoria was 18 so that the Duchess of Kent would never be regent: *'I trust to God that my life may be spared for nine months longer ... I should then have the satisfaction of leaving the exercise of the Royal authority to the personal authority of that young lady, heiress presumptive to the Crown, and not in the hands of a person now near me, who is surrounded by evil advisers and is herself incompetent to act with propriety in the situation in which she would be placed.'* Ten months later, he had a fatal heart attack.

JOHN QUINCY ADAMS
11 July 1767 – 23 February 1848

'This is the last of Earth! I am content!'

Attributed last words

John Quincy Adams was the son of President John Adams, and became the sixth President of the United States in 1825. In the presidential election, Andrew Jackson won more popular votes and more electoral votes, but Adams was elected by the House of Representatives because no one had a clear majority. When he took the oath of office he did not want to involve the Bible in politics, so he was sworn in with his hand on a book of law and the Constitution. Adams customarily took a nude early-morning swim in the Potomac River. Anne Royall, America's first professional journalist, knew of these swims, and after being refused interviews with the president time after time, she went to the river, gathered his clothes and sat on them until he relented.

In his eulogy on James Madison, Adams confirmed his view that '*A confederation is not a country.*' He is remembered as 'the Diplomat President' for his work as President Monroe's Secretary of State, arranging with England for the joint occupation of the Oregon country, obtaining from Spain the secession of the Floridas, and formulating the 'Monroe Doctrine'. He was anti-slavery, proclaiming: '*We know the redemption must come. The time and the manner of its coming we know not: It may come in peace, or it may come in blood; but whether in peace or in blood, LET IT COME ... Though it cost the blood of millions of white men, let it come. Let justice be done, though the heavens fall.*'

Following his electoral defeat by Andrew Jackson in 1829, Adams was unexpectedly elected by his home 11th District of Massachusetts to serve as a member of the House of Representatives, the only president to serve in that house after leaving office. Nineteen years later, aged 80, he collapsed from a stroke on the floor of the House, and was carried to the Speaker's Room where he died two days later. His last words have also been recorded as '*This is the end of the earth, but I am composed*', on 21 February, the day of his stroke.

EMILY JANE BRONTË
30 July 1818–19 December 1848

'No coward soul is mine'

Last poem

'No coward soul is mine,
No trembler in the world's storm-troubled sphere:
I see Heaven's glories shine,
And faith shines equal, arming me from fear.
O God within my breast,
Almighty, ever-present Deity!
Life – that in me has rest,
As I – undying Life – have power in thee!'

The second of the three Brontë sisters, Emily wrote the superb *Wuthering Heights* under the pseudonym of Ellis Bell. In ill health, she caught a cold during the funeral of her brother Bramwell in September, and developed tuberculosis. She refused any medical help until her dying moments, as recorded in Elizabeth Gaskell's *Life of Charlotte Brontë* (1857):

'But Emily was growing rapidly worse. I remember Miss Brontë's shiver at recalling the pang she felt when, after having searched in the little hollows and sheltered crevices of the moors for a lingering spray of heather – just one spray, however withered – to take in to Emily, she saw that the flower was not recognised by the dim and indifferent eyes. Yet, to the last, Emily adhered tenaciously to her habits of independence. She would suffer no one to assist her ... Charlotte and Anne, though full of unspeakable dread, had still the faintest spark of hope. On that morning Charlotte wrote thus – probably in the very presence of her dying sister: – "Tuesday – I should have written to you before, if I had had one word of hope to say; but I have not. She grows daily weaker. The physician's opinion was expressed too obscurely to be of use. He sent some medicine, which she would not take. Moments so dark as these I have never known. I pray for God's support to us all. Hitherto He has granted it." The morning drew on to noon. Emily was worse: she could only whisper in gasps. Now, when it was too late, she said to Charlotte, "If you will send for a doctor, I will see him now." About two o'clock she died.'

ANNE BRONTË
17 January 1820–28 May 1849

'Take courage, Charlotte, take courage'

Words from her deathbed to her sister

The youngest and most underestimated of the Brontë sisters, Anne wrote the grimly realistic *The Tenant of Wildfell Hall* after her first novel, *Agnes Grey*, was a success. She was only 29 when she died of tuberculosis. The death of her sister Emily, aged only 30, had affected her badly, and she caught influenza over the Christmas of that year. Worsening, she was sent to Scarborough to recover, but on 27 May asked her sister Charlotte if she could return to Haworth to die. On 28 May a doctor was consulted and told the sisters that death was already close. Seeing Charlotte's distress, Anne whispered to her to 'take courage' and died soon after. She was buried not in Haworth with the rest of her family, but in the graveyard of St Mary's Church, Scarborough.

Anne's final poem was 'Last Lines', where we read:

'Should death be standing at the gate,
Thus should I keep my vow;
But, Lord! Whatever be my fate,
Oh, let me serve Thee now!'

Charlotte noted, *'These lines written, the desk was closed, the pen laid aside – for ever.'* In June 1849 she wrote 'On the Death of Anne Brontë':

'There's little joy in life for me,
And little terror in the grave;
I've lived the parting hour to see
Of one I would have died to save.

Calmly to watch the failing breath,
Wishing each sigh might be the last;
Longing to see the shade of death
O'er those beloved features cast.'

'For this is England's greatest son'

From Alfred, Lord Tennyson, 'Ode on the Death of the Duke of Wellington', 1852

Wellesley fought in Flanders and India before being knighted and becoming an MP. He returned to serve in the Peninsular War against Napoleon, forcing the French to withdraw from Spain and Portugal. When Napoleon abdicated in 1814, Wellesley was made Duke of Wellington. With General Blücher he defeated Napoleon at Waterloo in 1815, and in 1828 became Prime Minister. His nickname, 'the Iron Duke', comes from his opposition to parliamentary reform. Later Foreign Secretary, he was given a state funeral, and Alfred, Lord Tennyson wrote these lines:

'Now, to the roll of muffled drums,
To thee the greatest soldier comes; ...
For this is England's greatest son,
He that gain'd a hundred fights,
Nor ever lost an English gun; ...
And underneath another sun,
Warring on a later day,
Round affrighted Lisbon drew
The treble works, the vast designs
Of his labour'd rampart lines,
Where he greatly stood at bay,
Whence he issued forth anew,
And ever great and greater grew,
Beating from the wasted vines
Back to France her banded swarms,
Till o'er the hills her eagles flew
Back to France with countless blows,

Beyond the Pyrenean pines,
Follow'd up in valley and glen
With blare of bugle, clamour of men,
Roll of cannon and clash of arms ...
A day of onsets of despair!
Dash'd on every rocky square
Their surging charges foam'd
    themselves away:
Last, the Prussian trumpet blew;
Thro' the long-tormented air
Heaven flash'd a sudden jubilant ray,
And down we swept and charged and
    over-threw
So great a soldier taught us there,
What long-enduring hearts could do
In that world-earthquake, Waterloo!'

SIR GEORGE CATHCART
12 May 1794–5 November 1854

'Have you no bayonets?'

Last words, at the Battle of Inkerman

Lord Raglan's ineffectual leadership during the Crimean War is remembered for his unnecessary destruction of the Light Brigade. Shortly afterwards, he again lost control of his forces during the counter-offensive at Mount Inkerman, as the Russians attempted to lift the siege of Sevastopol. Owing to the bravery of officers and men, however, the Russian attack proved unsuccessful, despite the fact that they outnumbered the British by five to one. A successful diplomat, Cathcart was over 60 when he died in the confusion of fog on the battlefield.

'On the English side, in the battle of Inkerman, there was no part for military science or skilful strategy to play. It was fought by the bravery and endurance of the private soldiers, whom their officers could assist only by their example ... Sir George Cathcart advanced rapidly with the 4th Division to cover the movement of the brigade of Guards, which was successfully brought back by General Bentinck, himself severely wounded. He threw them into their redoubt, where the Duke of Cambridge collected all the straggling parties within his reach. Lord Raglan came forward to this turning-point of the battle, and sent Sir George Cathcart with 400 men to check the approach of a Russian regiment marching on the position held by the Coldstreams. Thus detached from the main body of the 4th Division, its General found himself, with only these few companies of the 68th Regiment, surrounded by a large force coming up to support the advancing Russian regiments. "We have no more cartridges!" shouted the soldiers. "Have you no bayonets?" answered Cathcart with perfect composure, placing himself at their head to cut his way on foot through the masses that hemmed him in. He brought his men back to the 4th Division, but died when he reached it. As he fell, shot through the heart, his aide-de-camp, Colonel Charles Seymour, dismounted, and raised his chief from the ground. He also then received a mortal wound. The two friends were found side by side, trampled and defaced on the field of honour.'

CHARLOTTE BRONTË
21 April 1816–31 March 1855

'I am not going to die, am I? He will not separate us, we have been so happy.'

Last known words

The eldest of the three Brontë sisters, Charlotte wrote *Jane Eyre*. In June 1854, she married Arthur Bell Nicholls, her father's curate, and became pregnant soon afterwards. Her health declined rapidly, however, and she died nine months after her marriage, along with her unborn child. Of the six Brontë siblings, Charlotte alone had reached the ripe old age of 39.

Early in 1855, Charlotte 'was attacked by new sensations of perpetual nausea, and ever recurring faintness. After this state of things had lasted for some time, she yielded to Mr Nicholls' wish that a doctor should be sent for. He came, and assigned a natural cause for her miserable indisposition; a little patience, and all would go right. She, who was ever patient in illness, tried hard to bear up and bear on. But the dreadful sickness increased and increased, till the very sight of food occasioned nausea. "A wren would have starved on what she ate during those last six weeks," says one. Friends encouraged Charlotte with the thought of the baby that was coming. "I dare say I shall be glad some time," Charlotte would say, "but I am so ill, so weary ...'''

She wrote: '"I am not going to talk of my sufferings, it would be useless and painful. I want to give you an assurance, which I know will comfort you, and that is, that I find in my husband the tenderest nurse, the kindest support, the best earthly comfort that ever woman had. His patience never fails, and it is tried by sad days and broken nights." Wakening for an instant from this stupor of intelligence, she saw her husband's woe-worn face, and caught the sound of some murmured words of prayer that God would spare her. "Oh!" she whispered forth, "I am not going to die, am I? He will not separate us, we have been so happy."'

'God will pardon me. It is his trade.'

Last words, quoted in Alfred Meissner, *Heinrich Heine, Erinnerungen*, 1856

The German lyrical poet suffered terribly in the last eight years of his life, being bed-ridden in Paris. In his *Morphine* we read: '*Sleep is good, death is better; but of course, the best thing would be to never have been born at all.*' A 1997 analysis of his hair showed that Heine was suffering from chronic lead poisoning. His nephew wrote: '*Cramp-like vomitings, which were not to be repressed, began three days before his death ... his weakness grew worse, and the death pangs set in.*'

A letter from Heine's nurse Catherine Bourlois to Mrs Charlotte Embden dated 2 March 1858 reads:

'The day preceding his death my poor master said: "I am glad my family has come, for I shall never see them more." He regretted very much not to have written on Wednesday, because later he was no longer able to. During the last night he kept repeating, as he had repeated on Friday: "I am done for!" During that fatal night I had a watcher with me and I went to wake Miss Pauline [Heine's house-keeper] when I saw the end approaching. I could have easily called Madame, but the least noise might have made his last moments more painful, and I feared the effect that the death of a husband ought to produce on his wife, nevertheless Miss Pauline ran to Madame's room just before the final moment, and I only had time to tell her on the threshold of the door: "All is over!" A quarter of an hour before dying, Mr Heine had complete consciousness. I encouraged him and con-soled him as well as I could every moment, but he saw as we did that the medicines produced no relief whatever ... I should add that on Saturday at four or five in the afternoon Master called me three times in succession. He told me to write ... but not understanding the meaning of his words and not wishing to force him to repeat them, I answered Yes. I said to him a little later: when your vomiting ceases you must write yourself; he answered, I am going to die.'

JOHN BROWN
9 May 1800–2 December 1859

'The crimes of this guilty land will never be purged away but with blood'

Written on the morning of his execution in Virginia

Brown became an Abolitionist after the 1837 murder of the Abolitionist Presbyterian minister and journalist Elijah Parish Lovejoy by a mob in Illinois. Increasingly he moved away from pacifism and advocated and practised armed insurrection, including the Pottawatomie Massacre in Kansas in 1856, where five supporters of slavery were killed. In 1859 he captured the Federal Armoury at Harper's Ferry, now in West Virginia, intending to arm black slaves and begin a rebellion. Within 36 hours he and all his men had been killed, wounded or captured. The event is seen as a 'tipping-point' in escalating the tensions leading to civil war. Brown was tried for treason and hanged, but his impressive demeanour at his trial helped the Abolitionist cause. In his speech to the court on 2 November 1859, he said: *'Now, if it is deemed necessary that I should forfeit my life for the furtherance of the ends of justice, and mingle my blood further with the blood of my children and with the blood of millions in this slave country whose rights are disregarded by wicked, cruel, and unjust enactments, I submit; so let it be done!'*

Memorials were held in the North, church bells were rung, and Henry Thoreau and Ralph Waldo Emerson praised Brown's actions. The 1861 song that includes the lines *'John Brown's body lies a mould'ring in the grave, his soul is marching on'* was used as a marching song by Northern troops in the Civil War, which followed 16 months after his execution. At the end of the war, the noted black civil rights campaigner Frederick Douglass wrote: *'Did John Brown fail? John Brown began the war that ended American slavery and made this a free Republic. His zeal in the cause of freedom was infinitely superior to mine. Mine was as the taper light; his was as the burning sun. I could live for the slave; John Brown could die for him.'*

ELIZABETH BARRETT BROWNING
6 March 1806–29 June 1861

'How do I love thee? Let me count the ways.'

Opening line of her Sonnet No. 43

The above line sums up one of the greatest love stories in history. The poetess was sick, and in 1838 her physician sent her to recuperate in Torquay, where her brother died in a sailing accident. Her condition worsened, and she returned to live with her father at 53 Wimpole Street, London, hardly leaving her room for five years. Her 1844 *Poems* made her one of the most popular writers in the country and inspired the poet Robert Browning to write to her telling her how much he loved her work. An acquaintance arranged for Browning to meet Elizabeth in May 1845, and thus began one of the most famous courtships in literature, culminating in their secret marriage. Six years Browning's elder and an invalid, Elizabeth could not believe that he really loved her as much as he professed to, writing: '*He preferred ... of free and deliberate choice, to be allowed to sit only an hour a day by my side, to the fulfilment of the brightest dream which should exclude me in any possible world. I am still doubtful whether all the brightness can be meant for me. It is just as if the sun rose again at 7 o'clock PM ... I take it for pure magic, this life of mine. Surely nobody was ever so happy before.*'

Elizabeth had been disinherited, and in 1846 the couple fled to Italy. At the age of 45 she bore a son in a supremely happy marriage. After the death of an old friend and also her father, her health faded again, because of deteriorating lung function, and she died in her husband's arms. Browning wrote:

'Then came what my heart will keep till I see her again and longer – the most perfect expression of her love to me within my whole knowledge of her. Always smilingly, happily, and with a face like a girl's, and in a few minutes she died in my arms, her head on my cheek ... There was no lingering, nor acute pain, nor consciousness of separation, but God took her to himself as you would lift a sleeping child from a dark uneasy bed into your arms and the light. Thank God.'

HENRY DAVID THOREAU
(Born DAVID HENRY THOREAU)
12 July 1817–6 May 1862

'Moose ... Indian'

Last audible words

Thoreau had contracted tuberculosis in 1835, suffering intermittently until his condition worsened after an attack of bronchitis in 1859. Knowing he was dying, he spent his last three years editing his unpublished works, particularly *The Maine Woods* and *Excursions*, and asking publishers to print revised editions of *A Week* and *Walden*. His friends were alarmed at his deterioration, and surprised by his tranquil acceptance of death. Thoreau's biographer Henry Salt recorded:

'The thought of death was never a cause of anxiety to him; but terrible indeed to a man of Thoreau's temperament must have been the death-in-life of that long and dreary winter, when the daily walk and converse with nature, which had seemed necessities of his existence, were but memories of the past, and even the carefully kept journal must needs be discontinued, since there was in fact nothing to record. Yet of this outer life, in which for twenty-five years he had so faithfully and unremittingly busied himself, he now spoke no word, and we are told that no stranger could have imagined from his manner that "he ever had a friend in field or wood" ... It was on 6th May 1862, a beautiful spring morning, that the end came. At eight o'clock, shortly after enjoying the odour of a bunch of hyacinths from a friend's garden, he asked to be raised upright in his bed; his breathing became gradually fainter and fainter, until he died without pain or struggle in the presence of his mother and sister, his last audible words being "moose" and "Indian" – the thought still intent on the scenes that had detained it so long. He was buried, near his brother and sister, in "Sleepy Hollow", the quiet Concord burial-ground, close to the spot which became the grave of Nathaniel Hawthorne two years later. An address was given at the funeral by Emerson, and one of Thoreau's poems, "Sic Vita", was read by [Bronson] Alcott.'

'Let us cross over the river and sit under the shade of the trees'

Dying words

Jackson earned his nickname at the First Battle of Bull Run in 1861. As the Confederate lines began to fall back, his brigade provided crucial reinforcements. Brigadier General Bee exhorted his own troops to re-form by shouting, *'There is Jackson standing like a stone wall. Let us determine to die here, and we will conquer. Follow me!'* Jackson's own pickets accidentally shot him at the Battle of Chancellorsville in Virginia on 2 May 1863, and his left arm had to be amputated. General Robert E. Lee decided that he should recuperate in a safe refuge and ordered that he be taken about 30 miles from the front lines, writing to him: *'Could I have directed events, I would have chosen for the good of the country to be disabled in your stead.'* Jackson was expected to eventually recover, but pneumonia set in, and by Sunday, 10 May, it became clear that he would not last long. As he lay dying, Lee sent a message to his chaplain, B. Tucker Lacy, saying: *'Give General Jackson my affectionate regards, and say to him: he has lost his left arm but I my right.'*

On his deathbed Jackson remarked to his physician, *'It is the Lord's Day; my wish is fulfilled. I have always desired to die on Sunday'.* Dr Hunter McGuire wrote an account of his final hours: *'A few moments before he died he cried out in his delirium, "Order A. P. Hill to prepare for action! Pass the infantry to the front rapidly! Tell Major Hawks" – then stopped, leaving the sentence unfinished. Presently a smile of ineffable sweetness spread itself over his pale face, and he said quietly, and with an expression, as if of relief, "Let us cross over the river, and rest under the shade of the trees."'* His death was a severe setback for the Confederacy, affecting the morale of its army and of the general public.

'We made a good fight, but lost; thank God Virginia did its duty'

Battle command at Gettysburg, 3 July 1863, where he was fatally wounded

'Suddenly one of Pickett's brigade leaders, Lewis Armistead, led a hundred Virginians over the wall, exhorting his men, "Come forward, Virginians! Come on, boys, we must give them the cold steel! Who will follow me?" They grabbed the abandoned guns and even wheeled one around, but they couldn't fire it for lack of ammunition. Armistead, whose best friend before the war had been the Union corps commander Hancock, was shot and later died. His fellow brigade commanders James Marshall and Richard Garnett – the latter once court-martialed by Thomas J. "Stonewall" Jackson and conspicuously in search of redemption – also were killed. Pettigrew and Lowrance were wounded, and Trimble, Kemper, and Fry wounded and captured – all in a charge that reached this far but no farther. By day's end, Pickett's casualties, including killed, wounded, and captured, numbered 2,655, or about 42 per cent of his men. Pettigrew lost 2,700 men (62 per cent) and Trimble 885 (52 per cent).'

The mortally wounded Armistead was subsequently taken prisoner and moved to the rear of the Union line. Thomas H. Presnell of the 1st Minnesota wrote to a friend in 1890:

'After the battle was over, but while everything was confusion and excitement, I was returning from one of the wheat stacks to which I had assisted one of my comrades, toward the point occupied by Cushing's battery. I immediately saw that the occupant of the blanket was a Confederate officer, and was informed that he was Gen. Armistead. He seemed to be badly wounded in the head but was conscious and was talking, though rather incoherently. Among other things he asked was how Gen. Hancock was, and on being told that he was wounded, said: "I am sorry; he is a grand man." I remember he said this: "We made a good fight, but lost; thank God Virginia did its duty."'

SAMUEL 'SAM' HOUSTON
2 March 1793–26 July 1863

'Texas! Texas! Margaret ...'

Reported last words

A Virginian, Houston was badly injured three times fighting the English at the Battle of Horseshoe Bend. He practised law in Tennessee, and lived among the Cherokee, being named 'the Raven'. He became a congressman, then Governor of Tennessee in 1827. In 1836, Texas declared independence from Mexico, and Houston was elected Commander-in-Chief of its army, defeating Santa Anna and securing independence. He was the first President of the Republic of Texas, and after statehood in 1845 was elected Senator before becoming Governor. In 1861, he was deposed as Governor of Texas because he did not wish to secede from the Union. He forecast:

'To secede from the Union and set up another government would cause war. If you go to war with the United States, you will never conquer her, as she has the money and the men. If she does not whip you by guns, powder, and steel, she will starve you to death. It will take the flower of the country – the young men ... In the name of the constitution of Texas, which has been trampled upon, I refuse to take this oath. I love Texas too well to bring civil strife and bloodshed upon her ... I declare that civil war is inevitable and is near at hand ... For this reason I predict the civil war which is now at hand will be stubborn and of long duration.'

Houston was ill with pneumonia for five weeks, and died in Steamboat House, Huntsville, with his third wife Margaret and most of his children at his side. His last words have also been reported as '*Texas, Margaret, Texas*' (The *Huntsville Item*, 24 July 1988). An obituary appeared in the *Dallas Herald*, 5 August 1863, which read in part: '*Let us not shed tears to his memory due to one who has filled so much of our affections. Let the whole people bury with him whatever of unkindness they had for him.*' In 1936, in observance of the Texas Centennial, a marble marker was placed on his grave by the State of Texas, its inscription attributed to his friend Andrew Jackson. It reads: '*The World Will Take Care of Houston's Fame.*'

'They couldn't hit an elephant at this distance'

Words spoken moments before he was shot

Sedgwick was a Union Army general in the American Civil War, having fought in the Seminole Wars, the Mexican–American War, the Utah War and the Indian Wars. He was wounded in the leg and arm at Glendale, and almost surrounded by 'Stonewall' Jackson's forces at Antietam, where he was hit by three bullets with his division suffering 2,200 casualties. He took part in the battles of Chancellorsville, Salem Church and the Wilderness. At the Battle of Spotsylvania Court House, he was directing artillery emplacements, with Confederate sharpshooters causing his men to duck for cover. General McMahon was alongside him when he was shot dead, and recorded the moment:

'I gave the necessary order to move the troops to the right, and as they rose to execute the movement the enemy opened a sprinkling fire, partly from sharp-shooters. As the bullets whistled by, some of the men dodged. The general said laughingly, "What! What! Men, dodging this way for single bullets! What will you do when they open fire along the whole line? I am ashamed of you. They couldn't hit an elephant at this distance." A few seconds after, a man who had been separated from his regiment passed directly in front of the general, and at the same moment a sharp-shooter's bullet passed with a long shrill whistle very close, and the soldier, who was then just in front of the general, dodged to the ground. The general touched him gently with his foot, and said, "Why, my man, I am ashamed of you, dodging that way," and repeated the remark, "They couldn't hit an elephant at this distance." The man rose and saluted and said good-naturedly, "General, I dodged a shell once, and if I hadn't, it would have taken my head off. I believe in dodging." The general laughed and replied, "All right, my man; go to your place." For a third time the same shrill whistle, closing with a dull, heavy stroke, interrupted our talk; when, as I was about to resume, the general's face turned slowly to me, the blood spurting from his left cheek under the eye in a steady stream. He fell in my direction; I was so close to him that my effort to support him failed, and I fell with him.'

'She won't think anything about it'

Last words before his assassination

On Good Friday evening, 14 April 1865, the Lincolns went to Ford's Theatre to see *Our American Cousin*. Accompanying them were an engaged couple, Major Henry Reed Rathbone and Clara Harris. Mary Todd Lincoln recalled, '*During the drive he was so gay, that I said to him, laughingly, "Dear Husband, you almost startle me by your great cheerfulness." The President replied, "And well I may feel so, Mary, I consider this day, the war, has come to a close."*' However, John Wilkes Booth (1838–65), outraged by the Confederate defeat, the abolition of slavery and Lincoln's proposal to extend voting rights to emancipated slaves, was planning with co-conspirators to kill the President, Vice-President and Secretary of State. Although Robert E. Lee had surrendered the army of northern virginia four days earlier, the Confederate General Joseph Johnson's army had not surrendered, and Booth believed that the multiple assassination would destabilize the Union.

During the third act, Mary Lincoln whispered to her husband, who was holding her hand, '*What will Miss Harris think of my hanging on to you so?*' The President replied, '*She won't think anything about it,*' and laughed, just before John Wilkes Booth entered a narrow hallway between the President's box and the theatre's balcony, and barricaded the door. An actor, he was recognized by the employees at the Ford and able to gain easy access to the presidential party. Shortly after 10 p.m., he aimed his derringer and fired a single shot into the back of the President's head. As soldiers, civilians and physicians crowded into the presidential box, Mary Lincoln pleaded with Dr Charles Leale, '*Oh, Doctor, do what you can for my dear husband, do what you can for him.*'

The President never regained consciousness, and died at 7.22 the next morning. Secretary of War Edwin Stanton, who was on the death watch, said: '*Now he belongs to the Ages.*' Booth fled, breaking his leg as his horse fell, and was shot dead in a tobacco barn 11 days after the assassination. Four of his co-plotters were hanged. The assassination, together with the earlier loss of two of her sons, permanently unhinged Mrs Lincoln, and she wore black for the rest of her life.

JOHN WILKES BOOTH
10 May 1839–26 April 1865

'Tell mother, tell mother, I died for my country ... useless ... useless ...'

Dying words

John Wilkes Booth was a successful actor whose mother had made him promise not to fight for the Confederacy. He had attended the hanging of the Abolitionist John Brown in 1859, and worked with Confederate agents in the Civil War, planning to kidnap Lincoln and exchange him for Confederate prisoners-of-war. In 1865, Lee surrendered, but General Johnston was still fighting the Union, and Booth now plotted to kill the Union Commander-in-Chief General Ulysses S. Grant, Secretary of State William Seward, Vice-President Andrew Johnson and President Lincoln, thus removing the four Union leaders. On 14 April, he watched Lincoln give a speech outside the White House promising to free slaves, and remarked that it would be the last speech he would ever make.

After shooting Lincoln, Booth jumped from the 12-foot-high box to the stage of Ford's Theatre in Washington shouting, '*Sic semper tyrannis!*' ('*Thus always to tyrants!*'), the motto of the Commonwealth of Virginia. He fled the city with a co-conspirator, David Herold, and was later trapped by soldiers while hiding in a barn in Virginia. Herold gave himself up, but Booth refused to surrender, saying, '*Captain, this is a hard case, I swear. Give a lame man a chance. Draw up your men twenty yards from the door, and I will fight your whole command.*' His offer was refused, and he shouted, '*Well, my brave boys, you can prepare a stretcher for me.*' The soldiers had orders to capture Booth alive, so they set fire to the barn in an attempt to drive him from it. Booth began to shout, '*Kill me! Kill me!*' and in the confusion, at least one soldier shot into the barn. Booth collapsed, struck in the neck by a round, and was dragged from the flames, paralysed with a severed spinal cord.

In his dying moments he whispered, '*Tell my mother I died for my country.*' He then asked for his hands to be raised to his face so he could see them, and uttered his last words, '*Useless, useless.*'

EDMUND RUFFIN
5 January 1794–17 June 1865

'I here declare my unmitigated hatred to Yankee rule'
Final diary entry, 17 June 1865

A Virginian, as a farmer and agronomist Ruffin aided the Southern economy by proposing new ways to rotate and fertilize tobacco crops. In 1860 he wrote a book predicting an American civil war in 1868, starting with an attack on Fort Sumter in South Carolina, which would result in a victory for the Southern states. He came to hate the Union as it invaded his beloved Virginia, and is often credited with firing the first shot of the Civil War at Fort Sumter in 1861. There were three cannons fired, and he was certainly one of the men involved. He was also said to be the first man to enter Fort Sumter after it fell.

After Robert E. Lee's surrender on 9 April 1865, Ruffin wrote a short suicide note, in which he stated that he would *rather be dead than live in a country subjugated by the Yankee race*', then draped himself in a Confederate flag and shot himself in the head. His final diary entry reads in full:

'I here declare my unmitigated hatred to Yankee rule – to all political, social and business connection with the Yankees and to the Yankee race. Would that I could impress these sentiments, in their full force, on every living Southerner and bequeath them to every one yet to be born! May such sentiments be held universally in the outraged and down-trodden South, though in silence and stillness, until the now far-distant day shall arrive for just retribution for Yankee usurpation, oppression and atrocious outrages, and for deliverance and vengeance for the now ruined, subjugated and enslaved Southern States! ... And now with my latest writing and utterance, and with what will be near my latest breath, I here repeat and would willingly proclaim my unmitigated hatred to Yankee rule – to all political, social and business connections with Yankees, and the perfidious, malignant and vile Yankee race.'

LORD PALMERSTON, HENRY JOHN TEMPLE, THIRD VISCOUNT PALMERSTON
20 October 1784–18 October 1865

'That's Article 98; now go on to the next'
Dying words

'Pam' was in government office almost continuously from 1807 for 58 years until his death, serving twice as prime minister, and being the only prime minister who died in office. He is best remembered for his aggressive foreign policy, when England was at the height of its imperial power. In an 1864 letter he noted: '*Mackieson gave me the other day a buffalo hide whip from Africa called in those regions a Peace Maker and used as such in the households of chieftains. Our Peace Makers are our Armstrongs and Whitworths [rifles] and our engineers.*' He was also known as 'Lord Pumice Stone' for his abrasive style in debate, once replying: '*I will not talk of non-intervention, for it is not an English word*' to an MP who sought to correct him for saying '*non-interference*'.

His foreign policy and his actions towards hostile governments have given us the term 'gunboat diplomacy', and he forecast in his last few months that '*Russia will in due time become a power almost as great as the old Roman Empire ... Germany ought to be strong in order to resist Russian aggression.*' He saw the growing might of Prussia as a counter-balance to Russia. William Ewart Gladstone recounted a Frenchman trying to be complimentary to Palmerston, saying: '*If I were not a Frenchman, I should wish to be an Englishman.*' Palmerston coolly responded: '*If I were not an Englishman, I should be wish to be an Englishman.*'

In early October of 1865, Palmerston caught a chill and a violent fever, and in his delirium his last words were of diplomatic treaties. An apocryphal version of his last words is: '*Die, my dear doctor? That is the last thing I shall do.*' He was only the fourth non-royal person to be given a state funeral, following Newton, Nelson and Wellington. Walter Bagehot wrote a week after the prime minister's death: '*No man was better in action, but no man was more free from the pedantry of business ... England will never want statesmen, but she will never see in our time such a statesman as Viscount Palmerston.*'

'Give me 80 men and I'll ride through the whole Sioux nation'

Fetterman's claim before his death on the battlefield

In June 1866, Red Cloud, chief of the Oglala Sioux, could not agree with army negotiators to allow emigrants to settle on the last of the great Sioux hunting grounds. He sent out war parties that attacked emigrants, army patrols, settlers and grazing herds. These hit-and-run tactics were difficult for the army to deal with, as by the time they arrived on the scene the Sioux had disappeared. The 18th US Infantry Regiment, based at Fort Phil Kearney, was tasked with protecting emigrants travelling to the Montana goldfields. Its commander, Colonel Carrington, found Captain Fetterman to be a troublesome officer who wished for action, claiming that he could destroy the Sioux nation. Although a good Civil War officer, Fetterman had no experience of the guerrilla tactics of the Native Americans.

The Sioux continued their attacks to try to bait the US Cavalry into an ambush. Officers commanding patrols recognized the traps before they could be sprung, but Fetterman led a patrol that was fortunate to be rescued by Carrington on 7 December. A few days later, he made his fateful boast. On 21 December, Red Cloud himself led a large band of Cheyenne and Sioux, including the respected war leader Crazy Horse, pinning down a wood-supply train not far from Fort Phil Kearney. Fetterman demanded the relief assignment, based upon his seniority, but Carrington gave him explicit instructions not to pursue any Indians. Prophetically, Fetterman's column amounted to exactly 80 men, 27 from the 2nd Cavalry and the rest from the 18th Infantry. He gave the order to attack, ignoring his instructions not to venture beyond Lodge Trail Ridge, out of sight and support distance from the fort. The warriors rode away, and drew the soldiers into a clearing, surrounded by around 2,000 Sioux and Cheyenne, where they were all killed within 20 minutes in what became known as the Fetterman Massacre. Later that day, the stripped and mutilated bodies of the soldiers were found by a patrol led by Captain Ten Eyck. Not until Custer's Last Stand in 1876 would the US army suffer another such disaster.

'I do not have to forgive my enemies, I have had them all shot'

Words spoken on his deathbed when asked by a priest if he forgave his enemies

Six times prime minister of Spain from 1844, Narváez was born at Loja, Granada, a son of the first Count of Cañada Alta, and first saw active military service in Catalonia aged 22. He rose rapidly, becoming a general and statesman. He supported Isabella II on the death of her father Ferdinand VII in 1833, fighting for her forces from 1833 to 1839 and winning a great victory over the Carlist forces of Miguel Gomez Damas at the Battle of Majaceite in 1836. The Carlists were the followers of Isabella's younger brother Carlos, who wanted a King of Spain rather than the three-year-old Isabella. Maria Cristina de Bourbon, the widow of Ferdinand VII, acted as queen-regent for her daughter. Narváez then cleared La Mancha of bandits, and was given powerful military appointments. When Baldomero Espartero and the Progresista Party came to power in 1840, he was forced to flee to France for his part in the insurrection against them at Seville. Here he joined the partisans of the queen-regent. He returned to Spain in 1843, having planned an expedition to overthrow Espartero.

Narváez became President of the Council of Ministers (equivalent to prime minister) in 1844, being created a field marshal and the first Duke of Valencia in 1845. His reactionary policies led to his removal in 1846, and he became an ambassador at Paris. He was back in Spain as President of the Council of Ministers in 1847. He resigned in 1848, after a misunderstanding with the Queen-Regent, but was again President in 1856–57, and from 1866 until his death in Madrid. He was known as the 'strong man' of Isabelline Spain, and his authoritarian policies helped provoke an uprising shortly after his death, which led to the downfall of Queen Isabella a few months later. She was induced to abdicate in Paris in 1870 in favour of her son Alfonso XII, who reigned from 1875 to 1885.

HECTOR BERLIOZ
11 December 1803–8 March 1869

'And I say hourly to Death: "When you will." Why does he delay?'

Written five years before his death

In the last years of his life Berlioz felt isolated. Both of his wives had died, and a young woman with whom he had formed an attachment broke off their relationship. His son was lost at sea, and from financial necessity he was forced to conduct and write criticisms rather than compose. Many of his friends and family had died, including both his sisters. In 1863, he retired from composition and criticism, suffering from intestinal neuralgia, and became preoccupied with thoughts of death. In 1864 he wrote: '*I am in my 61st year; past hopes, past illusions, past high thoughts and lofty conceptions. My son is almost always far away from me. I am alone. My contempt for the folly and baseness of mankind, my hatred of its atrocious cruelty, have never been so intense. And I say hourly to Death: "When you will." Why does he delay?'*

His son's death in 1867 affected him terribly, leading him to write shortly before his own death: '*I believe in nothing.*' His intestinal pains had been gradually increasing, spreading to his stomach, and he passed his days in agony, with intense spasms of pain. He embarked on his second concert tour of Russia, and returned exhausted to Paris in 1868, with his health further damaged owing to the Russian winter. He went to Nice to recuperate but fell, possibly suffering a stroke, and returned as an invalid to Paris to die. His last words were said to be: '*Enfin, on va jouer ma musique*' ('*At last, they are going to play my music*'). Largely ignored in France, the romantic composer is best remembered for his *Symphonie fantastique, Romeo and Juliet, Te Deum* and the requiem *Grand messe des morts*. His *Treatise on Instrumentation* was a major work – he wrote elsewhere: '*Instrumentation is to music precisely what colour is to painting.*' His autobiography, *Mémoires*, was given to only a few friends in his lifetime, but has been called the most fascinating biography of any musician. An argumentative, under-appreciated and troubled man, his funeral was held at the Church of the Trinity a few days after Rossini's, at which the composer Gounod said, 'Here is he quiet, who never was quiet before.'

'It is no use'

Dying words

Robert E. Lee was an exceptionally capable general, who was invited by President Lincoln to take command of the entire Union army in early 1861. Because his home state of Virginia had seceded (against his wishes), Lee chose to join Jefferson Davis, and became commander of the Confederate army of Virginia. He fought McClellan to a standstill at Antietam, and beat Burnside at Fredericksburg and then Hooker at Chancellorsville. Launching his second invasion of the North, he lost at Gettysburg, mainly because of the power of the Union rifles. From the Wilderness to Petersburg he fought a retiring campaign against Grant in which he made full use of trenches, becoming known as 'Ace of Spades' Lee. Finally forced into a siege, he held on to Richmond and Petersburg for nearly 10 months before beginning his retreat to Appomattox, where he was forced to surrender. In 1975, Senator Byrd of Virginia brought a resolution, passed in Congress, to restore Lee's rights of US citizenship retrospectively to 13 June 1865. It was signed by President Ford on 24 July.

'Mrs Lee wrote thus of his last hours: ... He rarely spoke except when sleeping, and then his thoughts were with his much-loved soldiers on the "dreadful battlefields". Among his last words were, "Tell Hill he must come up." Once when General Custis Lee said something about his getting well, he shook his head and pointed upward. When his doctor said, to cheer him, "How do you feel to-day, General?" General Lee said slowly, "I feel better." The doctor then said: "You must make haste and get well. Traveler [Lee's old grey war-horse] has been standing so long in the stable that he needs exercise." The General made no reply, but shook his head and closed his eyes. Once or twice he put aside his medicine, saying, "It is no use." On October 10th, about midnight, he was seized with a chill and his pulse became feeble and rapid. The next day he was seen to be sinking. He knew those around him, but was not able to speak. Soon after nine o'clock on the morning of the 12th, he closed his eyes on earthly things and his pure soul took its flight to God.'

DR DAVID LIVINGSTONE
19 March 1813–1 May 1873

'Build me a hut to die in'
Instructions to his followers in his last days

The Scottish explorer and missionary was beset with health problems in his final years, but steadfastly refused to leave his beloved Africa. He had lost contact with Europe for six years before Stanley found him in 1871, and died less than two years later of malaria and internal bleeding caused by dysentery. This account of his last days was written by the *New York Herald* correspondent at Suez:

'[The] steamer arrived off Suez at eleven on Saturday night ... with the body of Livingstone. The great traveller had been ill with chronic dysentery for several months past, although well-supplied with stores and medicines; and he seems to have had a presentiment that this attack would prove fatal. He rode a donkey at first, but was subsequently carried, and thus arrived at Ilala, beyond Lake Bemba (Bangweolo), in Bisa Country, when he said to his followers, "Build me a hut to die in." The hut was built by his men, who first of all made him a bed. It is stated that he suffered greatly, groaning night and day. On the third day he said, "I am very cold: put more grass over the hut." His followers did not speak to or go near him. Kitumbo, chief of Bisa, however, sent flour and beans, and behaved well to the party. On the fourth day Livingstone became insensible, and died about midnight. Majahra, his servant, was present.

His last entry in the diary was on April 27. He spoke much and sadly of home and family. When first seized, he told his followers he intended to exchange every thing for ivory to give to them, and to push on to Djiji and Zanzibar, and try to reach England. On the day of his death these men consulted what to do, and the Nassick boys determined to preserve the remains. They were, however, afraid to inform the chief of Livingstone's death; and the secretary, therefore, removed the body to another hut, around which he built a high fence to insure privacy. Here they opened the body, and removed the internals, which were placed in a tin box, and buried inside the fence under a large tree.'

HANS CHRISTIAN ANDERSEN
2 April 1805–4 August 1875

'Most of the people walking after me will be children, so make the beat keep time with short steps'

Planning the music for his funeral, shortly before his death

The Dane was noted for his wonderful children's stories such as 'The Snow Queen', 'The Little Mermaid', 'The Ugly Duckling', 'The Emperor's New Clothes', 'The Princess and the Pea' and 'Thumbelina'. His poetry and stories have been translated into more than 150 languages. Andersen's father was a poor shoemaker and his mother a washerwoman who taught him about Danish folklore, which gave him the basis for his fables. Although his fairy-stories are seemingly for children, they have moral messages for adults.

A social misfit, with little success with the opposite sex, Andersen had risen from the bottom of Danish society to the top. Feted and honoured, he became the most widely travelled Danish writer of his day. Altogether he went on 29 trips abroad and spent over nine years of his life outside Denmark. Aged 62, he went to Paris, where he visited a brothel. It was neither his first visit nor his last, as his diaries reveal: '*Then [I] went suddenly up into a meat market – one of them was covered with powder; a second, common; a third, quite the lady. I talked with her, paid twelve francs and left, without having sinned in deed, though I dare say I did in my thoughts. She asked me to come back, said I was indeed very innocent for a man.*'

In the spring of 1872, Andersen fell out of bed and was severely hurt. He never fully recovered. By the time of his death, he was internationally renowned and received a stipend from the Danish government as a 'national treasure'. A large statue in his honour was being planned even before his death, and is prominently placed at the town hall square in Copenhagen.

'Hurrah boys, we've got them! We'll finish them up and then go home to our station.'

Custer's last known words, remembered by last survivor of the
Battle of Little Bighorn, Charles Windolph (1851–1950)

The Sioux and the Cheyenne were trying to resist white migration, and Custer and 655 men were sent to locate the villages of the Native Americans who had fought General Crook at Rosebud Creek. Custer refused the support offered by General Terry of an additional four companies of the Second Cavalry, stating that he '*could whip any Indian village on the Plains*' with his own regiment, and that extra troops would simply be a burden. At the same time, he left behind at Yellowstone a battery of Gatling guns, and before leaving the camp all his troops, including the officers, boxed their sabres and sent them back with the wagons. Through his field-glasses he saw a village 15 miles away, and thinking the Indians would be asleep, began organizing an attack, although his men and horses were exhausted from riding 70 miles in a short time. He divided his men to attack from three directions under himself, Captain Benteen and Major Reno.

Major Reno was the first to charge the village, but finding superior resistance, he retreated to the other side of the Little Big Horn River. He was later joined by Captain Benteen, and although they suffered heavy casualties they were able to fight off the Native Americans. Custer and his troop were forced to retreat into the bluffs to the east, where he was attacked by about 4,000 warriors. He died along with his two brothers, a brother-in-law and a nephew. The Sioux and Cheyenne had rifles as new as Custer's, and his entire force perished. Reno and Benteen were rescued by the arrival of General Terry. President Grant said: '*I regard Custer's Massacre as a sacrifice of troops, brought on by Custer himself, that was wholly unnecessary.*'

'Wild Bill, J.B. Hickok killed by the assassin Jack McCall in Deadwood, Black Hills, August 2, 1876. Pard, we will meet again in the happy hunting ground to part no more. Good bye, Colorado Charlie, C.H. Utter.'

Written by Hickok's friend on his wooden grave-marker in Deadwood

Hickok had been a skilled marksman and gunfighter, and had also scouted for Custer, hunted buffalo, appeared in Buffalo Bill's Circus, served as a lawman and gambled to excess. On 2 August 1876, he went to Nuttal & Mann's Saloon No. 10 in Deadwood to play low-stakes poker. Arriving late, he found his usual seat against the wall was already taken, so he sat with his back to one door and facing another. As he played, Jack McCall shot him in the back of the head with a Colt 45, revenge for killing his brother Lew in Abilene. Hickok was holding pairs of aces and eights, which became known as the 'dead man's hand'.

The first newspaper report of Hickok's death was published in Deadwood's only newspaper, the *Black Hills Pioneer*, on 5 August 1876:

'On Wednesday about 3 o'clock the report stated that J.B. Hickok (Wild Bill) was killed. On repairing to the hall of Nuttall and Mann, it was ascertained that the report was too true. We found the remains of Wild Bill lying on the floor. The murderer, Jack McCall, was captured after a lively chase by many of the citizens, and taken to a building at the lower end of the city, and a guard placed over him. As soon as this was accomplished, a coroner's jury was summoned, with C.H. Sheldon as foreman, who after hearing all the evidence, which was the effect that, while Wild Bill and others were at a table playing cards, Jack McCall walked in and around directly back of his victim, and when within three feet of him raised his revolver, and exclaiming, "Damn you, take that," fired; the ball entering at the back of the head, and coming out at the centre of the right check causing instant death, reached a verdict in accordance with the above facts.'

EDWARD 'NED' KELLY
June 1854/June 1855–11 November 1880

'His Honour then sentenced the prisoner to death in the usual form, ending with the words, "May the Lord have mercy on your soul." The prisoner: "I will go a little further than that, and say I will see you there when I go."'

Trial transcript

In 1869, aged 14, Ned was arrested for assaulting a Chinese pig farmer with the wonderful name of Ah Fook, and also for being an accomplice of bushranger Harry Power. He was found not guilty on both charges. In 1870 he was arrested for assault and sentenced to six months' hard labour. Three weeks after his release, he was arrested for having a stolen horse, and sentenced to three years' hard labour. On his release, he began cattle rustling with his brother Dan. In 1878, Ned's sister Ellen attracted the attentions of Constable Alexander Fitzpatrick, who assaulted her on a visit to the Kelly home. Fitzpatrick then accused Ned of attempted murder, and Ned went into hiding. When the police found him, he and his accomplices killed three of the officers before escaping. They robbed two banks at Euroa and Jerilderie in February 1879, then made suits of armour and helmets that they believed would protect them from the police. At this time, Ned dictated the 'Jerilderie letter', describing his view of his own activities and the treatment of his family and, more generally, of Irish Catholics by the police and the English and Irish Protestant squatters.

In July 1880, the police caught up with Ned at Glenrowan and he took hostages into the local hotel. The gang's armour was tough enough to repel bullets, but left the legs and arms unprotected. Three gang members and the hostages were killed before the hotel was burnt down. Ned was wounded several times, and sentenced to be hanged at Melbourne Gaol. He asked for a photograph to be taken of him. His mother's last words to him were reported to be: *'Mind you die like a Kelly.'* The newspapers *The Age* and *The Herald* reported his last words as: *'Such is life.'*

BENJAMIN DISRAELI, FIRST EARL OF BEACONSFIELD
21 December 1804–19 April 1881

'No, it is better not. She would only ask me to take a message to Albert.'

Dying words

A successful novelist, twice prime minister and a permanent parliamentary enemy of William Gladstone, Disraeli was famous for his friendship with Queen Victoria, remarking to Matthew Arnold: *'You have heard me accused me of being a flatterer. It is true. I am a flatterer. I have found it useful. Everyone likes flattery; and when you come to Royalty you should lay it on with a trowel.'*

'As the author of a runaway bestseller Disraeli purchased a seven-year lease on 19 Curzon Street, W1, in January 1881. It was the first time he had been able to purchase a house with his own money. Disraeli's health was already failing. The east wind cut into him as he made his way home on 22 March. The chill developed into bronchitis and the spiral of decline began. The house soon witnessed a procession of concerned visitors, including his old political rival Gladstone. Queen Victoria grew concerned. Before setting off for Osborne on 5 April she wrote this, her last, letter to Disraeli. It was accompanied by primroses from Windsor and the promise to send more primroses from Osborne. Victoria had thought of going to visit him but considered it better to let him rest and looked forward to seeing him when they returned. "You are ... constantly in my thoughts, & I wish I could do anything to cheer you." Disraeli's reputed final reference to Victoria, when asked if he wanted her to be called to his bedside, was "No, it is better not. She would only ask me to take a message to Albert." Disraeli died in the early hours of 19 April on the anniversary of Byron's death. At his bedside were Corry [his private secretary], who had returned from accompanying his sick sister to Algeria, Sir Philip Rose, Lord Barrington (Lord Derby's former secretary who was standing in for Corry) and his three doctors: Kidd (a homeopath), Bruce and Quain. His last recorded words were, "I had rather live but I am not afraid to die."'

'Who is it? Who is it?'

Last words before being shot

Billy the Kid was also known as Henry Antrim, Kid Antrim, William Antrim, Billy Bonney and William H. Bonney. In just four years, he fought in at least 16 shootouts, killed at least four men himself, and assisted in the murder of at least five others. A horse-rustler in Arizona, in 1877 he shot and killed his first man in a saloon. He fled to Lincoln County, New Mexico, where he found employment with the young rancher John Tunstall, who was embroiled in the bloody Lincoln County Range War. When Tunstall was murdered on 18 February 1878, Billy joined a force called the 'Regulators', who vowed vengeance. The men began killing those suspected of involvement in the assassination, including Lincoln County Sheriff William Brady. With a price on his head, Billy surrendered in exchange for amnesty. He soon took up rustling again, and in December 1880, after two of his partners were shot and killed, was captured by the new sheriff, Patrick Floyd Garrett. After standing trial for murder in New Mexico in April 1881, he was found guilty and sentenced to hang, but escaped from jail, killing the two men guarding him.

On 14 July, 'Pat' Garrett and two of his deputies were sitting in a darkened bedroom at the Fort Sumner ranch home of Billy's friend Pete Maxwell. Garrett was asking Maxwell about Billy's whereabouts when Billy, in his stockinged feet, unexpectedly entered the room, spotting but not recognizing Garrett in the dim light. *'Quién es? Quién es?'* ('Who is it? Who is it?') were his last words as Garrett shot him twice. Garrett made $2,500 from the killing, which he used to pay for a ranch. A biography, *The Authentic Life of Billy the Kid*, was published only two years after Billy's death, but the authors were his killer, Sheriff Garrett, and an alcoholic named Ash Upson, who ghost-wrote most of it. Garrett too drank heavily, and slid into debt. In February 1908 he was shot in an argument over the grazing of goats. His killer, a young cowboy named Jesse Wayne Brazel, was acquitted on the grounds of self-defence.

'In Loving Memory of my Beloved Son, Murdered by a Traitor and Coward Whose Name is not Worthy to Appear Here'

Epitaph written by his mother Zerelda James

A 'celebrity' while alive, Jesse James became even more so in death, when he was shot in the back of the head in his own home by fellow gang member Robert Ford. Jesse was born in Missouri, and along with his brother Frank was a Confederate guerrilla during the Civil War. After the war, the James brothers joined the Younger brothers, forming the James–Younger Gang, robbing banks, stagecoaches, and trains. With many of the gang dead, Jesse and Frank returned to Missouri, where Jesse rented a house in St Joseph, Frank moving on to hide out in Virginia. Charley Ford, the only other surviving gang member, came to live with Jesse, along with his brother Robert Ford. However, Robert had been negotiating secretly with Missouri Governor Thomas Crittenden to capture Jesse and Frank, with a $5,000 bounty for each of them.

On 4 April 1882, The *New York Times* reported:

'Charles, it is said, had lived with him in the shanty ever since November; Robert arrived 10 days ago, and the three have been making arrangements for a raiding expedition on which they were about to start tonight (3 April). James and the two Fords were in the front room together about 9 o'clock this morning. James took off his belt and laid his pistols on the bed, preparing to wash himself, when Robert Ford sprang up behind him and sent a bullet through his brain. The ball entered the head at the base of the right brain, coming out over the eye. The brothers at once made known what they had done and gave themselves up. They are now under guard at the Courthouse.'

KARL HEINRICH MARX
5 May 1818–14 March 1883

'Go on, get out. Last words are for fools who haven't said enough.'

On his deathbed, to his housekeeper

Marx was born in Prussia, but in 1849 settled in London, where he lived in poverty while developing his economic and political theories. It has been often said that he wrote so much that no individual has ever read all his writings, and intriguingly he wrote to Engels: *'All I know is that I am not a Marxist.'* He believed that philosophy ought to be employed in practice, to change the world. However, he is best known not as a philosopher but as a revolutionary communist, with his theory of history, historical materialism, stating that forms of society rise and fall as they improve, and then impede, the development of human productive power. He saw in this process the inevitable breakdown of capitalism, culminating in communism. His economic analysis of capitalism is based on his version of the labour theory of value, where he concludes that capitalist profit is the extraction of surplus value from the exploited proletariat (workers). The great historian Norman Davies contextualized Marxism thus: *'The intellectual rigour of Marxism proved to be far inferior to its emotive power ... Marx had unwittingly provided ... yet another substitute religion.'* (Marx, of course, had told us that religion was *'the opium of the people'*.)

After suffering from bronchitis and pleurisy for some years, Marx died and was buried in Highgate Cemetery, London. His tombstone is engraved with two messages. The first is: *'WORKERS OF ALL LANDS UNITE'*, taken from the closing words of the *Communist Manifesto*: *'Let the ruling classes tremble at a communist revolution. The proletarians have nothing to lose but their chains. They have a world to win. Working men of all countries, unite!'* The other is from Marx's *11th Thesis on Feuerbach*, of 1845: *'The philosophers have only interpreted the world in various ways – the point however is to change it.'*

ULYSSES S. GRANT (HIRAM ULYSSES GRANT)
27 April 1822–23 July 1885

'I don't want anybody to feel distressed on my account … Water.'

Last words, to his nurse, reported in *The New York Times*, 24 July 1885

General-in-chief of the Union Army from 1864 to 1869, Grant accepted the surrender of Robert E. Lee in the Civil War, and became the eighteenth President of the United States from 1869 to 1877. An officer once asked him if he ever felt fear on the battlefield, to which Grant responded: *'I never had the time.'* In 1884 he was bankrupted in a financial scam, and as he was suffering from terminal throat cancer, he began to write his memoirs to safeguard his family. Mark Twain, who published the memoirs, wrote in a letter to his wife on 1 July 1885: *'Manifestly, dying is nothing to a really great and brave man.'* As soon as he had finished writing, Grant told his doctor that he was at last ready to die: *'There is nothing more I should do to it now, and therefore I am not likely to be more ready to go than at this moment.'* On his last night:

> 'His last voluntary and irresponsive act of speech which embodied the idea that governed him in all his sufferings, and which will on that account stand probably as his last utterance, dates back to yesterday afternoon, when, noticing the grief that the family could not restrain, he said, whispering in little above a breath, yet quite distinctly: "I don't want anybody to feel distressed on my account." … Mrs Grant then pressed his hand and asked if he knew her. He replied with a look of reassurance. He was near collapse at the time, and Col. Grant [his son], thinking him possibly in distress, asked him if he suffered. He whispered a feeble "no". That question was asked several times with the same result. Once, about 3 o'clock, he seemed in need of something. The nurse bent over him and heard him say "Water." He did not speak after that.'

MARIAN 'CLOVER' HOOPER ADAMS
13 September 1843–6 December 1885

> **'If I had one single point of character or goodness, I would stand on that and grow back to life. Henry is more patient and loving than words can express.'**
>
> Letter to her sister

Known as 'Clover', the wife of Henry Adams was a society hostess and accomplished photographer, the inspiration for Henry James' *Daisy Miller* and *Portrait of a Lady*. She was only five when her mother died of tuberculosis. Her subsequent devotion to her father remained throughout her marriage. During their first long separation, when she was on her honeymoon in 1872 along the Nile, she suffered a brief nervous breakdown. The death of her father on 13 April 1885 began a period of mourning that evolved into mental depression, from which she did not recover. Her mother and grandmother had both suffered from depression, and as a child Clover had been present when her aunt had taken arsenic to end her own life and that of her unborn child. In addition, Clover suffered feelings of intellectual inferiority to her famous husband and a sense of frustration over his attention to another woman.

On 6 December 1885, Adams found his wife dead next to an opened vial of potassium cyanide, which she used in the processing of her photographs. He destroyed most of her letters and photos, but kept a letter to her sister that had not been posted. In part it read: '*If I had one single point of character or goodness, I would stand on that and grow back to life. Henry is more patient and loving than words can express – God might envy him – he bears and hopes and despairs hour after hour – Henry is beyond all words tenderer and better than all of you even.*' He never spoke her name or referred to her publicly again, even omitting her entirely from his autobiography, *The Education of Henry Adams*. Two years after Clover's suicide, her sister Ellen, grieving over the death of her husband, walked into the path of an oncoming train. Her brother Edward suffered a nervous breakdown as a result of that tragedy, and jumped from the third floor of his home. He survived briefly, but died two months later of pneumonia in an asylum.

WINFIELD SCOTT HANCOCK
14 February 1824–9 February 1886

'Oh Allie! Allie! Myra! Good ...'

Dying words

'Early Tuesday morning the stricken general's wife, who had kept a constant vigil at her husband's bedside, rose to leave the room to rest for a few moments. As she walked across the room, the patient's eyes followed her. When she reached the door and looked back, he struggled to speak to her: "Oh Allie! Allie! Myra! Good ..." He was unable to finish the sentence, the last words he ever spoke. He soon became unconscious ... An examination of the general's urine disclosed that he was suffering from diabetes ... [Dr] Janeway later told a reporter that "the general went down to the close of his life like a person descending a flight of stairs" ... The nation ... was shocked and saddened. President Cleveland spoke truly when he wrote to Allie: "The heroism and worth of your late husband have gathered to your side in this hour of affliction a nation of mourners" ... [General] Sherman ... one of Hancock's firmest friends, delivered a simple tribute of his own ... "I knew Hancock on the plains, where there was no chance of glory, no hope of fame, nothing but abuse and hardships, the same conscientious man, anxious to do right, anxious to fulfil the orders of his government, anxious to complete a job after which he had been dispatched, and generally successful." Not a bad epitaph for a soldier.'

They are not particularly inspiring last words, but were spoken by a man who should be immortalized. In fact, General Sherman had named Hancock 'one of the greatest soldiers in history'. After the Battle of Williamsburg, General McClellan telegraphed Washington that 'Hancock was superb today', and the nickname 'Hancock the Superb' stayed with him all his life. At Gettysburg his quick thinking and bravery saved the day for the Union, and he was also known as 'the Hero of Gettysburg'. When one of his subordinates protested, 'General, the corps commander ought not to risk his life that way', Hancock is said to have replied, 'There are times when a corps commander's life does not count.' Standing for president as a Democrat in 1880, he was defeated by Garfield by the closest popular vote margin in American history.

EMILY ELIZABETH DICKINSON
10 December 1830–15 May 1886

'I must go in, the fog is rising'

Last known words

'While her work still fascinated her, there came that morning in June, 1884, when Emily was smitten, as her father had been before her, and though she lived for two years after, "The green world went on a sudden blind" and it was impossible for her to write more than an occasional pencilled note. She wrote to her sister Sue at this time, "You must let me go first, Sue, because I live in the sea always now, and know the road." When the better days came, she still took out her writing and made her last corrections, playing with her beloved iridescent words to the last, but, in her own words, reminiscent of an oft-repeated family caution, "it was already growing damp" – "I must go in, the fog is rising," she warned, at the end of her briefest last message. Perhaps she was too elemental, too close to the very basis of being, to belong to mere humanity. It was on May 16, 1866, that her family gave her back to immortality with a strange relief, as of setting a winged thing free. At the simple funeral at the old house, Colonel Higginson read a poem of Emily Brontë's, the last words she ever wrote, prefacing it by saying "This poem on Immortality was a favourite of Emily Dickinson, who has just put it on – if she could have ever been said to have put it off."'

Of her mother's earlier death, Emily had said: '*Like a flake gathered by the wind, she is now part of the drift called Infinity. We don't know where she is, though many tell us.*' A wonderful innovative poet, Emily became confined to her bed, and less and less able to write. After several days of worsening symptoms, 'the Belle of Amherst' died. Her brother Austin wrote in his diary that '*the day was awful ... she ceased to breathe that terrible breathing just before the [afternoon] whistle sounded for six*'. Her physician gave the cause of death as Bright's disease (a kidney ailment now called nephritis). For much of her life she had been a recluse, always dressed in white. Very little of her work was published, until after her death, when her sister Lavinia found a cache of almost 1,800 poems. They were so different from the poems of her day that they were altered for publication, and it was not until the 1950s that Emily was accepted as a leading American poet.

'The most skilful gambler and nerviest, speediest, deadliest man with a six-gun I ever knew'

Recollections of Wyatt Earp

Nicknamed 'Doc', as he had been a dentist for around five years, Holliday was a gambler and gunfighter renowned for his friendship with Wyatt Earp, who recalled: *'I found him a loyal friend and good company. He was a dentist whom necessity had made a gambler; a gentleman whom disease had made a vagabond; a philosopher whom life had made a caustic wit; a long, lean blonde fellow nearly dead with consumption and at the same time the most skilful gambler and nerviest, speediest, deadliest man with a six-gun I ever knew.'* According to 'Bat' Masterson: *'Doc had but three redeeming traits. One was his courage; he was afraid of nothing on Earth. The second was the one commendable principle in his code of life, sterling loyalty to friends. The third was his affection for Wyatt Earp.'* The *Denver Republican* of 10 November 1887 reported on his death that *'Few men of his character had more friends or stronger champions.'* However, Doc O'Meara called him *'Without question a stone killer, an alcoholic and a whoremonger. He was known to cheat at cards'* (*Guns of the Gunfighters: Lawmen, Outlaws & Hollywood Cowboys,* 2003), while according to the *Las Vegas Optic* he was *'A shiftless, bagged-legged character – a killer and professional cut-throat and not a wit too refined to rob stages or even steal sheep'.*

Holliday developed consumption (tuberculosis) soon after starting his dental practice and moved from Atlanta to Texas to help his symptoms, trying to make a living as a professional gambler. In Dodge City he befriended the Earp family, and later moved to Tombstone, where he was on their side in the Battle at the OK Corral in 1881. He was then involved in the Earp Vendetta against the men who killed Morgan Earp and badly wounded Virgil. It was said that he hoped to die in a fight or with his boots on; dying in a hotel bedroom his last words were *'This is funny'* after noticing his bare feet.

GEORGE ENGEL
15 April 1836–11 November 1887

'Hurrah for anarchy! This is the happiest moment of my life!'

Last words from the scaffold, from the *Chicago Daily News* report on the
execution of George Engel, Albert Parsons, Adolph Fischer and August Spies

'Seldom, if ever, have four men died more gamely and defiantly than
the four who were strangled today. Engel smiled down at the crowd,
and then turning to Deputy Peters, who guarded him, he smiled grate-
fully toward him and whispered something to the officer that seemed
to affect him. "Hurrah for anarchy! Hurrah!" were the last words and
the last cheer of George Engel.'

There is some confusion about who said what on the gallows, with Lloyd
Chaisson reporting in *The Press on Trial: Crimes and Trials as Media Events* (1997):

'The heads of the men were covered with black hoods. Suddenly, Spies
called out from within his hood "There will come a time when our
silence will be more eloquent than the voices you strangle today!" Fifty-
year-old Adolph Fischer loudly proclaimed "Hurrah for anarchy! ..."
Before Fischer's shout ended, his companion George Engel cried "This
is the happiest moment of my life!" Confederate veteran and political
activist Albert Parsons pleaded "Will I be allowed to speak, O men of
America? Let me speak, Sheriff Matson! Let the voice of the people be
heard ..." Parsons' cry ended in mid-sentence. The trap doors fell open.
The ropes snapped taut. The four men struggled for a moment and
went limp, swaying before the spectators. The four deaths marked the
end of the beginning of the first nationwide "Red Scare"...'

The four men were executed as examples after the Haymarket Riot in Chicago,
although there were many witnesses to say that they could not have thrown any
bomb. On 1 May 1886, a strike in favour of the eight-hour day was held across
America. Employers were shocked by the levels of support from the workers.
Police shot and killed four workers at a meeting in Chicago, so August Spies
called for a mass protest meeting at Haymarket Square. A bomb was thrown from
a side alley killing eight policemen, and the police immediately attacked the
crowd, killing up to 30 people and wounding over 200.

> **'Shed not for her the bitter tear,**
> **Nor give the heart to vain regret;**
> **'Tis but the casket that lies here,**
> **The gem that filled it sparkles yet.'**

Epitaph by her daughter

Belle was born in Carthage, Missouri, and was an accomplished pianist. Growing up with Cole Younger, she later befriended the James brothers. When the outlaws of the James–Younger gang needed to hide out, they often stayed at her family's farm. In 1866, Belle Maybelle Shirley married Jim Reed, a former Confederate army guerrilla. Finding it difficult to make a living from subsistence farming, he joined the Starrs, a Cherokee Indian family known for horse stealing. With Belle's friends the James–Younger gang they began robbing, but Reed was killed while trying to escape from custody after being arrested for theft. Belle now took over the organizing and planning of robberies, and began fencing stolen goods. She bribed lawmen and sometimes seduced them to ensure no one was caught. In 1880 she married Sam Starr, and two years later both of them were convicted of stealing horses, being sentenced to a year in gaol.

Belle was murdered two days before she was to turn 41. She was shot in the back while riding home from the general store to her ranch near Eufaula, Oklahoma. She fell from her horse, which bolted, and was hit by a second blast from a shotgun as she lay on the ground. Her killer has never been identified. The main suspect was fugitive Edgar Watson, with whom Belle had been feuding over the land he was renting from her (she had been told by the authorities that she would lose her land if caught harbouring fugitives, and for once she was doing what she was told). Other suspects included an associate or lover, a Cherokee named Jim July, her son Ed, and even her daughter Pearl, all of whom had recently argued with her. Belle was buried on her ranch with a marble headstone on which was engraved a bell, her horse, a star and the above epitaph written by her daughter Pearl.

CROWFOOT
c.1830–25 April 1890

'What is life? It is a flash of a firefly in the night.'

Deathbed speech to his people, 25 April 1890

'A little while and I will be gone from among you. Whither, I cannot tell. From nowhere we came; into nowhere we go. What is life? It is the flash of a firefly in the night. It is the breath of a buffalo in the winter time. It is as the little shadow that runs across the grass and loses itself in the sunset.' Born a Blood Indian, Crowfoot grew up among the Blackfoot. As a teenager, he showed great bravery in a battle by advancing and striking a painted tipi in the hostile Crow camp. For this action he was given his dead elder brother's name, Isapo-muxika, meaning 'Crow Indian's Big Foot', shortened by interpreters to Crowfoot. He went to war 19 times and was wounded six times. In 1874 he welcomed the Mounted Police when they came to stamp out the whisky trade:

'My brother, your words make me glad. I listened to them not only with my ears but with my heart also. In the coming of the Long Knives, with their firewater and quick-shooting guns, we are weak and our people have been woefully slain and impoverished. You say this will be stopped. We are glad to have it stopped. We want peace. What you tell us about this strong power which will govern good law and treat the Indian the same as the white man, makes us glad to hear. My brother, I believe you, and am thankful.'

He was given a prominent role in peace negotiations in 1877: *'The Mounted Police have protected us as the feathers of the bird protect it from the frosts of winter. I wish all my people good and trust that all our hearts will increase in goodness from this time forward. I am satisfied. I will sign the Treaty.'* After the Blackfoot settled on their reserve in 1881, he became disillusioned with the Canadian government, but he refused to allow his people to join the 1885 North-West Rebellion, because he thought it was a losing fight. His last request to them was to be good and remain friendly to the whites.

VINCENT WILLEM VAN GOGH
30 March 1853–29 July 1890

'The sadness will last forever'

Last words, to his brother Theo the day before he died

The Dutch Post-Impressionist painter Van Gogh did not started painting until his late twenties, and most of his best-known works were produced during his final two years. On 27 July 1890, he was found injured in bed. Struggling with his lack of success as a painter, as well as depression and mental illness, he had gone out to a nearby field and shot himself in the chest. He survived the impact, and not realizing that his injuries were to be fatal, walked back to his room in the Ravoux Inn, where his brother Theo found him. Theo cared for him for two days, trying to persuade him that everything would be all right. Vincent answered, '*La tristesse durera toujours*' ('*The sadness will last forever*'), dying the following day. Although he had sent a letter to Theo only three days earlier, he was carrying another letter to his brother on his person when he shot himself, which is widely regarded as a suicide note:

'My dear brother, Thanks for your kind letter and for the 50-fr. note in contained. There are many things I should like to write you about, but I feel it useless. I hope you have found those worthy gentlemen favourably disposed toward you. Your reassuring me as to the peacefulness of your household was hardly worth the trouble, I think, having seen the weal and woe of it for myself ... Well, the truth is, we can only make our pictures speak ... Well, my own work, I am risking my life for it and my reason has half foundered because of it – that's all right – but you are not among the dealers in men as far as I know, and you can still choose your side, I think, acting with humanity, but que veux-tu?'

SITTING BULL (TATANKA IYOTAKA)
c.1831–15 December 1890

'**I am not going. Do with me what you like. I am not going. Come on! Come on! Take action! Let's go!**'

Attributed last words

This **Hunkpapa Lakota Sioux** holy man was the principal chief of the Dakota Sioux, who played a prominent role in defeating and massacring General Custer's party at Little Bighorn. Driven from their lands in the Black Hills by miners, they were forced to live on a reservation. In 1890, James McLaughlin, Indian Agent at Standing Rock Reservation, sent the Indian Constabulary to arrest Sitting Bull for fomenting unrest:

'Acting under these orders, a force of thirty-nine policemen and four volunteers ... entered the camp at daybreak on December 15th, proceeding direct to Sitting Bull's house, which ten of them entered, and Lieut. Bull Head announced to him the object of their mission. Sitting Bull accepted his arrest quietly at first, and commenced dressing for the journey to the Agency, during which ... considerable time his son, "Crow Foot", who was in the house, commenced berating his father for accepting the arrest and consenting to go with the police; whereupon Sitting Bull got stubborn and refused to accompany them.

Sitting Bull kept calling upon his followers to rescue him from the police; that if the two principal men, Bull Head and Shave Head, were killed the others would run away, and he finally called out for them to commence the attack, whereupon Catch the Bear and Strike the Kettle, two of Sitting Bull's men, dashed through the crowd and fired ... Catch the Bear's shot struck Bull Head in the right side, and he instantly wheeled and shot Sitting Bull, hitting him in the left side, between the tenth and eleventh ribs, and Strike the Kettle's shot having passed through Shave Head's abdomen, all three fell together. Catch the Bear, who fired the first shot, was immediately shot down by private of police Lone Man, and the fight then became general ...'

PHINEAS TAYLOR BARNUM
5 July 1810–7 April 1891

'Great And Only Barnum – He Wanted To Read His Obituary – Here It Is.'

Obituary printed two weeks before he died, in
the *New York Evening Sun* of 24 March 1891

Barnum was 15 years old when his father died, becoming a publisher and then a showman who presented a wizened black woman, the '161-year-old nurse to General George Washington'. Next, he bought the American Museum in New York City, turning it into a sensationalist 'freak show' of animals and people such as lambs with two heads, Siamese twins and the dwarf 'General Tom Thumb', and hoaxes such as the 'Feejee Mermaid'. He then risked his considerable fortune by bringing Jenny Lind, 'the Swedish Nightingale', to tour the USA, achieving a spectacular success. Calling himself 'the Prince of Humbugs', he was elected mayor of Bridgeport, Connecticut, fighting prostitution and union discrimination against blacks. In 1855 he published his autobiography, selling a million copies, and then allowing anyone to print it without copyright to achieve more publicity. Aged 60, he and James A. Bailey innovated the three-ring circus of Ringling Brothers and Barnum and Bailey. In partnership with Bailey, he made the American circus a gigantic spectacle, the 'Greatest Show on Earth'.

Aged 80 and knowing he was dying, Barnum asked the *New York Evening Sun* if he could see his own obituary, claiming that the press only said nice things about people after they died. He gave them permission to print the obituary so that he could read it, and it was run on the front page with the above headline. Two weeks later, Barnum died in his sleep in his Connecticut mansion. It is said that his last words were: '*Ask Bailey what the box office was at the [Madison Square] Garden last night*' (*The Independent*, 10 January 2004). The *Times* obituary read: '*He created the métier of showman on a grandiose scale ... He early realized that essential feature of a modern democracy, its readiness to be led to what will amuse and instruct it ... His name is a proverb already, and a proverb it will continue.*'

PYOTR ILICH TCHAIKOVSKY
7 May 1840–6 November 1893

'Tchaikovsky thought of committing suicide for fear of being discovered as a homosexual, but today, if you are a composer and not homosexual, you might as well put a bullet through your head'

Sergei Diaghilev

The Russian wrote the ballets *Swan Lake, The Sleeping Beauty* and *The Nutcracker;* the *1812 Overture,* seven symphonies, the opera *Eugene Onegin* and a famous piano concerto. In 1879 his marriage fell apart, and his wife Antonina kept changing her mind when Tchaikovsky wanted a divorce. He seemed to be terrified that she would reveal his true sexuality and wrote: *'I am a deceiver who married her in order to hide my true nature ... I insulted her every day, her sufferings at my hands were great ... she is appalled by my shameful vice, etc., etc.'*

While his death was traditionally thought to have been due to cholera, authorities today believe that he committed suicide. Allegedly, his fellow alumni of the St Petersburg Imperial School of Jurisprudence held a 'court of honour' and told him to kill himself because of his homosexuality. This theory first received widespread publicity when the Russian musicologist Alexandra Orlova came to the West in 1979, since when many other historians and musicologists seem to have agreed. Solomon Volkov wrote that even before Tchaikovsky's death, his final work, the Symphony No. 6, 'Pathétique', was regarded as his personal requiem to the world. One musical clue is that the trombone theme bears no relation to the music that precedes or follows it, and is taken from the Russian Orthodox Mass for the Dead, in which it is sung to the words: *'And may his soul rest with the souls of all the saints.'* Tchaikovsky conducted the symphony's première nine days before his death. In 2001, Roland John Wiley wrote: *'The polemics over death have reached an impasse ... Rumour attached to the famous die hard ... As for illness, problems of evidence offer little hope of satisfactory resolution: the state of diagnosis; the confusion of witnesses; disregard of long-term effects of smoking and alcohol. We do not know how Tchaikovsky died. We may never find out ...'*

ROBERT LEWIS (later altered to LOUIS)
BALFOUR STEVENSON
13 November 1850–3 December 1894

'What's that? Do I look strange?'

Dying words as he suffered a stroke

This novelist, travel writer and poet wrote *Treasure Island, The Strange Case of Dr Jekyll and Mr Hyde, The Master of Ballantrae* and *Kidnapped*. In poor health from 1880, he settled in Samoa in 1890 to recuperate, but probably died of a cerebral haemorrhage. His biographer wrote:

'The climate of Samoa had apparently answered the main purpose of preserving Stevenson from any disabling attacks of illness, and allowing him to lead a life of strenuous activity ... In all the time he was in Samoa he had but two or three slight haemorrhages, that were cured within a very few days. The consumption in his lungs was definitely arrested, but it seems certain that a structural weakening of the arteries was slowly and inevitably going on ... he gave up even the very moderate quantity of red wine which seemed to be a necessity of life to him, and worst deprivation of all he abandoned at these times the cigarettes which usually he smoked all day long. He wrote hard all that morning of the last day; his half-finished book, [Weir of] Hermiston, he judged the best he had ever written, and the sense of successful effort made him buoyant and happy as nothing else could ...

At sunset he came downstairs; rallied his wife about the forebodings she could not shake off; talked of a lecturing tour to America that he was eager to make, "as he was now so well", and played a game at cards with her to drive away her melancholy. He said he was hungry; begged her assistance to help him make a salad for the evening meal; and to enhance the little feast, he brought up a bottle of old Burgundy from the cellar. He was helping his wife on the verandah, and gaily talking, when suddenly he put both hands to his head, and cried out, "What's that?" Then he asked quickly, "Do I look strange?" Even as he did so he fell on his knees beside her. He was helped into the great hall, between his wife and his body-servant, Sosimo, losing consciousness instantly, as he lay back in the armchair that had once been his grand-father's ...'

WILLIAM MORRIS
24 March 1834–3 October 1896

'Do you ever think about death?'

Conversation with Bruce Glasier towards the end of his life

J.W. Mackail, who knew Morris, wrote his authorized biography *The Life of William Morris* in 1899. In it he related how the family doctor had diagnosed that Morris had *'died a victim of his enthusiasm for spreading the principles of socialism'*, believing that he had developed lung problems through constant exposure to the elements in travelling to and attending socialist meetings. An architect, furniture and textile designer, poet, writer, artist, translator, medievalist, printer, publisher, utopian socialist and leading socialist thinker, Morris founded the Pre-Raphaelite 'Brotherhood' with Edward Burne-Jones, which attracted like-minded people including Dante Gabriel Rossetti, Holman Hunt, Millais, and Ford Madox Brown. He also founded the Society for the Protection of Ancient Buildings, the English 'Arts and Crafts' movement and the Socialist League.

'One evening, probably the last I spent with him, sitting in the library, he asked abruptly: "Do you ever think about death? I hate to think about it, but my illness has forced the thought of it on me, worse luck. Yes, I hate it, but I don't fear it. I love life, I love the world. The world contains everything beautiful and joyful. I know of no happiness that I can desire, no life that I should wish to live, that could give me more happiness than this world and life can give. Barring human wrong-doing, and disease, decrepit old age, and death, I see no imperfection in it. Heaven, or another life beyond the grave, of which men dream and hope so fondly, could give me nothing which I possess the faculties to use or enjoy, that the present world and life cannot give, except maybe were it true reunion with those who have gone before or who will shortly afterwards follow. Human wrong-doing and perhaps disease can be got rid of: but old age and death are irremediable. Sometimes death appears to me awful, terrible, so cruel, so absurd. Yet there are times when I don't have that feeling and death seems sweet and desirable. I sometimes think how sweet it would be to lie in the earth at the feet of the grass and flowers, if only I could see the old church, and the meadow, and hear the birds and the voices of the village folk. But that, of course, would not be death; and I suppose that I should soon want to be up and doing. No, I cannot think it out. It is inexplicable."'

LEWIS CARROLL (CHARLES LUTWIDGE DODGSON)
27 January 1832–14 January 1898

'Take away those pillows – I shall need them no more'
Instructions given on the day before his death

The author of *Alice's Adventures in Wonderland* and *Through the Looking-Glass* was also a mathematician. He died of bronchitis. His nephew recorded Carroll's last hours:

'He determined to travel north the next day – but it was not to be so. An attack of influenza, which began only with slight hoarseness, yet enough to prevent him from following his usual habit of reading family prayers, was pronounced next morning to be sufficiently serious to forbid his undertaking a journey. At first his illness seemed a trifle, but before a week had passed bronchial symptoms had developed, and Dr Gabb, the family physician, ordered him to keep his bed. His breathing rapidly became hard and laborious, and he had to be propped up with pillows. A few days before his death he asked one of his sisters to read him that well-known hymn, every verse of which ends with "Thy Will be done". To another he said that his illness was a great trial of his patience. How great a trial it must have been it is hard for us to understand. With the work he had set himself still uncompleted, with a sense of youth and joyousness, which sixty years of the battle of life had in no way dulled, Lewis Carroll had to face death.

He seemed to know that the struggle was over. "Take away those pillows," he said on the 13th, "I shall need them no more." The end came about half-past two on the afternoon of the 14th. One of his sisters was in the room at the time, and she only noticed that the hard breathing suddenly ceased. The nurse, whom she summoned, at first hoped that this was a sign that he had taken a turn for the better. And so, indeed, he had – he had passed from a world of incompleteness and disappointment, to another where God is putting his beautiful soul to nobler and grander work than was possible for him here, where he is learning to comprehend those difficulties which used to puzzle him so much, and where that infinite Love, which he mirrored so wonderfully in his own life, is being revealed to him "face to face".'

'The G.O.M., when his life ebbs out, Will ride in a fiery chariot, And sit in state On a red-hot plate Between Pilate and Judas Iscariot.'

Contemporary limerick blaming the 'Grand Old Man'
for the death of General Gordon at Khartoum

Gladstone was Liberal prime minister in 1868–74, 1880–85, 1886 and 1892–94. After retiring in 1894 he wrote: *'I am thankful to have borne a part in the emancipating labours of the last sixty years; but entirely uncertain how, had I now to begin my life, I could face the very different problems of the next sixty years. Of one thing I am, and always have been, convinced – it is not by the State that man can be regenerated, and the terrible woes of this darkened world effectually dealt with.'*

Ill for some time, he suffered with mouth cancer for a year before it was diagnosed correctly. His doctors thought he had exaggerated the discomfort caused by 'nasal catarrh'. Patricia Jalland (*Death in the Victorian Family*, 1996) tells us that on 4 April he took final communion, as it was believed he was about to die: *'He thought his last hours were near, and sent for us all that were in reach, to give us his farewell blessing ... Physically, he seemed absolutely crushed under the dominion of pain – baffled, beaten, conquered – as he often said. But in the soul, the spirit, the Victory was absolute.'* Three weeks later there was another 'last words' event with Gladstone's doctors, his wife Mary listening from behind the door: *'He was very clear and definitely raised himself to ask them questions, – generally to bear testimony as to the gratitude he felt for all that was being done for him. He seemed deliberately to pull himself together, and mentioned by name and in what special particulars he owed thanks to Doctors, Nurses, servants, friends, relations and strangers.'* On 15 May, the 'Grand Old Man' slipped into a kind of coma but was still distressed with pain, and after more false alarms he finally died on 19 May. The future Edward VII and George V were pallbearers at Westminster Abbey.

OSCAR FINGAL O'FLAHERTIE WILLS WILDE
16 October 1854–30 November 1900

'I am dying as I have lived: beyond my means'
Attributed last words

Wilde is supposed to have said these words on his deathbed, while drinking a glass of champagne. However, their authenticity is complicated by his last-minute conversion to Catholicism, when a priest was with him to the very end. Another attribution, a month before his death, is *'My wallpaper and I are fighting a duel to the death. One or the other of us has to go.'* It is sometimes misquoted as *'Either that wallpaper goes, or I do.'* Wilde died of cerebral meningitis in the Hôtel d'Alsace in Paris. The wallpaper has since gone and the room has been refurbished in the style of one of his London flats, the hotel being renamed simply L'Hôtel.

A hugely successful playwright, poet and author, and the most celebrated wit of his day, Wilde wrote *Lady Windermere's Fan* and *The Importance of Being Earnest.* Some of his more celebrated quips are: *'To love oneself is the beginning of a lifelong romance'; 'I can resist everything except temptation'; 'A man who knows the price of everything and the value of nothing'; 'Experience is the name everyone gives to their mistakes'; 'Please do not shoot the pianist. He is doing his best';* and *'The only way to get rid of a temptation is to yield to it.'* In 1895 he was imprisoned in Reading Gaol after being convicted of homosexuality. On his release he left for France and never returned to the British Isles. His tomb in Père Lachaise cemetery was designed by Sir Jacob Epstein, and the epitaph is a verse from Wilde's *Ballad of Reading Gaol*:

> 'And alien tears will fill for him
> Pity's long-broken urn,
> For his mourners will be outcast men,
> And outcasts always mourn.'

The modernist angel on the tomb was originally complete with male genitalia, which were broken off and kept as a paperweight by a succession of cemetery keepers, but they have been lost and were replaced in 2000.

ANTON PAVLOVICH CHEKHOV
29 January 1860–15 July 1904

'It's a long time since I drank champagne'

Dying words to his wife

A practising physician, Chekhov is remembered as a superb and innovative playwright, and is considered to be one of the greatest short-story writers in history. He renounced the theatre after the poor reception of *The Seagull* in 1896, and later said: '*If I had listened to my critics, I'd have died drunk in the gutter.*' However, the play was revived in 1898 by the Moscow Art Theatre, which then also produced *Uncle Vanya, The Three Sisters* and *The Cherry Orchard.* Chekhov used the 'stream-of-consciousness' technique in his plays and stories, and did not attempt to set a moral tone, forcing audience as well as actors to think about the themes he raised.

By May 1904, he was terminally ill, his brother Mikhail recalling: '*Everyone who saw him secretly thought the end was not far off, but the nearer Chekhov was to the end, the less he seemed to realize it.*' A few months before he died, he told the writer Ivan Bunin that people might go on reading him for seven and a half years, which was not bad because he thought he had '*six years to live*'. In June he went with his wife Olga to Badenweiler, a spa town in the Black Forest. In 1908, Olga wrote this account of his dying moments:

'Anton sat up unusually straight and said loudly and clearly (although he knew almost no German): Ich sterbe [I'm dying]. The doctor calmed him, took a syringe, gave him an injection of camphor, and ordered champagne. Anton took a full glass, examined it, smiled at me and said: "It's a long time since I drank champagne." He drained it, lay quietly on his left side, and I just had time to run to him and lean across the bed and call to him, but he had stopped breathing and was sleeping peacefully as a child ...'

'On the contrary!'

Last words, after his nurse had told a visitor that he was feeling a little better

The Norwegian playwright, poet and theatre director is regarded as the founder of modern prose drama, and is ranked in the very top category of European playwrights. In 1901 his health began to decline, and he was ordered by his physician to abandon all mental effort. Suffering from depression and mental illness, he slowly declined and was bedridden. He died in Christiana (now Oslo) following a series of strokes, and was accorded a public funeral. The *Guardian* of 26 May 1906 announced his death:

'We regret to announce the death of Henrik Ibsen, which took place at Christiana yesterday afternoon ... The house in which he was born was destroyed in the great fire at Skien in 1886. It stood prominently in the market-place, face to face with the town hall, the church, the schools, the prison, the madhouse, and other visible symbols of that State-power which the future poet was so cordially to detest. But the roar of two neighbouring cataracts and the strident wail of the scores of sawmills they drove filled the air all day, begetting characteristically sombre fancies in the boy's mind. "When, at a later day," he tells us, "I read of the guillotine, I could not help thinking of those sawmills." Isolated as he seemed, his mind was yet in more vital touch than that of anyone else in Europe with the mind of this generation. Others have photographed reality with a more obvious fidelity, have created more amusing and agreeable characters, and had a more clear-cut philosophy to put in their mouths; Ibsen appalled us with sudden glimpses into the abysses of human nature at once unlike our experience and yet shooting across it vistas of interpreting and revealing light. Let it be added, strange as the tribute may sound to some who have not read him, that, having often to do with repugnant aspects of human nature, he uttered nothing base, and that, with many temptations to subserviency, he, like Hazlitt, wrote "not a line that licks the dust".'

GERONIMO, GOYATHLAY
16 June 1829–17 February 1909

'I think I could forget all the wrongs that I have ever received'

From his 1907 autobiography

This medicine man and war leader of the Chirichua Apache fought Mexican and American takeovers of his tribal lands for decades. On his deathbed, a prisoner in Oklahoma, he told his nephew that he regretted ever surrendering to the Americans, and in his autobiography wrote sadly:

'We are now held on Comanche and Kiowa lands, which are not suited to our needs ... There is no climate or soil which, to my mind, is equal to that of Arizona. We could have plenty of good cultivating land, plenty of grass, plenty of timber and plenty of minerals in that land which the Almighty created for the Apaches. It is my land, my home, my fathers' land, to which I now ask to be allowed to return. I want to spend my last days there, and be buried among those mountains. If this could be I might die in peace, feeling that my people, placed in their native homes, would increase in numbers, rather than diminish as at present, and that our name would not become extinct. I know that if my people were placed in that mountainous region lying around the head waters of the Gila River they would live in peace and act according to the will of the President. They would be prosperous and happy in tilling the soil and learning the civilization of the white men, whom they now respect. Could I but see this accomplished, I think I could forget all the wrongs that I have ever received, and die a contented and happy old man. But we can do nothing in this matter ourselves – we must wait until those in authority choose to act. If this cannot be done during my lifetime – if I must die in bondage – I hope that the remnant of the Apache tribe may, when I am gone, be granted the one privilege which they request – to return to Arizona.'

CHIEF RED CLOUD
1822–10 December 1909

'My sun is set. My day is done. Darkness is stealing over me.'

Farewell address to the Lakota people

'My sun is set. My day is done. Darkness is stealing over me. Before I lie down to rise no more, I will speak to my people. Hear me, my friends, for it is not the time for me to tell you a lie. The Great Spirit made us, the Indians, and gave us this land we live in. He gave us the buffalo, the antelope, and the deer for food and clothing. We moved our hunting grounds from the Minnesota to the Platte and from the Mississippi to the great mountains. No one put bounds on us. We were free as the winds, and like the eagle, heard no man's commands. I was born a Lakota and I shall die a Lakota. Before the white man came to our country, the Lakotas were a free people. They made their own laws and governed themselves as it seemed good to them. The priests and ministers tell us that we lived wickedly when we lived before the white man came among us. Whose fault was this? We lived right as we were taught it was right. Shall we be punished for this? I am not sure that what these people tell me is true ... Shadows are long and dark before me. I shall soon lie down to rise no more. While my spirit is with my body the smoke of my breath shall be towards the Sun for he knows all things and knows that I am still true to him.'

This war leader of the Oglala Lakota (Sioux) was one of the most capable of all the Native American chiefs, responsible for the Fetterman Massacre in 1866, and for the successful 'Red Cloud's War' in Wyoming and Montana (1866–68). The US finally agreed to withdraw from Lakota territory, and Red Cloud signed a treaty allowing them safe passage through Bozeman Pass, but from 1873 he was forced to live on reservations for the rest of his life. Charles A. Eastman recorded his words: *'They made us many promises, more than I can remember, but they never kept but one; they promised to take our land, and they took it.'*

‘Death, the only immortal, who treats us alike, whose peace and refuge are for all. The soiled and the pure, the rich and the poor, the loved and the unloved.’

Note found by his deathbed

Twain was travelling in Europe when his death was reported in the American press. There are many variations of his 'report of my death' quote, the original note from May 1897 reading: *'James Ross Clemens, a cousin of mine was seriously ill two or three weeks ago in London, but is well now. The report of my illness grew out of his illness, the report of my death was an exaggeration.'* This response to a premature obituary was sent to the *New York Times* on 2 June 1897. From 1896, Twain had been deeply depressed by the deaths of his favourite daughter Susy, then his wife Olivia in 1904, his great friend Henry Rogers in 1909 and his daughter Jean on Christmas Eve 1909. On 8 April 1910 in Bermuda, he suffered his second and almost fatal heart attack, and returned to Connecticut to recuperate.

In 1909, Twain had said: *'I came in with Halley's Comet in 1835. It is coming again next year, and I expect to go out with it. It will be the greatest disappointment of my life if I don't go out with Halley's Comet. The Almighty has said, no doubt: "Now here are these two unaccountable freaks; they came in together, they must go out together."'* His prediction was accurate, as he died several days after a third heart attack, and one day after the comet's closest approach to Earth. Albert Bigelow Paine's contemporary biography informs us: *'"Good-bye," he said, and Dr Quintard, who was standing near, thought he added: "If we meet" – but the words were very faint. He looked at her for a little while, without speaking, then he sank into a doze, and from it passed into a deeper slumber, and did not heed us any more.'* President Taft eulogized: *'Twain gave pleasure – real intellectual enjoyment – to millions, and his works will continue to give such pleasure to millions yet to come.'*

EDWARD VII, ALBERT EDWARD OF SAXE-COBURG AND GOTHA, KING OF THE UNITED KINGDOM AND THE BRITISH DOMINIONS, EMPEROR OF INDIA
9 November 1841–6 May 1910

'I am very glad'
Dying words

Before his accession in 1901, Edward had been Victoria's heir for a record 60 years, during which time he acquired a reputation as a playboy. In 1861, aged 20 and wishing to acquire army experience, he attended manoeuvres in Ireland. An actress, Nellie Clifton, was hidden in his tent by fellow officers. Queen Victoria and Prince Albert were horrified, and Albert, although ill, visited Edward at Cambridge to reprimand him, dying just two weeks after the visit. Queen Victoria was inconsolable. She blamed the Prince of Wales for her husband's death, and wore mourning clothes for the remaining 40 years of her rule. She regarded her son with distaste, and wrote to her eldest daughter, '*I never can, or shall, look at him without a shudder.*' The queen withdrew almost completely from public life, and Edward represented her at state occasions but was still not allowed to participate in affairs of state. He spent his days with mistresses including Lily Langtry, and eating, drinking, gambling, shooting, watching racing and sailing. In 1863, he married Princess Alexandra of Denmark and they had six children.

When he eventually succeeded to the throne, his reign brought sparkle to a monarchy that been extremely dour since his father's death 40 years earlier. Related to most European royalty, and being regarded as 'the Uncle of Europe', he assisted in foreign policy negotiations and helped pave the way for the Anglo-French Entente Cordiale of 1904. He regularly smoked 20 cigarettes and 12 cigars a day, so began suffering increasingly from bronchitis. He had several heart attacks, but refused to go to bed, saying, '*No, I shall not give in; I shall go on; I shall work to the end.*' On his deathbed, the Prince of Wales (the future George V) told Edward that his horse, Witch of the Air, had won at Kempton Park that afternoon. The king replied, '*I am very glad*', and died soon afterwards.

O. HENRY (WILLIAM SYDNEY PORTER)
11 September 1862–5 June 1910

'Turn up the lights; I don't want to go home in the dark'

Last words, quoting a 1907 song by Harry Williams

A writer of witty short stories with surprise endings, O. Henry's life included a spell in prison, his first wife dying and his second life leaving him. These factors and the pressures of success caused him to drink heavily, and he died of cirrhosis of the liver, diabetes complications and an enlarged heart. His biographer wrote:

> 'The end was near but not much nearer, I think, than he knew. To Mr Moyle he remarked with a shrug of the shoulders and a whimsical smile: "It'll probably be In the Good Old Summer Time." A few years before, the question of the after-life had come up casually in conversation and O. Henry had been asked what he thought of it. His reply was: "I had a little dog, and his name was Rover, / And when he died, he died all over."

During the last months the question emerged again. An intimate friend's father had died and O. Henry was eager to know how he had felt about the hereafter. "For myself," he said, "I think we are like little chickens tapping on their shells." On the afternoon of June 3, Mr Gilman Hall received a telephone message: "Can you come down right away, Colonel?" His friends were all Colonel or Bill to him. He had collapsed after sending the message and was lying on the floor when Mr Hall arrived. Dr Charles Russell Hancock was sent for and O. Henry was taken at once to the Polyclinic Hospital on East Thirty-Fourth Street ... He insisted on stopping to shake hands with the manager of the Caledonia and to exchange a cheery good-bye. He asked that his family be sent for and then quietly gave directions about the disposition of his papers ... "He was perfectly conscious until within two minutes of his death Sunday morning," said Doctor Hancock, "and knew that the end was approaching. I never saw a man pluckier in facing it or in bearing pain. Nothing appeared to worry him at the last." There was no pain now and just before sunrise he said with a smile to those about him: "Turn up the lights; I don't want to go home in the dark." ... He did not go home in the dark. The sun light was upon his face when he passed and illumines still his name and fame.'

COUNT LEV NIKOLAYEVICH 'LEO' TOLSTOY
9 September 1828–20 November 1910

'We all reveal ... our manifestations ... This manifestation is over ... That's all ...'

Dying words

One of the greatest novelists, the author of *War and Peace* and *Anna Karenina*, Tolstoy escaped from his ancestral estate at the age of 82 to begin a new life as a simple Russian peasant. He got as far as the small town of Astapovo, where he contracted pneumonia, dying a few days later in the stationmaster's house. According to the stationmaster, his last words were: '*But the peasants ... how do the peasants die?*' His close friend and secretary Vladimir Chertkov wrote his account of Tolstoy's death in a small booklet:

'On the eve of Tolstoy's death, at the request of the doctors, I administered oxygen to Tolstoy from a rubber bag. I did this for some time. When, at long last, I stopped, Tolstoy said: "Completely useless."... Leo Tolstoy's actual death was so quiet and so peaceful that I felt a certain sense of relief. After many hours, Tolstoy's heavy breathing suddenly became slight and superficial. Several minutes later, even this weak breathing came to an end. Then an interval of complete silence. No strain, no struggle. Then a barely audible, very deep, protracted, final sigh ... Looking at the shell of what was once Leo Nikolayevich Tolstoy, I recalled overhearing the night before some of the workings of his inner life. I was sitting alone with him by his bed. He was lying on his back, breathing heavily. Evidently giving expression to the thread of thoughts that occupied him, Tolstoy all of a sudden – as if arguing with himself – broke out in a loud voice: "We all reveal ... our manifestations ... This manifestation is over ... That's all ..." I remembered Tolstoy's conception of human life, namely, that man is a manifestation of the spirit of God temporarily imprisoned within the confines of his individual existence and seeking to break out and merge with the souls of others and with God. And I felt with especial force that life, understood in this way, was a blessing that was absolutely inviolate. In short, death was no more.'

DR HAWLEY HARVEY CRIPPEN
11 September 1862–23 November 1910

'My last prayer will be that God will protect her and keep her safe from harm and allow her to join me in eternity'

Statement on eve of execution, referring to his co-defendant Ethel le Neve

In a sensational trial, Dr Crippen was found guilty of murdering his wife. His mistress, Ethel le Neve, was found not guilty. A century later, in the *Daily Telegraph* of 7 June 2009, we read that

'The case of Dr Crippen could be referred to the Court of Appeal after the Criminal Cases Review Commission received an application relating to the homeopath. Should it be referred and subsequently overturned, it would mean a posthumous pardon 99 years after he was hanged and the longest miscarriage of justice in British history. Crippen, an American doctor, was accused of murdering his wife Cora when she disappeared from their London home after a party. Police conducted a search of the house and the remains of a human body were discovered buried under the brick floor of the basement. After attempting to flee the country with his mistress, Dr Crippen was arrested, subsequently found guilty and hanged in 1910. The centre of the case is DNA evidence that suggests the body discovered in the basement was not that of Cora Crippen but a man's. According to prosecutors at his Old Bailey trial in 1910, Dr Crippen poisoned his wife before dismembering her. Police found a corpse with no head, bones or genitals.

Dr Crippen had always protested his innocence and claimed his wife had returned to the USA. Acting for Patrick Crippen, a relative of the doctor, lawyer Giovanni Di Stefano, who was one of Saddam Hussein's defence team, told the *Observer* newspaper: "We have been told categorically that the case is being referred and we are now just waiting for the paperwork. The body was a man and so the pardon is deserved."'

CAPTAIN LAWRENCE EDWARD GRACE OATES
17 March 1880–17 March 1912

'I am just going outside and may be some time'

Journal entry, 17 March 1912 (Scott was unsure if it was 16 or 17 March)

Educated at Eton, Oates saw service in India, Egypt and South Africa, and was badly wounded in the Boer War. Owing to his injury, one leg was an inch shorter than the other. In 1910, he volunteered to join Robert Scott's expedition to the Antarctic, hoping to be the first men to reach the South Pole. He was accepted mainly on the strength of his experience with horses, and because he made a financial contribution of £1,000 towards the expedition. He wrote in his diary: '*Myself, I dislike Scott intensely and would chuck the whole thing if it were not that we are a British expedition ... He [Scott] is not straight, it is himself first, the rest nowhere ...*' Scott eventually selected Oates as one of the five-man party who would travel the last 167 miles to the Pole.

Despite malfunctioning equipment and terrible weather, the party, consisting of Scott, Wilson, Bowers, Evans and Oates, reached the South Pole on 17 January, only to find that the Norwegian explorer Roald Amundsen had arrived there a month earlier. Severe weather and lack of food and water affected the 800-mile return trip to the base camp. Evans died on 17 February, and their progress was further hampered by Oates' Boer War wound, aggravated by scurvy and frostbitten feet, which slowed the whole party. On 15 March, he told his companions that he could not go on and proposed that they leave him in his sleeping bag, which they refused to do. On the 17th – his thirty-second birthday – Oates, knowing he was a burden, left the tent and went willingly to his death. Scott wrote in his diary: '*We knew that poor Oates was walking to his death, but though we tried to dissuade him, we knew it was the act of a brave man and an English gentleman.*' The remaining party became trapped by blizzards and died within 11 miles of the base camp.

CAPTAIN ROBERT FALCON SCOTT
6 June 1868–29 March 1912

'For God's sake look after our people'

Last diary entry

'Thursday, March 29 – Since the 21st we have had a continuous gale from W.S.W. and S.W. We had fuel to make two cups of tea apiece and bare food for two days on the 20th. Every day we have been ready to start for our depot 11 miles away, but outside the door of the tent it remains a scene of whirling drift. I do not think we can hope for any better things now. We shall stick it out to the end, but we are getting weaker, of course, and the end cannot be far. It seems a pity, but I do not think I can write more. R. Scott. Last entry. For God's sake look after our people.'

Scott's first expedition, with Ernest Shackleton on the *Discovery* (1901–04), took him within 450 miles of the South Pole before he had to turn back. He later led the Terra Nova expedition (1910–13), which reached the pole on 17 January 1912, only to discover that Roald Amundsen had been there 35 days earlier. That day, Scott wrote in his journal: *'The worst has happened'* and *'Great God! This is an awful place.'* On the 800-mile return trip, team members Edgar Evans and Lawrence Oates died on 17 February and 16 March respectively. On 19 March, Scott, Dr Wilson and Lieutenant Bowers made their final camp, and on the 23rd, Scott gave up writing his diary, except for the above entry.

He also left the following Message to the Public, a defence of the expedition's organization ending on an inspirational note with these words:

'We took risks, we knew we took them; things have come out against us, and therefore we have no cause for complaint, but bow to the will of Providence, determined still to do our best to the last ... Had we lived, I should have had a tale to tell of the hardihood, endurance, and courage of my companions which would have stirred the heart of every Englishman. These rough notes and our dead bodies must tell the tale, but surely, surely, a great rich country like ours will see that those who are dependent on us are properly provided for. R. Scott.'

COLONEL JOHN JACOB ASTOR IV
13 July 1864–15 April 1912

'Ladies, you are next ... hold that boat'

Instructions given by Astor on board the *Titanic*

In an article entitled 'Astor Saved Us, Say Women', the *New York Times* of 22 April 1912 gave the following account:

'Mrs Ida S. Hippach and her daughter, Jean, survivors of the Titanic, who arrived home to-day, said that they were saved by Col. John Jacob Astor, who forced the crew of the last lifeboat to wait for them. "We saw Col. Astor place Mrs Astor in a boat and heard him assure her that he would follow later," said Mrs Hippach. "He turned to us with a smile and said 'Ladies, you are next.' The officer in charge of the boat protested that the craft was full and the seamen started to lower it. Col. Astor exclaimed, 'Hold that boat' in the voice of a man to be obeyed, and the men did as he ordered. The boat had been ordered past the upper deck, and the Colonel took us to the next deck below and put us in the boat, one after the other, through a porthole." Mrs Hippach said that after the impact the Titanic lay broadside on an iceberg that seemed, she said, to be a hundred feet high and extended farther than she could see.'

Astor was easily was the richest man in the world, worth around $40 billion in today's money. He owned over 700 prime Manhattan properties and was chairman of more than 20 different companies. In 1897 he built the Astoria, 'the world's most luxurious hotel', to adjoin his cousin William Waldorf Astor's Waldorf Hotel. The complex became known as the Waldorf–Astoria. When his new wife Madeleine became pregnant, Astor booked a passage from Cherbourg to New York on the maiden voyage of the *Titanic*. After the ship struck the iceberg, his wife was ushered to one of the last lifeboats. Astor asked if he could get into the boat too, on account of Madeleine's 'delicate condition', but was told to wait until all the women and children were taken off the sinking ship. He threw his gloves to Madeleine, saying that he would see her later. She survived, but Astor died, along with 1,500 other passengers, when the ship sank.

EMILY WILDING DAVISON
11 October 1872–8 June 1913

'So greatly did she care for freedom that she died for it'

Christabel Pankhurst, writing two days after Davison's death

Davison worked as a school teacher to raise enough money to study at St Hugh's College, achieving first-class honours in her final exams, although women were not given degrees at that time. She began teaching the children of a Berkshire family and in 1906 joined the Women's Social and Politican Union (WSPU), campaigning for votes and other rights for women. She was imprisoned seven times, and was force-fed when on hunger strike in Strangeways Prison. On one occasion she barricaded herself in a prison cell to escape the force-feeding. Her cell was flooded with ice-cold water, which drenched her while workmen broke down the door. Such treatment only made her even more determined. She threw herself down an iron staircase in Holloway Prison, to try to kill herself and draw attention to the cause, but was saved by wire netting thirty feet below. She sustained severe spinal damage in the attempt, which caused her pain for the rest of her life.

On 4 June 1913, she ran in front of the king's horse Anmer at the Epsom Derby and was trampled underfoot. Her skull was fractured and she sustained internal injuries. It is possible that she expected the horse to stop, and that she then hoped to drape the WSPU banner around it. The return train ticket in her coat pocket indicated that she did not intend to commit suicide.

After four days of lying unconscious, however, she died, and is buried in the churchyard of St Mary the Virgin, Morpeth, Northumberland. Her headstone bears the suffrage slogan '*Deeds Not Words*'. Herbert Jones, the King's jockey, suffered a mild concussion, but said he was '*haunted by that woman's face*' and committed suicide in 1951. Eleven years after Davison's death, at the suffragette Emmeline Pankhurst's funeral, Jones laid a wreath '*to do honour to the memory of Mrs Pankhurst and Miss Emily Davison*'. Emmeline herself had written in *My Own Story* that Emily had decided that only the loss of her life '*would put an end to the intolerable torture of women*'.

'As to me, I leave here tomorrow for an unknown destination'

Last line of last letter, sent to Blanche Partington on 26 December 1913

Another 'last letter', postmarked Chihuahua City and also dated 26 December 1913, was sent to Bierce's secretary/companion Carrie Christiansen in Washington. Christiansen destroyed the letter, but it is summarized in Richard O'Connor's biography: 'Trainload of troops leaving Chihuahua every day. Expect next day to go to Ojinaga, partly by rail.' Ojinaga, 125 miles north-east of Chihuahua City, across the Rio Grande from Presidio, Texas, was where Pancho Villa's revolutionaries had trapped federal troops.

In October 1913, at the age of 71, Bierce had decided to quit the United States and observe the Pancho Villa revolution in Mexico. The revolution lasted from 1910 until 1920. Before leaving, he wrote to his niece Lora:

'Dear Lora, I go away tomorrow for a long time, so this is only to say good-bye. I think there is nothing else worth saying; therefore you will naturally expect a long letter. What an intolerable world this would be if we said nothing but what is worth saying! And did nothing foolish – like going into Mexico and South America. I'm hoping that you will go to the mine soon. You must hunger and thirst for the mountains – Carlt [Lora's husband Carlton] likewise. So do I. Civilization be dinged! – It is the mountains and the desert for me. Good-bye – if you hear of my being stood up against a Mexican stone wall and shot to rags please know that I think that a pretty good way to depart his life. It beats old age, disease, or falling down the cellar stairs. To be a Gringo in Mexico – ah, that is euthanasia! With love to Carlt, affectionately yours, Ambrose.'

Lora received another short letter from Bierce on 6 November, reporting that he was in Laredo, Texas. It concluded: 'I shall not be here long enough to hear from you, and don't know where I shall be next. Guess it doesn't matter much. Adios, Ambrose.' She never heard from the humorous writer again, and his death remains a mystery.

ARCHDUKE FRANZ FERDINAND OF AUSTRIA
18 December 1863–28 June 1914

'It is nothing ... It is nothing ...'

Dying words whispered to Count Harrach as the Archduke
fell unconscious after being shot

Franz Ferdinand's last words were *'Sophie, Sophie! Don't die! Live for our children!'* followed by six or seven utterances of *'It is nothing ...'* This was followed by a long death rattle. The archduke was dead on arrival at the Governor's Residence. His wife Sophie died ten minutes later. In an earlier attack on the couple, a grenade had been thrown at their car. Ferdinand had deflected the grenade and it had detonated far behind them. Afterwards, he interrupted the mayor's welcome speech at Sarajevo Town Hall, angrily shouting: *'So you welcome your guests with bombs. What is the good of your speeches? I come to Sarajevo on a visit, and I get bombs thrown at me. It is outrageous!'* The royal couple decided to visit the injured in hospital, but on the way their driver got lost, and they were spotted by one of six assassins stationed along their route.

Franz Ferdinand, the nephew of Emperor Francis Joseph, was the heir to the Austro-Hungarian thrones and favoured the reorganization of Austria–Hungary to create a third kingdom in Bosnia. This had antagonized many Serbian nationals, who wished to annex Bosnia themselves. It was one of these revolutionaries, Gavrilo Princip, who spotted the royal couple's car. He approached and shot both Sophie, striking her in the abdomen, and Franz, who was hit in the jugular and was still alive when witnesses arrived to render aid.

The Serbian government had officially condoned and possibly funded the assassination. Austria responded by issuing an ultimatum to Serbia; both nations mobilized their armies, and Russia quickly did the same, declaring that she would fight alongside Serbia. Germany readied her own army in response to the Russian build-up and demanded that France, a Russian ally, should not mobilize her forces. When France refused to accede to the German demand, the German army began its march through Belgium, and the Great War began. If Franz Ferdinand's driver had not got lost, world history would have taken a different path.

RUPERT CHAWNER BROOKE
3 August 1887–23 April 1915

'If I should die, think only this of me …'

Last poem

Brooke's last poem, 'The Soldier', from the five-sonnet sequence *1914*, was written after his participation in the ill-fated five-day Antwerp Expedition in October 1914, in which 566 men died trying to relieve the city from the German advance.

> 'If I should die, think only this of me;
> That there's some corner of a foreign field
> That is for ever England. There shall be
> In that rich earth a richer dust concealed;
> A dust whom England bore, shaped, made aware,
> Gave, once, her flowers to love, her ways to roam,
> A body of England's breathing English air,
> Washed by the rivers, blest by suns of home.
> And think, this heart, all evil shed away,
> A pulse in the eternal mind, no less
> Gives somewhere back the thoughts by England given,
> Her sights and sounds; dreams happy as her day;
> And laughter, learnt of friends; and gentleness,
> In hearts at peace, under an English heaven.'

 A marble plaque on the Greek island of Skyros, where he was buried in an olive grove, commemorates Brooke's most famous sonnet. A junior naval officer, he was on his way to fight in the Dardanelles when he succumbed to acute food-poisoning and died in his cabin off the island of Lemnos. On the white cross on his grave was originally written in pencil: *'Here lies the servant of God, Sub-Lieutenant in the English Navy, who died for the deliverance of Constantinople from the Turks.'* Brooke also wrote the evocative poem about his home, 'The Old Vicarage, Grantchester', which contains the lines: *'Stands the church clock at ten to three? / And is there honey still for tea?'*

CHARLES FROHMAN
17 June 1860–7 May 1915

'Why fear death? It is the most beautiful adventure in life.'

Last words, before going down with the *Lusitania*

This American theatrical manager and producer became known for developing both playwrights and acting talent. In 1897 he leased the Duke of York's Theatre, London, introducing plays there as well as in the United States, with the subsequent exchange of successful plays across the Atlantic being largely a result of his efforts. At the time of his death he controlled six theatres in New York, over 200 across the rest of the United States and five in London, and had produced more than 700 shows. In 1915, his favourite playwright, J.M. Barrie, implored him to come to London to help out a faltering production. In the same year, Germany let it be known that it would use its new 'submarine' technology in the hostilities in Europe, and Americans were advised not to travel on ships with foreign registries. Actor John Drew pleaded with Frohman not to go while England was at war, stating that if he got himself blown out of the water, Drew would never forgive him. Frohman ignored his pleas and booked passage on the *Lusitania*.

After an uneventful crossing, the ship was torpedoed off the coast of Ireland. There was enough life-preserving equipment on board for all the passengers, but panic among the understaffed and poorly trained crew created a disaster. As Frohman helped the actress Rita Jolivet with her life-jacket he asked, '*Why fear death? It is the most beautiful adventure in life*', echoing the famous line from the Barrie play *Peter Pan*: '*To die would be an awfully big adventure.*' Calmly puffing a cigar as the ship was torpedoed, he met his end bravely. Miss Jolivet survived, and Frohman's body was recovered later. Several people had been meant to accompany him on the voyage but for various reasons had pulled out, including the great songwriter Jerome Kern, actress Ethel Barrymore, actor/playwright William Gillette and playwright Edward Sheldon. For his epitaph Frohman had asked that he be remembered as '*The man who gave Peter Pan to the world and Chantecler to America.*'

EDITH LOUISA CAVELL
4 December 1865–12 October 1915

'I must have no hatred or bitterness towards anyone'

Last words to her Anglican chaplain, the day before her execution by the Germans

After entering Brussels on 20 August 1914, the German occupying forces allowed the British nurse Edith Cavell to remain as matron of a teaching school, which was then converted into a Red Cross hospital. However, they began to supervise her work as she started to treat an increasing number of injured German soldiers alongside the Allied injured. During this time she helped around 200 Allied soldiers escape from Belgium into neutral Holland. After a year, her activities were discovered and she was tried for treason by a German court-martial in Brussels. Although not involved in espionage, she was condemned to face a firing squad. Her case was skilfully used by the British authorities of the day to boost the recruitment of soldiers at a time when there was no conscription. The Revd Gahan gave us her final words:

'On Monday evening, October 11th, I was admitted by special passport from the German authorities to the prison of St Gilles, where Miss Edith Cavell had been confined for ten weeks. The final sentence had been given early that afternoon. To my astonishment and relief I found my friend perfectly calm and resigned. But this could not lessen the tenderness and intensity of feeling on either part during that last interview of almost an hour ... She then added that she wished all her friends to know that she willingly gave her life for her country, and said: "I have no fear nor shrinking; I have seen death so often that it is not strange or fearful to me." She further said: "I thank God for this ten weeks' quiet before the end. Life has always been hurried and full of difficulty. This time of rest has been a great mercy. They have all been very kind to me here. But this I would say, standing as I do in view of God and eternity, I realize that patriotism is not enough. I must have no hatred or bitterness towards anyone."'

JOE HILL (JOEL EMMANUEL HÄGGLUND, JOSEPH HILLSTRÖM)
7 October 1879 or 1882–19 November 1915

'I die like a true blue rebel. Don't waste any time in mourning. Organize.'

Telegram sent before his execution

A Swedish-American itinerant worker, labour activist, poet and song-writer, Hill was an organizer for the Industrial Workers of the World (IWW). He was found guilty of murder after a controversial trial in Salt Lake City. Under Utah law he could either be executed by firing squad or hanged. He opted: 'I'll take the shooting. I've been shot a couple of times before and I think I can take it.' Luminaries such as the Swedish ambassador, Helen Keller and President Woodrow Wilson pleaded for clemency, but to no avail. Hill was executed by firing squad, and hearing the order, 'Ready, Aim', his last word was 'Fire!' Just before his execution, he sent a telegram to 'Big Bill' Haywood, the best-known IWW, saying: 'Goodbye Bill. I die like a true blue rebel. Don't waste any time in mourning. Organize. It is a hundred miles from here to Wyoming. Could you arrange to have my body hauled to the state line to be buried? I don't want to be found dead in Utah.'

It seems that on the night of the killing of a shopkeeper, Hill had been wounded in an argument over his sleeping with a married woman, keeping silent to protect her reputation, but always vowing that he was not guilty of the murder. His lawyer stated: 'The main thing the state had on Hill was that he was an IWW and therefore sure to be guilty. Hill tried to keep the IWW out of [the trial] ... but the press fastened it upon him.' Hill wrote his will the day before his execution:

> 'My will is easy to decide
> For there is nothing to divide
> My kin don't need to fuss and moan
> "Moss does not cling to a rolling stone."
> My body? – Oh – If I could choose
> I would to ashes it reduce
> And let the merry breezes blow
> My dust to where some flowers grow
> Perhaps some fading flower then
> Would come to life and bloom again
> This is my Last and final Will
> Good Luck to All of you, Joe Hill.'

THOMAS MACDONAGH (TOMÁS MAC DONNCHADHA)
1 February 1878–3 May 1916

'No person living is the worse off for having known Thomas MacDonagh'

Tribute paid by actor, author and friend James Stephens in 1916

The poet and playwright was a leader of the 1916 Easter Rising, having been a signatory of the Proclamation of the Irish Republic in 1915. He was married to Muriel Gifford and they had two children, Barbara and Donagh. Muriel was tragically drowned a few months after MacDonagh's execution. His sister-in-law married Joseph Plunkett, another leader of the rising, just minutes before Plunkett was executed. When MacDonagh laid down his arms to surrender, he said he *'would give anything to see Muriel once more'*. His wife was unable to reach him, but his sister, a nun, visited him in Kilmainham Gaol shortly before his death. When she entered the cell and saw that there was no water, she asked the guard for some, but the guard, acting under orders, refused the request. His sister gave MacDonagh a rosary that had belonged to their mother, and said she hoped that after his death they would return it to her. As MacDonagh put the rosary around his neck, he said: *'They will shoot it to bits.'* In fact only four beads were shot away, and his sister did eventually receive the rosary back. In his final letter to his wife, MacDonagh said: *'I am ready to die, and I thank God that I am to die in so a holy a cause. My country will reward my deed richly. I counted the cost of this, and I am ready to pay it.'*

MacDonagh's prophetic poem, 'Of a Poet Patriot', was first published in *Songs of Myself* (1910):

> 'His songs were a little phrase
> Of Eternal song,
> Drowned in the harping of lays
> More loud and long.
> His deed was a single word,
> Called out alone
> In a night when no echo stirred
> To laughter or moan.
> But his songs new souls shall thrill,
> The loud harps dumb,
> And his deeds the echoes fill
> When the dawn is come.'

SIR ROGER DAVID CASEMENT
1 September 1864–3 August 1916

‘**Self-government is our right, a thing born in us at birth, a thing no more to be doled out to us, or withheld from us, by another people than the right to life itself – than the right to feel the sun, or smell the flowers, or to love our kind**’

Speech from the dock after being found guilty of high treason, 29 June 1916

‘It is only from the convict these things are withheld, for crime committed and proven and Ireland, that has wronged no man, has injured no land, that has sought no dominion over others – Ireland is being treated today among the nations of the world as if she were a convicted criminal. If it be treason to fight against such an unnatural fate as this, then I am proud to be a rebel, and shall cling to my "rebellion" with the last drop of my blood ... Where all your rights have become only an accumulated wrong, where men must beg with bated breath for leave to subsist in their own land, to think their own thoughts, to sing their own songs, to gather the fruits of their own labours, and, even while they beg, to see things inexorably withdrawn from them – then, surely, it is a braver, a saner and truer thing to be a rebel, in act and in deed, against such circumstances as these, than to tamely accept it, as the natural lot of men ...’

Casement, an Irish nationalist, poet and diplomat was stripped of his knighthood when executed at Pentonville Prison. The hangman Albert Ellis recalled: ‘*He appeared to me the bravest man it fell to my unhappy lot to execute.*’ A former British consul, Casement had tried to smuggle arms from Germany for an Irish uprising in World War I. The government could find little legal basis upon which to convict him, so the seemingly forged ‘Black Diaries’ were discovered and published, making him out to be a homosexual and weakening his support from all strata of society. His body was buried in quicklime, but in 1965 his remains were repatriated to Ireland for a state funeral, when over half a million people filed past the coffin.

HECTOR HUGH MUNRO ('SAKI')
18 December 1870–14 November 1916

'Put that damned cigarette out!'

Attributed last words

Munro was born in Burma. When his family returned to England, his mother was killed by a runaway cow when he was two years old. He endured a miserable childhood, being regularly beaten by the aunts who brought him up. Allied to his homosexuality, which was then a penal offence, this gave him a jaundiced view of mankind. A misogynist, anti-Semite and reactionary who as an 'outsider' despised polite society, he never married.

Munro's pen-name of Saki was that of the cup-bearer in *The Rubaiyat of Omar Khayyam*. His newspaper columns and short stories satirized Edwardian society, being a mixture of the macabre and the humorous. Symptomatic of his works is the short story 'Tobermory', about a cat that observes country-house scandals, learns to talk and repeats the guests' vicious comments about each other. Among his works we can find such gems as: *'The cook was a good cook, as cooks go; and as cooks go she went'*; *'A little inaccuracy sometimes saves tons of explanations'*; *'People may say what they like about the decay of Christianity; the religious system that produced green Chartreuse can never really die'*; *'I always say beauty is only sin deep'*; *'Waldo is one of those people who would be enormously improved by death'*; and *'We all know that Prime Ministers are wedded to the truth, but like other married couples they sometimes live apart.'*

After the outbreak of World War I, although officially too old, Munro volunteered for the army, but refused a commission. Wounded and returning to action several times, on 14 November 1916 he was sheltering in a shell crater near Beaumont-Hamel on the Somme. His last words, according to several sources, were either: *'Put that damned cigarette out!'* or *'Put out that bloody cigarette!'* His voice and the smoke alerted a German sniper, and almost immediately Munro was shot dead. After his death, his sister Ethel destroyed most of his papers and wrote an account of their childhood. At Christmas 1915 he had sent her the following verse:

> 'While shepherds watched their flocks by night,
> All seated on the ground,
> A high-explosive shell came down
> And mutton rained around.'

MATA HARI (MARGARETHA GEERTRUIDA 'GRIETJE' ZELLE)
7 August 1876–15 October 1917

'It is unbelievable'

Last words, facing the firing squad

Margaretha left Holland at the age of 18, answering an advertisement from Rudolf John McLeod, a violent alcoholic army officer serving in the Dutch West Indies who was looking for a wife. The marriage was unhappy, McLeod giving her syphilis. Their two children were also infected. Margaretha studied Indonesian culture, joining a local dance company, and aged 21 wrote to her relatives that she had a new artistic name. It was Mata Hari, meaning 'eye of the day', i.e. the sun. In 1899 her son died, and three years later she left her husband. Penniless, she went to Paris and worked as a circus horse rider, artist's model and finally an exotic dancer. She became the mistress of rich men, posing as a Javanese Hindu princess. Her act involved stripping off all except her headdress, jewellery and brassiere, as she was conscious of her small breasts. She admitted: *'I could never dance well. People came to see me because I was the first who dared to show myself naked to the public.'*

When World War I began, Mata Hari, having neutral Dutch nationality, was able to travel across borders to perform and meet her lovers. However, on 13 February 1917, she was arrested in a Paris hotel, put on trial and convicted of spying for Germany and consequently causing the deaths of at least 50,000 soldiers. After exhausting multiple appeals, she donned a grey dress and straw hat and faced the firing squad at 5 a.m. on 15 October.

When asked if she had any last words, she responded, *'It is unbelievable.'* She then refused to be tied or blindfolded, and as the commands were given, she smiled and blew a kiss at the firing squad. Before her death, she allegedly told a nun who was comforting her: *'Death is nothing, nor life either, for that matter. To die, to sleep, to pass into nothingness, what does it matter? Everything is an illusion.'* Thirty years later, one of her prosecutors conceded the truth: *'There wasn't enough evidence to flog a cat.'*

❛I am the enemy you killed, my friend❜

From 'Strange Meeting', a poem written in 1918 and found among Owen's papers

'Foreheads of men have bled where no wounds were.
I am the enemy you killed, my friend.
I knew you in this dark; for so you frowned
Yesterday through me as you jabbed and killed.
I parried; but my hands were loath and cold.
Let us sleep now ...'

A leading war poet, Owen gives us some of the most shocking depictions of life in the trenches. In 'Insensibility' we read: '*Happy are men who yet before they are killed / Can let their veins run cold. / Whom no compassion fleers / Or makes their feet / Sore on the alleys cobbled with their brothers. / The front line withers. / But they are troops who fade, not flowers.*' His 'Anthem for Doomed Youth' asks us: '*What passing bells for these who die as cattle? / Only the monstrous anger of the guns. / Only the stuttering rifles' rapid rattle / Can patter out their hasty orisons.*' 'Futility' tells us more of death: '*Move him into the sun – / Gently its touch awoke him once, / At home, whispering of fields unsown. / Always it woke him, even in France, / Until this morning and this snow.*'

From 1 October 1918, Owen led units of the Second Manchesters in storming a number of enemy strong points. However, only one week before the end of the war, whilst attempting to traverse a canal, he was shot in the head and killed. He was awarded the Military Cross, the citation reading:

'2nd Lt, Wilfred Edward Salter Owen, 5th Bn. Manch. R., T.F., attd. 2nd Bn. – For conspicuous gallantry and devotion to duty in the attack on the Fonsomme Line on October 1st/2nd, 1918. On the company commander becoming a casualty, he assumed command and showed fine leadership and resisted a heavy counter-attack. He personally manipulated a captured enemy machine gun from an isolated position and inflicted considerable losses on the enemy. Throughout he behaved most gallantly.'

JOHN SILAS REED
22 October 1887–19 October 1920

'My dear little Honey, I would do anything I could for you, but don't ask me to be a coward'
Deathbed words

A poet and journalist, Reed became the hero of a generation of radical intellectuals. He was a close friend of Lenin and an eyewitness to the 1917 October revolution, which he recorded in his best-known book, *Ten Days That Shook The World* (1920). He had turned against the American capitalist system, and a four-month imprisonment in poor conditions in Finland had broken his health, before he returned to Russia and caught spotted typhus. He is buried with other Bolshevik heroes beside the Kremlin wall. His body lay in state for a week in the Labour Temple of Moscow, guarded by 14 soldiers, and a funeral holiday was arranged by the Soviet government for all the workers of Moscow to attend. On 14 November 1920, his partner Louise Bryant wrote a letter describing his last days, which was printed in *The Liberator*, February 1921.

'... At the funeral I suffered a very severe heart attack which by the merest scratch I survived ... Jack [John Reed] was ill twenty days. Only two nights, when he was calmer, did I even lie down. Spotted typhus is beyond description, the patient wastes to nothing under your eyes ... His clothes were just rags ... He told me of his cell, dark and cold and wet. Almost three months of solitary confinement and only raw fish to eat. Sometimes he was delirious and imagined me dead. Sometimes he expected to die himself, so he wrote on books and everywhere a little verse: "Thinking and dreaming / Day and night and day / Yet cannot think one bitter thought away – / That we have lost each other / You and I" ... Early in his sickness I asked him to promise me that he would rest before going home since it only meant going to prison. I felt prison would be too much for him. I remember he looked at me in a strange way and said, "My dear little Honey, I would do anything I could for you, but don't ask me to be a coward." I had not meant it so. I felt so hurt that I burst into tears and said he could go and I would go with him anywhere by the next train, to any death or any suffering. He smiled so happily then ...'

'Whatever happens, my fellow-countrymen won't kill me'

Comment to local National Army commander Joe Sweeney on 20 August
when warned that it was not safe to drive around County Cork

Collins had fought in the Easter Rising of the Irish Republican Brotherhood in 1916, and was interned in Wales before becoming commander-in-chief of the Irish Republican Army (IRA) throughout the Irish War of Independence. He pioneered urban guerrilla tactics, provoking British counter-terror by the 'Black and Tans', which polarized popular opinion behind the nationalist cause. Along with Arthur Griffith, in 1921 he undertook the thankless task of negotiating the Anglo-Irish Treaty, which partitioned Ireland between a rump Ulster and the semi-sovereign 'Irish Free State'. Collins knew that the IRA had been severely weakened, so control of the 26 Southern Counties was all that the nationalists could reasonably expect to obtain at that time. He defended the treaty during a referendum campaign, and then led the Free State army in the Irish Civil War against a dissident faction of the IRA led by Eamonn de Valera. De Valera's men wanted a unified Irish independence, rather than the partition compromise that Collins and Griffith had agreed to.

Collins had just signed the Anglo-Irish Treaty when he wrote in a letter: '*Think – what have I got for Ireland? Something which she has wanted these past 700 years. Will anyone be satisfied at the bargain? Will anyone? I tell you this – early this morning I signed my own death warrant. I thought at the time how odd, how ridiculous – a bullet may just as well have done the job five years ago.*' The following year he was seven minutes late for the handover from British military jurisdiction to the Irish Free State and remarked: '*We've been waiting 700 years; you can have the 7 minutes.*'

In 1922, two days after asserting that no Irishman would kill him, Collins was ambushed at Brandon, County Cork. He ordered his convoy to stop and return fire, rather than drive on or transfer himself to an accompanying armoured car. The great patriot was killed by a dum-dum bullet at the age of just 31.

ERSKINE ROBERT CHILDERS
25 June 1870–24 November 1922

'Take a step forwards, lads. It will be easier that way.'
Last words to his firing squad

Childers was the author of the popular novel *The Riddle of the Sands*, regarded variously as the first modern spy novel, a cautionary tale of the imminent war with Germany, and a great sailing and seamanship narrative. He served in the Boer War as a volunteer, but between 1903 and the outbreak of World War I took up the cause of Irish Home Rule, publishing tracts, making speeches and smuggling guns into Ireland. His mother was Irish, and Childers had lived with Irish relatives when his parents died. However, in 1914, when war was declared, he enlisted to fight for the British Empire, only to return to the campaign for Home Rule in 1918.

Childers had argued for peaceful Home Rule legislation, but now wanted only an immediate republic and became the main propagandist for de Valera's IRA irregulars. IRA actions included the assassinations of Dáil members, judges and Free State police. This violence produced a strong reaction from the new Free State Provisional Government. In its efforts to maintain control, and to provide a stable government and sound economy for the new country, it retaliated against the Republicans with military courts martial and firing-squad executions. Now believed to be the inspiration behind the Republican terrorist tactics, Childers was widely hunted by the Free State soldiers and was captured on his way to meet with de Valera in Dublin. He was summarily court-martialled, and sentenced to death by firing squad for treason. At his execution he shook each soldier's hand, and noted that he still loved his native England, although the British press, when reporting on his death, considered him a traitor. His leader, de Valera, even though he was arrested by the Free State in 1923, went on to serve as president of the Republic. Childers' son, also named Erskine, was elected fourth president of the Republic in 1973.

JOSÉ DOROTEO ARANGO ARÁMBULA
'PANCHO' VILLA
5 June 1878–20 July 1923

'Don't let it end like this. Tell them I said something.'

Said to be his last words

Also known as Francisco Villa, 'Pancho' was the nickname of this Mexican folk hero, variously described as a revolutionary general and a bandit. He advocated assistance for the poor and wanted agrarian reform. Having killed the owner of the estate where he worked because he had assaulted Villa's sister, as a young man Villa had fled to the mountains, then fought in the revolts against two dictators, Porfirio Díaz and Victoriano Huerta. He escaped from Mexico in 1912, but returned in 1913 and formed the famous División del Norte. In 1914, joining his force with that of Venustiano Carranza, they won a decisive victory over Huerta and entered Mexico City as the victorious leaders of a revolution. Villa's relationship with Carranza ended, and after several battles he and Emiliano Zapata fled to the northern mountains of Mexico. He was responsible for a raid on Columbus, New Mexico, in 1916, which was the first attack on US soil since 1812. After he executed 16 US citizens, President Wilson sent General Pershing to catch him, to no avail, as Villa knew the mountains and the people would not betray him. An officer in Carranza's army reported: *'I have the duty to inform you that Pancho Villa is everywhere and nowhere at the same time.'*

When the revolution ended in 1920, Villa retired to a hacienda in Chihuahua, Mexico. He was granted amnesty in return for laying down his arms, and promised to retire from all political and guerrilla activities, but the supporters of his long-time enemy, General Alvaro Obregon, suspected that he was going to make a comeback, and on 20 July 1923 Villa's Dodge car was ambushed on his way back from the bank in Parral. The revolutionary found himself lost for words, and as he lay dying pleaded with some journalists: *'Don't let it end like this. Tell them I said something.'*

'That's good. Go on, read some more.'

Last words to his wife

Harding's sudden death possibly saved him from impeachment. He had complained of severe cramps and indigestion, misdiagnosed as food-poisoning. A cross-country tour had exhausted him, so he cancelled scheduled speeches and was put to bed in San Francisco with a temperature of 102 degrees and a pulse rate of 120 bpm. He soon felt better, however, and listened contentedly as his wife read him an article from *The Saturday Evening Post*, 'A Calm View of a Calm Man', a flattering portrait of the his presidency by Samuel Blythe. '*That's good,*' Harding said. '*Go on, read some more.*' Mrs Harding finished the piece, then left the room for her own quarters across the hall of the hotel. Moments later, as Harding's nurse entered the room, the president's face suddenly twitched, his jaw dropped, and his head rolled to the right. His wife refused an autopsy, leading to suspicions of poisoning (he had had several mistresses).

Harding's death was greeted with glee by his critics. His presidency had been marked by scandals and bribes, and his speaking style was similar to that of a very recent president. '*The only man, woman or child who wrote a simple declarative sentence with seven grammatical errors is dead,*' wrote the poet e.e. cummings. H.L. Mencken described Harding's inaugural address: '*He writes the worst English that I have ever encountered. It reminds me of a string of wet sponges; it reminds me of tattered washing on the line; it reminds me of stale bean soup, of college yells, of dogs barking idiotically through endless nights. It is so bad that a sort of grandeur creeps into it. It drags itself out of the dark abysm of pish, and crawls insanely up the topmost pinnacle of posh. It is rumble and bumble. It is flap and doodle. It is balder and dash.*' Malcolm Gladwell has suggested that Harding became president only because '*he looked like a President*', and even Harding himself said: '*I am not fit for this office and should never have been here.*'

FRANZ KAFKA
3 July 1883–3 June 1924

'Dearest Max, my last request: Everything I leave behind me ... in the way of diaries, manuscripts, letters (my own and others'), sketches, and so on, [is] to be burned unread.'

Note to his friend Max Brod

Fortunately Brod ignored the request of one of the most influential writers of the twentieth century, and Kafka's friends published the bulk of his work posthumously, much of it incomplete. While alive, he had published only a part of his short fiction, which included in 1912 the novella *The Metamorphosis*, a story of a young man who is transformed into a huge disgusting insect. Kafka was born in the centre of Prague, then part of Bohemia, to a middle-class German-speaking Jewish family, and all his writing is in German. His works include *In the Penal Colony, The Trial, The Castle* and *Amerika*. From 1917 he began suffering from tuberculosis, and spent the rest of his life going to various sanatoria, also suffering from depression. He died in a sanatorium near Vienna, apparently from starvation, as his condition made it too painful for him to eat.

In December 1913, Kafka wrote: '*To die would mean nothing else than to surrender a nothing to the nothing, but that would be impossible to conceive, for how could a person, even only as a nothing, consciously surrender himself to the nothing, and not merely to an empty nothing but rather to a roaring nothing whose nothingness consists only in its incomprehensibility.*' His three sisters were all killed by the Nazis in the Lodz Ghetto or at Auschwitz, and Bertolt Brecht (*Time*, 18 July 1983) noted that '*Kafka described with wonderful imaginative power the future concentration camps, the future instability of the law, the future absolutism of the state Apparat.*' On Kafka's grave in the Jewish Straschnitz Cemetery is written: '*Writing is a deeper sleep than death. / Just as one wouldn't pull a corpse from its grave, / I can't be dragged from my desk at night.*' His parents were later buried in the same plot.

'Because it is there'

Reply when asked why he wanted to climb Mount Everest

Mallory had taken part in the first two British expeditions to Mount Everest, and it was on the third, in June 1924, that he and his young climbing partner Andrew Irvine vanished high on the North-East Ridge during their attempt to make the first conquest of the world's highest mountain. The pair were last seen a few hundred yards from the summit. A colleague, Noel Odell reported:

> 'At 12.50, just after I had emerged from a state of jubilation at finding the first definite fossils on Everest, there was a sudden clearing of the atmosphere, and the entire summit ridge and final peak of Everest were unveiled. My eyes became fixed on one tiny black spot silhouetted on a small snow-crest beneath a rock-step in the ridge; the black spot moved. Another black spot became apparent and moved up the snow to join the other on the crest. The first then approached the great rock-step and shortly emerged at the top; the second did likewise. Then the whole fascinating vision vanished, enveloped in cloud once more.'

Mallory was 37 years old and knew it was his last opportunity to climb Everest. His partner was only 21 but immensely fit and strong. A first attempt by Mallory and Geoffrey Bruce, the expedition leader, failed, as did another by Norton and Somervell. On 8 June, Mallory and Irvine decided to try to reach the top via the North Col route. The pair used oxygen, Mallory having been converted from his original scepticism by his failure on the initial assault. After their disappearance, several expeditions tried to find their bodies. In 1999, Mallory's frozen remains were found at 26,760 feet (8,160 m) on the North Face, directly below where Irvine's axe was discovered by the Welsh climber Percy Wyn-Harris in 1933. If Irvine's body or a camera is found, it may be possible to ascertain whether they reached the summit, with poor kit and almost 30 years before the Hunt expedition.

SERGEI ALEXANDROVICH YESENIN
3 October 1895–28 December 1925

'There's nothing new in dying now / Though living is no newer'

Written in his own blood, and given to a friend the day before he hanged himself

'Goodbye, my friend, goodbye
My love, you are in my heart.
The promised destinies are weaving
the thread from parting to a meeting
Good-bye, my dear, no hand or word,
Do not be sad, don't cloud your brow,
There's nothing new in dying now
Though living is no newer.'

Yesenin began to write poetry at the age of 9. In 1915 he moved to St Petersburg, gaining a reputation as a poet and publishing two collections in 1915 and 1916. He became one of the most popular poets of the time, writing about love and the simple life, and for a time supported the Bolshevik Revolution before becoming disillusioned and criticizing it. In 1922 he married his third wife, Isadora Duncan, and accompanied her on a tour of Europe, but the marriage only lasted a year because of his alcoholism and drunken rages. Back in Moscow, his behaviour was increasingly erratic, and he continued writing, marrying at least twice more (another probable wife committed suicide at his grave in 1926).

After a mental breakdown, Yesenin was hospitalized for a month. Two days after his release for Christmas, he allegedly cut his wrist and wrote a farewell poem in his own blood. The following day he hanged himself with a suitcase strap from the heating pipes on the ceiling of his room in the Hôtel Angleterre in St Petersburg. He was only 30 years old. Most of his work was banned under the regimes of Stalin and Khrushchev, but his Bohemian love-life and early death have left an enduring image. A great lyrical poet, he was not appreciated by Russia's literary elite, and had written: '*I am a stranger in my own land*' and '*My poems are no longer needed now, and myself I am unwanted.*'

RUDOLPH VALENTINO (RODOLFO ALFONSO RAFFAELLO PIERO GUGLIEMI DE VALENTINA D'ANTONGUOLLA)
6 May 1895–23 August 1926

'Don't worry, Chief, I will be all right'
Last words to his studio chairman

Valentino had been incensed in July 1926 by an article in the *Chicago Tribune* complaining that he was *'feminizing men'*. H.L. Mencken responded defending Valentino in the *Baltimore Sun*, a week before the star's death in August 1926: *'Here was a young man who was living daily the dream of millions of other men. Here was one who was catnip to women. Here was one who had wealth and fame. And here was one who was very unhappy.'* Valentino had challenged the incognito writer to a boxing match in order to defend his masculinity, but the writer never came forward, and the fight never took place. The movie star, thoroughly stressed, travelled to Manhattan for the New York première of his final film, *The Son of the Sheik*. There he participated in a public sparring match with sportswriter Frank O'Neill, whom he grounded with two punches. After an all-night party in his honour, on 15 August Valentino crashed to the floor in his suite at the Ambassador Hotel, where he was found writhing in agony.

'With a burst appendix and violent pain, severe uremic poisoning had spread through-out his body by the time he went into surgery. Valentino fought bravely, refusing to face his perilous condition and told his visiting studio chairman, Joseph M. Schenck, "Don't worry, Chief, I will be all right." Those were his last words.' Valentino fell into a coma and on 23 August died of peritonitis and septic endocarditis, surrounded by three doctors and two weeping nurses. The death of the 31-year-old 'Latin Lover', the star of *The Sheik* and *The Four Horsemen of the Apocalypse*, caused mass hysteria, with two women attempting suicide outside the hospital. A song was quickly written, 'There's a New Star in Heaven Tonight', recorded by the popular singer Rudy Vallée, and was a massive hit. Over 100,000 people lined the streets of New York to pay their respects at Valentino's funeral.

HARRY HOUDINI (born ERIK WEISZ)
24 March 1874–31 October 1926

'I'm tired of fighting, Dash. I guess this thing is going to get me.'

Last words, to his brother Theo, the day before his death

The Hungarian–American magician gained worldwide fame for his Chinese water-torture cell escape, suspended straitjacket escape and other acts of showmanship. Kenneth Silverman in *Houdini: The Career of Ehrich Weiss*, recalled the magician's last days:

'Around noon on Oct. 22, 1926, Houdini was in his dressing room at a Montreal theater. Lying on a couch, he chatted with three students from McGill University. One of them, a ruddy six-footer, asked if it was true that Houdini could take the hardest punches to his stomach. "Would you mind if I delivered a few blows to your abdomen?" he asked. Houdini's escapes were gut-wrenching. He had kept his little Hercules physique tuned for them by years of running, swimming and acrobatics, but he was now 52, and for more than a week he had limped through his 2-$^1/_2$ hour program in a splint and leg brace ... Hovering over Houdini, elbow bent, the student began forcibly punching him in the stomach. The shots caught Houdini as he started to rise off the pillows bolstering him. According to later sworn testimony, another student protested, "Hey there, you must be crazy. What are you doing?"

At that evening's performance, Houdini retired to his couch during intermissions in a cold sweat. After the show, he was unable to dress himself. He completed his Montreal engagement the next evening, then with his assistants caught a late-night train to begin a run in Detroit. On board, though, he experienced severe stomach pains. He managed in the morning to reach a Detroit hotel, but for a half hour he shook with chills. Still, he was determined to go on for opening night. At curtain time, his temperature was 104. When he left the stage after act one, he fell down. He revived, gave the rest of his show, and collapsed again. The next afternoon, Oct. 25, Houdini's appendix was removed at Grace Hospital. It had ruptured and produced peritonitis. Doctors gave him an experimental serum, and four days later operated again. But the sepsis had taken over his system. "I can't fight anymore," he told his brother.'

BARTOLOMEO VANZETTI
11 June 1888–23 August 1927

'If you could execute me two times, and if I could be reborn two other times, I would live again to do what I have done already'

Last speech to Judge Webster Thayer, 19 April 1927, at
Norfolk County courthouse, Dedham, Massachusetts

'I would not wish to a dog or a snake, to the most low and misfortunate creature of the earth – I would not wish to any of them what I have had to suffer for things that I am not guilty of. But my conviction is that I have suffered for things that I am guilty of. I am suffering because I am a radical, and indeed I am a radical; I have suffered because I am an Italian, and indeed I am an Italian ... If you could execute me two times, and if I could be reborn two other times, I would live again to do what I have done already.'

Vanzetti and Ferdinando Nicola Sacco (born 22 April 1891) were Italian-born labourers and anarchists who were sentenced to the electric chair for a 1920 armed robbery and double murder in Braintree, Massachusetts. Judge Thayer was extremely prejudiced against their Californian defence counsel, and the case was riddled with bad judicial practice and conflicting prosecuting evidence. Their seven years in gaol fighting the death sentence made them a cause célèbre. Sacco's last words to his son Dante were:

'So son, instead of crying, be strong, so as to be able to comfort your mother ... take her for a long walk in the quiet country, gathering wild flowers here and there, resting under the shade of trees ... But remember always, Dante, in this play of happiness, don't you use all for yourself only ... help the persecuted and the victim because they are your better friends ... In this struggle of life you will find more love and you will be loved.'

Vanzetti commented to a reporter before their execution: '*Never in our full life can we hope to do such work for tolerance, justice, for man's understanding of man, as now we do by accident. Our words – our lives – our pains – nothing! The taking of our lives – lives of a good shoemaker and a poor fish peddler – all! That last moment belong to us – that agony is our triumph.*'

ANGELA ISADORA DUNCAN
26 May 1878–14 September 1927

'Farewell, my friends. I go to glory!'

Last words according to Mary Desti

Born in San Francisco, Isadora Duncan is con-sidered to be one of the founders of the free expressionism of modern dance. Although never very popular in the United States, she entertained throughout Europe, performing a new style of dance that she said was based on the figures found on Greek vases. She flouted traditional morality, and her bisexual private life caused scandal. Duncan had two illegitimate children. In 1913, the children were in a car with their nurse. The driver stalled while attempting to avoid a collision and got out to hand-crank the engine, but he had forgotten to set the emergency brake and the car rolled down the embankment into the River Seine below. The children and the nanny all drowned. In 1922, Duncan married the Russian poet Sergei Yesenin, who was 18 years her junior. His alcoholism resulted in drunken rages, with repeated destruction of the interiors of their hotel rooms, bringing Duncan more bad publicity. On her last US tour in 1922–23, she waved a red scarf and bared her breast on stage in Boston, shouting, *'This is red! So am I!'* At her death she was a Russian citizen, and her will was the first of a Soviet citizen to be probated in the United States.

On the day she died, before getting into the car of a handsome mechanic, Benoît Falchetto, in Nice, Duncan said to her friend Mary Desti and others, *'Adieu, mes amis. Je vais à la gloire!'* (*'Farewell, my friends. I go to glory!'*) However, according to the American novelist Glenway Westcott, Desti admitted that she had lied about Duncan's last words. Actually Duncan had said, *'Je vais à l'amour!'* but Desti considered this too embarrassing to be remembered as her last words, as it suggested that she and Falchetto were going to her hotel for sex. As Falchetto drove off, Duncan's large silk scarf, a gift from Desti, became entangled around one of the vehicle's open-spoked wheels and rear axle. She was yanked from the car, almost decapitated and died either from strangulation or from hitting the pavement.

'With the publication of his Private Papers in 1952, he committed suicide 25 years after his death'

Lord Beaverbrook's judgement on Haig

Thankfully, leaders of armies are no longer always accepted as heroes by all historians of their native countries. Haig was the senior commander of British forces in World War I, having undermined Sir John French's position by political intriguing and his closeness to George V. A cavalry man through and through, he did not rate the war's new weaponry, decrying the use of the tank and saying in 1915 that *'the machine gun is a much over-rated weapon'*. His decision to attack at the Somme in 1916 saw the British army suffer the highest number of casualties in its history: 60,000 on one day alone. From 1 July to the calling off of the offensive on 18 November there was little achieved. His forces sustained 420,000 casualties and gained seven miles, which they lost later in the war. The following year saw the campaign at Passchendaele (the Third Battle of Ypres) from July to November, which ultimately ground down German resistance, although at heavy cost in terms of British manpower. When Haig asked the Canadian Corps commander Arthur Currie to capture Passchendaele Ridge during the final month of the battle, Currie told him: *'It's suicidal. I will not waste 16,000 good soldiers on such a hopeless objective.'* In the event he lost over 15,000 men. Fortunately for Haig, the American entry into the war saved the Anglo-French cause, as German offensives had regained all their lost ground. Known as the 'Butcher of the Somme', Haig never visited the front lines, and Churchill accused him of blocking German machin-gun-fire with *'the breasts of brave men'*. Lloyd George likened him to *'the blind King of Bohemia at Creçy'*.

On 6 February 1928, *Time* magazine reported: *'Characteristically the last formal act of his life was to address a Boy Scout rally, last week on his estate. "Stand up for England when people speak disrespectfully of her!" he said. On the evening of the next day, as Earl Haig stood up to put on his pyjamas and then sat down on the edge of his bed, he was stricken with heart failure, and died instantly.'*

ARNOLD 'THE BRAIN' ROTHSTEIN
17 January 1882–4 November 1928

'You stick to your trade I'll stick to mine … Me mudder did it.'

Words on deathbed to police who asked him who had
shot him, observing the Mafia code of *omerta*

A New York Jewish businessman and inveterate gambler, Rothstein led organized crime in the days of Prohibition. He was also thought to have been behind baseball's 'Black Sox Scandal' when the 1919 World Series was fixed. The Chicago White Sox 'threw' the series, but the Grand Jury believed Rothstein when he stated that he had been framed. Rothstein was responsible for transforming organized crime from *'thuggish activity by hoodlums into a big business, run like a corporation, with himself at the top'.* By 1910, aged 18, he had established a gambling casino in Manhattan, and during Prohibition bought up 'speakeasies'. He also made money from fixing races at a Maryland racetrack he owned. During Prohibition he diversified into bootlegging and narcotics, becoming the *'spiritual father of American organized crime'*, and known as 'the Fixer', 'the Little Man', 'the Man Uptown', 'Mr Big', 'the Big Bankroll' and 'the Brain'. His attorney described his client thus: *'Arnold Rothstein is a man who waits in doorways – a mouse, waiting in the doorway for his cheese.'*

Rothstein was known as the man who could fix anything – of 6,902 Rothstein-era liquor cases, 400 never came to trial and 6,074 ended in dismissal. However, in a poker game lasting from 8 to 10 September 1928, he lost $320,000 and refused to pay the debt, saying the game was fixed. The underworld was shocked, and it seems that another gangster, Dutch Schulz, had him shot, although the main suspects were men who played in the game. Rothstein died the next day, refusing to incriminate anyone. He had never been convicted of breaking any law. Meyer Lansky and Lucky Luciano took over as the new Mafia Godfathers. Rothstein's colourful life inspired the fictional characters Meyer Wolfsheim in *The Great Gatsby*, and Nathan Detroit in *Guys and Dolls*.

'Nothing's so sacred as honour and nothing's so loyal as love'

Epitaph on tombstone of Wyatt and Josie Earp in the
Jewish cemetery, Colma, California

After working as a stagecoach driver and buffalo hunter, Earp stole horses and ran a brothel before serving as deputy marshal in Wichitaand Dodge City, Kansas, and becoming friendly with 'Bat' Masterson and 'Doc' Holliday. In Tombstone, Arizona, he acquired the gambling concession at the Oriental Saloon, meeting his third wife, the German-Jewish Josie Marcus. In 1881, a feud with the Clanton gang ended with the famous Gunfight at the OK Corral. Three of the Clanton gang were killed, but the three Earp brothers survived, along with Doc Holliday. The Clanton gang took revenge by ambushing Wyatt and Morgan Earp in a saloon, killing Morgan. Wyatt Earp and Doc Holliday then raided various outlaw hideouts, killing individuals whom they suspected of participating in Morgan's death. Wyatt himself said: '*Shooting at a man who is returning the compliment means going into action with the greatest speed of which a man's muscles are capable, but mentally unflustered by an urge to hurry or the need for complicated nervous and muscular actions which trick shooting involves.*' Bat Masterson reported: '*I think it was the distinguishing trait of Wyatt Earp, the leader of the Earp brothers, that more than any man I have ever known, he was devoid of physical fear. He feared the opinion of no one but himself and his self respect was his creed.*'

Between 1885 and 1887, Wyatt and Josie arrived in San Diego, where Wyatt invested heavily in real estate and gambling saloons, in what is now the Gaslamp Quarter. In 1897 they operated a saloon in Nome at the height of the Alaska Gold Rush. In 1901 they moved on to a gold strike in Nevada, and Earp spent his final years working mining claims in the Mojave Desert. He and Josie summered in Los Angeles, where they befriended early Hollywood actors. Western actors Tom Mix and William S. Hart were pallbearers at his funeral. Josie was too grief-stricken to attend.

THOMAS ALVA EDISON
11 February 1847–18 October 1931

'It is very beautiful over there!'

Words spoken in the days before his death

These are often reported as Edison's last words, but they were actually spoken several days before his death, as he awoke from a nap, gazing upwards, as reported by his physician Dr Hubert S. Howe. With only three months of formal education, Edison became one of the greatest industrial leaders in history. He obtained 1,093 US patents, the most issued to any individual. His greatest contribution was the first practical electric lighting, inventing the first successful electric light bulb, and also setting up the first electrical power distribution company. He invented the phonograph, and made improvements to the telegraph, telephone and motion-picture technology. He also founded the first modern research laboratory. He was a superb businessman, creating companies worldwide for the manufacture and sale of his inventions, and helping make the United States a world industrial power. He became friends with Henry Ford after encouraging him to use the gasoline-powered engine for his automobiles. He was ruthless too, and would fight viciously to defeat his competitors.

Edison believed that inventing useful products offered everyone the opportunity for fame and fortune while benefiting society. He was honest about the advantages of hard work, telling a press conference in 1929: *'None of my inventions came by accident. I see a worthwhile need to be met and I make trial after trial until it comes. What it boils down to is one per cent inspiration and ninety-nine per cent perspiration.'* He also said: *'Through all the years of experimenting and research, I never once made a discovery. I start where the last man left off ... All my work was deductive, and the results I achieved were those of invention pure and simple.'* His work ethic was again demonstrated when he said: *'Restlessness is discontent – and discontent is the first necessity of progress. Show me a thoroughly satisfied man – and I will show you a failure.'*

GILES LYTTON STRACHEY
1 March 1880–21 January 1932

'If this is dying, I don't think much of it'

Among his last words on his deathbed to Dora Carrington and friends

Strachey revolutionized biographical writing with a realistic exposure of hypocrisy in his *Eminent Victorians* (1918) and works on Elizabeth I and Queen Victoria. The homosexual writer and critic was part of the 'Bloomsbury Set', a group of writers, intellectuals and artists, including J.M. Keynes, Virginia Woolf, E.M. Forster, Duncan Grant, Roger Fry and Vanessa Bell, who met regularly in Bloomsbury, London, for informal discussions. Strachey had a particular friendship with the artist Dora Carrington, to whose husband he was attracted. Strachey and Carrington lived together for 16 years, despite his homosexuality and her marriage and affairs, at least one of which was with a woman.

In late 1931, Strachey was suffering from acute pain, but stomach cancer was not diagnosed until his last days. On his death, the devoted Carrington wrote in her diary, 16 February 1932:

> 'At last I am alone. At last there is nothing between us ... Now there is nothing left. All your papers have been taken away. Your clothes have gone. Your room is bare. In a few months no traces will be left. Just a few book plates in some books and never again, however long I look out of the window, will I see your tall thin figure walking across the path past the dwarf pine past the stumps, and then climb the ha-ha and come across the lawn. Our jokes have gone for ever ... I feel as if I was in a dream, almost unconscious, so much of me was in you ... In a few years what will be left of him? A few books on some shelves, but the intimate things that I loved, all gone. And soon even the people who knew his pale thin hands and the texture of his thick shiny hair, and grisly beard, they will be dead and all remembrance of him will vanish. I watched the gap close over others but for Lytton one couldn't have believed (because one did not believe that it was ever possible) that the world would go on the same.'

Soon afterwards, Carrington tried to commit suicide by inhaling car exhaust fumes, but her husband found her in time. She succeeded at the second attempt, shooting herself on 11 March, unable to live without her soulmate.

GEORGE EASTMAN
12 July 1854–14 March 1932

'To my friends, My work is done, why wait?'

Suicide note

In 1880, Eastman had perfected a process for making dry plates for photography and organized the Eastman Dry Plate and Film Company for their manufacture. He invented roll film, helping to bring photography to the masses, and enabling the development of the motion-picture industry. He also invented a simple, hand-held box camera, and the first Kodak camera was marketed in 1888. Costing $25, it contained a 100-exposure roll of paper stripping film. The entire camera was sent back to the manufacturer for developing, printing, and even reloading, when the film was used up. Eastman coined the marketing phrase, '*You press the button, we do the rest.*' By 1896, however, only 100 Kodak cameras had been sold. Eastman's Brownie camera, which was originally meant for children, was introduced in 1900 and sold for $1, becoming a global success, and earning Kodak a virtual monopoly in cameras and film for many years. He also registered the trademark Kodak, understanding the need for international marketing and branding. Marketers have usually followed his advice from this time when developing brands. His three principal concepts in creating the name were: it must be short, it could not be mispronounced and it could not resemble anything else or be associated with anything other than itself.

During his lifetime, Eastman gave away $100 million, mostly to MIT and the University of Rochester, and usually under the alias of Mr Smith. He pioneered profit-sharing as an employee incentive, and in 1924 alone donated half his fortune in gifts amounting to $75 million. In his final two years, he was in terrible pain, suffering from a degenerative disorder affecting his spine. He had trouble standing, walking became a slow shuffle and he grew depressed. He wished to control how he died, so he committed suicide in his bedroom, placing a folded towel over his chest and shooting himself with an automatic Luger.

JOHN CALVIN COOLIDGE
4 July 1872–5 January 1933

'I feel I am no longer fit in these times'

Words spoken to an old friend just before his death from a heart attack

When told of the death of Coolidge, Dorothy Parker quipped, *'How could they tell?'* which is unfair to the memory of one of the better American presidents. He deliberately chose a quiet persona, believing that he was less important than the nation he served. A lawyer by profession, he and his wife Grace were invited to many parties, where the stories of 'Silent Cal' originated. In private he was a man of few words, and it is said that Dorothy Parker, seated next to him at a dinner, said, *'Mr Coolidge, I've made a bet against a fellow who said it was impossible to get more than two words out of you.'* His reply was: *'You lose.'* He seemed ill at ease amongst fashionable Washington society, and when asked why he continued to attend so many of their dinner parties, he replied, *'Got to eat somewhere.'* He wrote later: *'The words of a President have an enormous weight, and ought not to be used indiscriminately.'* He told Ethel Barrymore, *'I think the American people want a solemn ass as a President, and I think I will go along with them.'*

Coolidge spoke out in favour of the civil rights of African Americans and Catholics, and the Ku Klux Klan lost most of its influence during his term. He refused to run for a third term as president, saying: *'Ten years in Washington is longer than any other man has had it – too long!'* In his memoirs, Coolidge explained his decision not to run: *'The Presidential office takes a heavy toll of those who occupy it and those who are dear to them. While we should not refuse to spend and be spent in the service of our country, it is hazardous to attempt what we feel is beyond our strength to accomplish.'* Despite his reputation as a quiet and even reclusive politician, Coolidge used the new medium of radio and made radio history several times while president.

GARETH RICHARD VAUGHAN JONES
13 August 1905–12 August 1935

'What luck! There are great events here.'

Last diary entry

This Welsh investigative journalist was in Leipzig when Hitler was appointed Chancellor, and a few days later flew with the Führer to Frankfurt, reporting on Hitler's ecstatic acclamation there. Jones was the first foreign journalist to report on starvation in Stalin's Russia, after travelling through the Ukraine. He interviewed Lenin's widow, and his accounts were at extreme odds with those of the Russian sympathizers such as George Bernard Shaw and the Pulitzer Prize-winning Walter Duranty of the *New York Times,* who echoed what the Communist Party told them, never venturing out of Moscow to see the reality.

Jones was in Inner Mongolia, and checking upon reports that Japan was going to invade China, when he was killed by a bullet in the back of the head, almost certainly by the Japanese secret service rather than by Chinese bandits. The NKVD – the Soviet secret police – were also suspected of the shooting: Jones had been travelling with a Nazi-affiliated German who was spared. As well as exposing Stalin's Five-Year Plan and its consequent 6–11 million deaths, Jones predicted that World War II would begin in the Polish Corridor, that it would involve all Europe and that Japan would enter the war. The final words he wrote in his diary before he was murdered were: '*What luck! There are great events here. I am witnessing the changeover of a big district from China to Manchukuo ... There are two roads to Kalgan to where we go back; over one 200 Japanese lorries have travelled; the other is infested by bandits.*' In 1935, Lloyd George commented: '*That part of the world is a cauldron of conflicting intrigue and one or other interests concerned probably knew that Mr Gareth Jones knew too much of what was going on ... He had a passion for finding out what was happening in foreign lands wherever there was trouble, and in pursuit of his investigations he shrank from no risk ... I had always been afraid that he would take one risk too many.*'

'God, don't let me die. I have so much left to do.'

Dying words

Governor of Louisiana and a US senator, Long is remembered for his 'Share Our Wealth' platform during the Great Depression, with the motto 'Every Man a King', proposing wealth redistribution via huge taxes on corporations and rich individuals. Demonized by powerful corporations and corrupt politicians as a revolutionary, he was revered as a champion of the common man. In a land of plenty, Huey Long believed that no American should be without an education, a home, an automobile and a job that paid a decent living wage. He implemented an unprecedented programme of modernization and reform in Louisiana – building roads and bridges, providing free public education, expanding voting rights to all citizens and creating economic opportunities for the poor and unemployed. He was the first to champion social security, veterans' benefits, student financial aid and public works. Long split with Roosevelt in June 1933, claiming that his 'New Deal' policies were 'inadequate'. The President privately said of Long that along with General Douglas MacArthur, he was *'one of the two most dangerous men in America'*. Long's first autobiography, *Every Man a King*, was published in 1933, priced to be affordable by poor Americans and laying out his wealth-sharing programme. In July 1935 he revealed a plot to assassinate him, which had been discussed in New Orleans' De Soto Hotel. His second book, *My First Days in the White House*, was published posthumously. In it he described his ambitions for the presidential election of 1936.

On 8 September 1935, Long was in Baton Rouge for a special session of the Louisiana legislature, pushing through bills including one to gerrymander opponent Judge Benjamin Pavy out of his job. Pavy's son-in-law, Dr Carl Weiss, approached Long in a corridor and shot him at close range in the abdomen. Long said, *'I wonder why he shot me'* and ran to safety as his bodyguards opened fire. Weiss was killed instantly, and Long was rushed to a nearby hospital, where he died two days later from internal bleeding.

'God damn you!'

Last words to his nurse

George joined the Royal Navy at the age of 12, but had to leave when the Prince of Wales died and he became heir to the throne. He married his elder brother's fiancée, Princess Mary of Teck, and together they preferred the simple life. Harold Nicolson wrote in his diary of George's time as Duke of York: *'He may be all right as a young midshipman and a wise old king, but when he was Duke of York ... he did nothing at all but kill animals and stick in stamps.'* The duke set world-record prices building up the royal philatelic collection, and in 1913 shot over 1,000 pheasants in six hours. On a state visit to India in 1911 he killed 21 tigers. He became king in 1910, and public respect for him increased during World War I, when he made many visits to the front line, hospitals, factories and dockyards. Kaiser Wilhelm II, a hate figure for the British public, was the king's first cousin, and in 1917, anti-German feeling led George to adopt the family name of Windsor, replacing Saxe-Coburg-Gotha.

A heavy smoking habit gave the king recurrent pulmonary problems. In 1928, he fell seriously ill, and retired for a brief period to the seaside resort of Bognor Regis. In his final days he was told that he would soon be well enough to revisit the town, and he supposedly replied: *'Bugger Bognor!'* In 1936, he was close to death. His physician, Lord Dawson, issued a bulletin: *'The King's life is drawing peacefully to a close.'* Dawson's private diary revealed that George's last words were addressed to his nurse when she gave him a sedative on the night of his death, a mumbled *'God damn you!'* Dawson also wrote that he hastened the king's end by giving him a lethal injection of cocaine and morphine, to prevent further strain on the family and so that his death could be announced in the morning edition of *The Times*.

FEDERICO GARCÍA LORCA
5 June 1898–19 August 1936

'Friends, carve a monument out of dream stone for the poet in the Alhambra ...'

From 'The Crime was in Granada', Antonio Machado's
poem for the assassinated poet

Lorca was one of 130,000 people killed by General Franco's death-squads during the Spanish Civil War and in the years that followed. Bones are still being discovered across Spain, and in October 2009 a possible burial place for Lorca was found. The 2007 Law of Historical Memory gave relatives of Franco's victims state assistance to unearth the remains of their loved one. The family of Francisco Galadi, a bullfighter thought to have been executed along-side Lorca, has requested that the mountainside site be investigated, and it is guarded around the clock. Lorca is the most famous of the 'disappeared' persons, one of the country's greatest poets and dramatists. His 'crime' was to be a homosexual and to produce work that enraged conservatives. His works in the 1930s included *The House of Bernardo Alba*, *Blood Wedding* and *Yerma*, in which a peasant woman murders her husband and denies God.

In an interview with Luis Bagaría, 'Diágolos de un caricaturista salvaje', published in *El Sol*, Madrid, on 10 June 1936, Lorca stated: '*As I have not worried to be born, I do not worry to die.*' Intellectuals were thought dangerous by Franco's Nationalists, and along with a schoolmaster and two bullfighters, Lorca was dragged into a field at the foot of the Sierra Nevada Mountains, shot, and thrown into an unmarked grave. He had recently told a Spanish journalist: '*I still consider myself a true novice, and I'm still learning my profession ... One has to ascend one step at a time ... [One shouldn't] demand of my nature, my spiritual and intellectual development, something that no author can give until much later ... My work has just begun.*' After his death, Lorca's writings were outlawed and burned, and even his name was forbidden. The young poet quickly became an international symbol of the politically oppressed, but his plays were not revived until the 1940s, and some bans on his work remained in place until as late as 1971.

'Listen folks; I'm gonna have to stop for a minute, because I've lost my voice. This is the worst thing I've ever witnessed.'

Herbert 'Herb' Morrison (1905–89): eyewitness account on WLS Radio of the airship LZ 129 Hindenburg bursting into flames

'It's practically standing still now. They've dropped ropes out of the nose of the ship; and (uh) they've been taken ahold of down on the field by a number of men. It's starting to rain again; it's ... the rain had (uh) slacked up a little bit. The back motors of the ship are just holding it (uh) just enough to keep it from ... It's burst into flames! It burst into flames, and it's falling, it's crashing! Watch it! Watch it! Get out of the way! Get out of the way! Get this, Charlie; get this, Charlie! It's fire ... and it's crashing! It's crashing terrible! Oh, my! Get out of the way, please! It's burning and bursting into flames and the ... and it's falling on the mooring mast. And all the folks agree that this is terrible; this is the one of the worst catastrophes in the world. [Indecipherable] its flames ...

Crashing, oh! Four or five hundred feet into the sky and it ... it's a terrific crash, ladies and gentlemen. It's smoke, and it's in flames now; and the frame is crashing to the ground, not quite to the mooring mast. Oh, the humanity! and all the passengers screaming around here. I told you; it – I can't even talk to people Their friends are out there! Ah! It's ... it ... it's a ... ah! I ... I can't talk, ladies and gentlemen. Honest: it's just laying there, mass of smoking wreckage. Ah! And everybody can hardly breathe and talk and the screaming. Lady, I ... I ... I'm sorry. Honest: I ... I can hardly breathe. I ... I'm going to step inside, where I cannot see it. Charlie, that's terrible. Ah, ah ... I can't. Listen, folks; I ... I'm gonna have to stop for a minute because [indecipherable] I've lost my voice. This is the worst thing I've ever witnessed.'

The airship was destroyed within a minute of attempting to dock to a mooring mast in New Jersey, killing 36 people with 62 survivors.

JOHN DAVISON ROCKEFELLER
8 July 1839–23 May 1937

'Goodbye, I'll see you in heaven'

Farewell to Henry Ford shortly before Rockefeller's death

Ron Chernow's magisterial biography of Rockefeller examines the industrialist's character: '*In truth, John D. Rockefeller, Sr, had left behind a contradictory legacy – an amalgam of godliness and greed, compassion and fiendish cunning.*' In his 40 years of retirement, Rockefeller donated millions to charity, and created the Rockefeller Foundation, Rockefeller University, the University of Chicago, and the General Education Board. His foundations pioneered the development of medical research, and were important in the eradication of yellow fever and hookworm. Chernow noted: '*The fiercest robber baron had turned out to be the foremost philanthropist.*' In a meeting between Henry Ford and a frail Rockefeller shortly before his death at the age of 97, Rockefeller said, '*Goodbye, I'll see you in heaven.*' Ford replied, '*You will, if you get in.*'

Rockefeller was the son of a medicine pedlar and a deeply religious mother, and these contradictory influences became the foundation for his actions. He once said: '*I believe it is a religious duty to get all the money you can, fairly and honestly; to keep all you can and to give away all you can.*' He slowly squeezed out competitors by cutting deals with railroads to provide cheaper shipments to customers. He founded Standard Oil (ESSO) in 1870 and ran it aggressively until his retirement in 1897. By the time his Standard Oil Trust was at its peak in 1882, it controlled 90 per cent of the nation's oil refining and distribution. Rockefeller became the first American billionaire, possibly the richest man in history. Later, President Theodore Roosevelt's anti-monopoly campaign resulted in Standard Oil being dissolved in 1911 by the US Supreme Court.

Rockefeller adhered to total abstinence from tobacco and alcohol (which he called '*the right hand of the devil*') . Aged 86, he wrote a poem to summarize his life:

> 'I was early taught to work as well as play,
> My life has been one long, happy holiday;
> Full of work and full of play –
> I dropped the worry on the way –
> And God was good to me everyday.'

'We must be on you, but cannot see you – but gas is running low'

Part of last radio communication

Amelia Earhart was the first woman to receive the Distinguished Flying Cross, awarded for being the first female aviator to fly the Atlantic solo. She set many flying records, and wrote best-selling books about her experiences. In 1937, with Fred Noonan as navigator, she attempted to circumnavigate the globe in a Lockheed L-10 Electra. Leaving Miami on 1 June, they made stops for fuel in South America, Africa and Asia, arriving in Lae, New Guinea, on the 29th. They had completed 22,000 miles, and their final 7,000 miles would all be over the Pacific Ocean.

On 2 July, they took off from Lae, making for Howland Island 2,556 miles away. The island is not much more than a mile long by 500 yards wide and only 10 feet high. The US Coast Guard cutter *Itasca* was stationed there, to guide them to the island once they arrived in the vicinity. The final approach to Howland was not successful. *Itasca* received clear voice transmissions from Earhart identifying her plane, but she was unable to hear voice transmissions from the ship. At 7.42 a.m. she radioed: '*We must be on you, but cannot see you – but gas is running low. Have been unable to reach you by radio. We are flying at 1,000 feet.*' Her next transmission, at 7.58 a.m., said that she couldn't hear the *Itasca* and asked them to send voice signals so she could try to take a radio bearing. *Itasca* could not send voice signals at the frequency she asked for, so Morse code signals were sent instead. Earhart received these but said she was unable to determine their direction. In her last known transmission, at 8.43 a.m., she broadcast: '*We are on the line 157 337. We will repeat this message. We will repeat this on 6210 kilocycles. Wait.*' There may have been one last communication a few minutes later: '*We are running on line north and south.*' Her plane has never been found.

GEORGE GERSHWIN (JACOB GERSHOWITZ)
26 September 1898–11 July 1937

'George Gershwin died last week. I don't have to believe it if I don't want to.'

Reaction of author John O'Hara

Gershwin's compositions spanned both popular and classical genres, and his best-known melodies are universally familiar. He wrote most of his vocal and theatrical works, including more than a dozen Broadway shows, in collaboration with his elder brother, lyricist Ira Gershwin. In 1924, he composed his first major classical work, the wonderful *Rhapsody in Blue*, for orchestra and piano. Also in 1924, George and Ira collaborated on a musical comedy, *Lady Be Good*, which included such }future standards as 'Fascinating Rhythm'. A series of musicals followed, and in 1931 *Of Thee I Sing* was the first musical comedy to win a Pulitzer Prize. George stayed in Paris and wrote *An American in Paris*, before composing in 1935 the sublime and ambitious *Porgy and Bess*, from which we remember 'I Got Plenty o' Nuttin', 'Summertime' and 'It Ain't Necessarily So'. A critic wrote at the time: *'With a libretto that should never have been accepted on a subject that should never have been chosen, a man who should never have attempted it has written a work that has a considerable power.'*

Early in 1937, Gershwin complained of blinding headaches and a constant smell of burned rubber. Doctors discovered that he had developed a type of cystic malignant brain cancer. However, in recent years their diagnosis of glioblastoma multiforme has been questioned, with the surgeon's description being more consistent with a low-grade brain tumour, pilocytic astrocytoma. Gershwin had complained of feeling unwell for 20 years, suffering from chronic gastrointestinal symptoms, which he called his 'composer's stomach'. He died aged only 38 after surgery to remove the tumour, and received posthumously his only Oscar nomination, for the song 'They Can't Take That Away From Me'. According to Fred Astaire's letters to his sister Adele, Gershwin whispered Astaire's name before passing away. In 2005, the *Guardian* newspaper determined using 'estimates of earnings accrued in a composer's lifetime' that George Gershwin was the wealthiest composer of all time.

THOMAS CLAYTON WOLFE
3 October 1900–15 September 1938

'I've seen the dark man very close'

Letter to Maxwell Perkins, 12 August 1938

William Faulkner called Wolfe the finest writer of their generation, but less than half of his work was published in his own lifetime. His wonderful novel *You Can't Go Home Again* was published two years after his death. He developed pneumonia and later was diagnosed with tuberculosis of the brain. Worried over the author's condition, Wolfe's old editor Maxwell Perkins sent him a barrage of letters, despite Wolfe not having spoken to him for three years after a literary dispute. Wolfe was on his deathbed when he realized that Perkins had been his closest friend and supporter. On 12 August, he finally wrote back to Perkins from hospital in Seattle:

> 'Dear Max: I'm sneaking this against orders, but "I've got a hunch" – and I wanted to write these words to you. I've made a long voyage and been to a strange country, and I've seen the dark man very close; and I don't think I was too much afraid of him, but so much of mortality still clings to me – I wanted most desperately to live and still do, and I thought about you all a thousand times, and wanted to see you all again, and there was the impossible anguish and regret of all the work I had not done, of all the work I had to do – and I know now I'm just a grain of dust, and I feel as if a great window has been opened on life I did not know about before – and if I come through this, I hope to God I am a better man, and in some strange way I can't explain, I know I am a deeper and a wiser one. If I get on my feet and out of here, it will be months before I head back, but if I get on my feet, I'll come back ...'

Perkins travelled to Wolfe's bedside. The writer had developed tubercular meningitis, and his surgeon hoped that instead of many tubercles, there might be just one, which could be removed in a second operation. On 12 September, the doctor broke the news that Wolfe's brain was infested with 'myriads' of tubercles. There was nothing more that could be done for him, and he died three days later, still unconscious.

MUSTAFA KEMAL ATATÜRK
1881–10 November 1938

'Today I am not sad, for 15 years have taught me that Atatürk will never die'

Elderly officer at the fifteenth anniversary remembrance of Atatürk's death

Atatürk was the only undefeated Ottoman commander during World War I, and after its defeat he led the Turkish national movement in the Turkish War of Independence. He liberated Turkey and became its first president, embarking upon political, economic and social reforms.

'At five minutes past 9 one morning last week, in the capital city of Ankara, a bugler blew a blast, and all over the nation's 296,000 square miles, 21 million Turks stood motionless for five minutes. Only the delayed shriek of jet formations broke the silence. Then cannon began to boom at five-minute intervals as Kemal Atatürk, the Father of the Turks – dead 15 years this day – began his last voyage ... Behind a military band playing Chopin's Funeral March slowly marched 80,000 Turks, including the President, the Premier, every Cabinet minister, every parliamentary deputy, every provincial governor and every foreign diplomat. Many of the 7,000 marching Turkish soldiers wore their Korean war decorations. Ten generals and two admirals escorted the coffin, while another admiral guarded a velvet cushion which bore the Medal of Independence, the only decoration Atatürk ever wore. After $3\frac{1}{2}$ hours, the procession reached the top of a hill overlooking Ankara – the modern city built by Atatürk – and stopped before a square-pillared mausoleum, set in a 148-acre park ... The sarcophagus was lit only by the light from a huge wrought-iron window. There last week, covered with earth from each of Turkeys 64 provinces, the Father of the Turks finally came to rest. His grateful people had spent $12 million and laboured nine years to build their tribute to the dictator who modernized his ancient land and bequeathed it democracy. An elderly officer standing by spoke quietly to a friend: "I was on active duty during his funeral, when I shed bitter tears at the finality of death. Today I am not sad, for 15 years have taught me that Atatürk will never die."'

SIGMUND FREUD
6 May 1856–23 September 1939

**'My dear Schur, you remember our first talk.
You promised me then not to forsake me when my
time comes. Now it is nothing but torture and
makes no sense any more.'**

Last words to his doctor Max Schur

Sigismund Schlomo Freud was born in Freiberg, Moravia, now Pribor in the Czech Republic. A neurologist and psychologist, he was the founder of the psychoanalytic school of psychology. His family moved to Leipzig and then settled in Vienna, where Freud was educated. The family were Jewish, but Sigmund was non-practising. In 1930, he received the Goethe Prize in appreciation of his contribution to psychology and to German literary culture. Three years later the Nazis took control of Germany and Freud's books were among those burned and destroyed. In March 1938, Nazi Germany annexed Austria, and Freud was permitted to move to London after paying a large ransom *'to die in freedom'*. Listening to an idealistic broadcaster proclaiming this to be the last war, Freud commented, *'My last war.'*

He regularly smoked 20 cigars a day, and had undergone over 30 operations to remove tumours and fit prostheses after being diagnosed with cancer of the jaw in 1923. After specialists finally reported that it was useless to operate again, Freud remarked that *'It is tragic when a man outlives his body.'* On 22 September, he read Balzac's *La Peau de chagrin* in a single sitting. Bedridden, he pressured his friend and personal physician, Dr Max Schur, for relief from the intense pain. Schur administered three large doses of morphine over many hours in an assisted suicide, which resulted in Freud slipping into a coma and dying the following day. It has also been recorded that he mumbled, *'Das ist absurd! Das ist absurd!'* as he lost consciousness. He is alternatively reported to have said: *'The meagre satisfaction that man can extract from reality leaves him starving.'*

ISAAC EMMANUILOVICH BABEL
13 July 1894–27 January 1940

'I am only asking for one thing – let me finish my work'
Last words at his trial

As a child, Babel survived Odessa's 1905 pogrom with the help of Russian Orthodox neighbours, and became a Soviet journalist, playwright and short-story writer. According to his daughter, Nathalie Babel Brown, '*The young writer burst upon the literary scene and instantly became the rage in Moscow. The tradition in Russia being to worship poets and writers, Babel soon became one of the happy few, a group that included Soviet writers who enjoyed exceptional status and privileges in an otherwise impoverished and despotic country. In the late 1930s, he was given a villa in the writer's colony of Peredelkino, outside Moscow.*' However, he had an affair with the wife of the NKVD (secret police) chief Nikolai Yezhov, who put him under surveillance. Babel had also been heard to say of Trotsky: '*It's impossible to imagine the charm and strength of his influence on anyone who encounters him.*'

The new chief of the NKVD, Beria, was determined to outdo Yezhov in his zealousness in killing 'enemies of Stalin', and in May 1939, Babel was arrested at his dacha in Peredelkino and tortured, as evidenced by his bloodstained 'confession paper'. His daughter described his trial and execution:

'As we now know, his trial took place on January 26, 1940, in one of Lavrenti Beria's private chambers. It lasted about twenty minutes. The sentence had been prepared in advance and without ambiguity: death by firing squad, to be carried out immediately. Babel had been convicted of "active participation in an anti-Soviet Trotskyite organization", and of "being a member of a terrorist conspiracy, as well as spying for the French and Austrian governments". Babel's last recorded words in the proceedings were, "I am innocent. I have never been a spy. I never allowed any action against the Soviet Union. I accused myself falsely. I was forced to make false accusations against myself and others ... I am asking for only one thing – let me finish my work." He was shot the next day and his body was thrown into a communal grave.'

'I feel this time they have succeeded. I do not want them to undress me. I want you to undress me.'

Last words to his wife

Stalin seized control of the Soviet Union after Lenin died in 1924 and began killing all possible rivals. Trotsky, Lenin's principal assistant, fled from Russia in 1929, and Mexico agreed that he could settle there in exile. Stalin, however, had ordered his assassination. Trotsky became friends with Frank Jackson, who was actually Ramon Mercader, a Spanish communist sent by Stalin. One day, while Trotsky was meeting with 'Jackson' at his home, Mercader struck him in the back of the head with a mountaineer's ice axe. Trotsky's wife Natalia wrote:

'Not more than three or four minutes had elapsed when I heard a terrible, soul-shaking cry and without so much as realizing who it was that uttered this cry, I rushed in the direction from which it came. Between the dining room and the balcony, on the threshold, beside the door post and leaning against it stood ... Lev Davidovich. His face was covered with blood, his eyes, without glasses, were sharp blue, his hands were hanging ... "You know, in there" – his eyes moved towards the door of his room – "I sensed ... understood what he wanted to do ... He wanted to strike me ... once more ... but I didn't let him." He spoke calmly, quietly, his voice breaking ...

The ambulance pulled up at the hospital. It stopped. A crowd milled around us. "There may be enemies," it flashed through my mind, as was always the case in similar situations. "Where are our friends? They must surround the stretcher ..." They then began to remove the remaining garments without cutting them, and he said to me then, "I don't want them to undress me ... I want you to do it." He said this quite distinctly, only very sadly and gravely. These were the last words he spoke to me. When I finished I bent over him and touched his lips with mine. He answered me. Again ... It was our final farewell. But we were not aware of it.'

'I should not fear the historian's verdict'

Written a few days before his death

As Conservative prime minister from 1937 to 1940, Chamberlain is remembered for his appeasement policy towards Hitler, in particular his signing of the Munich Agreement in 1938. The Sudetenland region of Czechoslovakia was ceded to Nazi Germany, and Chamberlain famously declared: *'I believe it is peace in our time.'* Hitler continued his aggression, and Chamberlain continued his 'containment' policy until declaring war after the invasion of Poland on 3 September 1939. Recent historians agree that his policies allowed Britain time to move to a war footing.

In declaring war, Chamberlain said: *'We have a clear conscience, we have done all that any country could do to establish peace. The situation in which no word given by Germany's rulers could be trusted, and no people or country could feel themselves safe has become intolerable ... Now may God bless you all. May He defend the right. It is the evil things we shall be fighting against – brute force, bad faith, injustice, oppression, and persecution – and against them I am certain that the right will prevail.'* Later in the day he addressed Parliament: *'Everything that I have worked for, everything that I have hoped for, everything that I have believed in during my public life has crashed into ruins. There is only one thing left for me to do: that is devote what strength and power I have to forwarding the victory of the cause for which we have sacrificed so much.'*

Less than six months after his resignation as prime minister, Chamberlain died of bowel cancer. A few days before his death he wrote: *'So far as my personal reputation is concerned, I am not in the least disturbed about it. The letters which I am still receiving in such vast quantities so unanimously dwell on the same point, namely without Munich the war would have been lost and the Empire destroyed in 1938 ... I do not feel the opposite view ... has a chance of survival. Even if nothing further were to be published giving the true inside story of the past two years, I should not fear the historian's verdict.'*

'So we beat, boats against the current, borne back ceaselessly into the past'

Last lines of *The Great Gatsby*, inscribed on the grave
of Fitzgerald and his wife Zelda

From 1919, Fitzgerald had suffered with tuberculosis, having a severe attack in 1929 and then being affected by insomnia, depression and guilt over his wife Zelda being committed to an asylum. He developed alcoholism, partly because of an oversecretion of insulin. In 1936, he described himself as '*a cracked plate ... Now the standard cure for one who is sunk is to consider those in actual destitution or physical suffering. This is an all-weather beatitude for gloom in general, but at 3 o'clock in the morning the cure doesn't work and in a real dark night of the soul it is always 3 o'clock in the morning.*' A reporter asked him what he thought had become of the jazz-mad, gin-drinking generation he wrote of in *This Side of Paradise*. He answered: '*Some became brokers and threw themselves out of windows. Others became bankers and shot themselves. Still others became newspaper reporters. And a few became successful authors.*'

In late 1940, Fitzgerald suffered two heart attacks. After the first, he was ordered by his doctor to avoid strenuous exertion, so he moved in with Sheilah Graham, who had a ground-floor apartment in Hollywood near his, which had two flights of stairs. Three weeks after the first attack, they went to the theatre. Fitzgerald felt dizzy and had trouble leaving the theatre, allegedly saying to Graham, '*They think I am drunk, don't they?*' The following day, Graham saw him jump from his armchair, grab the mantelpiece, and fall, dying of a massive heart attack. At the time of Fitzgerald's death, the tax appraisers considered his copyrights worthless. Three of his four novels were out of print, and of *The Great Gatsby*, Matthew Bruccoli wrote that a second printing of 3,000 copies in 1925 did not sell well either: '*when Fitzgerald died fifteen years later there were still unsold copies ... The novel was never out of print; it had simply stopped selling ... F. Scott Fitzgerald died believing himself a failure ... The obituaries were condescending and he seemed destined for literary obscurity.*'

JAMES AUGUSTINE ALOYSIUS JOYCE
2 February 1882–13 January 1941

'Does nobody understand?'

Last utterance before his death in Zurich

Joyce's last words seem to give meaning to his reply for a request for a plan of *Ulysses*: '*If I gave it all up immediately, I'd lose my immortality. I've put in so many enigmas and puzzles that it will keep the professors busy for centuries arguing over what I meant, and that's the only way of insuring one's immortality.*' His books are notoriously 'difficult' but were a breakthrough in English literature, altering the possibilities of the 'form' of the novel. According to Stanley Kunitz, after Joyce left Ireland in 1902, his '*story for the next quarter of a century is the history of one long struggle for publication, a struggle probably unmatched in the annals of literature*'. Joyce completed *Dubliners* in 1902, but it was not published until 1914. From 1914 until 1921 he worked on developing a short story from *Dubliners*, struggling with its complexity until the famous last word, '*Yes*', of his magnum opus *Ulysses*. The first legal edition in the English language was not published until 1934, because of censorship battles. *Finnegans Wake* took eight years to write and revise, before Joyce would allow it to be published in 1939. His daughter died insane, and over the last ten years of his life Joyce became blind. In 1940 he was forced to leave his self-imposed exile in France because of the German occupation.

Now living in Zurich, on 11 January 1941 he underwent surgery for a perforated ulcer, and died two days later. The Irish government declined his widow's offer to repatriate his remains. Richard Ellmann reports that when the arrangements for Joyce's burial were being made, a Catholic priest tried to convince his widow that there should be a funeral mass. She replied, '*I couldn't do that to him.*' Joyce had written: '*I confess that I do not see what good it does to fulminate against the English tyranny while the Roman tyranny occupies the palace of the soul.*'

VIRGINIA WOOLF (*née* STEPHEN)
25 January 1882–28 March 1941

‛I feel certain that I'm going mad again’

Opening lines of suicide note to her husband

Virginia Stephen married writer and publisher Leonard Woolf in 1912, and in 1937 wrote in her diary: '*Love-making – after 25 years can't bear to be separate ... you see it is enormous pleasure being wanted: a wife. And our marriage so complete.*' However, in March 1941, fearing that she was on the brink of the latest in a series of breakdowns, she committed suicide by loading her overcoat pockets full of stones and wading into the River Ouse near her home. Her body was not found until 18 April. Her suicide note told her husband that she would rather die than endure another such episode.

'I feel certain that I am going mad again. I feel we can't go through another of those terrible times. And I shan't recover this time. I begin to hear voices, and I can't concentrate. So I am doing what seems the best thing to do. You have given me the greatest possible happiness. You have been in every way all that anyone could be. I don't think two people could have been happier 'til this terrible disease came. I can't fight any longer. I know that I am spoiling your life, that without me you could work. And you will I know. You see I can't even write this properly. I can't read. What I want to say is I owe all the happiness of my life to you. You have been entirely patient with me and incredibly good. I want to say that – everybody knows it. If anybody could have saved me it would have been you. Everything has gone from me but the certainty of your goodness. I can't go on spoiling your life any longer. I don't think two people could have been happier than we have been. V.'

'So I close in saying that I might have been given a bad break, but I've got an awful lot to live for. Thank you.'

Farewell speech to 61,808 cheering fans at Yankee Stadium, 4 July 1939

'Fans, for the past two weeks you have been reading about the bad break I got. Yet today I consider myself the luckiest man on the face of the earth. I have been in ballparks for seventeen years and have never received anything but kindness and encouragement from you fans. Look at these grand men. Which of you wouldn't consider it the highlight of his career just to associate with them for even one day? Sure, I'm lucky. Who wouldn't consider it an honor to have known Jacob Ruppert? Also, the builder of baseball's greatest empire, Ed Barrow? To have spent six years with that wonderful little fellow, Miller Huggins? Then to have spent the next nine years with that outstanding leader, that smart student of psychology, the best manager in baseball today, Joe McCarthy? Sure, I'm lucky. When the New York Giants, a team you would give your right arm to beat, and vice versa, sends you a gift – that's something. When everybody down to the groundskeepers and those boys in white coats remember you with trophies – that's something. When you have a wonderful mother-in-law who takes sides with you in squabbles with her own daughter – that's something. When you have a father and a mother who work all their lives so that you can have an education and build your body – it's a blessing. When you have a wife who has been a tower of strength and shown more courage than you dreamed existed – that's the finest I know. So I close in saying that I might have been given a bad break, but I've got an awful lot to live for. Thank you.'

Called 'the Iron Horse', Gehrig set a record for consecutive baseball games played until halted by illness, a record that stood for 56 years. He also set a record for the most career grand slams. After 2,130 games, with his powers fading, he was diagnosed with the fatal neuromuscular disease amyotropic lateral sclerosis, since called Gehrig's disease.

JOHN GILLESPIE MAGEE, JR
9 June 1922–11 December 1941

'Oh! I have slipped the surly bonds of Earth.'

From his poem 'High Flight', 3 September 1941

'Oh! I have slipped the surly bonds of Earth
And danced the skies on laughter-silvered wings;
Sunward I've climbed, and joined the tumbling mirth
Of sun-split clouds, – and done a hundred things
You have not dreamed of – wheeled and soared and swung
High in the sunlit silence. Hov'ring there,
I've chased the shouting wind along, and flung
My eager craft through footless halls of air ...
Up, up the long, delirious burning blue
I've topped the wind-swept heights with easy grace
Where never lark, or ever eagle flew –
And, while with silent, lifting mind I've trod
The high untrespassed sanctity of space,
Put out my hand, and touched the face of God.'

Born in Shanghai, Magee was an American who at the age of 18 enlisted with the Royal Canadian Air Force. After a year of flight training, he was posted to Fighter Squadron 412 in England, arriving in 1941. He was promoted to pilot officer after several missions over England and in France, and on 3 September 1941 he flew a high-altitude test flight in a newer model of the Spitfire V. As he climbed upwards, he was inspired to write a poem. Once back on the ground, he wrote a letter to his parents: '*I am enclosing a verse I wrote the other day. It started at 30,000 feet, and was finished soon after I landed.*' On the back of the letter, he jotted down his poem 'High Flight'. Just three months later, on 11 December 1941 (only three days after the United States entered the war), he was killed in a mid-air collision over Lincolnshire in his beloved Spitfire V. Buried in Lincolnshire, his grave is inscribed with the first and last lines of the poem. 'High Flight' was quoted by President Reagan after the *Challenger* space shuttle disaster on 28 January 1988.

DAVID HILBERT
23 January 1862–14 February 1943

'We must know. We will know.'

Epitaph on his tombstone in Göttingen

Hilbert's epitaph is taken from the closing lines of his retirement address to the Society of German Scientists and Physicians in Königsberg on 8 September 1930: *'We must not believe those, who today, with philosophical bearing and deliberative tone, prophesy the fall of culture and accept the ignorabimus. For us there is no ignorabimus, and in my opinion none whatever in natural science. In opposition to the foolish ignorabimus our slogan shall be: We must know – we will know!'* The Latin maxim *'ignoramus et ignorabimus'*, meaning *'we do not know and will not know'*, stood for a position on the limits of scientific knowledge in nineteenth-century thought. Hilbert refused to believe that it could apply to what he called *'the global culture'* of mathematics. He had been deeply angered by the Nazi removal of all the Jewish members of his University of Göttingen. In 1929, he had been seated at a banquet next to the new Minister of Education, Bernhard Rust. When Rust asked, *'How is mathematics in Göttingen now that it has been freed of the Jewish influence?'* Hilbert bravely replied, *'Mathematics in Göttingen? There is really none any more.'* As he said, *'Mathematics knows no races or geographic boundaries; for mathematics, the cultural world is one country.'*

Hilbert was one of the most influential and universal mathematicians of the nineteenth and early twentieth centuries, discovering and developing a broad range of fundamental ideas, including the theory of Hilbert Spaces (one of the foundations of functional analysis), proof theory, mathematical logic and invariant theory. His 'finiteness theorem' of 1888 was dismissed with the comment: *'This is not Mathematics. This is Theology'*, but came to be accepted later. Hilbert said: *'One can measure the importance of a scientific work by the number of earlier publications rendered superfluous by it.'* His logical mind is demonstrated in his statement: *'If one were to bring ten of the wisest men in the world together and ask them what was the most stupid thing in existence, they would not be able to discover anything so stupid as astrology.'*

ROBERT LAURENCE BINYON
10 August 1869–10 March 1943

'They shall grow not old, as we that are left grow old'

Recited on Remembrance Day, from his poem 'For the Fallen', 1914

'They shall grow not old, as we that are left grow old:
Age shall not weary them, nor the years condemn.
At the going down of the sun and in the morning
We will remember them.'

This is the stanza of Binyon's best-known poem, written in 1914 about the bloodbath of World War I. It was published in *The Times* in September, after the huge casualties of the Battle of the Marne, in which two million men fought and over 500,000 were killed or wounded. The poem is still recited at cenotaphs and church services on the eleventh hour of the nearest Sunday to the eleventh day of the eleventh month, which was when the war ended. Although too old to enlist, in 1915 Binyon volunteered for work in a British hospital for French soldiers. His poems 'Fetching the Wounded' and 'The Distant Guns' were inspired by his hospital service. On 11 November 1985, Binyon was among 16 poets of World War I commemorated on a slate stone in Westminster Abbey's Poets' Corner. The inscription on the stone, written by Wilfred Owen, reads: *'My subject is War, and the pity of War. The Poetry is in the pity.'*

Binyon was a poet, dramatist, literary writer and art scholar. While Keeper of Oriental Art at the British Museum, he became a published and renowned expert on Japanese and Chinese art. He inspired his friends Ezra Pound and W.B. Yeats, and after retiring from the British Museum was Norton Professor of Poetry at Harvard.

'What have I lived for?'

Last words to his nurse

Towards the end of his tormented life, the lyricist said: *'Talent is beautiful.'* Hart believed that despite his own talents he was ugly, something that caused him much grief. He was only five feet tall, with a normally proportioned head but a childlike body, hands and feet. The noted lyricist Alan Jay Lerner said that *'because of his size, the opposite sex was denied him, so he was forced to find relief in the only other sex left'*. Frederick W. Nolan's biography notes that Hart was ambivalent about his sexuality, compulsively drowning himself in an unending round of parties and alcohol. Of his famed Broadway song-writing partnership with Richard Rodgers, Nolan quotes a 'close friend' of Hart's who said: *'Poor Larry. What a shame he had to fall in love with Dick.'* Hart suffered great emotional turmoil, and his increasing alcoholism and struggle with homosexuality caused friction between him and Rodgers. There was a brief break-up in 1943, and Rodgers started working with Hart's school-friend Oscar Hammerstein II. However, in the autumn, Rodgers and Hart teamed for a final time for the revival of *A Connecticut Yankee*. Five days after the show opened, Hart died alone in New York City of pneumonia caused by exposure and aggravated by alcoholism.

From 1920 to 1930, Rodgers and Hart wrote an amazing array of musical comedies for Broadway and London's West End, creating an average of four new shows a year. In 1930 they relocated to Hollywood, where they wrote the scores for several movie musicals, before returning to New York. Hart's contribution to the canon of American popular music cannot be underestimated. His hundreds of songs included 'The Lady is a Tramp', 'Blue Moon', 'The Most Beautiful Girl in the World', 'Isn't It Romantic', 'Mountain Greenery', 'Falling in Love with Love', 'This Can't Be Love' and 'My Funny Valentine'. His lyrics were witty and technically sophisticated, and his advocacy of internal rhyme and multisyllabic rhyming is seen in: *'I'm wild again, beguiled again / A simpering, whimpering child again / Bewitched, bothered and bewildered – am I.'*

ALUN LEWIS
1 July 1915–5 March 1944

'A bullet stopped his song'

From his poem 'All Day it Has Rained'

Lewis' best-known poem was written in memory of the poet Edward Thomas, who died in World War I and whom he greatly admired.

> 'And I can remember nothing dearer or more to my heart
> Than the children I watched in the woods on Saturday
> Shaking down burning chestnuts for the schoolyard's merry play
> Or the shaggy patient dog who followed me
> By Sheet and Steep and up the wooded scree
> To the Shoulder o' Mutton where Edward Thomas brooded long
> On death and beauty – till a bullet stopped his song.'

Regarded by many as Britain's finest Second World War poet, Lewis joined the army in 1940 although he was a pacifist. In 1942 he was sent to India with the South Wales Borderers. As an intelligence officer in Burma, he could have stayed safely at headquarters, but he repeatedly asked to be sent to the front. According to the war diary of the 6th Battalion, he went to a latrine at the bottom of a steep bank, fell heavily in his hurry to get there and accidentally shot himself in the head.

Some critics see Lewis as the last of the great Romantic poets, a twentieth-century Keats. He was prone to depression, and in his last letter to his wife Gweno, written at the end of February, he wrote: *'The long self-torture I've been through is resolving itself now, into a discipline of the emotions and hopes of you and me ... I feel my grasp is broader and steadier than it's been for a long time. I hope it's true, because that's how I want to be: and the rest of me is invulnerable. I want you to know that.'*

FIELD MARSHAL ERWIN JOHANNES EUGEN ROMMEL
15 November 1891–14 October 1944

'In about half an hour there will come a telephone call from Ülm to say that I have had an accident and am dead'

Last words to his aide Captain Hermann Aldinger

Rommel was a war hero in World War I and the Second World War invasion of France, and was known as the Desert Fox for his exploits in North Africa. He was a co-conspirator in the von Stauffenberg 20 July plot to kill Hitler, and because of his prestige was allowed to commit suicide rather than be strung up with piano wire like the other plotters.

'After a moment General Burgdorf said that he wished to speak to the Field Marshal [Rommel] alone ... As he [Rommel] was taking leave of his wife, [his 15-year-old son] Manfred entered the room cheerfully, to see what had become of his father. The generals were waiting for him. Rommel said good-bye to his son also. Then he turned and went into the room next door. Manfred followed at his heels. Rommel called for his soldier servant and sent him to find [Captain] Aldinger. To Aldinger he explained what was in store for him. He was now quite calm but Aldinger could hear Frau Rommel sobbing in her room. Aldinger was not disposed to take it like this.

Aldinger said we could at least shoot Burgdorf and Maisel. "No," said Rommel, "they have their orders. I have Manfred and my wife to think of." Then he told me that he had been promised that no harm should come of them if he took the first choice. A pension would be paid. He was to be given a state funeral. He would be buried at home in Herrlingen. "I have spoken to my wife and made up my mind," he said, "I will never allow myself to be hanged by that man, Hitler!! I planned no murder. I only tried to serve my country, as I have done all my life, but now this is what I must do. In about half an hour there will come a telephone call from Ülm to say that I have had an accident and am dead."'

'If only there were no other people in the world'

Final words in her last diary entry, 1 August 1944,
three days before she was arrested

'... I just can't keep it up any more, because when everybody starts hovering over me, I get cross, then sad, and finally end up turning my heart inside out, the bad part on the outside and the good part on the inside, and keep trying to find a way to become what I'd like to be and what I could be if ... if only there were no other people in the world.'

Anne Frank was one of the German-Jewish victims of Nazi persecution during World War II. After Germany invaded the Netherlands in 1940, increasingly severe anti-Jewish measures were enforced there. The Frank family tried to escape deportation by going into hiding. In July 1942, Otto Frank, Edith Frank-Hollander and their daughters Margot and Anne hid in an annexe of rooms at the back of Otto's office in Amsterdam. They were later joined by Mr and Mrs Daan, their son Peter and a Mr Dussel. After more than two years the group was betrayed and deported to various Nazi concentration camps.

The 15-year-old Anne and her sister Margot both died of typhus in Bergen-Belsen in March 1945, only a few weeks before the camp was liberated. Their father was the only member of the group to survive. During her time in hiding, Anne had kept a diary, in which she described daily life in the back annexe, the isolation and the fear of discovery. After the betrayal, the diary was found by Miep Gies, Otto Frank's former secretary and one of the family's helpers. When it was confirmed that Anne would not be returning, it was given to Otto. The first Dutch edition appeared in 1947, since when the diary has been published in more than 55 languages. Anne Frank's House is now a tourist attraction.Anne wished for a career as a writer, and one of her diary entries reads: '*Perhaps through Jewish suffering the world will learn good.*'

'This is the end – for me the beginning of life'

Message given to a fellow prisoner to pass on to Bishop George Bell of Chichester

This German Lutheran pastor and theologian was important in the resistance movement against Nazism. In 1933 he co-wrote 'The Bethel Confession', affirming God's faithfulness to the Jews as his chosen people, in opposition to the official Nazi-supported 'German Christian' church. However, it was watered down by opposition church leaders and he refused to sign it. He now founded the new Confessing Church, insisting that Christ, not the Führer, was its head. From 1935, most of his activities, devoted to opposition to Hitler, were by necessity underground as the Nazis suppressed the new church and closed its seminaries. Banned from Berlin, Bonhoeffer went to the United States in 1939 and was asked to stay there by his friends. However, he was determined to return to Germany, and came back on the last scheduled steamer to cross the Atlantic.

Back in Germany, Bonhoeffer was forbidden to speak in public and had to report his activities to the police. He secretly joined the Abwehr, a German military intelligence organization, which was also the centre of anti-Hitler resistance. On 6 April 1943, he was arrested, and later sent to concentration camps. Know-ing the war was lost, Hitler decided to take revenge on all his suspected assassination plotters. On 8 April 1945, Bonhoeffer was condemned to death, and the next day he was stripped naked and hanged with thin wire, along with other Abwehr conspirators, at Flossenbürg. The camp doctor who witnessed the execution wrote:

> 'I saw Pastor Bonhoeffer ... kneeling on the floor praying fervently to God. I was most deeply moved by the way this lovable man prayed, so devout and so certain that God heard his prayer. At the place of execution, he again said a short prayer and then climbed the few steps to the gallows, brave and composed. His death ensued after a few seconds. In the almost fifty years that I worked as a doctor, I have hardly ever seen a man die so entirely submissive to the will of God.'

❛Be careful❜

Last words to his daughter

In his biography of FDR, Conrad Black wrote that the President was sitting for a portrait when he put his left hand to the back of his head and said: '*I have a terrific pain in the back of my head.*' As he was carried to his bed by several people, he was understood by his daughter Laura to say, only semi-consciously, '*Be careful.*' These were his last words before he died of a massive cerebral haemorrhage. Throughout his life, from his catching poliomyelitis in 1921, he had shown terrific courage, fighting to hide his disability and illnesses from the American people.

The only US president elected to more than two terms, FDR won the first of four presidential elections in 1932, while the United States was in the depths of the Great Depression. He brought hope as he promised prompt, vigorous action, and asserted in his inaugural address, '*The only thing we have to fear is fear itself.*' There were 13 million unemployed, and almost every bank was closed. In his first '100 Days', he proposed, and Congress enacted, a massive programme to bring recovery to business and agriculture, and relief to the unemployed and to those in danger of losing farms and homes. He declared that his 'New Deal' was for '*the forgotten man at the bottom of the economic pyramid*'. He is credited with keeping the country's economic crisis from developing into a political crisis.

When the Second World War broke out, FDR kept the USA neutral while devoting massive resources to its military capability. When France fell in 1940, leaving Britain alone fighting German expansion, he began to send all possible aid, short of actual military involvement, claiming that '*The best immediate defence of the United States is the success of Great Britain defending itself.*' When the Japanese attacked Pearl Harbor on 7 December 1941, he directed organization of the nation for global war, dying in office when the conflict was almost ended.

BENITO AMILCARE ANDREA MUSSOLINI, IL DUCE, HIS EXCELLENCY BENITO MUSSOLINI, HEAD OF GOVERNMENT, DUCE OF FASCISM, AND FOUNDER OF THE EMPIRE
29 July 1883–28 April 1945

'I await the end of the tragedy'

Interviewed in 1945 by Madeleine Mollier, just before
he was captured and executed

'Seven years ago I was an interesting person. Now I am a corpse ... Yes, madam, I am finished. My star has fallen. I work and I try, yet know that all is but a farce ... I await the end of the tragedy and – strangely detached from everything – I do not feel any more an actor. I feel I am the last of spectators.'

After Allied forces landed in Sicily in 1943, Mussolini was deposed by the Fascist Grand Council and was the most hated man in Italy. Anxious to prevent a possible rescue attempt by the Germans, the new government moved him around the country, finally settling on a remote ski resort. However, in September he was taken from his makeshift prison in a daring glider raid without a shot being fired. Two weeks later, he flew back to his homeland in a fighter plane borrowed from the Luftwaffe, to become the figurehead of a puppet government controlled by Hitler. Almost immediately the Germans deported the Jewish population of Rome, and forced Mussolini to execute those who had deposed him, including his own son-in-law. Learning of the execution, Mussolini confessed to his wife, *'From that morning I have begun to die.'*

In 1945, Mussolini and his mistress Clara Petacci joined the retreating Germans, but were recognized as they headed to Switzerland to board a plane for Franco's Spain. Mussolini was wearing a German uniform. The next day the pair and most of their 15 accompanying personnel were summarily shot by Communist partisans. As Petacci fell, Mussolini opened his jacket and screamed, *'Shoot me in the chest!'* He fell down, but it took another bullet to kill him. On 29 April 1945, the bodies were strung up on meat hooks in a Milan square, and stoned by the civilian population.

ADOLF HITLER
20 April 1889–30 April 1945

'*I myself and my wife – in order to escape the disgrace of deposition or capitulation – choose death*'
From his will

Hitler typed his will in his bunker at 4 a.m. on 29 April 1945, the day before he and Eva Braun committed suicide.

'As I did not consider that I could take responsibility, during the years of struggle, of contracting a marriage, I have now decided, before the closing of my earthly career, to take as my wife that girl who, after many years of faithful friendship, entered, of her own free will, the practically besieged town in order to share her destiny with me. At her own desire she goes as my wife with me into death. It will compensate us for what we both lost through my work in the service of my people. What I possess belongs – in so far as it has any value – to the Party. Should this no longer exist, to the State; should the State also be destroyed, no further decision of mine is necessary. My pictures, in the collections which I have bought in the course of years, have never been collected for private purposes, but only for the extension of a gallery in my home town of Linz on Donau. It is my most sincere wish that this bequest may be duly executed. I nominate as my Executor my most faithful Party comrade, Martin Bormann.

He is given full legal authority to make all decisions. He is permitted to take out everything that has a sentimental value or is necessary for the maintenance of a modest simple life, for my brothers and sisters, also above all for the mother of my wife and my faithful co-workers who are well known to him, principally my old Secretaries Frau Winter etc. who have for many years aided me by their work. I myself and my wife – in order to escape the disgrace of deposition or capitulation – choose death. It is our wish to be burnt immediately on the spot where I have carried out the greatest part of my daily work in the course of a twelve years' service to my people.'

DR PAUL JOSEPH GOEBBELS
29 October 1897–1 May 1945

'I have nowhere to go because with little children I will not be able to make it'

Farewell words to Vice-Admiral Voss

'Later on 1 May, Vice-Admiral Hans-Erich Voss saw Goebbels for the last time: "Before the breakout [from the bunker] began, about ten generals and officers, including myself, went down individually to Goebbels's shelter to say goodbye. While saying goodbye I asked Goebbels to join us. But he replied: 'The captain must not leave his sinking ship. I have thought about it all and decided to stay here. I have nowhere to go because with little children I will not be able to make it.'"'

The Reichsminister of Propaganda in Nazi Germany from 1933 to 1945, Goebbels earned his doctorate for a thesis on eighteenth-century romantic drama. He remained with Hitler in Berlin in his bunker to the end, and following the Führer's suicide he became the Third Reich's Chancellor for one day. On 30 April, with the Russians advancing to within a few hundred yards of the bunker, Goebbels was one of four witnesses to Hitler's will. After the Führer had shot himself, Goebbels commented: *'The heart of Germany has ceased to beat. The Führer is dead.'*

Vice-Admiral Voss recalled: *'When Goebbels learned that Hitler had committed suicide, he was very depressed and said: "It is a great pity that such a man is not with us any longer. But there is nothing to be done. For us, everything is lost now and the only way left for us is the one which Hitler chose. I shall follow his example."'* At eight o'clock on the evening of 1 May, Goebbels arranged for an SS doctor to kill his six children by injecting them with morphine and, when they were unconscious, crushing ampoules of cyanide into their mouths. Goebbels and his wife Magda then went up to the garden of the Chancellery, where they killed themselves. Joachim Fest commented: *'What he seemed to fear more than anything else was a death devoid of dramatic effects ... Whatever he thought or did was always based on this one agonizing wish for self-exaltation, and this same object was served by the murder of his children ... They were the last victims of an egomania extending beyond the grave.'*

'Shakespeare, Here I Come!'

Intended dying words, told to H.L. Mencken

The American novelist and journalist helped pioneer the realist-naturalist school of writing. He specialized in characters who were underdogs, to some extent ignoring a moral code in order to overcome obstacles. Towards the end of his life he came to the attention of the American public more for his political views than his creative works. In 1941 he wrote *America is Worth Saving*, an anti-war diatribe, partially because of his misplaced admiration for Russia. Since Russia at that time was aligned with Germany, he felt that joining England in the fight against Fascism would also lead America into a war against Communist Russia. However, Japan's attack at Pearl Harbor and Hitler's attack on Russia forced a modification of his views.

In 1944 he received the Award of Merit from the American Academy of Arts and Letters for *Sister Carrie*, *Twelve Men* and *An American Tragedy*, among other books. In July 1945, he joined the Communist Party, stating: '*Belief in the greatness and dignity of Man has been the guiding principle of my life and work. The logic of my life and work leads me therefore to apply for membership in the Communist Party.*' A superb novelist, he fought with censors for a more equitable society and for freedom of expression, at the cost of his personal reputation and book sales.

Dreiser died of heart failure with only the last chapter of *The Stoic* unfinished. At his funeral service, his friend Charlie Chaplin read from Dreiser's poem 'The Road I Came'. H.L. Mencken eulogized: '*the fact remains that he is a great artist, and that no other American of his generation left so wide and handsome a mark upon the national letters. American writing, before and after his time, differed almost as much as biology before and after Darwin. He was a man of large originality, of profound feeling, and of unshakable courage. All of us who write are better off because he lived, worked, and hoped.*'

'Yes, Yes, as God wills it. May God reward you for it. May God protect the dear fatherland. Go on working for him ... oh, you dear Saviour!'

Dying words in hospital

From a distinguished Westphalian family, the 'Lion of Münster' was beatified in 2005. A German count (*graf*), he was the Roman Catholic Bishop of Münster from 1933, in the strongly Catholic region of Westphalia and Lower Rhine. He consistently spoke out against the Third Reich. In 1935, he led a mass protest against the Fascist leader Rosenborg speaking in Münster. The police stopped crowds coming to support the bishop, and he spoke from his cathedral pulpit: *'Can the shepherd be severed from his flock? Can the police divide Catholics from their own bishop by ropes and chains?'* In Berlin, his sermons were regarded as *'the strongest attack against the German political leadership for decades'*.

On 13 July 1941, von Galen publicly attacked the Gestapo, disappearances without trial, the closing of Catholic institutions and the fear imposed on all honest Germans. On 20 July 1941, he informed the faithful that all written protests against Nazi hostilities had been useless, and that members of religious orders were still being deported or jailed. He declared that the German people were being destroyed not by Allied bombing, but by negative forces within Germany. In a third 1941 sermon he complained of the continued desecration of Catholic churches, and the deportation and euthanasia of mentally ill people, usually in prison camps. His sermons were reproduced and sent to families all over Germany, and to German soldiers on the Western and Eastern Fronts. They were even dropped over Germany by Allied planes. One Nazi official proposed that the bishop should be executed, and Hitler wanted him arrested, but Goebbels warned of the deleterious effect upon the morale of German Catholic troops and on the 40 million German-speaking Catholics. It may be that von Galen's sermons inspired the formation of the anti-Nazi White Rose group. He was made a cardinal in Rome in February 1946, to rapturous applause from the congregation, and died a few days after his return to Germany, from an appendix infection.

JOHN MAYNARD KEYNES, FIRST BARON KEYNES
5 June 1883–21 April 1946

'I should have drunk more champagne'

His last words, when asked if he regretted anything

This economist influenced both economic theory and practice, advocating interventionist government, using both fiscal and monetary policies to smooth business cycles. He helped the world out of recession by overturning neoclassical economist ideas that free markets would automatically provide full employment, as long as workers were flexible in their wage demands. His economic policies were adopted by leading Western economies, especially during the 1950s and 1960s. However, his ideas were ignored from the 1970s onwards, as Milton Friedman-influenced governments allowed the 'invisible hand of market forces' to take control. Unrestrained capitalism led to the largely global recession of 2008, and Keynesian policies were used across the world to haul economies back into financial shape.

Part of London's bohemian Bloomsbury group, Keynes dined with such luminaries as Virginia Woolf and E.M. Forster. For most of his life he was simultaneously a don, a diplomat and a highly successful currency speculator. As his stature grew, his sexuality shifted, and in 1925 he married the beautiful Russian ballerina Lydia Lopokova, their marriage lasting for the rest of his life. Keynes suffered a series of heart attacks trying to secure an American loan for Britain after World War II, a process he described as *'absolute hell'*. He had his first severe heart attack on 19 March 1946, on the train to Washington, dying a month later. His *Times* obituary of 22 April 1946 informs us: *'To find an economist of comparable influence, one would have to go back to Adam Smith.'* In 1999, *Time* magazine named him one of the 100 most important people of the twentieth century, stating that *'His radical idea that governments should spend money they don't have may have saved capitalism.'* It was Keynes who told us: *'The long run is a misleading guide to current affairs. In the long run we are all dead.'*

GERTRUDE STEIN

3 February 1874–27 July 1946

❛"What is the answer?" (I was silent.) "In that case, what is the question?"❜

Last words, spoken to Alice B. Toklas

An American writer who spent most of her life in France, Stein became a catalyst in the development of modern art and avant-garde literature. She shared her literary salon at 27 rue de Fleurus, Paris, first with her brother Leo from 1874, and then with her partner Alice B. Toklas from 1903 until Stein's death in 1946. The salon became home to her extensive modern art collection, including works by her friends Picasso, Bracque, Matisse, Renoir, Cézanne, Toulouse-Lautrec, Daumier, Bonnard and Gauguin. F. Scott Fitzgerald and Ernest Hemingway visited, and to some extent Stein influenced Hemingway's style of writing. In 1925 she wrote to Fitzgerald: '*One does not get better but different and older and that is always a pleasure.*'

Despite her German-Jewish parentage, she announced that Hitler should be awarded the Nobel Peace Prize: '*I say that Hitler ought to have the peace prize, because he is removing all the elements of contest and of struggle from Germany. By driving out the Jews and the democratic and Left element, he is driving out everything that conduces to activity. That means peace ... By suppressing Jews ... he was ending struggle in Germany*' (*New York Times* magazine, 6 May 1934). Stein stayed in France throughout World War II. She and Toklas were both Jews, but placed under the protection of Marshall Pétain. Her written works, such as *The Autobiography of Alice B. Toklas* (which brought her international fame), *Three Lives* and *Tender Buttons,* were meant to be the literary counterparts of her beloved Cubism, and divide critics as to whether they are masterworks or failed experiments.

Stein died from stomach cancer in Neuilly-sur-Seine, being interred in Paris in the Père Lachaise cemetery. As she was being wheeled into the operating theatre for surgery, she enigmatically asked Toklas: '*What is the answer?*' Toklas struggled for a reply, and before she could speak, Stein went on: '*In that case, what is the question?*'

'There is nothing to be said in mitigation'

Judgment of the International Military Tribunal
for the Trial of German Major War Criminals

'Goering is indicted on all four counts. The evidence shows that after Hitler he was the most prominent man in the Nazi Régime. He was Commander-in-Chief of the Luftwaffe, Plenipotentiary for the Four Year Plan, and had tremendous influence with Hitler, at least until 1943 when their relationship deteriorated, ending in his arrest in 1945. He testified that Hitler kept him informed of all important military and political problems ... Although their extermination was in Himmler's hands, Goering was far from disinterested or inactive, despite his protestations in the witness box. By decree of 31st July, 1941, he directed Himmler and Heydrich to bring "about a complete solution of the Jewish question in the German sphere of influence in Europe" ... There is nothing to be said in mitigation. For Goering was often, indeed almost always, the moving force, second only to his leader. He was the leading war aggressor, both as political and as military leader; he was the director of the slave labour program and the creator of the oppressive program against the Jews and other races, at home and abroad. All of these crimes he has frankly admitted. On some specific cases there may be conflict of testimony, but in terms of the broad outline, his own admissions are more than sufficiently wide to be conclusive of his guilt. His guilt is unique in its enormity. The record discloses no excuses for this man.'

A World War I fighter ace with 22 confirmed kills, Goering was one of Hitler's closest acolytes. After his trial, he made an appeal, offering to accept the court's death sentence if he were shot as a soldier instead of hanged as a common criminal, but the court refused. He committed suicide with a potassium cyanide capsule the night before he was to be hanged. The poison was hidden in jars of the opaque skin cream he used for his dermatitis. His body was displayed next to the gallows for the witnesses of the executions.

'I believe in Germany'

Last words of last war criminal hanged

The following were all hanged on the same day for war crimes following the Nuremberg War Trials of 1945–46. Stalin had proposed executing 50,000–100,000 German staff officers, but only 10 were executed. Martin Bormann was sentenced to death in absentia and Goering committed suicide the night before he was due to be hanged. Sadly, General Jodl was acquitted on all counts, six years after his hanging. He had requested a firing squad.

01:11 a.m. Joachim von Ribbentrop – *'My last wish is that Germany realize its entity and that an understanding be reached between East and West. I wish peace to the world.'*
c.01:22 a.m. Field Marshal Wilhelm Keitel – *'I call on God Almighty to have mercy on the German people. More than two million German soldiers went to their death for the fatherland before me. I follow now my sons – all for Germany.'*
01:36 a.m. Ernest Kaltenbrunner – *'I have loved my German people and my fatherland with a warm heart. I have done my duty by the laws of my people and I am sorry this time my people were led by men who were not soldiers and that crimes were committed of which I had no knowledge. Germany, good luck.'*
01:47 a.m. Alfred Rosenberg – *'No.'* (asked if he had any last words)
c.01:56 a.m. Hans Frank – *'I am thankful for the kind treatment during my captivity and I ask God to accept me with mercy.'*
02:05 a.m. Wilhelm Frick – *'Long live eternal Germany.'*
02:12 a.m. Julius Streicher – *'Heil Hitler!'* ('Ask the man his name.') *'You know my name well. Julius Streicher! Now it goes with God. Purim Fest 1946! The Bolsheviks will hang you one day! I am with God. Adele, my dear wife.'*
02:20 a.m. Fritz Sauckel – *'I am dying innocent. The sentence is wrong. God protect Germany and make Germany great again. Long live Germany! God protect my family!'*
c.02:09 a.m. General Alfred Jodl – *'My greetings to you, my Germany.'*
02:38 a.m. Artur Seyss-Inquart – *'I hope that this execution is the last act of tragedy of the Second World War and that the lesson taken from this world war will be that peace and understanding should exist between peoples. I believe in Germany.'*

DAMON RUNYON (ALFRED DAMON RUNYAN)
4 October 1884–10 December 1946

'You can keep the things of bronze and stone, and give me one man to remember me just once a year'

Note sent to his friends shortly before he died

Early in his career as a newspaperman, humorist and writer, a typographical slip altered Runyan to Runyon and he kept the name. He was a legendary reporter who gained fame with his tales of the gambling, racing and criminal world – a companion to Al Capone, Jack Dempsey, Babe Ruth, Arnold Rothstein and Walter Winchell. His best friend was the mobster accountant Otto Berman, whom he used in several of his stories under the alias 'Regret, the horse player'. When Berman was killed in a hit on his Mafia boss, 'Dutch' Schultz, Runyon was quick to correct press releases stating that Berman was one of Schultz's gunmen, saying: *'Otto would have been as effective a bodyguard as a two-year-old.'*

He was best known for his short stories celebrating the world of Broadway in the Prohibition era. His characters such as Lemon Drop Kid, Dave the Dude, Harry the Horse, Dream Street Rose and Izzy Cheesecake reflected city life, and 16 stories and one play were turned into movies. Runyon warns us: *'One of these days in your travels, a guy is going to come up to you and show you a nice brand-new deck of cards on which the seal is not yet broken, and this guy is going to offer to bet you that he can make the Jack of Spades jump out of the deck and squirt cider in your ear. But, son, do not bet this man, for as sure as you are standing there, you are going to end up with an earful of cider.'*

A life-long chain-smoker, Runyon contracted throat cancer in 1938. He held nightly meetings with friends and colleagues at Lindy's restaurant, but in 1944 an operation left him unable to speak. He continued his meetings, communicating by written notes. A national celebrity, he died two years later, on 10 December 1946. His ashes were scattered out of a plane over Broadway, by the World War I air ace Eddie Rickenbacker.

W.C. FIELDS (CLAUDE WILLIAM DUKENFIELD)
29 January 1880–25 December 1946

'Here lies W.C. Fields. I would rather be living in Philadelphia.'

His own suggested epitaph

This actor, juggler and writer's comic persona as a misanthrope will last for ever. Hugely successful in the first half of the twentieth century with his portrayal of a drunkard who cared for no one and hated politicians, women, children and pets, his film and performing careers slowed in the 1940s. He suffered many illnesses, mostly rooted in his alcoholism, which confined him to brief guest-star appearances in other people's films. His last radio appearance was in 1946, and just before his death he recorded a spoken-word album, delivering his comic 'Temperance Lecture' and 'The Day I Drank a Glass of Water' monologues. His vision had deteriorated so much that he read his lines from large-print cue cards. His attitude to alcohol was: '*Some weasel took the cork out of lunch.*'

Suffering from liver cirrhosis and then pneumonia, Fields was hospitalized for his final weeks. A friend visited and saw him reading the Bible, although he was an atheist. The friend asked him why, and Fields replied: '*I'm checking for loop-holes.*' As he lay dying, his long-time lover, Carlotta Monti, went outside and turned a hose on to the roof, to allow Fields to hear his favourite sound of falling rain. His last words were allegedly: '*Goddamn the whole friggin' world but you, Carlotta!*' According to the documentary *W.C. Fields Straight Up*, he winked and smiled at a nurse, put a finger to his lips, and died. It was Christmas Day, a day he despised in his act. There are many stories that tell how he wanted his grave marker to read: '*On the whole, I would rather be in Philadelphia*', his home town. This is similar to a line he used in *My Little Chickadee*: '*I'd like to see Paris before I die ... Philadelphia would do!*' Some say he wanted the line because of the old vaudeville joke among comedians that '*I would rather be dead than play Philadelphia*', a notorious 'graveyard' for comics.

MOHANDAS KARAMCHAND GANDHI
2 October 1889–30 January 1948

'The light has gone out of our lives'

Jawaharlal Nehru's radio broadcast, 30 January 1948,
following Gandhi's assassination

'Friends and comrades, the light has gone out of our lives, and there is darkness everywhere, and I do not quite know what to tell you or how to say it. Our beloved leader, Bapu [Father] as we called him, the father of the nation, is no more. Perhaps I am wrong to say that; nevertheless, we will not see him again, as we have seen him for these many years, we will not run to him for advice or seek solace from him, and that is a terrible blow, not only for me, but for millions and millions in this country.'

The political and spiritual leader of Indian independence from Britain evolved a system of mass civil dis-obedience. It inspired similar campaigns and civil rights movements throughout the word, and he is honoured in India as the 'Father of the Nation'. He led the Indian National Congress from 1921, and campaigned for ending 'untouchability' and poverty, establishing women's rights, building ethnic and religious harmony and increasing economic self-reliance. From 1930 he conducted his famous non-violent independence campaign, declaring: *'I cannot teach you violence, as I do not believe in it. I can only teach you not to bow your heads before any one, even at the cost of your life'*; and *'I object to violence because when it appears to do good, the good is only temporary: the evil it does is permanent.'*

Gandhi was shot while having his nightly public walk in New Delhi, by an extremist Hindu assassin who thought that he was weakening India by wishing to pay Pakistan compensation. Speaking in 1946 of the forthcoming conflict between India and Pakistan, between Hindus and Muslims, Gandhi had said: *'Religions are different roads converging to the same point. What does it matter that we take different roads, so long as we reach the same goal. Wherein is the cause for quarrelling?'* His memorial bears the epigraph *'Hē Ram'*, meaning *'Oh God'*, believed to be his last words after he was shot.

GEORGE BERNARD SHAW
26 July 1856–2 November 1950

‘Sister ... you're trying to keep me alive as an old curiosity, but I'm done, I'm finished, I'm going to die.’

Dying words

In 1950 *Time* magazine reported on Shaw's last hours:

> '"Sister," the old man told Nurse Gwendoline Howell, "you're trying to keep me alive as an old curiosity, but I'm done, I'm finished, I'm going to die." Before the next dawn, George Bernard Shaw had lapsed into final unconsciousness. A little over 24 hours later, the 94-year-old philosopher, playwright, professional pixie and self-styled "Bishop of Everywhere" was dead. The end that came so peacefully and quietly to Bernard Shaw, in bed at Ayot St Lawrence last week, was not unwelcome. "I am longing for my eternal rest," Shaw told a friend just after his 94th birthday. The broken thighbone that sent Shaw into the hospital when he slipped and fell in his garden last September had shown signs of knitting better than his doctors dared hope, but the Shavian spirit was broken for good. When Shaw guessed that he might live only to become a bedridden invalid, he lost interest in the business. Last week Lady Astor drove down from London to pay him a visit. "Oh, Nancy," Shaw murmured to his long-time friend as she sat gently stroking the parchment skin on his still defiantly bearded white head, "I want to sleep, to sleep." These quiet words were among the last that voluble Bernard Shaw was heard to speak. When the end came, Shaw met it with a faint quizzical smile that might have been construed as satisfied.'

Shaw told Nancy Astor, *'I want my ashes mingled with those of my wife. After that, you may bury me wherever you like.'* In Shaw's parlour in the tiny village where he had spent the last 44 years of his life, there was a brief service, held by the Revd R.J. Davies. The vicar later said, *'Mr Shaw was not really an atheist. I would call him rather an Irishman.'* Shaw was said to have composed his own epitaph – *'I knew if I stayed around long enough, something like this would happen.'* He wrote more than 60 plays, winning the 1925 Nobel Prize for Literature.

GEORGE VI, ALBERT FREDERICK ARTHUR GEORGE, KING OF THE UNITED KINGDOM AND THE BRITISH DOMINIONS, EMPEROR OF INDIA, HEAD OF THE COMMONWEALTH
14 December 1895–6 February 1952

'Take care of Lilibet for me'

Last known words

George VI was born on the anniversary of the death of his great-grandfather, Prince Albert. His father, then the Prince of Wales, knew that Queen Victoria was always *'greatly distressed'* on that particular day, but she was cheered by the proposal to name the new baby Albert, and wrote: *'I am all impatience to see the new one, born on such a sad day but rather more dear to me, especially as he will be called by that dear name which is a byword for all that is great and good.'* His Highness Prince Albert of York was always known within the Royal Family as 'Bertie'. King George V was disappointed with his heir, Albert's elder brother Edward, who had many affairs with married women. He felt that Bertie would be a far better king, and he adored Bertie's elder daughter, Princess Elizabeth. The king nicknamed her 'Lilibet' and she called him 'Grandpa England'. George presciently said of Edward: *'After I am dead, the boy will ruin himself within 12 months ... I pray to God my eldest son will never marry and have children, and that nothing will come between Bertie and Lilibet and the throne.'*

In 1936, Albert became king following the sudden abdication of his brother, Edward VIII, to marry Mrs Simpson. As George VI, he supported Prime Minister Neville Chamberlain's policy of appeasement towards Germany and Italy, but then worked hard with Prime Minister Churchill to keep up public morale throughout World War II. A heavy smoker, from 1948 his health deteriorated, and in 1951 he had an operation for lung cancer. On 31 January 1952, he went to the airport to see off Princess Elizabeth, who was going on a tour of Australia via Kenya. Before takeoff he said to 'Bobo' Macdonald, Elizabeth's childhood nanny who was accompanying her, *'Take care of Lilibet for me.'* He died six days later and was succeeded by his daughter, who became Elizabeth II.

MARÍA EVA DUARTE DE PERÓN, 'EVITA'
7 May 1919–26 July 1952

'Eva is leaving'

Last words, to her sister Elisa

Known affectionately by her people as Evita (Little Eva), the wife of the President of Argentina never forgot her humble background and fought for the poor of her country, the *descamisados* (shirtless ones). Over a period of seven years, she brought the working classes into a position of political power never witnessed before, and earned the enmity of the upper classes and the military. She was working for charities and women's suffrage until the end of her short life. Not knowing that she was suffering from cervical cancer (the same disease that killed President Juan Perón's first wife as well as Evita's own mother), she weighed only 79 pounds (36 kg) when she died. For her last public appearance, at her husband's second inauguration, she made a speech to the masses from the presidential balcony, with the aid of morphine to help her withstand the pain, and the support of her husband and a plaster and wire frame hidden under her fur coat.

Seven weeks later Eva was dead: '*On Saturday morning, July 26, 1952, a damp grey winter's day, Evita said to her maid, "I never felt happy in this life. That is why I left home. My mother would have married me to someone ordinary and I could never have stood it, Irma; a decent woman has to get on in the world."*' Tens of thousands of people travelled to her funeral, but in 1955 her embalmed body disappeared after a military coup deposed President Perón. She represented the people's independence, and her body was buried for 16 years in Italy under an assumed name. When Perón returned from exile to take power again, he had her body returned. In 1976, Evita was entombed in the Duarte family museum in Buenos Aires, and a plaque there reads: '*Don't Cry for Me*' in Spanish, from the 1978 musical *Evita*.

'Then came that fateful day'

From a scrap of paper found on the floor of the car in which the singer died

> 'We met we lived and dear we loved
> Then came that fateful day
> The love that felt so dear
> Fades so far away
> Tonight we both are all alone
> And here's all that I can say
> I love you still and always will
> But that's the price we had to pay.'

Aged only 29, Hank Williams died in a car somewhere between Knoxville, Tennessee, and Canton, Ohio. He had recently been fired from the *Grand Ol' Opry* a weekly country music concert, broadcast from Nashville since 1925, because of his drug and alcohol abuse, and was scheduled to perform a show in Canton. *Opry* star Roy Acuff had told him: *'You've got a million-dollar voice, son, but a ten-cent brain.'* When his 17-year-old chauffeur stopped for petrol, he found Williams dead in the back seat along with a few empty beer cans and the lyrics to an unfinished song, 'Then Came That Fateful Day'. The circumstances of his death are mysterious, with some claiming that he was dead when placed in the car. The official cause of death was heart failure.

An icon of country music, the singer-songwriter had 300 songs published and is admired today by luminaries such as Bob Dylan and Leonard Cohen. His Number 1 hits included: 'Long Gone Lonesome Blues', 'Your Cheatin' Heart', 'Lovesick Blues', 'Why Don't You Love Me?', 'Moanin' the Blues', 'Hey, Good Lookin'', 'Cold, Cold Heart', 'Jambalaya', 'Take These Chains From My Heart', 'I'm So Lonesome I Could Cry' and the prophetic 'I'll Never Get Out of This World Alive'. His epitaph in Oakwood Cemetery, Montgomery, Alabama, reads:

> 'Thank you for all the love you gave me.
> There could be no one stronger.
> Thank you for the many beautiful songs.
> They will live long and longer.'

JOSEPH HILAIRE PIERRE RENÉ BELLOC
27 July 1870–16 July 1953

❛When I am dead, I hope it may be said / "His sins were scarlet, but his books were read"❜

His own epitaph, from 'On His Books', 1923

Belloc's obituary in *Life*, 27 July 1953, noted: '*He was the last of the Edwardian giants and the most versatile of them all. He published at least 153 books, sometimes three or four a year – "because", he explained, "my children are howling for pearls and caviar".*' A.P. Herbert called him '*the man who wrote a library*'. At his funeral mass, Monsignor Ronald Knox observed, '*No man of his time fought so hard for the good things.*' Belloc's writings show his contempt for the political, literary and social establishments of the day, and he is now recognized as one of the great writers of English prose and verse. He stood down as an MP, disillusioned with party politics, He had demanded in Parliament that the finances of parties be subject to public audits, and his 'Epitaph on the Politician Himself' reads:

> 'Here richly, with ridiculous display,
> The Politician's corpse was laid away.
> While all of his acquaintance sneered and slanged
> I wept: for I had longed to see him hanged.'

He summarized his feelings about Westminster as:

> 'The accursed power which stands on Privilege
> (And goes with Women, and Champagne, and Bridge)
> Broke – and democracy resumed her reign:
> (Which goes with Bridge, and Women, and Champagne).'

He was also a wonderful comic writer, and we remember:

> 'I shoot the Hippopotamus
> With bullets made of platinum,
> Because if I use leaden ones
> His hide is sure to flatten 'em.'

'Born in a goddam hotel room and dying in a hotel room'

Self-written obituary

When this superb playwright and Nobel Laureate died in Room 401 of the Sheraton Hotel, now the Shelton Hall dorm at Boston University (91 Bay State Road), he had already written this obituary notice. Alternatively his last words have been reported as: '*I knew it. I knew it. Born in a hotel room, and God damn it, died in a hotel room*' (Louis Sheaffer, *O'Neill: Son and Artist*, 1973). Students at the university have attributed inexplicable events to his ghost.

O'Neill was born in a Broadway hotel room in Times Square, now a Starbucks (1,500 Broadway, north-east corner of 43rd and Broadway). His father was the famous actor and matinée idol James O'Neill. A commemorative plaque on the building is inscribed: '*Eugene O'Neill, October 16, 1888 – November 27, 1953. America's greatest playwright was born on this site then called Barrett Hotel. Presented by Circle in the Square.*' His parents and elder brother Jamie (who drank himself to death at the age of 45) died within three years of one another, and O'Neill turned to writing as a form of escape. After suffering for years from health problems such as alcoholism and depression, he had a severe tremor in his hands, attributed to Parkinson's disease, which made it impossible for him to write. He found that he was unable to dictate his works, so for the last ten years of his life he was frustrated at his inability to work on a major literary project, a cycle of 11 plays detailing the life of a family over a century. He managed to complete only two of the plays, *A Touch of the Poet* and *More Stately Mansions*. As his health worsened, he struggled to produce three largely autobiographical plays, *The Iceman Cometh*, *A Moon for the Misbegotten* and his masterpiece, *Long Day's Journey into Night*. Drafts of many other uncompleted plays were destroyed by his wife Carlotta at his request. Lately it has been discovered that he was not suffering from Parkinson's disease, but from late-onset cerebellar cortical atrophy.

ALBERT EINSTEIN
14 March 1879–18 April 1955

‘I want to go when I want. It is tasteless to prolong life artificially. I have done my share, it is time to go. I will do it elegantly.’

Last words after refusing surgery

On 12 April 1955, Einstein realized that his abdominal aortic aneurysm had finally burst, and agreed to be admitted to the Princeton Hospital because he felt he was becoming too much of a burden at home. He had had an operation to repair the problem five years previously. Now his surgeon recommended resection of the aneurysm, even though the operation was new, using cadaver grafts to replace the aorta. Einstein refused surgery, saying it was time for him to go, and died the next morning. During the autopsy the hospital pathologist took Einstein's brain without the permission of the family, hoping that neuroscience in future years could discover why he was such a genius. It was only returned to them 40 years later. Einstein took into hospital with him the draft of a speech he was writing to celebrate the seventh anniversary of the state of Israel. It ends with an unfinished sentence:

'In essence, the conflict that exists today is no more than an old-style struggle for power, once again presented to mankind in semireligious trappings. The difference is that, this time, the development of atomic power has imbued the struggle with a ghostly character; for both parties know and admit that, should the quarrel deteriorate into actual war, mankind is doomed. Despite this knowledge, statesmen in responsible positions on both sides continue to employ the well-known technique of seeking to intimidate and demoralize the opponent by marshalling superior military strength. They do so even though such a policy entails the risk of war and doom. Not one statesman in a position of responsibility has dared to pursue the only course that holds out any promise of peace, the course of supranational security, since for a statesman to follow such a course would be tantamount to political suicide. Political passions, once they have been fanned into flame, exact their victims ... Citater fra ...'

JAMES BYRON DEAN
8 February 1931–30 September 1955

'It is now ten o'clock, Friday the 23rd of September, 1955. If you get in that car you will be found dead in it by this time next week.'

Alec Guinness's warning to James Dean a week before he died in a car crash

Dean made only three films: *Rebel Without a Cause*, which cemented his place as a cultural icon for troubled teenagers, *East of Eden* and *Giant*. He remains the only person to have two posthumous Academy Award acting nominations, and was the first actor to receive a posthumous Oscar. His great love was racing cars. During the filming of *Giant*, he was contractually barred from racing them. When filming *Rebel Without a Cause*, he bought a Porsche 550 Spyder to compete at a sports car race in Salinas in California. It was customized by the man who went on to design the Batmobile for the *Batman* TV series, with its nickname 'Little Bastard' painted on it. Dean introduced himself to Alec Guinness outside a restaurant, and asked him to take a look at the Spyder. Guinness thought the car was 'sinister', telling Dean that it would kill him within a week.

A week later, Dean and his mechanic set off for Salinas. Dean was given a speeding ticket in Kern County for driving at 65 mph (105 km/h) in a 55 mph (89 km/h) zone. He was then driving west near Cholame, California, when a 1950 Ford Custom Tudor coupe, driven from the opposite direction by a 23-year-old student, attempted to take the fork on to the road. The student crossed into Dean's lane without seeing him, and the two cars hit almost head on. Dean's mechanic was thrown from the Porsche, but survived with a broken jaw and other injuries. Dean was taken to Paso Robles War Memorial Hospital, where he was pronounced dead on arrival. His last known words, uttered just before impact, were: '*That guy's gotta stop ... He'll see us!*' The student had minor bruising and was not cited by police for the accident. The mechanic died in a road accident in Germany in 1981 after surviving several suicide attempts.

'Goodbye, Spence'

Last words to Spencer Tracy, the night before he died

'[Kathryn] Hepburn, in an interview, described the last time she and Spencer Tracy saw Bogart (the night before he died): Spence patted him on the shoulder and said, "Goodnight, Bogie." Bogie turned his eyes to Spence very quietly and with a sweet smile covered Spence's hand with his own and said, "Goodbye, Spence." Spence's heart stood still. He understood.'

The film star was a heavy smoker and drinker, but refused to see a doctor until January 1956. He was diagnosed with cancer of the oesophagus a few weeks later, and on 1 March had surgery to remove his oesophagus, a rib and two lymph-nodes. The cancer kept spreading, even after chemotherapy and further surgery. In great pain but uncomplaining, he became too weak to walk up and down stairs and joked: 'Put me in the dumbwaiter and I'll ride down to the first floor in style.' He was visited by friends like Sinatra, Hepburn and Tracy until the end, when he weighed just 80 pounds and sank into a coma. His simple funeral was attended by all the stars of Hollywood. Bogart's wife, Lauren Bacall, asked Spencer Tracy to give the eulogy, but Tracy was too upset, so John Huston gave it, saying:

'Himself, he never took too seriously – his work most seriously. He regarded the somewhat gaudy figure of Bogart, the star, with an amused cynicism; Bogart, the actor, he held in deep respect ... In each of the fountains at Versailles there is a pike which keeps all the carp active; otherwise they would grow overfat and die. Bogie took rare delight in performing a similar duty in the fountains of Hollywood. Yet his victims seldom bore him any malice, and when they did, not for long. His shafts were fashioned only to stick into the outer layer of complacency, and not to penetrate through to the regions of the spirit where real injuries are done ... He is quite irreplaceable. There will never be another like him.'

'Well, I hope your ol' bus freezes up'

Last known conversation, with Waylon Jennings, 3 February 1959

Buddy Holly had only 18 months of success, when the singer-songwriter from Lubbock, Texas, helped pioneer rock 'n roll, and influenced countless groups. His agent was slow in paying him record royalties, so to make money Holly had set up a gruelling schedule of concerts, known as the Winter Dance Party Tour, covering 24 cities in three weeks. Waylon Jennings, a friend from Lubbock, and Tommy Allsup were the backup musicians in his Crickets band. Also on the bill was Ritchie Valens, one of the hottest artists of the time, with the huge hits 'Come On', 'Let's Go' and 'Donna', with its flip side, 'La Bamba'. Jiles P. Richardson, known to his fans as the Big Bopper, who had found success in 1958 with 'Chantilly Lace', and Dion and the Belmonts were on the list of performers too.

The tour bus developed heating problems, and when they arrived at the Surf Ballroom in Clear Lake, Iowa, they were all freezing and suffering from lack of sleep. Holly had had enough of the unheated bus and decided to charter a plane to take him and two of the others to the next show in Moorhead, Minnesota. Waylon Jennings gave his seat up to the Big Bopper, as Richardson was running a fever and had trouble fitting his large frame comfortably into the bus seats. When Holly learned that Jennings was not going to fly with him, he said, '*Well, I hope your ol' bus freezes up.*' Jennings responded with a laugh, '*Well, I hope your ol' plane crashes*', a phrase that haunted him in the following years. Buddy's other friend Tommy Allsup was asked by Ritchie Valens to toss a coin for the remaining seat, and Valens won. The plane took off a little after 1 a.m., bound for Fargo, North Dakota, and crashed in snow near the airport, killing all on board – Holly, Valens, Richardson and the pilot. Don McLean wrote in his wonderful song 'American Pie' that it was 'the day the music died'. Waylon Jennings would go on to become a hugely popular country singer, and Tommy Allsup still plays guitar, 60 years after his first public performance. Holly's own pioneering hits included 'That'll be the Day', 'Peggy Sue', 'Raining in My Heart', 'Love is Strange', 'Oh Boy!', 'Everyday', 'Not Fade Away', 'It Doesn't Matter Any More', 'Heartbeat' and 'Rave On'.

ERROL LESLIE FLYNN
20 June 1909–14 October 1959

'I shall return'

Last words before his death from a heart attack

A favourite saying of Flynn's was: *'I like my whisky old and my women young.'* He began going out with Beverley Aadland when she was just 15. After his death, her mother Florence wrote an account of the relationship. On 9 October 1959, Flynn flew with Beverley to Vancouver , to lease his yacht *Zaca* to millionaire George Caldough. On 14 October, Caldough was driving them back to the airport when Flynn felt unwell. He was taken to the apartment of Caldough's friend, Dr Grant Gould. A party began, with Flynn back in fine form relating anecdotes and doing impressions. He felt ill again, announced, *'I shall return'*, and went to a bedroom to rest. Half an hour later, Beverley checked on him and discovered him unconscious. He died from a heart attack. He is interred in Forest Lawn Cemetery in Glendale, California, allegedly sharing his coffin with six bottles of whisky given by his drinking partners.

A handsome Tasmanian film actor, Flynn came into the movies by accident. *'I hadn't the least idea of what I was doing, except that I was supposed to be an actor,'* he said after working three weeks on *In the Wake of the Bounty,* his first film. A romantic and athletic swashbuckler in Hollywood cinema, he was noted for his flamboyant lifestyle, having amongst others Fidel Castro as a drinking partner. As his looks and career faded, he said in the *New York Times,* 'My main problem is reconciling my gross habits with my net income.' David Niven said: 'He was an enchanting creature. I had more fun with Errol than everybody else put together ... It was never-ending fun.' Flynn wrote in his 1959 autobiography *My Wicked Wicked Ways*: 'So, come all you young men. With your wicked, wicked ways. Sow your wild oats in your younger days. So that we may be happy when we grow old. Yes! Happy and happy when we grow old. For the day's getting on and the night's getting long. Darling please gimme your arm and we'll joggle along, yes, we'll joggle and joggle and joggle along.'

'Oh God, here I go!'

Last words, said to his physician when suffering fatal heart attack

'Madcap Maxie' had a career as an actor, entertainer, professional wrestler and referee, and for a short time was heavyweight boxing champion of the world. In June 1933, he stopped the German heavyweight Max Schmeling in the tenth round at the Yankee Stadium. Baer's trunks had embroidered on them a Star of David, and he then vowed to wear them for every match. For Baer, fighting was just a job that paid the bills, and he said: '*Some guys string electrical wire for a living. I punch people with my fists.*' In 1934, he knocked down the huge Primo Carnera no fewer than 11 times to win the world title, but he only held it for a year because he hardly bothered to train. In a huge upset he lost the title in a 15-round decision to James J. Braddock, clowning around.

On 18 November 1959, Baer refereed a nationally televised ten-round boxing match in Phoenix, Arizona. At the end of the match, he vaulted out of the ring and joined boxing fans in a cocktail bar. The next day he was due to appear in several television commercials in Hollywood. Upon his arrival on the 19th, he booked into the Hollywood Roosevelt Hotel. As he was shaving on the morning of the 21st, he felt chest pains, called the front desk and asked for a doctor. Supposedly the desk clerk answered that '*a house doctor would be right up*'. Baer joked, '*A house doctor? No, dummy, I need a people doctor.*' The doctor gave Baer medication and a fire department rescue squad administered oxygen. His chest pains subsided. He told the doctor that he had come through two similar but lighter attacks earlier in Sacramento, California, and he was showing signs of recovery when he suffered a second attack. He exclaimed: '*Oh God, here I go!*', slumped on his left side, turned blue and died within a matter of minutes.

'Well, what is the sense of ruining my head and erasing my memory, which is my capital, and putting me out of business? It was a brilliant cure but we lost the patient.'

Comment to his friend and biographer A.E. Hotchner

Hemingway was suffering from various injuries, diabetes, high blood pressure, liver problems caused by alcoholism, hypertension, paranoia (he was being watched by the FBI), depression and possible haemochromatosis. Additionally, his eyesight was failing and his home and possessions in Cuba had been lost. He checked in at the Mayo Clinic in Minnesota for electro-convulsive therapy for depression, then went to Sun Valley Hospital, before returning to the Mayo Clinic. It was after this second series of electro-shock treatments that he complained about his head being 'ruined'. Released in late June, he returned to his home in Ketchum, Idaho, put the barrel of his favourite shotgun in his mouth and pulled the trigger. A memorial to Hemingway in Ketchum is inscribed with a 1939 eulogy, which he wrote for a friend, Gene van Guilder:

> 'Best of all he loved the fall
> The leaves yellow on the cottonwoods
> Leaves floating on the trout streams
> And above the hills
> The high blue windless skies
> Now he will be a part of them forever.'

The writer and journalist had won the Pulitzer Prize in 1953 for *The Old Man and the Sea*. In 1951 he had completed the draft in only eight weeks and considered it *'the best I can write ever for all of my life'*. He was too ill to attend his award of the Nobel Prize for Literature in 1954, so his acceptance speech was read by the US Ambassador John C. Cabot: *'Writing, at its best, is a lonely life. Organizations for writers palliate his loneliness but I doubt if they improve his writing. He grows in public stature and as he sheds his loneliness often his work deteriorates. For he does his work alone and if he is a good enough writer he must face eternity, or the lack of it each day ...'*

WILLIAM CUTHBERT FAULKNER (born FALKNER)
25 September 1897–6 July 1962

> **'It is my aim, and every effort bent, that the sum and history of my life, which in the same sentence is my obit and epitaph too, shall be them both: He made the books and he died.'**
>
> From a letter to Malcolm Cowley, 11 February 1949

Later in the same year that he wrote the above, Faulkner won the Nobel Prize, and belatedly began to be recognized as one of the most important writers in the history of American literature. A relative unknown until 1949, most of his works are set in Mississippi, where he was born. In the 1940s he was invited by Howard Hawks to Hollywood to collaborate on film scripts, and as well as novels he wrote short stories and poetry. Faulkner drank to excess, often while writing, saying that it helped fuel his creative process. However, critics believe that much of his drinking was an escape from constant financial pressures. An unkind obituary in the *New York Times* stated: '*Mr Faulkner's writings showed an obsession with murder, rape, incest, suicide, greed and general depravity that did not exist anywhere but in the author's mind.*'

After falling from his horse twice and being hospitalized both times, Faulkner was in constant pain, and on 5 July 1962 asked to be taken to hospital. Less than eight hours later, he suffered a heart attack and could not be resuscitated. He was buried on 7 July at St Peter's Cemetery in Oxford, Mississippi. A huge gathering of the media was at the funeral, shouting to family members to find out how Faulkner had died. A representative relayed to them a message from the family: '*Until he's buried he belongs to the family. After that, he belongs to the world.*'

'The woman is perfected / Her dead / Body wears the smile of accomplishment.'

Opening lines of her last poem before she committed suicide

From Boston, Massachusetts, the poet wrote the semi-autobiographical novel *The Bell Jar*, based on her own suicide attempt. After her third year at college, when she won a contest to be guest editor at *Mademoiselle* magazine, Plath experienced her first breakdown and famously disappeared for some time. This was followed by a suicide attempt with sleeping pills in 1953. She was then hospitalized in a mental institution and treated with shock therapy, which she described as a *'time of darkness, despair, and disillusion – so black only as the inferno of the human mind can be – symbolic death, and numb shock – then the painful agony of slow rebirth and psychic regeneration'.* Winning a scholarship to Cambridge, she met the poet Ted Hughes and they married in 1956. The relationship was difficult, and Hughes began an affair with Assia Wevill. Plath and Hughes separated in late 1962.

In early 1963, Plath sealed with *'wet towels and cloths'* the rooms between herself and her sleeping children, aged one and two. She then took a bottle of sleeping pills and stuck her head in the gas oven in the kitchen. Her downstairs neighbour, knocked out by gas seeping through the floor, believed she had intended him to rescue her when he smelled it. Her gravestone in Heptonstall Church is inscribed: *'Even amidst fierce flames the golden lotus can be planted.'* The stone has been repeatedly vandalized by some of Plath's supporters, who have chiselled off the name 'Hughes', believing him somehow responsible for her death. In 1969, Wevill, who had lived with Hughes and his children for much of the intervening period, also gassed herself, and their four-year-old daughter Shura. This left Hughes to look after his two children with Plath, Frieda and Nicholas. Ted Hughes died of cancer in 1998, and in 2009 Professor Nicholas Hughes, suffering from depression, hanged himself.

POPE JOHN XXIII (ANGELO GIUSEPPE RONCALLI)
25 November 1881–3 June 1963

'I am able to follow my own death step by step. Now I move softly towards the end.'

Remarks made two days before his death

Elected as 261st Pope and Sovereign of Vatican City on 28 October 1958, John XXIII was the pope with the common touch, appealing to all religions as a humane, warm, humorous, peaceful and charitable man. Patriarch of Venice, he was surprised to be elected, and observers believed that he was a 'stopgap pope' because of his age. On Christmas Day, two months after his election, he became the first pope since 1870 to make pastoral visits in Rome, visiting polio-infected children in two hospitals. On Boxing Day he went to Rome's Regina Coeli prison, telling the prisoners: *'You could not come to me, so I came to you.'* He wrote in his diary that this caused *'... great astonishment in the Roman, Italian and international press. I was hemmed in on all sides: authorities, photographers, prisoners, wardens ...'*

In September 1962, Pope John was diagnosed with gastric carcinoma, following nearly eight months of occasional stomach haemorrhages. The news was kept secret, but his public appearances were reduced. Looking unwell, in April 1963 he said to visitors, *'That which happens to all men perhaps will happen soon to the Pope who speaks to you today.'* In May he had another haemorrhage and required blood transfusions. However, the cancer had perforated the stomach wall, and peritonitis and the spread of the cancer meant that his death was imminent. At 11 a.m. on 3 June he said: *'I had the great grace to be born into a Christian family, modest and poor, but with the fear of the Lord ... My time on earth is drawing to a close. But Christ lives on and continues his work in the Church. Souls, souls, ut omnes unum sint* [that they may all be one] *...'* The Papal Sacristan Petrus Canisius van Lierde then anointed his eyes, ears, mouth, hands and feet. Overcome by emotion, he forgot the right order of anointing, and Pope John gently helped him before bidding van Lierde and all the other bystanders a last farewell.

ÉDITH PIAF (ÉDITH GIOVANNA GASSION)
19 December 1915–10 October 1963

---

⁶She died as if consumed by the fire of her fame⁹

Epitaph by Jean Cocteau on French radio

In her 'Letter from Paris', dated 23 October 1963, Janet Flanner of the *New Yorker* reported the death of this cultural icon:

> 'Edith Piaf died at seven o'clock in the morning in Paris, and a few hours later on that same recent Friday her friend Jean Cocteau, in his nearby country house at Milly-la-Forêt, suffered a final heart attack, provoked by the news of her demise, and himself died at one o'clock. Yet at noon his incisive, familiar voice, already quasi-posthumous, was heard on the national radio among the hastily collected hommages to Piaf's memory, saying, "She died as if consumed by the fire of her fame." This epitaph for her had, in fact, been premature, originally prepared and recorded by him a few months earlier, when, as had been frequent lately, she seemed to be perishing and was given up as lost. But on this precise Friday, by a melodramatic coincidence, her intended epitaph suddenly became apropos for them both, in a confusion of mortal destinies.'

Piaf was regarded as France's greatest popular singer, with songs like 'Milord', 'Le Légionnaire', 'L'Accordéoniste' and 'Je ne regrette rien'. In 1961, though nearly unable to stand, she appeared at the Paris Olympia, but within 18 months was dead of liver cancer. Suffering from pain for years after a car crash, she wrote: *'For four years I lived almost like an animal or a madwoman: nothing existed for me beyond the moment I was given my injection and felt at last the soothing effect of the drug.'* She described how she would inject herself through her skirt and stockings, moments before going on stage. When asked why she took morphine, she said: *'Because it helps me to ignore my body'* (*The Wheel of Fortune: The Auto-biography of Edith Piaf*, 1958). She was forbidden a mass by the Archbishop of Paris because of her lifestyle, but her ceremony at Père Lachaise cemetery was attended by 40,000 Parisians. It was the only time since the end of World War II that Parisian traffic had come to a complete stop.

JOHN FITZGERALD KENNEDY
29 May 1917–22 November 1963

❛Mr President, you certainly cannot say that Dallas does not love you❜

Last words to the President

Nellie Connally (1919–2006), the wife of Texas governor John Connally, was seated with her husband in front of John and Jackie Kennedy in the open-top presidential limousine when she turned round to comment on the cheering crowds. The above version of her words is from a Fox TV interview of 2003 and from her book of that year. The book was based on contemporary notes she made, which were locked away for 33 years. A previous version was *'You certainly can't say that the people of Dallas haven't given you a nice welcome, Mr President.'*

There is some also confusion whether the President actually answered her. In one account he replied, *'That's obvious'* and in another, *'No, you certainly can't'*, just before he was hit by the first bullet. In her TV interview, Mrs Connally said that JFK just grinned widely and waved at the crowds. She is also said to have heard the President say to his wife, *'My God, I'm hit.'* In the Fox News interview, 'The Big Story with John Gibson', 21 November 2003, she was asked for her strongest memory of the day and responded: *'The whole day is a strong memory. I'll never forget after it was over, I'll never forget Jackie's red roses all over the car, my yellow roses all over the car, blood all over the roses of John's and Jack's. Horrible. Hideous.'*

John Fitzgerald Kennedy, thirty-fifth president of the United States, was assassinated by Lee Harvey Oswald as he was travelling by motorcade through the streets of Dallas. He was visiting the city in preparation for his coming election campaign. Nellie Connally's husband, John Connally, later Secretary of the Treasury, was seriously wounded in the attack. After being shot, Governor Connally shouted: *'My God, they are going to kill us all!'*

‘You made one mistake. You married me.’

Last words, to his wife on his deathbed

Behan saw that it paid to be drunk. His public wanted the witty 'broth of a boy', who cared nothing about how he was perceived and scorned the authorities. In turn, he said, *'There's no bad publicity except an obituary.'* Because of alcoholism, his health suffered terribly, with blackouts, diabetic comas and seizures occurring regularly. Towards the end he had become an embarrassment to his adoring public, being frequently thrown out of pubs. He knew that his literary career was just about finished – he could no longer write great prose or poetry. Whether it was due to alcoholism, or whether he was using alcohol to cloak his disappointment, is open to debate.

He collapsed in the Harbour Lights bar, and was taken to hospital in Dublin, where he was given emergency treatment for severe liver disease and said, *'Bless you, Sister. May all your sons be bishops'* to a nursing nun as she was taking his pulse. One of his drinking cronies smuggled a bottle of brandy into the hospital, which Behan drank, inducing another diabetic coma. He was given a tracheotomy to help him breathe, and later awoke briefly to tell his wife that she had made a mistake in marrying him.

Behan had served time in Borstal as an IRA member, and after some time in Paris returned to Dublin in 1950, becoming a hard-drinking rabble-rouser. In 1954, his play *The Quare Fellow* was produced, and after it was shown in London in 1956 he began to receive constant media attention. Joan Littlewood's production of *The Hostage* (1958) led to further success in London and New York. A famous line from the play runs: *'When I came back to Dublin, I was court-martialled in my absence and sentenced to death in my absence, so I said they could shoot me in my absence.'* Behan's autobiographical *Borstal Boy* also appeared in 1958. An IRA guard of honour escorted his coffin, in one of the biggest funerals Ireland has seen.

GENERAL DOUGLAS MACARTHUR
26 January 1880–5 April 1964

'The shadows are lengthening for me'
Last public appearance

MacArthur made his last appearance in 1962 at West Point Military Academy, where he made a speech accepting an award for outstanding service to the nation:

> 'The shadows are lengthening for me. The twilight is here. My days of old have vanished, tone and tint. They have gone glimmering through the dreams of things that were. Their memory is one of wondrous beauty, watered by tears, and coaxed and caressed by the smiles of yesterday. I listen vainly, but with thirsty ears, for the witching melody of faint bugles blowing reveille, of far drums beating the long roll. In my dreams I hear again the crash of guns, the rattle of musketry, the strange, mournful mutter of the battlefield. But in the evening of my memory, always I come back to West Point. Always there echoes and re-echoes: Duty, Honour, Country. Today marks my final roll call with you, but I want you to know that when I cross the river my last conscious thoughts will be of The Corps, and The Corps, and The Corps. I bid you farewell.'

When, as commander of American forces in the Philippines, he was ordered to evacuate to Australia in 1942, he famously said: '*I came out of Bataan and I shall return*', repeated in a later speech: '*I came through and I shall return.*' On landing in Leyte in 1944, he announced: '*People of the Philippines; I have returned.*' President Harry Truman relieved the general from military duties in 1951 for 'insubordination', after MacArthur issued an ultimatum to the Chinese Communists to withdraw from conflict in Korea or risk attacks upon their coastal areas and interior bases. Truman's advisers suggested it might be better to allow MacArthur to resign, but Truman is said to have replied, '*The son of a bitch isn't going to resign on me, I want him fired.*' MacArthur returned to the United States for the first time in 11 years of service, and made a wonderful farewell address to the US Congress, including the lines: '*Old soldiers never die; they just fade away ... And like the old soldier of that ballad, I now close my military career and just fade away – an old soldier who tried to do his duty as God gave him the light to see that duty. Goodbye.*'

'Jakie, is it my birthday or am I dying?'

Last words on her deathbed to her son John Jacob 'Jakie' Astor and her other
children, when she momentarily woke up and saw them standing around her

A wealthy Virginian, and the wife of Waldorf Astor,
Second Viscount Astor, Nancy Astor was the first woman to
serve as a Member of Parliament. In 1919 she was elected
to represent the Conservative Party in the Plymouth Sutton
constituency. Incredibly self-opinionated, and with a scath-
ing wit, she antagonized both her own party and her family
so much that by 1945 both advised her not to stand for
Parliament again after 24 years of being an MP. Although
vehemently anti-Catholic, she had a close relationship with
Joseph P. Kennedy Sr, who held similar opinions: *'As fiercely anti-Communist
as they were anti-Semitic, Kennedy and Astor looked upon Adolf Hitler as a welcome
solution to both of these "world problems" (Nancy's phrase) ... Kennedy replied that he
expected the "Jew media" in the United States to become a problem, that "Jewish
pundits in New York and Los Angeles" were already making noises contrived to "set a
match to the fuse of the world".'*

When war was declared, Astor admitted that she had made mistakes in supporting Hitler, but fellow MPs were still hostile to her. She had contributed little
enough to Parliament over the previous two decades, and some termed her 'the
Honourable Member for Berlin'. In addition, a lifetime of alcoholic dinner-parties
and an inability to reason rationally had made some of her speeches only semi-
comprehensible. With an increasing phobia of Catholics, she made a speech
claiming that a Catholic conspiracy was subverting the Foreign Office. She also
insulted Stalin's role as an ally during the war. Her speeches became rambling,
and Harold Nicolson noted in 1943 that debating with her had become *'like
playing squash with a dish of scrambled eggs'.* Not content with homophobia, anti-
Semitism and anti-Communism, she also managed to insult the men of the
Eighth Army in North Africa and those fighting the Japanese in Burma.

JOHN BURDON SANDERSON HALDANE FRS
5 November 1892–1 December 1964

'Cancer's a Funny Thing'

Poem written when ill with cancer

An evolutionary biologist and geneticist, Haldane was one of the founders of population genetics and famously atheistic: '*My practice as a scientist is atheistic. That is to say, when I set up an experiment I assume that no god, angel, or devil is going to interfere with its course; and this assumption has been justified by such success as I have achieved in my professional career. I should therefore be intellectually dishonest if I were not also atheistic in the affairs of the world.*' Whilst dying of cancer in hospital in his last year of life, Haldane wrote the poem 'Cancer's a Funny Thing':

> 'I wish I had the voice of Homer
> To sing of rectal carcinoma,
> This kills a lot more chaps, in fact,
> Than were bumped off when Troy was sacked ...
> I know that cancer often kills,
> But so do cars and sleeping pills;
> And it can hurt one till one sweats,
> So can bad teeth and unpaid debts.
> A spot of laughter, I am sure,
> Often accelerates one's cure;
> So let us patients do our bit
> To help the surgeons make us fit.'

Haldane declared: '*I have no doubt that in reality the future will be vastly more surprising than anything I can imagine. Now my own suspicion is that the Universe is not only queerer than we suppose, but queerer than we can suppose.*' He also acknowledged the problem of scientific progress: '*I suppose the process of acceptance will pass through the usual four stages:(i) this is worthless nonsense; (ii) this is an interesting, but perverse, point of view; (iii) this is true, but quite unimportant; (iv) I always said so.*'

SIR WINSTON LEONARD SPENCER CHURCHILL
30 November 1874–24 January 1965

> **'I am ready to meet my Maker. Whether my Maker is ready for the ordeal of meeting me is another matter.'**
>
> Said on his seventy-fifth birthday, 30 November 1949

The end of Churchill's last major speech in the House of Commons on 1 March 1955 gives us an idea of what came to be known as 'Churchillian rhetoric': *'The day may dawn when fair play, love for one's fellow men, respect for justice and freedom, will enable tormented generations to march forth triumphant from the hideous epoch in which we have to dwell. Meanwhile, never flinch, never weary, never despair.'* After seeing military action in India, the Sudan, the Second Boer War and World War I, he worked as a war correspondent before entering a political career, leading Britain through the dark days and eventual victory of World War II. Chapter 32 of his *Second World War*, Volume III, is entitled 'Pearl Harbor', and notes his relief when the United States entered the war:

'No American will think it wrong of me if I proclaim that to have the United States at our side was to me the greatest joy. I could not foretell the course of events. I do not pretend to have measured accurately the martial might of Japan, but now at this very moment I knew the United States was in the war, up to the neck and in to the death. So we had won after all! ... Hitler's fate was sealed. Mussolini's fate was sealed. As for the Japanese, they would be ground to powder.'

Prime minister from 1940 to 1945 and from 1951 to 1955, he was also an historian, writer and artist, and won the Nobel Prize for Literature. General Lafayette was the first person to be made an Honorary Citizen of the United States, in 1784; Churchill became only the second, after a special Act of Congress. In 1949 he had a mild stroke, then a more severe one in 1953, news of which was kept from the public and from Parliament. His powers diminished, he retired as prime minister in 1955. After another stroke in 1956, his final, fatal attack was in 1965.

'It is a time for martyrs now, and if I am to be one, it will be for the cause of brotherhood. That's the only thing that can save this country.'

Speech in New York City, 19 February 1965, two days before he was assassinated

Malcolm X was a Muslim cleric and human rights activist. By the time he was 13, his father had been murdered and his mother was in a mental hospital. In prison he saw a route out of crime, and became the public face of the Nation of Islam. To many, he was a great advocate for the rights of African-Americans, indicting white America for its crimes against blacks. He has been described as one of the most influential African-Americans in history, but others accuse him of preaching black supremacy and violence. In a 1965 conversation with Gordon Parks, just two days before his assassination, Malcolm said: '*Listening to leaders like Nasser, Ben Bella, and Nkrumah awakened me to the dangers of racism. I realized racism isn't just a black and white problem. It's brought bloodbaths to about every nation on earth at one time or another.*' After leaving the Nation of Islam, he disavowed racism in all its forms.

A year later, Malcolm X was speaking to a meeting of the Organization of Afro-American Unity, which he had recently founded. A disturbance broke out in the crowd of 400, and a man yelled, '*Nigger! Get your hand outta my pocket!*' as two men pretended to argue, to distract attention from three approaching assassins. Malcolm's last words have been reported as '*Brothers! Brothers, please! This is a house of peace!*' and '*Now, now, brothers, break it up, be cool, be calm.*' As he and his bodyguards moved to quell the disturbance, a man rushed forward and shot him in the chest with a sawn-off shotgun. Two other men charged the stage and fired handguns, hitting him 16 times. Malcolm was thought to be dead before his body struck the floor.

'Fancy being remembered around the world for the invention of a mouse!'

Said during his last illness

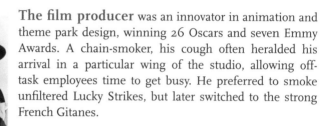

The film producer was an innovator in animation and theme park design, winning 26 Oscars and seven Emmy Awards. A chain-smoker, his cough often heralded his arrival in a particular wing of the studio, allowing off-task employees time to get busy. He preferred to smoke unfiltered Lucky Strikes, but later switched to the strong French Gitanes.

Disney was in bad health for a few months, before he finally entered hospital on 2 November 1966, complaining of pain in his neck and back. An X-ray revealed a tumour on his neck, and his left lung was riddled with tumours the size of walnuts. A workaholic, he checked out to finish some studio business. Songwriter Robert B. Sherman wrote:

'He was up in the third floor of the animation building after a run-through of *The Happiest Millionaire*. He usually held court in the hall-way afterward for the people involved with the picture. And he started talking to them, telling them what he liked and what they should change, and then, when they were through, he turned to us and with a big smile, he said, "Keep up the good work, boys." And he walked to his office. It was the last we ever saw of him.'

He re-entered the hospital on 6 November. Surgery was performed the next day and his left lung was removed. On 30 November, Disney collapsed in his home, but was revived and taken back to hospital. The actor Kurt Russell confirmed a long-standing industry legend, that the last thing Walt Disney did before he died was write the words 'Kurt Russell'. No announcements of his funeral were made and only close relatives were in attendance. His daughter Diane once quoted her father as saying: *'When I'm dead I don't want a funeral. I want people to remember me alive.'*

‘I'm getting a lot of bloody row in here ... I can't see anything ... I'm going ... oh!’

Last words spoken moments before his fatal accident

The full version of Campbell's last words via radio intercom on his final run for a world water speed record is:

> 'Pitching a bit down here ... Probably from my own wash ... Straightening up now on track ... Rather close to Peel Island ... Tramping like mad ... er ... Full power ... Tramping like hell here ... I can't see much ... and the water's very bad indeed ... I can't get over the top ... I'm getting a lot of bloody row in here ... I can't see anything ... I'm going ... oh!'

An alternative version is: *'The water's dark green and I can't see a bloody thing. Hallo, the bow is up. I'm going. I'm on my back. I'm gone.'*

Campbell broke eight world speed records in the 1950s and 1960s, and is the only person to set both land and water speed records in the same year (1964). His father, Sir Malcolm Campbell, had set 13 world speed records in cars and boats in the 1920s and 1930s, nine on land and four on water. Between 1955 and 1963, Donald Campbell's *Bluebird K7* set six world water speed records. Then, in July 1964, Campbell set a land speed record of 403 mph (690 km/h), but was disappointed as the conditions meant that he could not go any faster. As it was, he peaked at 440 mph (710 km/h) at the finish of the measured mile. The land speed record was soon overtaken by a jet car, Craig Breedlove's *Spirit of America,* but Campbell's record for a wheel-driven car remained unbeaten until 2001. Campbell set another world water speed record on 31 December 1964, when he reached 276 mph (445 km/h) in Western Australia. In 1966, he decided to go for an eighth water speed record, with *Bluebird K7* being fitted with a lighter and more powerful jet engine. The trials at Coniston Water did not go well, and in 1967 he was killed when *Bluebird K7* flipped and disintegrated at a speed in excess of 300 mph (480 km/h) on her second run. She had completed a perfect north–south run at an average of 297.6 mph (478.9 km/h), with a peak speed of 315 mph (507 km/h). The boat and Campbell's body were not recovered until 2001.

'Excuse my dust'

One of her several suggestions for her epitaph

'*This is on me*' was another of her suggestions for her tombstone inscription. In the *New Yorker* (1929) she also wrote: '*That would be a good thing for them to cut on my tombstone: Wherever she went, including here, it was against her better judgment.*'

The satirical poet, film scriptwriter, playwright, noted wit and short-story writer began her career as *Vanity Fair*'s drama critic (1917–20) and then became the *New Yorker*'s theatre and book reviewer (1927–33). Politically left-wing, she co-founded the Hollywood Anti-Nazi League, and after World War II was blacklisted by the House Un-American Activities Committee. Asked to used the word 'horticulture' in a quiz show, she answered: '*You can lead a horticulture, but you can't make her think.*' Other aphorisms include: '*This is not a novel to be tossed aside lightly. It should be thrown with great force*'; '*There is no cure for curiosity*'; '*Men seldom make passes/At girls who wear glasses*'; '*That woman speaks eighteen languages, and can't say No in any of them*'; and '*Katharine Hepburn delivered a striking performance that ran the gamut of emotions, from A to B.*'

Parker died of a heart attack, leaving her estate to the Martin Luther King Foundation. On his assassination, her estate was passed on to the National Association for the Advancement of Colored People. In 1988, the organization claimed her ashes and designed a memorial garden for them outside their Baltimore headquarters. The plaque reads:

'Here lie the ashes of Dorothy Parker (1893–1967) humorist, writer, critic. Defender of human and civil rights. This memorial garden is dedicated to her noble spirit which celebrated the oneness of humankind and to the bonds of everlasting friendship between black and Jewish people. Dedicated by the National Association for the Advancement of Colored People. October 28, 1988.'

ERNESTO 'CHE' GUEVARA
(ERNESTO GUEVARA DE LA SERNA)
14 June 1928–9 October 1967

'I know you have come to kill me. Shoot, coward. You are only going to kill a man.'

Last words to his executioner

These were reportedly Guevara's last words, to his executioner Sergeant Jaime Terán, after he had been wounded and captured in Bolivia with the assistance of the CIA. The ninth bullet, through the throat, was what eventually killed him. His last words to Colonel Parada, who delivered the official report on his death, were: *'I knew you were going to shoot me; I should never have been taken alive. Tell Fidel that this failure does not mean the end of the revolution, that it will triumph elsewhere. Tell Aleida [his second wife] to forget this, remarry and be happy, and keep the children studying. Ask the soldiers to aim well.'* Earlier, General Ovando, the chief of the Bolivian armed forces, had declared that Che had died in battle, and that just before he died had declared: *'I am Che Guevara and I have failed.'*

Guevara was an Argentine Marxist revolutionary, politician, author, physician, military theorist and guerrilla leader. In 1956, along with Fidel Castro and a handful of men, he invaded Cuba and overthrew the dictator Fulgencio Batista. Two years later, after a guerrilla campaign in which Guevara displayed such leadership that he was named 'comandante', the rebels entered Havana.

Following his execution, he became both a stylized countercultural icon and a symbol of rebellion for leftist movements worldwide. His farewell letter to Fidel Castro, published on 1 April 1965, stated: *'In a revolution, one triumphs or dies (if it is a true revolution) ... I feel that I have fulfilled the part of my duty that tied me to the Cuban revolution in its territory, and I say farewell to you, to the comrades, to your people, who now are mine ... I have lived magnificent days ... Other nations of the world summon my modest efforts of assistance.'* His 'Last Letter from Papa', written to his children in 1965, to be opened in the event of his death, ends: *'Above all, try always to be able to feel deeply any injustice committed against any person in any part of the world. It is the most beautiful quality of a revolutionary.'*

'Mine eyes have seen the glory of the coming of the Lord'

Line from 'The Battle Hymn of the Republic'; closing words of his speech
the evening before he was assassinated

Dr King's flight to Memphis had been delayed by a bomb threat, and in the last words of his speech to supporters and striking workers, he seemed to foretell his death the following day:

'... And then I got to Memphis. And some began to say the threats, or talk about the threats that were out. What would happen to me from some of our sick white brothers? Well, I don't know what will happen now. We've got some difficult days ahead. But it doesn't matter with me now. Because I've been to the mountaintop. And I don't mind. Like anybody, I would like to live a long life. Longevity has its place. But I'm not concerned about that now. I just want to do God's will. And He's allowed me to go up to the mountain. And I've looked over. And I've seen the promised land. I may not get there with you. But I want you to know tonight, that we, as a people, will get to the promised land. So I'm happy, tonight. I'm not worried about anything. I'm not fearing any man. Mine eyes have seen the glory of the coming of the Lord.'

Arrested more than 20 times for preaching racial equality, King was the youngest man ever to receive the Nobel Peace Prize. He gave the award money to further the Civil Rights movement. Martin Luther King Day was established as a US National Holiday in his memory in 1986. He was shot while standing on his motel's balcony. Jesse Jackson claimed that his last words were to musician Ben Branch, who leant over him: '*Ben, make sure you play "Take My Hand, Precious Lord" in the meeting tonight. Play it real pretty.*' The King family believe that James Earl Ray (1928–98), who was convicted for the killing, had nothing to do with it. Ray's ashes were flown to Ireland, as he was disgusted at being refused the right of a retrial.

'No! No!'

Last words before losing consciousness

The younger brother of President John F. Kennedy was US Attorney-General from 1961 to 1964, when he resigned to become senator for New York. He publicly disagreed with President Johnson over the Vietnam War, and at a meeting on 6 February 1967, Johnson told Kennedy: *'I'll destroy you and every one of your dove friends. You'll be dead politically in six months.'* In a television interview later that year, Kennedy said:

> 'We're going in there and we're killing South Vietnamese, we're killing children, we're killing women, we're killing innocent people because we don't want a war fought on American soil, or because [the Viet Cong are] 12,000 miles away and they might get 11,000 miles away. Do we have the right, here in the United States, to say we're going to kill tens of thousands, make millions of people ... refugees, killing women and children, as we have?'

He began campaigning for the presidency in March 1968. Jackie Kennedy told Arthur Schlesinger in New York: *'Do you know what I think will happen to Bobby?'* When Schlesinger replied that he didn't, she said: *'The same thing that happened to Jack.'* William W. Turner believed that Kennedy was going to reopen the investigation into the killing of his brother once he had been elected president, and probably also that of his friend Martin Luther King.

On 4 June, Kennedy defeated Eugene McCarthy in the California presidential primary. On the 5th, he made a short victory speech just after midnight at the Ambassador Hotel in Los Angeles. He was then heading for the Colonial Room for a press conference when it was suggested that he take a short cut through the kitchen. Eight shots were fired, with five people injured, and Kennedy was hit three times. A Palestinian immigrant, Sirhan Sirhan, was overpowered, but all eyewitnesses said that it would have been impossible for him to have fired the point-blank fatal shot into the back of Kennedy's head, as he was always in front of him and never near enough. Medical attendants arrived and lifted Kennedy on to a stretcher, prompting him to exclaim, *'No! no!'* He lost consciousness shortly afterwards, surviving another 26 hours.

'Things seemed to go too wrong too many times'

Suicide note sent to Edward Joffe

The comedian left two suicide notes, both addressed to his friend and producer Edward Joffe. The first one said: '*Dear Eddie, This is quite rational please give my love to my mother, but there was nothing left to do. Things seemed to go too wrong too many times. Tony.*' The second added: '*Ed – Please send my mother this, I am so sorry to cause her any more grief as she has already had enough – but please pass on this message to her – ... that the soul is indestructible ... Please send her my love as deeply as possible.*' The *Independent* of 24 December 2005 states that part of the note read: '*Nobody will ever know I existed. Nothing to leave behind me. Nothing to pass on. Nobody to mourn me. That's the bitterest blow of all.*'

Joffe recounts: '*I found him sitting at a table on which, set out like a New York skyscape, were on-end 200-pack cartons of cigarettes and several bottles of vodka. My last memory of him is haunted by the sunken, staring eyes.*' The comedian Spike Milligan recalled in 1989 that Hancock was a '*very difficult man to get on with. He used to drink excessively. You felt sorry for him. He ended up on his own. I thought, he's got rid of everybody else, he's going to get rid of himself. And he did.*' Elsewhere Milligan commented: '*He shut the door on all the people he knew, and then he shut the door on himself.*'

His career in decline, Hancock had gone to Australia to film a 13-part series, which had not gone well, with him forgetting lines. He committed suicide by overdose in Sydney, being found dead in his flat with an empty vodka bottle and an empty bottle of sleeping pills at his side. Cliff Goodwin wrote: '*On that final day of shooting – and unknown to Hancock – executives at Channel 7 decided that, however bad the episodes they already had in the can, it was worth taking a chance and commissioning a second series. The producer had been informed. Most of the crew knew. But no one thought to tell their star ...*'

MEHER BABA (born MERWAN SHERIAR IRANI)
25 February 1894–31 January 1969

'Do not forget that I am God'

Last words, conveyed by gestures to his followers

The son of a Persian Zoroastrian who had been a wandering Sufi Dervish, and who married a Zoroastrian Indian in Pune, India, Baba spent seven years in training with spiritual masters before beginning public work. One of his first followers gave him the name Meher Baba, meaning Compassionate Father. From 10 July 1925 to his death 43 years later, he maintained silence, communicating with his growing band of disciples with an alphabet board or by unique hand gestures. He spent long periods in seclusion, meditating and often fasting. He worked for charities, the poor, lepers and the mentally ill.

In 1931, he made the first of many visits to the West. The message '*Don't worry, be happy*' was often cabled to followers there, leading to its adoption in the 1960s by the hippy movement. He wrote: '*Happiest is he who expects no happiness from others. Love delights and glorifies in giving, not receiving. So learn to love and give, and not to expect anything from others.*' On 10 February 1954, he declared that he was the Avatar, an incarnation of God, descended from the higher realm to do good on Earth. He told his female disciples: '*I am the last Avatar in this present cycle of twenty-four, and therefore the greatest and most powerful. I have the attributes of five. I am as pure as Zoroaster, as truthful as Ram, as mischievous as Krishna, as gentle as Jesus, and as fiery as Muhammad.*'

After being badly injured as a passenger in two car crashes, Baba's ability to walk became limited and his health steadily deteriorated. However, he continued to undertake long periods in seclusion, fasting and meditating. In late July 1968, he emerged from a rigorous period of seclusion, saying that his work was '*completed 100% to my satisfaction*'. Racked with muscular spasms, he died seven months later, and his tomb has become a pilgrimage shrine.

BERTRAND ARTHUR WILLIAM RUSSELL, THIRD EARL RUSSELL
18 May 1872–2 February 1970

'I was told the Chinese might bury me ... I might have become a god, which would have been very chic for an atheist.'

From his autobiography

A genius and a polymath, Russell was born and died in Wales. He was noted globally as a mathematician, philosopher, logician, social theorist, socialist and pacifist, fighting to the end for his beliefs. In November 1969 alone, at the age of 97, he protested about show trials in Czechoslovakia, US war crimes in Vietnam and the expulsion of Solzhenitsyn from the Writers' Union. On 31 January 1970, two days before his death from influenza, Russell issued a statement condemning Israeli aggression in the Middle East, read out at a conference in Cairo the day after his death. The concluding words were: *'What Israel is doing today cannot be condoned, and to invoke the horrors of the past to justify those of the present is gross hypocrisy.'*

Imprisoned for pacifist activities in World War I, Russell abandoned this stance against Hitler, declaring that war was *'the lesser of two evils in such extreme circumstances'*. In 1950, he was awarded the Nobel Prize for Literature, *'in recognition of his varied and significant writings in which he champions humanitarian ideals and freedom of thought'*. In 1962, his international reputation was such that Nikita Khrushchev responded to his correspondence by telegram during the Cuban Missile Crisis. Aged 84, Russell added a short prologue to a new edition of his autobiography. It was entitled 'What I Have Lived For', and reads in part:

'Three passions, simple but overwhelmingly strong, have governed my life: the longing for love, the search for knowledge, and unbearable pity for the suffering of mankind ... always pity brought me back to earth ... Children in famine, victims tortured by oppressors, helpless old people a hated burden to their sons, and the whole world of loneliness, poverty, and pain make a mockery of what human life should be. I long to alleviate the evil, but I cannot, and I too suffer. This has been my life. I have found it worth living, and would gladly live it again if the chance were offered me.'

HAROLD CLAYTON LLOYD
20 April 1893–8 March 1971

'I am just turning 40 and taking my time about it'

Response when asked his age when 77 years old

The film actor and producer was most famous for starring in silent movies, but he also pioneered the use of colour in films. Like Buster Keaton and Charlie Chaplin, he left an indelible mark on the industry, making almost 200 'silents' and 'talkies'. He is well remembered for his 'Glasses Character', a resourceful, success-seeking go-getter in 1920s America, and his movies frequently contained 'thrill sequences' of extended chase scenes and daredevil physical feats. Lloyd founded his own film company in 1924. He held on to the copyrights and became one of the wealthiest men in Hollywood, making more money from his films than Chaplin. In 1953 he was given an honorary Academy Award for being a 'master comedian and good citizen'. The 'good citizen' citation was a snub to Chaplin, who was being investigated by the Un-American Activities Committee, and whose amorality was well known. At the time, Chaplin had had his entry visa into the United States revoked.

Lloyd died of prostate cancer in March 1971. *Time* magazine tersely recorded:

'Died. Harold Lloyd, 77, comedian whose screen image of horn-rimmed incompetence made him Hollywood's highest-paid star in the 1920s; of cancer; in Hollywood. He usually played a feckless Mr Average who triumphed over misfortune. "My character represented the white-collar middle class that felt frustrated but was always fighting to overcome its shortcomings," he once explained. Lloyd usually did his own stunt work, as in *Safety Last* (1923), in which he dangled from a clock high above the street; he was protected only by a wooden platform two floors below.'

In 1919, Lloyd had injured himself during the filming of *Haunted Spooks*, when an accident with a prop bomb resulted in the loss of the thumb and index finger of his right hand, which makes his hanging from window ledges, flagpoles and gutterings even more remarkable. The injury was disguised on film with the use of a special prosthetic glove.

'Medal of Honor'

Citation on tombstone

'AUDIE L. MURPHY
TEXAS
MAJOR INFANTRY
WORLD WAR II
JUNE 20 1924
MAY 28 1971
MEDAL OF HONOR
DSC – SS & OLC
LM – BSM & OLC
PH & 2 OLC'

Medal of Honor is the US military's highest award for valour; DSC = Distinguished Service Cross; SS = Silver Star; LM = Legion of Merit; BSM = Bronze Star Medal; PH = Purple Heart; OLC = Oak Leaf Cluster. Murphy was awarded an additional 32 US and foreign medals and citations.

One of the most decorated American soldiers of World War II, the son of poor Texas sharecroppers, Murphy lied about his age to serve in the war. He tried to enlist after Pearl Harbor, but was only 15 years old. His sister then adjusted his birth date to make him appear 18, not 16, which accounts for the discrepancy upon his gravestone from his real date of birth. After being turned down by the Marines and paratroopers because he was of slight build, baby-faced and under 5 feet 6 inches, he was accepted by the army. His company commander tried to have him transferred into a non-combat job, but Murphy refused and fought the system to take his place in the front line. Credited with killing over 240 of the enemy, while wounding and capturing many others, he was a legend in the 3rd Infantry Division. From being a private, he rose to the rank of staff sergeant, and was given a battlefield commission as 2nd lieutenant. Wounded three times, he fought in nine major campaigns across Europe. Suffering from post-traumatic stress disorder, he managed to become an actor, appearing in 44 American films. His best movies were *The Red Badge of Courage* and *To Hell and Back*, a movie about his war experiences. He was killed in a plane crash in Virginia.

GEORGE HENRY SANDERS
3 July 1906–25 April 1972

'Dear World, I am leaving because I am bored. I feel I have lived long enough. I am leaving you with your worries in this sweet cesspool. Good luck.'

Suicide note

In 1975, David Niven related in the second volume of his autobiography, *Bring On the Empty Horses*, how in 1937 his friend George Sanders, at the age of 31, had predicted that he would commit suicide when he was 65. On 23 April 1972, Sanders checked into a hotel in Castelldefels, on the coast near Barcelona. He was found dead two days later, having taken five bottles of the barbiturate pills Nembutal. He was 65 years old. What is less well known is that he left a second suicide note to his sister Margaret, who had grown up with him in St Petersburg: *'Dearest Margoolinka. Don't be sad. I have only anticipated the inevitable by a few years.'*

Sanders' film career spanned four decades and included *Rebecca, Forever Amber* and *All About Eve*, for which he won an Oscar. He was married four times, and his wives included two of the Gabor sisters, Zsa Zsa and Magda. His last marriage, to Magda, lasted only six weeks, after which he began drinking heavily. In his later years he suffered from bewilderment and bouts of anger, worsened by waning health, having had a minor stroke. In his 1979 biography, *A Dreadful Man*, his friend Brian Aherne wrote that Sanders moaned: *'I can't speak straight and I can't think.'*

Sanders' sister Margaret went to take care of him. One morning she found that he had ordered the servants to drag his piano into the garden, where he chopped it to pieces with an axe. When Margaret protested, he pushed her away, saying, *'I can't play the damned thing any more, so why should I keep it?'* Aherne saw Sanders a month before his death, when Sanders was downing glasses of straight vodka and asking about pills: *'How many would it take? ... Everything I do is wrong. I can't do right. I must be crazy!'* Sanders' opinion of the acting profession is given in a 1937 letter to Aherne, calling *'the actor, strutting and orating away his youth and his health, alienated from reality, disingenuous in his relationships, a muddle-headed peacock forever chasing after the rainbow of his pathetic narcissism'*.

PABLO PICASSO (PABLO DIEGO JOSÉ FRANCISCO
DE PAULA JUAN NEPOMUCENO MARÍA DE LOS
REMEDIOS CIPRIANO DE LA SANTÍSIMA
TRINIDAD RUIZ Y PICASSO)
25 October 1881–8 April 1973

'Drink to me, drink to my health, you know I can't drink any more'

Attributed last words, to friends visiting him and his wife Jacqueline Roque

Among Picasso's last words, spoken to his bachelor doctor, were these, quoted by his biographer Patrick O'Brian: *'You are wrong not to marry. It's useful.'* Picasso's second wife Jacqueline prevented his children from a former marriage, Claude and Paloma, from attending his funeral. Grief-stricken after his death, in 1986 she shot herself, aged 60. All his life Picasso maintained a number of mistresses in addition to his wife or primary partner, and had four children by three women, none of them with Jacqueline Roque.

The most famous painter of the twentieth century, Picasso co-founded Cubism with Georges Braque, and was also a sculptor. For many of us, his abstract works are difficult to understand, something he explained as:

'Everyone wants to understand painting. Why don't they try to understand the song of the birds? Why do they love a night, a flower, everything which surrounds man, without attempting to understand them? Whereas where painting is concerned, they want to understand ... Those who attempt to explain a picture are on the wrong track most of the time ... How can you expect a beholder to experience my picture as I experienced it? A picture comes to me a long time beforehand; who knows how long a time beforehand, I sensed, saw, and painted it and yet the next day even I do not understand what I have done. How can anyone penetrate my dreams, my instincts, my desires, my thought, which have taken a long time to fashion themselves and come to the surface, above all to grasp what I put there, perhaps involuntarily?'

SALVADOR ALLENDE (SALVADOR ISABELINO DEL SAGRADO CORAZON DE JESUS ALLENDE GOSSENS) 26 June 1908–11 September 1973

'Long live Chile! Long live the people! Long live the workers!'

Last known words, at the end of a radio broadcast on the morning of the day he was killed

This socialist was President of Chile from November 1970 up until his death during the 1973 coup. In his last broadcast to the people of Chile, as General Pinochet's forces were sacking the country, he said: *'I have faith in Chile and in its destiny. Other men will overcome this dark and bitter moment, when treason stands to conquer. May you go forward in the knowledge that, sooner rather than later, the great avenues will open once again along which free citizens will march in order to build a better society.'* A North American Congress of Latin America editorial of July 2003 noted that Allende's *'Popular Unity government represented the first attempt anywhere to build a genuinely democratic transition to socialism – a socialism that, owing to its origins, might be guided not by authoritarian bureaucracy, but by democratic self-rule.'*

Allende redistributed land and wealth in Chile, and nationalized the banks and the copper industry. However, his government was seen by Henry Kissinger as being against US interests: *'Of all of the leaders in the region, we considered Allende the most inimical to our interests. He was vocally pro-Castro and opposed to the United States. His internal policies were a threat to Chilean democratic liberties and human rights.'* In 1970, President Nixon asked Kissinger to organize a coup against the Chilean government. The CIA tried to persuade Chile's Chief of Staff General Schneider to overthrow Allende. He refused, and on 22 October 1970, his car was ambushed and he was killed. A military coup was organized by General Pinochet, in which large numbers of civilians were killed or imprisoned. Upon being offered by a general a chance to flee, Allende said: *'Tell General von Schouwen that the president of Chile does not flee in a plane. As he knows how a soldier should act, I will know how to fulfil my duty as president of the republic.'* The presidential palace in Santiago was strafed by air force planes, and then overrun by soldiers, Allende dying in the fighting. Years of military dictatorship under Pinochet were to follow.

JACK BENNY (BENJAMIN KUBELSKY)
14 February 1894–26 December 1974

'Jack Benny's timing was all wrong. He left us much too soon.'

Bob Hope's funeral eulogy

Trying to explain the success of his life and career, Benny declared: '*Everything good that happened to me happened by accident. I was not filled with ambition nor fired by a drive toward a clear-cut goal. I never knew exactly where I was going.*' Beginning in vaudeville, he became one of the greatest comic personas of all time, taking the part of a miser and often accompanied by his violin, which he deliberately played badly. Performing until he was over 80, he always insisted upon being 'thirty-nine' years old. Despite his vainglorious and mean comic image, he performed free to benefit worthy causes and raised millions of dollars for charities, One of his best-remembered jokes is when a thug holds him up and says: '*This is a stickup! Now come on! Your money or your life!*' When pressed again, after a long pause Benny responds: '*I'm thinking it over.*'

In October 1974 Benny cancelled a performance after feeling dizzy, but nothing was diagnosed. In December he complained of stomach pains and was discovered to have pancreatic cancer. He died two weeks later, after visits from his great friends Bob Hope, George Burns, Johnny Carson and Frank Sinatra. Burns was supposed to read the funeral elegy but broke down, and a shaken Bob Hope took over, saying: '*For a man who was the undisputed master of comedy timing, you'd have to say that this was the only time when Jack Benny's timing was all wrong. He left us much too soon.*'

Benny's wife, Mary, recalled: '*I don't think Jack ever had a true inner sense of his own worth. He knew people liked him, but I don't think he ever realized just how much people adored him ... loved him. And he was the most patient, gracious man I ever met. Whenever he went, if a fan stopped him, he'd always stand and chat as long as they wanted to talk.*' In his will, Benny arranged for a single long-stemmed red rose to be delivered to Mary every day for the rest of her life.

JAMES RIDDLE (JIMMY) HOFFA
14 February 1913–disappeared 30 July 1975, pronounced legally dead 1982

'I don't need bodyguards'
Last interview, with Jerry Stanecki

 **Attorney-General Robert Kennedy** called the International Brotherhood of Teamsters *'the most powerful institution in this country – aside from the United States Government itself'* and claimed that with a membership of 1.7 million truck-drivers and warehousemen, *'the Teamster union under Hoffa is often not run as a bona fide union. As Mr Hoffa operates it, this is a conspiracy of evil'* (Robert Kennedy, *The Enemy Within*, 1960). *Life* magazine called Hoffa America's 'Public Enemy Number One'.

In July 1975 Hoffa disappeared from the parking lot of the Machus Red Fox restaurant in Michigan, where he was the most regular celebrity visitor. Thirty years later, in the *New York Times* of 21 May 2006, Jerry Stanecki commented on Hoffa's sudden disappearance:

'Back in 1975, Hoffa was angry. He wanted to serve notice to the mob [Mafia] and brother Teamsters who had betrayed him when he went to prison for bribery. Jimmy was coming back to run the union. It was his do-or-die mission, one he outlined as he sat across the table from me in his newly remodelled kitchen, drinking instant coffee. "Tell the rats to get off the ship because I'm coming back," he said. He was tough, all right – thought he was indestructible, and it was that ego that got him killed. Hoffa disappeared on July 30, 1975, and word on the street was that he'd given me "insurance" papers in case something happened to him. He hadn't, but no one knew that except me. For a while, I started my car by reaching in through the window, figuring it was better to lose an arm than be blown to bits.'

'Though I have not been able to be active for several years, I want you to know that I am the same Paul, dedicated as ever to the worldwide cause of humanity for freedom, peace and brotherhood'

Last public message, taped and played to 3,000 people in the Carnegie Hall celebration of his seventy-fifth birthday

Paul Robeson was a famous African-American athlete, singer, actor, and advocate for the civil rights of people around the world. Only the third black student at Rutgers University, he excelled at sports and academically, and went to Columbia Law School. He stopped practising when a white secretary refused to take dictation from him, and took up acting and singing, becoming a role model for all subsequent black American entertainers. At a 1937 rally for the anti-Fascist forces in the Spanish Civil War, he declared, '*The artist must elect to fight for Freedom or for Slavery. I have made my choice. I had no alternative.*'

Robeson died of a stroke following 'complications from a severe vascular disorder', after many years of ill health. His son believed that he had been poisoned by the CIA in 1961, and he was under surveillance as a 'Communist' for over 30 years, with attacks by the House Un-American Activities Committee almost ending his career. According to Martin Duberman:

'The white press, after decades of harassing Robeson, now tipped its hat to a "great American", paid its gingerly respect in editorials that ascribed the vituperation levelled at Robeson in his lifetime to the "Bad Old Days" of the Cold War, implied those days were forever gone, downplayed the racist component central to his persecution, ignored the continuing inability of white America to tolerate a black maverick who refused to bend.'

The *New York Amsterdam News*, an African-American newspaper, called Robeson '*Gulliver among the Lilliputians*', and stated that his life would '*always be a challenge and a reproach to white and Black America*'.

ELVIS AARON (born ARON) PRESLEY
8 January 1935–16 August 1977

'He said "I'm going into the bathroom to read" and that's the last thing he ever said to me. I didn't want to think that he was dead. God wouldn't want to take him so soon.'

Last words to Ginger Alden

There is still confusion about Elvis' last night. Allegedly at the final concert of his last tour in 1977 he told the audience: *'I hope I haven't bored you'* and *'I may not look good tonight, but I'll look good in my coffin.'* He weighed around 230 lb (104 kg) at the time. His last words to anyone outside his home, Graceland, were to his first cousin and assistant, Billy Smith, about his upcoming series of concerts: *'Billy, son, this is gonna be my best tour ever.'* At 10.30 on 15 August, Elvis went to the dentist, returning to Graceland at midnight. At 2.15 a.m. on 16 August he called his doctor for more painkillers. At 4 he woke his cousin Billy up to play racquetball, then at 5 and 7 in the morning took two packs of prescription pills. At 8 he took a third pack; at 9.30 a.m. he went to the bathroom. His girlfriend Ginger Alden woke up at 1.30 p.m. to find him unconscious on the bathroom floor. An ambulance was called and Elvis was taken to hospital.

Elvis had said something about not being able to sleep and going into the bathroom to 'read'. As Ginger and others understood it, this meant that he was about to take more prescription drugs. Another version of his last words is that Ginger told him, *'Don't fall asleep in there'*, and he replied, *'Okay, I won't.'* Ginger then went back to sleep before waking up and finding him. The *Commercial Appeal* quoted his doctor as saying on the way to the hospital, *'Breathe, Presley, breathe!'* At 4 p.m. his father Vernon appeared on the steps of Graceland to tell reporters: *'My son is dead.'* The coroner's report lists 'cardiac arrhythmia', but the real cause of death was a cocktail of ten prescribed drugs, taken in doses no doctor would allow: two painkillers, two tranquillizers, an antihistamine, two opiates, a sleeping pill, a barbiturate and a depressant.

**'Here lies Groucho Marx – and lies and lies and lies.
ps He never kissed an ugly girl.'**

His own suggestion for an epitaph

The eldest Marx brother, Manfred, died in infancy, but the others formed a comedy group and became huge vaudeville and then radio and film stars. They were Herbert 'Chico' (1887–1961), Adolph, later changed to Arthur 'Harpo' (1888–1964), 'Groucho', Milton 'Gummo' (1892/93–1977) and Herbert 'Zeppo' (1901–79). Three hit plays featuring their comedy routines were performed on Broadway, and Groucho emerged as the main 'front man' for the act, although Chico arranged the finances. Groucho starred in 26 films, 13 of them with his brothers Chico and Harpo. He developed an act as a wise-cracking hustler with an ever-present cigar, prominent glasses, a distinctive bent-forward walk, and an exaggerated greasepaint moustache and eyebrows, improvising insults to all and sundry, especially the dim and stuffy dowager played by Margaret Dumont. A typical quip was: '*He may look like an idiot and talk like an idiot but don't let that fool you. He really is an idiot.*'

Erudite and extremely witty, Groucho later had a successful solo career, notably as the host of the radio and television game shows *Tell It To Groucho* and *You Bet Your Life*. He joked: '*I find television very educational. Every time someone switches it on I go into another room and read a good book.*' Woody Allen called him '*the best comedian this country ever produced ... He is simply unique in the same way that Picasso or Stravinsky are.*' Towards the end of his life, Marx's children thought that his companion Erin Fleming was pushing him beyond his capabilities. He started comeback shows at a sell-out in Carnegie Hall in 1972, and in 1974 made his last public appearance, accepting an honorary Oscar on behalf of the Marx Brothers and Margaret Dumont. He died of pneumonia in Los Angeles at the age of 86. He had also suggested an epitaph saying '*Excuse me, I can't stand up*', but his grave bears only his stage name, birth and death dates and the Star of David.

'He was an average guy who could carry a tune'

His own suggested epitaph

Crosby sang from 1926 until his death 51 years later, and was the best-selling artist until the era of rock 'n roll, selling more than half a billion records. Of the rock era, he noted: *'I think popular music in this country is one of the few things in the twentieth century that have made giant strides in reverse.'* On his phenomenally successful single 'White Christmas', he said: *'A jackdaw with a cleft palate could have sung it successfully.'* He inspired Frank Sinatra, Perry Como and Dean Martin to become crooners, and in 1948 polls stated that he was *'the most popular man alive'*. From 1934 to 1954 he had the greatest record sales, radio ratings and motion-picture gross takings. His clever investments made him one of Hollywood's richest men. Apart from *White Christmas* and other films, he starred with Bob Hope in seven immortal *'Road to...'* movies. Crosby joked about their relationship: *'There is nothing in the world I wouldn't do for Hope, and there is nothing he wouldn't do for me ... We spend our lives doing nothing for each other.'* In his turn, Hope commented on *The Jack Benny Show* on Crosby's wealth: *'He's up in Nevada looking over Boulder Dam – his piggy bank is filled. He's so loaded, you know, he uses Howard Hughes for a bell boy.'*

Golf Digest, celebrating the hundredth anniversary of Crosby's birth in May 2003, related how, walking off a Spanish golf course near Madrid after shooting 85 and winning a $10 bet, Crosby suffered a heart attack, during which he said: *'That was a great game of golf, fellas.'* He once laughed, *'My golf is woeful but I will never surrender.'* His last concert had been in Brighton with Gracie Fields, just two days before, and he had flown to Spain to enjoy his favourite pastime. He was buried nine feet deep to allow his second wife to be buried with him.

ARCHBISHOP ÓSCAR ARNULFO ROMERO
Y GALDÁMEZ
15 August 1917–24 March 1980

'Let my blood be a seed of freedom'

Words spoken before he was murdered by a paramilitary death-squad

Appointed Archbishop of San Salvador in 1977, Romero spoke out against government violations of human rights, and helped the poor and the victims of the civil war. He openly condemned both Marxism and capitalism. In 1977, the assassination of his friend, the Jesuit priest Rutilio Grande, who had been helping to create self-reliance groups for the poor, forced Romero to action: *'When I looked at Rutilio lying there dead I thought, "If they have killed him for doing what he did, then I too have to walk the same path."'* He urged the government to act, but nothing happened and with press censorship he was powerless. He travelled to Europe, trying to gain international interest, and on 2 February 1980 at Louvaine University, Belgium, denounced the persecution of his Church:

> 'In less than three years, more than fifty priests have been attacked, threatened and slandered. Six of them are martyrs, having been assassinated; various others have been tortured, and others expelled from the country. Religious women have also been the object of persecution. The archdiocesan radio station, Catholic educational institutions and Christian religious institutions have been constantly attacked, menaced, threatened with bombs. Various parish convents have been sacked.'

Also in February, Romero wrote to President Carter asking him to halt military aid to San Salvador because it legitimized terror and assassinations, and would *'undoubtedly sharpen the injustice and the repression inflicted on the organized people, whose struggle has often been for their most basic human rights'*. The United States continued its aid, fearing a situation like that in Nicaragua. Romero was killed by a shot to the heart while celebrating mass at a small chapel in a hospital called La Divina Providencia. The previous day he had called on Salvadorean soldiers, as Christians, to obey God's higher order and to stop carrying out the government's repression. According to an audio recording, he was shot while holding up the Host, and his blood spilled over the altar. At is funeral mass, which was attended by more than 250,000 mourners, between 30 and 50 people died from gunshots.

'I'm shot'

Last words spoken before collapsing

As one half of one of the greatest song-writing partnerships in history, and one quarter of the Beatles, Lennon changed the face of popular music for ever. On 6 December 1980, two days before his murder, he was interviewed for the BBC by Andy Peebles, who told him that David Bowie had said that he could walk the streets of New York safely. Lennon responded: *'That's what made me finally stay here ... Yes you can walk on the street.'* At 1 p.m. on the 8th, at his apartment in the Dakota in New York, Lennon was interviewed by Dave Sholin of RKO Radio, saying: *'I've always considered my work one piece whether it be with Beatles, David Bowie, Elton John, or Yoko Ono. And I consider that my work won't be finished until I'm dead and buried and I hope that's a long, long time.'* He enthused about his new album, *Double Fantasy*, his first in five years. *'His focus was not on all the Beatle stuff that he'd been through a zillion times,'* Sholin recalled later. *'The focus was on his time with Sean, his relationship with Yoko, the new album. We had a great interview.'*

At about 5 p.m. John and Yoko left the Dakota to go to the recording studios; they did this at the same time every day, so that fans knew when to get autographs and pictures. Additionally, three weeks before his murder, John had fired his bodyguards. As the couple left the building, Mark Chapman silently handed Lennon a copy of the new album to sign, and Lennon asked him, *'Is this all you want?'* Chapman nodded silently. Later that day, the Lennons returned to the Dakota in time to say goodnight to five-year-old Sean. Chapman shot Lennon four times in the back using hollow-point bullets, which expand upon entering the target and severely disrupt maximum tissue as they travel through the body. Lennon staggered up the steps to the reception area, said, *'I'm shot'*, and collapsed. The doorman shouted at Chapman, *'Do you know what you've done?'* to which Chapman calmly replied, *'Yes, I just shot John Lennon.'* He then sat down to wait for the police. Lennon's new album *Double Fantasy*, marking his comeback, won the 1981 Grammy Award for Album of the Year.

ROBERT NESTA 'BOB' MARLEY
6 February 1945–11 May 1981

'Money can't buy you life'

Last words, to his son Ziggy, according to the official Bob Marley website

The lead singer, songwriter and guitarist for the reggae band the Wailers, Marley is credited with bringing reggae and Rastafarianism to worldwide attention. His wonderful 'Redemption Song' and 'No Woman, No Cry', along with 'Jamming', 'Get Up, Stand Up', 'One Love', 'I Shot the Sheriff' and 'Could You Be Loved' are known across the world, and a compilation album released three years after his death, *Legend*, has sold over 20 million copies. In 1999, *Time* magazine chose *Exodus* by Bob Marley and the Wailers as the greatest album of the twentieth century. Marley fathered 13 children by nine different women, telling an interviewer in 1973: '*I don't really settle down with lady. Me not ready.*' He did not make a will, which has caused massive legal problems.

In 1977 Marley survived an assassination attempt in Jamaica. In the same year in London, he hurt a toe while playing football. The wound became cancerous, and a form of malignant melanoma was diagnosed, but he refused amputation for religious reasons. It continued to fester until he had belated treatment in Miami, but by 1980, cancer, in its most virulent form, had begun to spread through Marley's body. He fought the disease for eight months, taking treatment at the clinic of Dr Joseph Issels in Bavaria. Issels' treatment was controversial and non-toxic and Marley's condition seemed to stabilize. Eventually, however, the battle proved too much and at the start of May 1981, Issels told Marley that there was no more hope. Bob Marley left Germany to die in Jamaica, but had to be taken to Miami for urgent medical attention. The cancer had spread to his lungs and brain. He was too ill to travel to Jamaica and died in a Miami hospital, surrounded by his family. A state funeral was held in Jamaica.

'Everyone has got to die, but I have always believed an exception would be made in my case. Now what?'

Statement to the Associated Press, 13 May 1981, for publication after his death

An Armenian-American author and dramatist, Saroyan worked rapidly, hardly bothering with editing his text, and drinking and gambling to excess, causing periods of near-poverty. Though many of his works are set in his native Fresno, California, from 1958 on he mainly resided in a Paris apartment, and wrote in 1961: '*I am an estranged man, said the liar: estranged from myself, from my family, my fellow man, my country, my world, my time, and my culture. I am not estranged from God, although I am a disbeliever in everything about God excepting God indefinable, inside all and careless of all.*'

Saroyan died in Fresno of prostate cancer, in his will asking for half of his ashes to be buried in California, and the remainder in Armenia. Twenty years later his Fresno ashes were found sitting in obscurity on a chapel shelf. They were eventually buried on the occasion of Fresno's first Saroyan Festival in 2001, held to honour the city's most famous native son. At a Broadway memorial tribute to Saroyan in October 1983, José Quintero said: '*A great man for the arts should be celebrated not because of the past, but for the future.*' Strangely, Saroyan's work is not well remembered today, and a *Los Angeles Times* article by Peter H. King in 1997, entitled 'Saroyan's Literary Quarantine', states:

'For whatever reasons, Saroyan today is held under book-land quarantine. Few of his titles are in print. He's barely taught in schools. His own plans for literary legacy – a writers-in-residence program, posthumous publication of many works – have been scrapped or stalled. They did name a theatre after him in Fresno, the one thing he expressly requested not be done. Those who remain under the Saroyan spell can only hope that the world will come around. His work simply seems too extraordinary, and universal, to be cleared from the shelves.'

'I'm not a dreamer ... but I believe in miracles. I have to.'

Letter to the Canadian Cancer Society, planning his fund-raising run
across Canada, 15 October 1979

'My name is Terry Fox. I am 21 years old, and I am an amputee. I lost
my right leg two-and-a-half years ago due to cancer ... I was rudely
awakened by the feelings that surrounded and coursed through the
cancer clinic. There were the faces with the brave smiles, and the ones
who had given up smiling. There were the feelings of hopeful denial,
and the feelings of despair. My quest would not be a selfish one. I could
not leave knowing these faces and feelings would still exist, even
though I would be set free from mine. Somewhere the hurting must
stop ... and I was determined to take myself to the limit for this cause.
I feel now is the time to make good my promise. I have been training
for eight months, running on an artificial leg. Starting with half a mile,
I have now worked up to thirteen-and-a-half a day, adding half a mile
weekly. By April next year [1980] I will be ready to achieve something
that for me was once only a distant dream reserved for the world of
miracles; to run across Canada to raise money for the fight against
cancer. The running I can do, even if I have to crawl every last mile.
But there are some barriers I cannot overcome alone. We need your
help. The people in cancer clinics all over the world need people who
believe in miracles. I am not a dreamer and I'm not saying that this will
initiate any kind of definitive answer or cure to cancer, but I believe in
miracles. I have to. '

Fox began his 'Marathon of Hope' despite being told that a heart condition could kill him if he exerted himself. Crowds watched him run every day,
but after 143 days and 3,339 miles (over 23 miles a day), he was forced to stop
because of cancerous lumps on each lung. Eight days later, a nationwide telethon
raised more than his target of $1 for each Canadian. Fox died the following year,
not yet 23 years old.

'I'll be around here a little longer so I'm going to take better care of myself'

Said two months before he died of a drug overdose

Belushi was a well-known musician, comedian and actor, remembered for his work on *Saturday Night Live, National Lampoon's Animal House* and *The Blues Brothers*. He was renowned for his excessive lifestyle, partying, overeating and taking prodigious quantities of alcohol and drugs. On the night of 4 March he began drinking and taking cocaine in his room at the Chateau Marmont hotel, on Sunset Strip, Los Angeles, and then went on to a secret club on the Strip (On the Rox, above the Roxy) that caters for stars and celebrities. He returned to his rooms at the hotel to continue partying, and was visited by Robin Williams and Robert DeNiro amongst others, and Cathy Evelyn Smith. Belushi asked Smith to *'shoot him up with a speedball'* (inject him with a combination of heroin and cocaine). A former backing singer for the Band, Smith had become a drug-dealer to pay for her own addiction, and hung out around celebrities. Belushi received several injections over the course of the night, Next morning he was found naked, dead on his bed.

The verdict was an accidental overdose of *'acute cocaine and heroin intoxication'*. Smith was released after questioning, but two months later gave an interview to the *National Enquirer*, admitting that she had injected Belushi. She was charged with murder, plea-bargained and had to serve 18 months in prison for involuntary manslaughter. Belushi's friend and co-star in *Blues Brothers*, Dan Aykroyd, led the funeral procession on a motorbike, and played loud guitar music at the memorial service, which he had earlier promised to do if Belushi predeceased him. Aykroyd and Belushi were due to present an Oscar a few weeks later, and Ackroyd did it alone, saying: *'My partner would have loved to have been here to present this award, given that he was something of a visual effect himself.'* Belushi's tombstone reads: *'I may be gone, but Rock and Roll lives on.'*

ALEXANDER COFFIN
1958–11 January 1983

'My own consolation lies in knowing it was not the will of God that Alex died'

Eulogy given by his father Revd William Sloane Coffin

This was one of Coffin's most requested sermons, inspired by the death of his 24-year-old son, who died in a car crash on 11 January 1983. William Sloane Coffin was a progressive Christian minister who gained international stature campaigning against nuclear weapons and the Vietnam and Iraq Wars, and in support of gay and civil rights and the peace movement. This is all the more remarkable as he was a former CIA agent.

'When a person dies there are many things that can be said, and there is at least one thing that should never be said ... The night after Alex died, a kind woman came into the house carrying about 18 quiches, saying sadly, "I just don't understand the will of God." I exploded, "I'll say you don't, lady. Do you think it was the will of God that Alex never fixed that lousy windshield wiper, that he was probably driving too fast in such a storm, that he probably had had a couple of beers too many? Do you think it is God's will that there are no streetlights on that road and no guardrail separating that right-angle turn from Boston Harbour?" For some reason, nothing so infuriates me as the incapacity of seemingly intelligent people to get it through their heads that God doesn't go around this world with his finger on triggers, his fist on knives, his hands on steering wheels. Deaths that are untimely and slow and pain-ridden raise unanswerable questions ... Never do we know enough to say that a death was the will of God ... My own consolation lies in knowing it was not the will of God that Alex died; that when the waves closed over the sinking car, God's heart was the first of all our hearts to break ... And finally I know that when Alex beat me to the grave, the finish line was not Boston Harbour in the middle of the night. If a week ago last Monday, a lamp went out, it was because, for him at least, the Dawn had come. So I shall – so let us all – seek consolation in that love which never dies, and find peace in the dazzling grace that always is.'

ARTHUR KOESTLER
5 September 1905–1 March 1983

'I wish my friends to know that I am leaving their company in a peaceful frame of mind'

From the joint suicide note of the writer and his wife Cynthia, dated June 1982

A Hungarian Jew, Koestler escaped from France to England at the start of World War II. In 1940, his virulently anti-Communist novel *Darkness at Noon* brought him international fame. In 1976 he was diagnosed with Parkinson's disease, and then later with terminal cancer. He told his friends that he was afraid not of death, but of the process of dying, losing control over his body and mind, and they were not surprised by his suicide from an overdose of barbiturates.

'To whom it may concern. The purpose of this note is to make it unmistakably clear that I intend to commit suicide by taking an overdose of drugs without the knowledge or aid of any other person. The drugs have been legally obtained and hoarded over a considerable period. Trying to commit suicide is a gamble the outcome of which will be known to the gambler only if the attempt fails, but not if it succeeds. Should this attempt fail and I survive it in a physically or mentally impaired state, in which I can no longer control what is done to me, or communicate my wishes, I hereby request that I be allowed to die in my own home and not be resuscitated or kept alive by artificial means ... After a more or less steady physical decline over the last years, the process has now reached an acute state with added complications which make it advisable to seek self-deliverance now, before I become incapable of making the necessary arrangements. I wish my friends to know that I am leaving their company in a peaceful frame of mind, with some timid hopes for a de-personalised after-life beyond due confines of space, time and matter and beyond the limits of our comprehension. This "oceanic feeling" has often sustained me at difficult moments, and does so now, while I am writing this. What makes it nevertheless hard to take this final step is the reflection of the pain it is bound to inflict on my surviving friends, above all my wife Cynthia. It is to her that I owe the relative peace and happiness that I enjoyed in the last period of my life – and never before. Since the above was written in June 1982, my wife decided that after thirty-four years of working together she could not face life after my death.'

JOHN CHARLES ELTON LE MESURIER
DE SOMERYS HALLILEY
5 April 1912–15 November 1983

'John le Mesurier wishes it to be known that he conked out on November 15th. He sadly misses family and friends.'

Self-penned obituary

Commissioned in World War II, the actor served as a captain in the Royal Tank Regiment. Most famous for his role as Sergeant Arthur Wilson in the popular BBC comedy *Dad's Army* (1968–77), he also appeared in over 100 films from 1948, including *Private's Progress, I'm All Right Jack,* and *Carlton Brown of the FO.* When his second wife, Hattie Jacques, left him for a younger man, Le Mesurier allowed the press to blame him for the break-up in order to save the comedienne's public image. He had been married to his third wife, Joan, for just six months when she began her affair with his great friend Tony Hancock. Hancock had only been married (to his second wife) for three months. Hancock and Joan told John straight away, and he more or less overlooked the affair. Joan later said: *'John was a lovely man, a gentleman. He was born looking old, with his long face and big soulful eyes. But he wasn't exactly passionate. He wouldn't tell me he loved me. He would pat me on the head and say, "I'm awfully fond of you, my little friend." Tony was different. He swept me off my feet.'* The affair lasted for two years, off and on, until Hancock killed himself in 1968. Joan went back to John permanently and stayed with him until his death, aged 71.

Much of this was kept secret from the general public at the time, for the sake of the reputations of all parties. In his private life, this gentle man was a heavy drinker. He gave up alcohol on medical advice but despite this became seriously ill, and lost a great deal of weight. He returned to drinking and had seven more years of life, reportedly regaining his *joie de vivre.* He died of a stomach haemorrhage brought on by cirrhosis of the liver. His last words before slipping into a coma were reportedly: *'It's all been rather lovely.'*

> **'I don't mind if my life goes in the service of the nation. If I die today every drop of my blood will invigorate the nation.'**
>
> Last public speech, at Orissa, 30 October 1984

Indira was the daughter of Jawaharlal Nehru, independent India's first prime minister (1947–64), and she spent her life in politics, being elected to Parliament in 1964. She was married to Feroze Gandhi (1912–60) and had two sons. The younger of the two, Sanjay (1946–80), was a controversial figure in her government before he was killed in a plane crash. The elder, Rajiv (1944–91), succeeded her as India's prime minister in 1984 before being killed in a bombing.

Indira Gandhi became India's first female prime minister in 1966, winning four successive elections. The successful prosecution of the Indo-Pakistan War (1971) under her guidance led to the creation of Bangladesh. In 1984 she used the military to suppress Sikh rebels and ordered an attack on the Golden Temple shrine in Amritsar. Over 1,000 Sikhs died, despite her maxim *'You cannot shake hands with a clenched fist.'* A few months later, the day after she made the above remark at a rally in Orissa, she was in the garden of the prime minister's residence in New Delhi, waiting to be interviewed by Peter Ustinov, when she was murdered by two Sikh bodyguards in revenge for the attack on the temple. Her body was riddled with 28 entry and exit wounds. She had also said: *'If I die a violent death, as some fear and a few are plotting, I know that the violence will be in the thought and the action of the assassins, not in my dying'* and *'Martyrdom does not end something, it is only a beginning.'*

Known as the 'Iron Lady', Gandhi led India to become one of the fastest-growing economies in the world. Her ascension to the highest position in the world's most populous democracy was especially significant for Indian women, who have traditionally been subservient to men.

'Dance like you're in percussion heaven'

Instructions to his cast the day he died

Bob Fosse won eight Tony awards for choreography, as well as one for direction. He was also nominated for an Academy Award four times, winning for his direction of *Cabaret* in 1973. In fact in that year he received an Oscar, three Emmy awards for directing, producing and choreographing Liza Minnelli's TV special *Liza With a Z*, and two Tony awards for directing and choreographing the Broadway show *Pippin*. He was one of the most innovative and influential choreographers of the twentieth century, changing the course of Broadway musicals with his distinctively slinky, sexy style of dancing. In 1979, when he was editing his film *All That Jazz*, and his musical *Dancin'* was due to open at the Shubert Theater, he said: *'All I want to do is to have someone remember me as a dancin' man.'*

Fosse had been diagnosed with epilepsy in 1961, and suffered from heart problems. He had a heart attack as a revival of his musical *Sweet Charity* was opening at the National Theater, collapsing in the next street as the show was beginning nearby. Gwen Verdon, the dancer who was his third wife, was with him, and cradled his head, thinking he was having an epileptic seizure. A crowd gathered and a doctor loosened Fosse's shirt and began to pound at his heart, but Fosse whispered, *'Please stop. You're hurting me. I'm alright. Don't worry about me.'* The ambulance took so long to arrive that he died in hospital. *'One member of the cast, Fred Mann, said, "We learned about this after what he would have considered a glorious time, a standing ovation." Mr Mann said the cast was told of Mr Fosse's death on the stage after the curtain went down at the end of the show. Another dancer, Patricia Ben Peterson, said, "Bob said today at rehearsal, 'Dance like you're going to percussion heaven,' and that's where he is."'* In his will Fosse left 66 friends $400 each, to *'go out and have dinner on me'.*

KENNETH CHARLES WILLIAMS
22 February 1926–15 April 1988

'...what's the bloody point?'

The end of the last sentence Williams wrote in his diary, 14 April 1988

The troubled comic actor kept meticulous diaries from the age of 14 until his death 48 years later. He claimed that writing them eased the loneliness he often felt. Williams adored his supportive mother Louisa ('Lou'), but hated his homophobic father. In 1962 his father was taken to hospital in agony after drinking carbon tetrachloride from a cough mixture bottle. Williams refused to visit him in hospital and carried on performing. He was later denied a visa to visit America because Scotland Yard considered him a suspect in his father's death.

From the mid 1950s up until his own death, Williams always lived in small flats in north London, with his mother close by. He insisted he was celibate, and his diaries suggest this was so, mainly because he found his homosexuality emotionally difficult to deal with. He lived alone all his adult life and appears never to have had a close companion other than his mother, nor a romantic relationship of any great significance, though he often holidayed with homosexuals. He starred in 26 *Carry On* films, more than anyone else. Highly intelligent and witty, he wrote disparagingly that the work required little talent, and critically of his role in the films, but he was friendly with most of the cast. The series producer, Peter Rogers, worked hard to keep him onside in the series: '*Kenneth was worth taking care of, because while he cost very little – £5,000 a film – he made a very great deal of money for the franchise.*'

In later life Williams' health declined, along with that of his elderly mother, and his depression deepened. He took an overdose of barbiturates, and was discovered by his mother, who was living in the next-door flat. Despite the fact that as far back as his earliest diaries he regularly wrote that he could not see any point in existence, an open verdict was returned. His last diary entry ended: '*By 6.30 pain in the back was pulsating as it's never done before ... so this, plus the stomach trouble combines to torture me – oh – what's the bloody point?*' His mother died three years later.

ʿI do not believe in my deathʾ

TV interview in 1958 affirming that he believed in the immortality of his art

On the same TV show, asked about why he thought death was beautiful, Dalí replied: *'Everything is erotic.'* The Spanish Catalan, from Figueres, is best remembered for his bizarre surrealist paintings and his striking appearance – he considered himself both a work of art and a genius. He acted the part of a dandy, in colourful clothes and with grandiose manners, always appearing with pomaded hair, long cape, walking stick and upturned waxed moustache.

He stated: *'Every morning upon awakening, I experience a supreme pleasure: that of being Salvador Dalí, and I ask myself, wonderstruck, what prodigious thing will he do today, this Salvador Dalí.'* Most people remember his 1931 painting of soft, melting pocket watches, called *The Persistence of Memory*. The limp watches, some being eaten by insects, and expanding landscape make us reject the assumption of time as being deterministic or rigid.

In 1929 Dalí met his future wife Gala, then a married woman years older than him. His father was so upset by the affair and his son's eccentric behaviour that he called him *'a perverted son on whom you cannot depend for anything'* and forever banned him from the family homes. Dalí became completely dependent on Gala, marrying her in 1934. He said: *'Without Gala, divine Dalí would be insane.'* After World War II, he became close to Franco, thanking the dictator for *'clearing Spain of destructive forces'*.

In 1980 Dalí's health worsened. Gala had allegedly been dosing him with a dangerous cocktail of unprescribed medicines that damaged his nervous system, causing his right hand to tremble. After her death, Dalí lost much of his will to live. In 1984 a fire broke out in his bedroom that may have been a suicide attempt. It is alleged that Dalí was forced by his guardians to sign blank canvases that would after his death be used in forgeries and sold as originals. His 1964 *Diary of a Genius* records: *'It is not necessary for the public to know whether I am joking or whether I am serious, just as it is not necessary for me to know it myself.'*

'Tomorrow there will be a battle'

Last words to his family

The physicist had been the youngest-ever member of the Academy of Sciences and helped develop the hydrogen bomb, but he annoyed Khrushchev from 1962, protesting about human rights and the testing of nuclear bombs. He was the first Soviet citizen to receive the Nobel Peace Prize, in 1975, the Nobel committee calling him '*the conscience of contemporary mankind*'. In his Nobel acceptance speech, he stated: '*We need reform, not revolution. We need a flexible, pluralist, tolerant society, which selectively and experimentally can foster a free, undogmatic use of the experiences of all kinds of social systems. What is detente? What is rapprochement? We are concerned not with words, but with a willingness to create a better and more decent society, a better world order ... We must make good the demands of reason and create a life worthy of ourselves and of the goals we only dimly perceive.*'

In 1980 he was exiled to Gorky, where in 1982 he declared: '*I shall continue to live in the hope that goodness will finally triumph.*' His banishment inspired worldwide protest, and in 1986, after Gorbachev's rise to power, both Sakharov and his wife were pardoned. Sakharov helped Mikhail Gorbachev find the courage to press home *glasnost* and *perestroika*, the twin pillars of revolution. During a visit to the United States in 1988, doctors at Massachusetts General Hospital performed cardiovascular tests, because of his angina, and determined that Sakharov did not need heart surgery or a pacemaker. In 1989 he was elected to the Soviet parliament, briefly serving before he died. According to the *Victoria Sun*:

> 'Yefrem Yankelovich, Sakharov's son-in-law, said Sakharov's last words to his family were: "Tomorrow there will be a battle" – a reference to his plans to press again for an end to the Communist Party's monopoly on power. He then went to prepare for the Friday's session of Congress, the parliament to which he was elected this year ... Sakharov, who suffered angina, had looked tired in recent months, which were filled with foreign trips and work as a deputy.'

He died that night of a heart attack, fighting to the end for human rights.

'The reports of my death are greatly exaggerated'

Written when he was dying, mimicking the words of Mark Twain

From Richmond, Virginia, Ashe won three tennis Grand Slam titles, the Australian Open, the American Open and Wimbledon, but succumbed to a heart attack from a hereditary heart condition in 1979. After a quadruple bypass operation, he was training to return to professional tennis, but developed chest pains while running and abandoned the attempt. In 1988 he discovered that he had contracted HIV from blood transfusions during one of his two heart operations. He and his wife kept his illness private until April 1992, when reports that a newspaper was about to publish a story about his condition forced him to make a public announcement that he had the disease. He was already known for his work for social causes and civil rights, and in the last year of his life called attention to AIDS sufferers across the world and founded a charity to help healthcare delivery. He died of an AIDS-related infection after almost completing his autobiography *Days of Grace*. It is not a traditional memoir but rather a collection of observations on sport, race, patriotism, sexual ethics, the individual's obligation to his family, and coping with terminal illness without bitterness. In it he wrote a message for his then six-year-old daughter Camera:

'I may not be walking with you all the way, or even much of the way, as I walk with you now. Don't be angry with me if I am not there in person, alive and well, when you need me. I would like nothing more than to be with you always. Do not feel sorry for me if I am gone. When we were together, I loved you deeply and you gave me so much happiness I can never repay you. Camera, wherever I am when you feel sick at heart and weary of life, or when you stumble and fall and don't know if you can get up again, think of me. I will be watching and smiling and cheering you on.'

'It's better to burn out than to fade away'

Line from Neil Young's song 'Out of the Blue' in Cobain's suicide note

'Thank you all from the pit of my burning, nauseous stomach for your letters and concern during the past years. I'm too much of an erratic, moody baby! I don't have the passion anymore, and so remember, it's better to burn out than to fade away.

Peace, love, empathy,

Kurt Cobain

Frances and Courtney, I'll be at your altar.

Please keep going Courtney, for Frances.

For her life, which will be so much happier without me.

I LOVE YOU, I LOVE YOU!'

Kurt Cobain was the singer-songwriter lead guitarist leader of the grunge rock group Nirvana. The band's second album, *Nevermind* (1991), with the terrific 'Smells Like Teen Spirit' track and single, made Cobain's reputation across the globe. He struggled with stomach pains and drug addiction, as well as personal and public pressures, and after a failed suicide attempt, he agreed to undergo a detox programme. On his arrival at the clinic he was visited by his daughter Frances. That night, 30 March, he scaled a six-foot-high fence and flew from Los Angeles to his home town of Seattle. On 3 April his wife, Courtney Love, contacted a private investigator to find him. On 8 April, Cobain's body was discovered at his home at Lake Washington by an electrician who had arrived to install a security system. A high concentration of heroin and traces of Valium were found in his body. Some conspiracy theorists believe that he did not commit suicide by shotgun, but was murdered by a killer hired by his wife. The suicide note found by his body seems to be a peculiar letter to someone else, with the last lines being additions in a different handwriting.

RICHARD MILHOUS NIXON
9 January 1913–22 April 1994

'I think, with the exception of his inexcusable continuation of the war in Vietnam, Nixon really will get high marks in history'

Verdict of his defeated opponent George McGovern

A complex man, Nixon was the thirty-sixth vice-president of the United States, its thirty-seventh president, and the only president ever to resign the office. Running for the House of Representatives in 1950, he called his Democratic opponent 'pink right down to her underwear', and she responded by calling him 'Tricky Dick', a term that stayed attached to him. A strongly anti-Communist senator, he became Eisenhower's vice-presidential candidate. When the *New York Post* disclosed that a secret cash fund had been set up for him by campaign donors, in return for political influence, he defended himself in the famous 'Checkers speech', saying that he was not going to return a dog that had been given to him as his daughters loved it. In 1960 he narrowly lost the presidential campaign to Kennedy, and called a halt to challenging the results to avoid a constitutional crisis – it appears that both sides had been guilty of vote-rigging. In 1962 he lost the election for Governor of California, blaming the media and seemingly retiring from public life: '*You won't have Nixon to kick around anymore because, gentlemen, this is my last press conference.*'

Nixon became president in 1969. At the beginning of his second term, Vice-President Agnew resigned because of charges of money-laundering, bribery and tax evasion. In that same year 'Watergate' broke, and Nixon told the press: '*People have got to know whether or not their President is a crook. Well, I'm not a crook. I've earned everything I've got.*' With the possibility of impeachment, however, he resigned on 9 August 1974. In 1977, he received $600,000 for interviews with David Frost. He said: '*I did abuse the power I had as president ... I said things that were not true ... I brought myself down. I gave them a sword and they stuck it in. And they twisted it with relish. And, I guess, if I'd been in their position, I'd have done the same thing.*' Bob Dole in a 1983 speech stated: '*History buffs probably noted the reunion at a Washington party a few weeks ago of three ex-presidents: Carter, Ford and Nixon – See No Evil, Hear No Evil, and Evil.*'

❛"Is it true that you still surround yourself with beautiful young women?" "That's true." "What does your doctor say about all of this?" "My doctor is dead."❜

One of his last comic routines

Burns performed from the days of vaudeville until his death, a comedian with a trademark arched eyebrow and a cigar, whose happiest years were when performing with his wife, Gracie Allen. After a long battle with heart disease, Allen had a fatal heart attack in 1964, aged only 69. Burns wrote that he found it impossible to sleep after her death, until he decided to sleep in the bed she used during her illness. To get over her death, he immersed himself in work, touring all over playing nightclubs and theatres, and in 1974 he starred in the film *The Sunshine Boys*. He recalled years later: '*The happiest people I know are the ones that are still working. The saddest are the ones who are retired. Very few performers retire on their own. It's usually because no one wants them. Six years ago Sinatra announced his retirement. He's still working.*' In a celebration for Burns' ninety-ninth birthday, Los Angeles renamed a road 'Gracie Allen Drive' off a road they had previously named after George. Burns was present at the unveiling ceremony and said, '*It's good to be here at the corner of Burns and Allen. At my age, it's good to be anywhere!*'

In 1988 he had booked himself to play Caesar's Palace and the London Palladium for his hundredth birthday in 1996, but was not able to do so. In July 1994, he fell in his bathtub and his health began to decline. In December 1995 he reportedly caught influenza at Sinatra's Christmas party, and was weakened for his hundredth birthday three weeks later. Burns had said that he looked forward to death, believing that the day he died he would be with Gracie again in heaven. He was buried alongside her, with the crypt's marker being changed to '*Gracie Allen & George Burns – Together Again*'. He had said that he wanted Gracie to have top billing, after so many years of performing as 'George Burns and Gracie Allen'.

JACQUES-YVES COUSTEAU
11 June 1910–25 June 1997

'Commander Jacques-Yves Cousteau has rejoined the world of silence'

Announcement of his death by the Cousteau Foundation;
Cousteau had written *The Silent World* in 1953

This naval officer co-developed the aqua-lung and pioneered ocean conservation upon his ship *Calypso*. He was an ecologist, explorer, scientist, photographer, researcher, author and film-maker who inspired many to take an active interest in the ecosystem of the seas. Even in his eighty-eighth year, he gave an interview saying:

> 'I said that the oceans were sick but they're not going to die. There is no death possible in the oceans – there will always be life – but they're getting sicker every year ... We have to prepare for what life could become in 40 years. We need to outline what is possible and what is impossible with the non-renewable resources of the Earth. What role will technological improvement play? Taking all this into account, what kind of life can we produce in the best way for 10 billion people? That's a problem that needs to be solved.'

A few months before his death, in January 1997, Cousteau accepted an award in Florida, saying: '*The future of civilization depends on water, I beg you all to understand this.*' Cousteau envisioned solving the global energy crisis by channelling the sea's tides and temperatures, and by extracting essential raw materials from the ocean floor. He hoped for a day when the world's population could be fed by plantations hundreds of feet beneath the surface. He is remembered by millions as the first man who opened up the mysteries of the deep to television viewers, pioneering maritime photography with over 100 films. At his funeral, Notre-Dame Cathedral in Paris was filled with thousands of mourners, including President Jacques Chirac, and President Clinton stated: '*While we mourn his death, it is far more appropriate that we celebrate his remarkable life. Captain Cousteau showed us both the importance of the world's oceans and the beauty that lies within.*'

'God has forgotten me'

Referring to her 120th birthday

Jeanne Calment lived all her life in Arles, France, and has the longest known lifespan, of 122 years and 164 days. At the age of 113 she was celebrated as the last living person to have met Van Gogh. He had come to her uncle's shop in 1888 to buy paint, and she described him as *'very ugly, ungracious, impolite, sick'*, and also *'dirty, badly dressed and disagreeable'*. Calment remembered selling coloured pencils to him, and also seeing the Eiffel Tower being built. Her marriage in 1896 to her second cousin, a rich store owner, enabled her to live comfortably, playing tennis, swimming, cycling, playing the piano and attending the opera. Aged 85, she took up fencing, and at 100 she was still riding a bicycle. Calment lived on her own until shortly before her 110th birthday, when she needed to be moved to a nursing home, after a cooking accident started a small fire in her flat. However, she was able to walk daily until, aged almost 115, she fractured her femur in a fall, which required surgery. After her operation, she became confined to a wheelchair and began losing weight.

She officially gave up smoking aged 117, but had an occasional puff after her 118th birthday. She ascribed her longevity and relatively youthful appearance to olive oil, which she poured over all her food and rubbed on to her skin. She said: *'I've only got one wrinkle and I'm sitting on it.'* Her other health tips were to drink port before lunch and dinner every day, and to eat nearly two pounds of chocolate a week. After her 122nd birthday, it was decided she would not do any more public speaking, as her health had seriously deteriorated. A notary public, André-François Raffray, had purchased her apartment, promising to pay $500 per month until Jeanne died. He paid twice the market value for the apartment before predeceasing her in December 1995. Calment commented: *'In life, one sometimes makes bad deals.'* She also stated: *'I took pleasure when I could. I acted clearly and morally and without regret. I'm very lucky.'*

LADY DIANA FRANCES MOUNTBATTEN-WINDSOR, *née* SPENCER, PRINCESS OF WALES
6 July 1961–31 August 1997

'My God. What's happened?'
Last words, according to police files

The daughter of Viscount Althorp, Diana was descended from illegitimate offspring of Charles II and James II. Prince Charles proposed to her in February 1982, when she was 19 years old and he was 32, and they married in July. When their engagement was announced, Anthony Carthew of ITN asked the royal couple how they felt, then enquired: *'And I suppose – in love?'* Diana immediately answered: *'Of course.'* Charles hesitated, then replied: *'Whatever "in love" means.'*

By the early 1990s, after Diana had given birth to the princes William and Harry, adultery on both sides had ended the marriage. The royal couple formally separated in 1992 and divorced in 1996. On 20 November 1995, Martin Bashir asked the princess on the BBC TV *Panorama* programme: *'Do you think Mrs Parker-Bowles was a factor in the breakdown of your marriage?'* Diana responded: *'Well, there were three of us in this marriage, so it was a bit crowded ... She won't go quietly, that's the problem. I'll fight to the end, because I believe that I have a role to fulfil, and I've got two children to bring up ... I'd like to be a queen of people's hearts, in people's hearts, but I don't see myself being Queen of this country. I don't think many people will want me to be Queen.'* Prince Charles went on to marry his long-term mistress Camilla Parker-Bowles in 2007. Lady Diana died in a car crash with her lover Dodi Al Fayed in Paris in 1997. An inquest was not held until 2004, ending in 2008, at which it was concluded that she died through the grossly negligent driving of the French chauffeur, but rumours of conspiracy still surround the death. At her funeral, her brother, the ninth Earl Spencer, was publically critical of the royal family, and his broadcast speech was sensationally cheered by the massive crowds outside Westminster Abbey.

MOTHER TERESA OF CALCUTTA
(AGNESË GONXHE BOJAXHIU)
26 August 1910–5 September 1997

'She is the United Nations. She is peace in the world.'

Tribute from former UN Secretary-General Javier Pérez de Cuéllar

An Albanian Roman Catholic nun, Mother Teresa took Indian citizenship and founded the Missionaries of Charity in Calcutta (Kolkata) in 1950. She said that its aim was to care for '*the hungry, the naked, the homeless, the crippled, the blind, the lepers, all those people who feel unwanted, unloved, uncared for throughout society, people that have become a burden to the society and are shunned by everyone*'. It began as a small order, with 13 members, and now has more than 4,000 nuns, 300 brothers and over a million co-workers running orphanages, schools, hospices and charity centres in 123 countries, caring for refugees, the blind, disabled, aged, dying, alcoholics, AIDS victims, the poor and homeless, and victims of floods, epidemics and famine.

In 1979 Mother Teresa was awarded the Nobel Peace Prize: '*for work undertaken in the struggle to overcome poverty and distress, which also constitutes a threat to peace*'. She refused the ceremonial banquet given to laureates, and asked that the $192,000 funds be given to the poor in India, stating that earthly rewards were important only if they helped her to help the world's needy. When she received the prize, she was asked, '*What can we do to promote world peace?*' She answered: '*Go home and love your family.*' In her Nobel lecture, she said: '*Around the world, not only in the poor countries, but I found the poverty of the West so much more difficult to remove. When I pick up a person from the street, hungry, I give him a plate of rice, a piece of bread, I have satisfied. I have removed that hunger. But a person that is shut out, that feels unwanted, unloved, terrified, the person that has been thrown out from society – that poverty is so hurtable and so much, and I find that very difficult.*' In 1996 she was proclaimed an Honorary Citizen of the United States. In ill health, on 13 March 1997 she stepped down as head of the Missionaries of Charity and died six months later.

FRANCIS ALBERT 'FRANK' SINATRA
12 December 1915–14 May 1998

'I'm losing'

Last words, according to his daughter Nancy Sinatra, as told to
Variety magazine columnist Army Archerd

Sinatra's final words after his fatal heart attack, spoken as attempts were made to stabilize him, were posted on 20 May 1998 on CNN's website under the heading '*Hollywood bids Sinatra last farewell*'. Other sources quote him as saying, '*I'm losin' it.*' Nancy Sinatra was angered that she had not been at her father's deathbed, blaming Sinatra's last wife, the former Barbara Marx. His death was confirmed by the Sinatra family on their website with a statement accompanied by a recording of the singer's version of 'Softly As I Leave You'. The next night the lights on the Las Vegas Strip were dimmed in his honour. It is said that Sinatra was buried with a flask of Jack Daniels whiskey, a roll of ten dimes (in reference to the kidnapping of his son, when he had to contact the kidnappers from payphones), a Zippo lighter (which may refer to his Mafia connections) and a packet of Camel cigarettes. The words '*The Best is Yet to Come*' are imprinted on his tombstone. Sinatra had not been seen in public since a heart attack in January 1997, and had been in and out of hospital several times since then. His final attack, in Los Angeles, followed a long battle with coronary heart disease, kidney disease, bowel cancer and senility. He was buried a few miles away from Palm Springs, next to his parents in Desert Memorial Park in Cathedral City.

The crooner, nicknamed 'Ol' Blue Eyes', started entertaining as a singing waiter. He became one of the world's richest and best-loved singers, with songs like 'My Way', 'Strangers in the Night' and 'New York, New York' becoming classics associated with him. He was also a film star, appearing in a series of films including *From Here to Eternity*, for which he won an Oscar. Stephen Holden called him '*the first modern pop superstar ... Sinatra transformed popular singing by infusing lyrics with a personal, intimate point of view that conveyed a steady current of eroticism ... his 1950s recordings ... were instrumental in establishing a canon of American pop song literature.*'

'I'm just wandering, I think of things and then they go away for ever'

Speaking in September 1996 of her inability to write, quoted in *The Times*
on 5 February 1997, when it was announced she was suffering from
Alzhemer's disease

The Irish-born author and philosopher was best known for her novels such as *Under the Net* and *The Bell*, specializing is stories about relationships, the power of the unconsciousness and morality. At Oxford in 1956, she met and married John Bayley, a professor of English literature and also a novelist. She went on to produce 25 more novels, and other works of philosophy and drama. From the mid-1990s she suffered from Alzheimer's disease, the first signs of which were seen on visits to Israel, where she had difficulties answering questions from audiences. Her last novel was *Jackson's Dilemma* (1995), a psychological thriller. A critic wrote in the *New York Times* that Murdoch's prose was afflicted with imprecision and redundancies: for example the phrase '*then suddenly*' appeared three times in a single paragraph.

In 1995 Murdoch told an interviewer that she was experiencing severe writer's block, with the struggle to write leaving her in '*a hard, dark place.*' She was, Murdoch confided to one of her friends, '*sailing into the darkness.*' In 1996 John Bayley announced to the public that Murdoch had Alzheimer's disease. Over the next few years Bayley wrote '*Elegy for Iris*', not just a love story but a sad record of watching of a loved one diminish, with Murdoch not understanding what was happening to her. In this memoir, Bayley wrote that Murdoch became like '*a very nice 3-year-old,*' and needed to be fed, bathed and changed. In the book he portrayed the last years of his brilliant wife lovingly but unsentimentally: '*She was a superior being, and I knew that superior beings just did not have the kind of mind that I had ... Every day we are physically closer ... She is not sailing into the dark. The voyage is over, and under the dark escort of Alzheimer's, she has arrived somewhere. So have I.*' The 2001 film *Iris*, starring Judi Dench and Kate Winslet, is based upon Bayley's book.

'No, I think he's writing'

Last *Peanuts* cartoon strip, 13 February 2000

In the last ever *Peanuts* strip, which appeared the day after Schulz's death, Charlie Brown speaks the above words into a telephone, while Snoopy lies on top of the doghouse writing the following letter:

> 'Dear Friends, I have been fortunate to draw Charlie Brown and his friends for almost fifty years. It has been the fulfillment of my childhood ambition. Unfortunately, I am no longer able to maintain the schedule demanded by a daily comic strip. My family does not wish Peanuts to be continued by anyone else, therefore I am announcing my retirement. I have been grateful over the years for the loyalty of our editors and the wonderful support and love expressed to me by fans of the comic strip. Charlie Brown, Snoopy, Linus, Lucy ... how can I ever forget them.'

Peanuts ran for nearly 50 years and appeared in more than 2,600 newspapers in 75 countries. In November 1999 Schulz suffered a stroke, when it was discovered that he had colon cancer. Because of chemotherapy treatment, and the fact that he could not read or see clearly, he announced his retirement on 14 December 1999. This was difficult for Schulz; as he said on the *Today Show*: *'I never dreamed that this would happen to me. I always had the feeling that I would stay with the strip until I was in my early eighties, or something like that. But all of sudden it's gone. I did not take it away. This has been taken away from me.'* He had predicted that the strip would outlive him, as comic strips are usually drawn weeks before their publication. In the event, it survived him by only one day. He was asked if, for his final *Peanuts* strip, Charlie Brown would finally get to kick that football after so many decades. His answer was: *'Oh, no! Definitely not! I couldn't have Charlie Brown kick that football; that would be a terrible disservice to him after nearly half a century.'*

THOMAS EDWARD BURNETT, JR
29 May 1963–11 September 2001

'I know we're all going to die ... there's a group of us who are going to do something about it. I love you, honey.'

Last words to his wife Deena

Burnett was the VP and COO of a medical devices company who was travelling on United Airlines Flight 93 from Newark to San Francisco when terrorists took over the plane. He and other passengers had been informed by cell phones that the World Trade Center and the Pentagon had already been hit by hijacked airlines, so they decided to fight the terrorists hand-to-hand. The plane had been redirected towards Washington DC, where the hijackers planned to crash it into the Camp David presidential retreat, the White House or Capitol Hill; because of the passengers' resistance, it actually impacted near a strip mine in Shanksville, Pennsylvania, the only one of four hijacked aircraft not to hit a US landmark. The men involved in the desperate struggle, breaking into the cabin, were Burnett (aged 38), Mark Bingham (31), Jeffery Glick (31) and Todd Beamer (32). Beamer was heard via a cell phone uttering the now famous '*Let's roll!*' as they moved to attack. Faced with being overpowered, the hijackers nose-dived the plane, and all 45 people on board died on impact.

The attacks, usually now referred to as 9/11, were a series of suicide missions by al-Qaeda terrorists. Two planes flew into the Twin Towers of the World Trade Center in New York City, causing both buildings to collapse within two hours, and destroying nearby buildings. A third airliner crashed into the Pentagon. The terrorists used box-cutter knives to kill crew and passengers, and teargas or pepper sprays to keep passengers away from the first-class accommodation while they took over the flight cabins. Altogether there were 2,973 deaths in New York, Pennsylvania and Washington.

TERENCE ALAN PATRICK SEÁN ('SPIKE') MILLIGAN KBE
16 April 1918–27 February 2002

'I told you I was ill'
'Love, Light, Peace'

His own epitaph

Born in India to an Irish father and an English mother, Milligan was the greatest comic genius of his age. Although suffering from severe bipolar disorder, he was a consummate actor, musician, artist, poet, author, script-writer and comedian. The principal writer of *The Goon Show*, he said after fellow Goon Harry Secombe's death, *'I'm glad he died before me, because I didn't want him to sing at my funeral.'* A recording of Secombe singing was played at Milligan's memorial service. Two years after Milligan died, aged 83, relatives erected a headstone on his grave in Winchelsea, East Sussex, bearing the above epitaph. They had been unable to agree on a headstone, and finally settled on the Gaelic text to meet with approval from the Chichester Diocese, which had refused to allow the English words, but were happy with the translation.

In a BBC poll in August 1999, Spike Milligan was voted the 'funniest person of the last 1,000 years'. In 2006 it was reported that Professor Richard Wiseman had identified Milligan as the writer of the world's funniest joke, as decided by the Laughlab project. It was based on a 1951 *Goon Show* sketch: *'Two hunters are out in the woods when one of them collapses. He doesn't seem to be breathing and his eyes are glazed. The other guy whips out his phone and calls the emergency services. He gasps, "My friend is dead! What can I do?" The operator says, "Calm down. I can help. First let's make sure he's dead." There is a silence, then a shot is heard. Back on the phone, the guy says, "OK, now what?"'* Among some of his other jokes are: *'Contraceptives should be used on every conceivable occasion'*; *'Policemen are numbered in case they get lost'*; *'I have the body of an eighteen-year-old. I keep it in the fridge'*; and *'My father had a profound influence on me; he was a lunatic.'* Milligan's last words were *'Come on out.'*

'I will probably be found dead in the woods'

Conversation with David Broucher in February 2003

Born in Llwynypia in Wales, Dr Kelly was acknowledged as one of the world's leading experts on biological and chemical weapons. As a member of the UNSCOM team, he visited Iraq 37 times, with his success in uncovering Iraq's biological weapons programme leading to a nomination for the Nobel Peace Prize. Kelly was unhappy about the 2002 claim in a government dossier that Iraq was capable of firing battlefield biological and chemical weapons within 45 minutes of an order to use them, and queried its inclusion. On the BBC *Today* programme in May 2003, journalist Andrew Gilligan reported that the 45-minute claim was dubious, and the whole might of the establishment pressed to find who had leaked this information. Kelly was interrogated fiercely and humiliatingly before a parliamentary committee, one member saying to him, '*You have been set up, haven't you?*' Two days after this public appearance, Kelly sent an email to a *New York Times* journalist claiming that there were '*many dark actors playing games*'. At 3 p.m. that day he went for his daily walk to local woodlands, where he allegedly ingested up to 29 painkillers and then cut his left wrist with a knife.

Kelly's wife reported him missing shortly after midnight and he was found dead early the next morning. The government immediately announced that Lord Hutton would lead the judicial inquiry into the events leading up to the death. (Usually inquiries take months to set up.) A British ambassador, David Broucher, reported a conversation with Kelly in Geneva in February 2003. Broucher had asked Kelly what would happen if Iraq were invaded, and Kelly had replied, '*I will probably be found dead in the woods.*' Medical experts do not believe that it was suicide, for a number of reasons, including lack of blood loss, and uniquely there was no inquest, as is normal with violent deaths. There were no fingerprints on the knife, and suicide was also against Kelly's Baha'i faith. An MI5 operative took his mobile phone from the body, and MI5 officers went to his house an hour before the body was found and removed his computer, upon which he had written 46,000 words about the false reasons for going to war with Iraq. Both phone and computer have vanished. In a highly unusual move, the vital evidence of Dr Kelly's post-mortem will be kept secret until 2073.

'I now begin the journey that will lead me into the sunset of my life'

Letter to the American people, 5 November 1994

In August 1994, at the age of 83, Ronald Reagan was diagnosed with Alzheimer's disease. In November of that year, he informed the nation through a handwritten letter:

'My fellow Americans, I have recently been told that I am one of the millions of Americans who will be afflicted with Alzheimer's disease. Upon learning this news, Nancy and I had to decide whether as private citizens we would keep this a private matter or whether we would make this news known in a public way. In the past, Nancy suffered from breast cancer and I had my cancer surgeries. We found through our open disclosures we were able to raise public awareness. We were happy that as a result, many more people underwent testing. They were treated in early stages and able to return to normal, healthy lives. So now we feel it is important to share it with you. In opening our hearts, we hope this might promote greater awareness of this condition. Perhaps it will encourage a clearer understanding of the individuals and families who are affected by it. At the moment I feel just fine.

I intend to live the remainder of the years God gives me on this Earth doing the things I have always done. I will continue to share life's journey with my beloved Nancy and my family. I plan to enjoy the great outdoors and stay in touch with my friends and supporters. Unfortunately, as Alzheimer's disease progresses, the family often bears a heavy burden. I only wish there was some way I could spare Nancy from this painful experience. When the time comes, I am confident that with your help she will face it with faith and courage. In closing, let me thank you, the American people, for giving me the great honour of allowing me to serve as your president. When the Lord calls me home, whenever that day may be, I will leave with the greatest love for this country of ours and eternal optimism for its future. I now begin the journey that will lead me into the sunset of my life. I know that for America there will always be a bright dawn ahead. Thank you, my friends. May God always bless you.'

'He was a very real contender for a Superman hero figure'

Tribute by actress Susannah York, 11 October 2004

The actor, film director, producer and screenwriter, who starred as Superman, became a quadriplegic on 27 May 1995 after breaking his neck when falling from his horse. He required a wheelchair and breathing apparatus for the rest of his life and became an advocate for spinal cord injury research. In his last years he regained sensation in some parts of his body. He finally suffered a cardiac arrest at his New York home and slipped into a coma. His friend, the Democratic presidential candidate John Kerry, led the tributes to the actor and campaigner for funding for stem-cell research: '*He was an inspiration to all of us and gave hope to millions of Americans who are counting on the life-saving cures that science and research can provide. He met every challenge with a courage and character that broke new ground in this struggle.*'

Susannah York, the actress who played Superman's mother, said on BBC radio on 11 October that Reeve had '*enormous goodness of soul and courage. I felt terribly proud to play his mother. When I was doing the film I thought, "Wow, this guy is terrific." He was a very real contender for a Superman hero figure, because of his courage and generosity of spirit. He was fun. I think he was great ... what he set out to do since his accident ... I admired him incredibly.*'

Professor Colin Blakemore, Chief Executive of the Medical Research Council, told BBC Radio 4's *Today* programme that it took commitment like Reeve's to carry research forward: '*It takes extraordinary individuals like Reeve to recognise that investment and effort is worthwhile in the long run to work for others. He always said that he was working for himself and was convinced that there would be a cure, but I think probably deep in his mind he knew his efforts would be far more likely to pay off for others than for him.*' Tragically, his wife Dana, who encouraged and inspired him through his illness, contracted lung cancer in 2005, although a non-smoker, and died on 6 March 2006 aged only 44.

'I found something I always wanted to do, and I have enjoyed every single minute of it'

Farewell statement on final *Tonight Show*

The comedian hosted the *Tonight Show* for 30 years, becoming a much-loved American institution. Later shows began with music and the announcement '*Heeeeeere's Johnny!*' followed by a brief monologue by Carson. His trademark was a phantom golf swing at the end of his monologues, aimed 'stage left' towards the *Tonight Show* band. On the emotional occasion of his retirement, his 4,531st and final show on 22 May 1992, handing over to Jay Leno, he said:

> 'And so it has come to this: I, uh ... am one of the lucky people in the world; I found something I always wanted to do, and I have enjoyed every single minute of it. I want to thank the gentlemen who've shared this stage with me for thirty years, Mr Ed McMahon ... Mr Doc Severinsen ... and ... you people watching, I can only tell you that it has been an honour and a privilege to come into your homes all these years and entertain you – and I hope when I find something that I want to do, and I think you would like, and come back, that you'll be as gracious in inviting me into your home as you have been. I bid you a very heartfelt good night.'

A chain-smoker, in 1999 he suffered a severe heart attack at his home in Malibu, and was rushed to hospital in nearby Santa Monica, where he underwent quadruple-bypass surgery. On 23 January 2005 he died in hospital in Los Angeles from respiratory arrest arising from emphysema. In early *Tonight Shows*, he would often smoke cigarettes on air, saying as far back as the 1970s: *'These things are killing me.'*

HUNTER STOCKTON THOMPSON
18 July 1937–20 February 2005

'Relax – This won't hurt'

Note left by Thompson for his wife Anita, 16 February 2005

'Football season's over. No More Games. No More Bombs. No More Walking. No More Fun. No More Swimming. 67. That is 17 years past 50. 17 more than I needed or wanted. Boring. I am always bitchy. No Fun – for anybody. 67. You are getting Greedy. Act your old age. Relax – This won't hurt.'

Four days after writing this suicide note, Thompson shot himself in the head at his 'fortified compound' of Owl Farm, Woody Creek, near Aspen, Colorado. He had suffered weeks of pain from physical problems that included a broken leg and a hip replacement. His son, daughter-in-law and grandson were visiting for the week-end at the time of his suicide. They were in an adjacent room when they heard the gunshot, which they at first mistook for the sound of a book falling. Thompson's wife Anita, who was at a gym at the time of his death, was on the phone to Thompson when he ended his life.

A journalist and author of repute, in 1971 Thompson wrote *Fear and Loathing in Las Vegas,* which the *New York Times* called the *'greatest book of the dope decade'.* His heavily subjective, flamboyant style, whereby the writer becomes a central figure, and fiction and non-fiction are blurred, became known as 'Gonzo journalism'. An anti-authoritarian user of drugs, alcohol and firearms, his ashes were blown into the sky in Woody Creek to the sound of 'Spirit in the Sky' amid fireworks on 20 August, fired from a cannon on top of a 153-foot tower of Thompson's own design. The funeral was financed by his friend the actor Johnny Depp, who told an Associated Press reporter: *'All I'm doing is trying to make sure his last wish comes true. I just want to send my pal out the way he wants to go out.'*

'I have no regrets'

Michael Parkinson, reporting an interview with George Best

'I asked him once on the programme, given the chance to live his life again, what he would change. "Not a thing. I keep reading people who describe my life as a tragedy and I don't see it like that at all. I have no regrets," he said. But he left us too soon and I still miss him,' Parkinson added. Pelé called Best *'the greatest footballer in the world'*, and he is remembered for his dazzling skills for Man-chester United and Northern Ireland. He inspired his club to win the Football League Championships in 1965 and 1967, and the European Cup in 1968, when he was named European Footballer of the Year. Northampton player Roy Fairfax, who marked Best when he scored six goals in an 8–2 FA Cup win in 1970, said: *'The closest I got to him was when we shook hands at the end of the game.'* Footballer Rodney Marsh summed him up: *'He was everything a man wanted to be, and everything a woman wanted.'*

Best himself said: *'In 1969 I gave up women and alcohol – it was the worst 20 minutes of my life'* and *'I spent a lot of money on booze, birds and fast cars. The rest I just squandered.'* An Irish hotel employee brought champagne to Best's five-star hotel suite to find him and the current Miss World sprawled on a bed covered with his casino winnings, and famously asked: *'So George, where did it all go wrong?'* On a TV chat show, George commented: *'I used to go missing a lot ... Miss Canada, Miss United Kingdom, Miss World'*, and on another occasion: *'I've stopped drinking, but only while I'm asleep.'* He played for short periods for another 11 clubs, and became an alcoholic and a bankrupt, being imprisoned in 1984 for drink-driving and assaulting a policeman. He was evicted from his flat in 1998, and in 2002 had a liver transplant. However, he began drinking again, and on 20 November 2005, at his own request, the *News of the World* published a picture showing him in his hospital bed, along with his final message: *'Don't die like me.'*

'I am returning home, to the Earth, to the place of my origins'

End of suicide note

'To my friends and supporters to help them make sense of all these events that have happened so quickly: Certain human cultures have been waging war against the Earth for millennia. I chose to fight on the side of bears, mountain lions, skunks, bats, saguaros, cliff rose and all things wild. I am just the most recent casualty in that war. But tonight I have made a jail break – I am returning home, to the Earth, to the place of my origins. Bill, 12/21/05 (the winter solstice).'

The environmental campaigner was arrested on 7 December 2005 by the FBI during Operation Backfire, and was charged with ecoterrorist activities. He denied the allegations but committed suicide in his one-person cell in Flagstaff, Arizona, using a plastic bag over his head. A bookstore owner from Prescott, Arizona, he was charged with six others with firebombing a federal Animal and Plant Health Inspection Service facility outside Olympia, Washington, causing $1.2 million of damage. He was also named as a suspect in the arson of the University of Washington Center for Urban Horticulture in 2001, causing $1.5 million of damage, and a string of arson attacks in the Pacific Northwest. Rodgers had been scheduled to be transported to Seattle to face the charges. Lt Charlie Wong of the Flagstaff police said: '*There was no indication of any distress. He was completely normal.*' According to the *Seattle Times* (23 December 2005):

'FBI agents, in testimony and affidavits, said the government had recorded Rodgers admitting he was planning an arson attack. The government also claimed Rodgers had attended a meeting of Earth Liberation Front members in western Colorado where the arson of a Vail ski resort was planned. The federal government also claimed to have a recording of another person saying he found a manual, written by Rodgers, called "Setting Fires with Electronic Timers", in the offices of a New York environmental group, according to affidavits unearthed by the Rocky Mountain News in Denver.'

ALEXANDER VALTEROVICH LITVINENKO
23 November 1962–23 November 2006

'The bastards got me, but they won't get everybody'

Interview on day of his death

Litvinenko fell out with Russian President Vladimir Putin, then head of the FSB (the Federal Security Service), in the late 1990s, after leading an investigation into corruption in the FSB and its links with the Russian Mafia. Like Putin, he had served first in Russia's KGB, and then its successor, the FSB. In 1998 he publicly accused his superiors of ordering the assassination of Russian tycoon Boris Berezovsky, who fled Russia for self-imposed exile in the UK. Litvinenko was arrested in 1999, acquitted, rearrested and acquitted again. He then managed to flee with his family to London, where he was granted political asylum, becoming a journalist. He wrote two books, one of which accused the FSB of staging the 1999 Russian apartment-block bombings that killed more than 300 people. The attacks helped swing public opinion behind Russia's second war in the breakaway Chechen republic. Putin maintained the blasts were the work of Chechen separatists, and together with other terrorist acts, they helped to bring him easily to power, succeeding President Boris Yeltsin. Litvinenko denounced the war in Chechnya as a crime, called for Russian troops to be withdrawn, and declared that compensation should be paid to the Chechens. He also alleged that al-Qaeda number two Ayman al-Zawahiri was trained by the FSB in Dagestan, in the years before the 9/11 attacks.

The Times reported in May 2005 that someone had tried to push a pram loaded with petrol bombs through Litvinenko's front door, and he also believed that an FSB assassination squad had been formed to kill him. The month before Litvinenko himself was killed, he accused Putin of ordering the murder of the dissident journalist Anna Politkovskava (7 October 2006), claiming that after being handed documents relating to Politkovskaya's murder, he was taken ill. On 1 November 2006, Litvinenko became unwell after meeting two former KGB agents. In hospital it was discovered that he had been poisoned by radioactive polonium-210. After three weeks in intensive care, he died. A posthumous statement attributed his murder to President Putin. British investigation into his death resulted in a request to Russia for the extradition of the 'former KGB agent' Andrey Lugovoi. Russia refused.

JAMES JOSEPH BROWN JR
3 May 1933–25 December 2006

'I'm going away tonight'

Last words, to Paul Sargent moments before his death

As early as 1983, Brown said: '*Sometimes I look back on my life and wonder just how one man could achieve all I've done.*' He was variously known as 'the Godfather of Soul', 'Soul Brother Number One', 'Mr Dynamite', 'the King of Funk', 'the Original Disco Man', 'Minister of the New New Super Heavy Funk' and 'the Hardest Working Man in Show Business'. Known for his strenuous live performances, showmanship and dancing, the singer-songwriter and bandleader became a pivotal force in popular music. It is said that what became known as soul music in the sixties, funk in the seventies and rap in the eighties are all directly attributable to him. He transformed gospel fervour into the taut, explosive intensity of rhythm and blues, combined with precision choreography, defining the direction black music would take from the release of his first R&B hit ('Please Please Please') in 1956 to the present day. Other massive hits included 'Cold Sweat', 'Papa's Got a Brand New Bag' and 'I Got You (I Feel Good)'. His career was littered with brushes with the law, but he made a significant contribution to the rise of black equality in the 1960s and 1970s.

On 23 December 2006, in ill health, Brown went to his dentist in Atlanta, several hours late for an appointment. The dentist saw that he looked '*very bad … weak and dazed*', and advised him to go and see a doctor immediately. According to his manager, Brown had been sick and suffering with a cough since his November European tour. He said that Brown was often ill, never complaining, and often performed when feeling sick. Brown was confident he would leave hospital in time to perform his New Year's Eve shows in New York, but his condition worsened and he died early on Christmas Day of heart failure arising from pneumonia complications. His agent Frank Copsidas and friend Paul Sargent were at his bedside when Brown whispered, '*I'm going away tonight*', took three long, quiet breaths and died.

LUCIANO PAVAROTTI
12 October 1935–6 September 2007

'I believe that a life lived for music is an existence spent wonderfully, and this is what I have dedicated my life to'

Last words to his manager, Terri Robson

The Italian lyric tenor was considered one of the finest bel canto opera singers of the twentieth century. His concerts, recordings and television appearances gained him a global following. He gave his last 'live' performance, a masterful rendition of 'Nessun Dorma', at the opening ceremony of the Turin Winter Olympics in 2006, on a cold winter's night. In actual fact the whole performance was pre-recorded, as it had been decided not to risk his health. In July 2006 he was diagnosed with pancreatic cancer, while undertaking an 'international farewell' tour. He fought back, undergoing major abdominal surgery, but his health deteriorated severely in August 2007, when he was treated for a fever and a chest infection. He left hospital, but lapsed into unconsciousness and suffered kidney failure. He died at home in Modena, the place of his birth, surrounded by his family.

Within hours of his death, his manager, Terri Robson, noted in an e-mail statement, *'The Maestro fought a long, tough battle against the pancreatic cancer which eventually took his life. In fitting with the approach that characterized his life and work, he remained positive until finally succumbing to the last stages of his illness.'* Pavarotti had recently assured his fans that he was in good health, and had even joked about his sickness. The previous month, he phoned a concert on the island of Ischia to assure the public that he was about to release a new album of choral work, and that he looked forward to teaching his pupils again. *'Up until a few weeks before his death, he committed several hours each day to teaching his pupils at his summer villa in Pesaro on Italy's Adriatic Coast,'* said Robson. *'He remained optimistic and confident that he would overcome the disease and had been determined to return to the stage to complete his Worldwide Farewell Tour, which he was halfway through before being struck down by illness.'*

DAME ANITA LUCIA RODDICK (*née* PERILLI)
23 October 1942–10 September 2007

'I have hepatitis C. It's a bit of a bummer, but you groan and move on.'

Announcement to the media, 14 February 2007

'The Body Shop founder, Dame Anita Roddick, has revealed she is carrying the hepatitis C virus. Dame Anita, 64, also said she was suffering from cirrhosis of the liver, one of the long-term effects of the virus. Describing it as "a bit of a bummer", she said she contracted the virus through a blood transfusion while giving birth to her youngest daughter in 1971. The entrepreneur pledged to campaign to increase people's knowledge of the virus, dubbed "the silent killer" because of the few symptoms it causes. Dame Anita announced she has become a patron of the Hepatitis C Trust, a UK charity she turned to two years ago when she discovered she had the virus. She called for the condition to be taken more seriously as a "public health challenge" and questioned the success of a government awareness campaign. People infected with hepatitis C often show no symptoms initially, but long-term consequences can include liver damage and cancer. Men are more than twice as likely to be infected with the disease as women. The virus is transmitted by infected body fluids, and drug-users who share needles are particularly at risk. Dame Anita said: "I have hepatitis C. It's a bit of a bummer, but you groan and move on. I had no idea that I had this virus. I was having routine blood tests when it showed up. What I can say is that having 'hep C' means that I live with a sharp sense of my own mortality, which in many ways makes life more vivid and immediate. It makes me even more determined to just get on with things." Dame Anita called for more public money to be spent on raising awareness of the disease. She said: "Well, I've always been a bit of a 'whistleblower' and I'm not going to stop now."'

Roddick founded the Body Shop in 1976, producing and retailing cosmetic products. Her company was one of the first to prohibit the use of ingredients tested on animals, be environmentally friendly, and promote 'Fair Trade', pioneering the model of ethical consumerism.

'Dammit, I can't sleep'

Said to Christopher Plummer while shooting his last film

'Leaving England, says [Christopher] Plummer, "Heath was in very high spirits. He was just enjoying himself tremendously. It's a rather fanciful script, and he was wonderful in this role." Confirming earlier reports that Ledger hadn't been feeling well on set, Plummer says, "We all caught colds because we were shooting outside on horrible, damp nights. But Heath's went on and I don't think he dealt with it immediately with the antibiotics ... I think what he did have was the walking pneumonia. On top of that, he was saying all the time, 'Dammit, I can't sleep' ... and he was taking all these pills." As well as the damp cold and lack of sleep, Plummer describes the shoot as rigorous. "We had to shoot every second we were out there ... there was hardly any time to go into the tent or the car to keep warm. We just kept shooting ... boom, boom, boom ... there was no pause. It was very, very hard work."'

The Australian TV and film actor was halfway through filming *The Imaginarium of Doctor Parnassus* when he died. He had been nominated for an Academy Award for his role in *Brokeback Mountain* in 2005, and had recently completed the *Batman* film *The Dark Knight*, in which he played the Joker and received a posthumous Oscar. He was found naked on the floor near his bed in a Manhattan apartment, dying from a *'toxic combination of prescription drugs'* that included oxycodone, hydrocodone, diazepam, temazepam, alpazolam and doxylamine. Ledger told Sarah Lyall of the *New York Times* (4 November 2007) that he saw the Joker as a *'psychopathic, mass murdering, schizophrenic clown with zero empathy'*, and that in preparing for the role: *'I ended up landing more in the realm of a psychopath – someone with very little to no conscience towards his acts.'* Because of the stress of filming: *'Last week I probably slept an average of two hours a night ... I couldn't stop thinking. My body was exhausted, and my mind was still going.'* He took sleeping pills but they left him in *'a stupor, only to wake up an hour later, his mind still racing'*.

'Murder has become the primary tool whereby the state seeks to control the organs of liberty ... I hope my murder will be seen not as a defeat of freedom but an inspiration.'

Editorial published three days after his killing

This anti-government politician and journalist predicted his own assassination by the Sri Lankan government in an editorial in the Sri Lanka paper the *Sunday Leader* titled 'And Then They Came For Me', published posthumously on 11 January 2009. He had been on Amnesty International's endangered list since 1998, when anti-tank shells were fired into his house, and had been badly beaten up twice, with no police inquiries. He was shot while he was on his way to work. Four gunmen riding motorcycles blocked his vehicle before breaking open his window and shooting him in the head. No one has been arrested or charged, and attacks against media personnel continue.

'We find ourselves in the midst of a civil war ruthlessly prosecuted by protagonists whose bloodlust knows no bounds. Terror, whether perpetrated by terrorists or the state, has become the order of the day. Indeed, murder has become the primary tool whereby the state seeks to control the organs of liberty. Today it is the journalists, tomorrow it will be the judges. For neither group have the risks ever been higher or the stakes lower. Why then do we do it? I often wonder that ... When finally I am killed, it will be the government that kills me ... It has long been written that my life would be taken, and by whom. All that remained to be written was when ... That the *Sunday Leader* will continue fighting the good fight, too, is written. For I did not fight this fight alone. Many more of us have to be – and will be – killed before the *Leader* is laid to rest. I hope my assassination will be seen not as a defeat of freedom but an inspiration for those who survive to step up their efforts. Indeed, I hope that it will help galvanise forces that will usher in a new era of human liberty in our beloved motherland. I also hope it will open the eyes of your president to the fact that however many are slaughtered in the name of patriotism, the human spirit will endure and flourish.'

FARRAH FAWCETT
2 February 1947–25 June 2009

'I'm happy. I'm ready.'

Last words, passed in a note from her deathbed to Ryan O'Neill

Formerly married to the 'Six-Million-Dollar Man' and known as Farrah Fawcett Majors, she rose to inter-national fame in *Charlie's Angels* from 1976. A poster of her in a red swimsuit sold over 10 million copies and made her a global blonde sex symbol. The actress endured an erratic career after leaving the hit TV show, and had a long relationship with the film actor Ryan O'Neill. Drugs and violence littered her personal life, affecting her looks. By 1997, she seemed to be losing a sense of reality, appearing in *Playboy* rolling naked in paint, and speaking in a semi-coherent way on the *David Letterman Show*. She courageously took part in a TV documentary, *Farrah's Story*, after she was diagnosed with anal cancer in 2006. It showed her fight to the death to try to beat the illness. At the end of the film, she aims a camera at the audience and asks: '*How are you? What are you fighting for?*'

In an interview for *Today* with Meredith Viera (21 July 2009), Ryan O'Neill was asked about the atmosphere when Fawcett was dying:

'It was horrible. It was horrible. It was – he thought that she would live just another couple of hours, and she lived a couple of days. So I had a bed put in the room for me. And I just lay by her side. And she wouldn't – move on. She wouldn't pass. She just – she just looked at us with – with a slight smile. Was awful. And then – and then all the machines flat lined. After about – 16 hours. And she was – she was gone ... I said I'd see her soon. And I see her every day. And I write to her. I write in my journal now, to her ... but we all kissed her goodbye and hugged her and held her. And didn't want to let her go. It was something that I had never experienced, and I'd done a movie about it. But I'd never experienced it.'

MICHAEL JOSEPH JACKSON
29 August 1958–25 June 2009

'I love you more'

Last words to his film crew, the day before he died

Michael Joseph Jackson, the self-styled 'King of Pop', was one of the most commercially successful entertainers in history. Despite a troubled private life, he had an immense influence on popular music and dance, and his *Thriller* (1982) is the best-selling album of all time. He collapsed and died of suspected cardiac arrest at his rented mansion in Los Angeles, having been administered with propofol, lorazepam and midazolam.

The *Daily Express* reported Jackson shouting, '*This is it, this really is it*' as he got into a limousine after his last official public appearance, at London's O2 centre on 5 March 2009. He went to Los Angeles to rehearse for a scheduled 50 shows in the UK, despite worries about his health. '*I don't know how I'm going to do fifty shows. I'm not a big eater – I need to put some weight on,*' he said to fans gathered outside the rehearsal studio. It seems he was a reluctant participant, driven back to the stage as a last resort in order to pay off overwhelming debts. Promoter Randy Phillips, head of AEG Live, dismissed rumours of Jackson's frailty, declaring on 21 May: '*I would trade my body for his tomorrow. He's in fantastic shape.*'

'*The night before he died we had completed all of the physicality of the show as it would have been staged at the O2,*' said Kenny Ortega, producer and director of *This Is It*, the film based on footage of Jackson's last rehearsals. '*Michael stood out at the front of the stage that night with me and looked out into the empty arena and said, "This is the dream. We did it good, Kenny. We did it." There was this feeling in the air, and in our minds we were already on the plane. Michael said, "You can feel London. You can smell it."*' Associate producer and choreographer Travis Payne revealed that as Jackson was leaving for his waiting car after rehearsal, he shouted '*I love you*' to him, and Jackson smiled back and said '*I love you more.*'

'Am I dying? Am I giving up? Am I on my deathbed? Am I saying goodbye to people? No way.'

Last interview, 7 January 2009

The singer-songwriter, actor and dancer is best remembered for his romantic leading roles in *Dirty Dancing* and *Ghost*, and in 1991 was named by *People* magazine as the 'Sexiest Man Alive'. A chain-smoker, he was diagnosed with stage IV pancreatic cancer in January 2008. The cancer spread to his liver and he developed pneumonia. He helped raise cancer awareness across the world with his public battle against the illness. In the live television event 'Stand Up To Cancer' in September 2008, he received a standing ovation, saying: '*I keep dreaming of a future, a future with a long and healthy life, a life not lived in the shadow of cancer, but in the light. Together, we can make a world where cancer no longer means living with fear, without hope, or worse.*' In February 2009 his article in the *Washington Post* titled 'I'm Battling Cancer. How About Help, Congress?' urged politicians to increase funding for the National Institute of Health: '*My hope is that one day the words "a cure" won't be followed by the words "is impossible".*'

Swayze had brutal chemotherapy and experimental treatments at Stanford University Medical Center, with his wife and partner of 34 years, Lisa Niemi, accompanying him. He said: '*Hope is a very, very fragile thing in anyone's life, and the people I love do not need to be having that hope robbed from them.*' Meanwhile, despite debilitating side effects, he continued to act, launching a demanding new TV action series, *The Beast*. In late July 2008, six months after reportedly being given just weeks to live by medical experts, Swayze was asked by reporter in Los Angeles airport about his health. He replied, '*I'm cooking. I'm a miracle dude. I don't know why.*' In his last TV interview, with Barbara Walters, the actor said: '*One thing I'm not gonna do is chase staying alive. You spend so much time chasing staying alive, you won't live.*'' The tabloid headline he envisioned for himself, '*Swayze's Kicking It*', did not come to pass.

KEITH FLOYD
28 December 1943–14 September 2009

'I've not felt this well for ages'

Last words to his friend Celia Martin

Married four times and bankrupted once, this convivial author, restaurateur and chef hosted many TV cookery programmes. He had originally joined the army, mainly because he had seen the film *Zulu*, and served as a second lieutenant in the Royal Tank Regiment. Deciding that he and the army were 'mutually incompatible', he decided that his future lay in fine cuisine. Floyd was famed for his haphazard cooking style, which involved frequent 'quick slurps' of any local alcoholic beverage. He took cooking out of the studio, and began presenting programmes al fresco all over the world, cooking regional dishes and sampling local wines and beers. After suffering heart problems and undergoing operations for bowel cancer, Floyd was told by his doctor that his treatment was going well. To celebrate the news, as well as the birthday of his close friend Celia Martin, they went for a gourmet feast at the restaurant of a fellow celebrity chef, Mark Hix, at Lyme Regis in Dorset. Floyd finished off his meal with relish, and then smoked some cigarettes. Afterwards:

> 'They went home for a siesta, looking forward to watching Floyd on television in an interview with Keith Allen. Floyd died in his sleep before the programme started. Mrs Martin, who says that they had a close but platonic relationship, said: "It was my 65th birthday yesterday and we started off by going to see the specialist to do with his cancer. He had some very good news and he was very optimistic of his chances of beating it. We then went to have a pub lunch in Lyme Regis. He said, "I have not felt this well for ages." He had a very good last day.'

Floyd's final lunch consisted of:

Hix Fix Cocktail – a morello cherry soaked in apple eau de vie with champagne (£11.50)
Glass of Pouilly-Vinzelles white Burgundy 2006 (£49 a bottle)
Oysters with potted Morecambe Bay shrimps and toast (£12.70)
One bottle, shared, of Côtes du Rhone red wine (£21.50)
Red-legged partridge with bread sauce, rowan jelly and celeriac crisps (£21.50)
Perry Jelly with apple pie – pear cider made into a jelly (£6.50)

References

p.6: W.J. Serschol and E.A. Wallis Budge, *The Dwellers on the Nile: Chapters on the Life, History and Customs of the Ancient Egyptians*, 1912

p.7: *Mahaparinibbana Sutta* 6:8

p.8: Herodotus, *The Histories*, 450s–20s BCE

p.9: *The Histories of Herodotus*, Book 7, *c.*440 BCE

p.10: Bernadotte Perrin, *Plutarch's Greek Lives Vol. 2 Cimon and Pericles*, 1910

p.11: Plato, *Phaedo*

p.12: Stringfellow Barr, *The Mask of Jove: a history of Graeco-Roman civilization from the death of Alexander to the death of Constantine*, 1966

p.13: Plutarch, *Parallel Lives*

p.14: Plutarch, *Demosthenes*, *c.*75 CE (trans. John Dryden)

p.15: Plutarch, *Parallel Lives*

p.16: Livy, *Ab Urbe Condita*, Book XXXIX

p.17: Will Durant, *Heroes of History: A Brief History of Civilization from Ancient Times to the Dawn of the Modern Age*, 2001

p.18: William Shakespeare, *Julius Caesar*, first performed 1599

p.19: Cassius Dio, *Roman History*, Book LI

p.20: Horace, *Odes*, Book 3, No. 30, Lines 1 and 6, *c.*23 BCE

p.21: Mark 15:34–5 and Matthew 27:46

p.22: Suetonius, *The Lives of the Twelve Caesars: Nero*, *c.*121 CE

p.23: Suetonius, *The Lives of the Twelve Caesars: Vespasian*, *c.*121 CE

p.24: Suetonius, *The Lives of the Twelve Caesars: Titus*, *c.*121 CE

p.26: Henry Dwight Sedgwick, *Marcus Aurelius: A Biography*, 1921

p.27: Edward Gibbon, *The Decline and Fall of the Roman Empire*, 1776–1788, Chapter 7

p.28: Paul Edward Dutton (ed.), *Carolingian Civilization: A Reader*, 2nd edn, 2004

p.29: J.W. Bowden, *The Life and Pontificate of Gregory VII*, 1840

p.30: Robert Fabyan, *The New Chronicles of England and France*, Vol. I, 1516

p.31: Edwin A. Abbot, *St. Thomas of Canterbury*, 1898

p.32: Harold Lamb, *Genghis Khan: The Emperor of All Men*, 1928

p.33: Sir Walter Scott, *The Ministrelsy of the Scottish Borders*, 1803/04

p.35: William M. Bowsky, *The Black Death: A Turning Point in History?*, 1971

p.36: Morris Bishop (trans.), *Letters from Petrarch*, 1966

p.37: John Foxe, *The Book of Martyrs*, 1563

p.38: John Foxe, *The Book of Martyrs*, 1563

p.40: Paul Murray Kendall, *Richard III*, 1956

p.41: William Roscoe, *The Life of Lorenzo de' Medici, Called the Magnificent*, 1803

p.42: Johann Burchard, *Liber Notarum 1483–1506*, 1906

p.45: Peter Loring, *The Chevalier Bayard: A Study in Fading Chivalry*, 1929

p.47: William Roper, *The Life of Sir Thomas More*, 1554 (published 1626)

p.49: Christopher Hibbert, *Tower of London: A History of England from the Norman Conquest*, 1971

p.52: Agnes Strickland, *Lives of the Queens of Scotland and English Princesses*, 1851

p.53: Susan Brigden, *New Worlds, Lost Worlds*, 2000

p.54: Aidan Reynolds and William E. Charlton, *Arthur Machen: A Short Account of His Life and Work*, 1964 (p.186)

p.55: Diarmaid MacCulloch, *Thomas Cranmer: A Life*, 1996

p.57: Raphael Holinshed, *The Chronicles of England, Scotland and Ireland*, Vol. III, 1587

p.58: J.A. de Chavigny, *La première Face du Janus François*, Lyon, 1594

p.59: George R. Preedy, *The Life of John Knox*, 1940

p.60: Fulke Greville, *Life of Sir Philip Sidney*, 1652, quoted in John Addington Symonds, *Sir Philip Sidney*, 1902

p.62: *Notes by William Drummond, of Conversations with Ben Jonson, at Hawthornden in January 1619*; from a manuscript entitled *Informations by Ben Jonson to W. D., when he came to Scotland upon foot*, 1619

p.64: Pierre Gassendi, *Tycho Brahe*, 1654

p.65: F. Chamberlin, *Sayings of Queen Elizabeth*, 1923

p.66: *Dictionary of National Biography*, 1917

p.69: William Stebbing, *Sir Walter Raleigh*, 1891

p.72: Benjamin Chapman, *The History of Gustavus Adolphus and of the Thirty Years' War up to the King's Death*, 1856

p.74: Giuseppe Marc'Antonio Baretti, *Italian Library*, 1757

p.75: Bishop White Kennet, *Compleat History of England*, 1706

p.77: George Buchanan, *The History of Scotland*, 1827

p.78: Samuel Pepys, *Diary*, 13 October 1660

p.80: John Watkins, *Anecdotes of Men of Learning*, 1808

p.81: Thomas Babington Macaulay, *History of England*, 1849

p.82: Thomas Babington Macaulay, *History of England*, 1849

p.86: *Mémoire sur la mort de Louis XIV*, from Philippe, Marquis de Dangeau, *Memoirs of Philippe de Courcillon* (1638–1720), 1858

p.88: H.-F. de Bassewitz, *Russkii arkhiv 3*, 1865

p.91: *Notes and Queries*, 28 April 1855

p.92: Jean-Jacques Rousseau, *The Confessions, Book II, 1728–31*

p.94: Joseph Spence, *Anecdotes, Observations and Characters of Books and Men*, *c.*1740

p.96: Horace Walpole, *Memoirs of King George II*, 1846

p.97: Horace Walpole, *Memoirs of King George II*, 1846

p.98: Francis Parkman, *Montcalm and Wolfe*, 1884

p.99: *Notes and Queries*, 28 April 1855

p.100: E. Cobham Brewer, *Dictionary of Phrase and Fable*, 1898

p.101: J.H. Jesse, *George Selwyn and his Contemporaries*, 1843–44

p.102: Maria Hall Campbell, *Revolutionary Services and Civil Life of General William Hull; Prepared from his Manuscripts*, 1848

p.103: Jeremy Black, *Pitt the Elder*, 1992

p.104: Parton's *Life of Voltaire*, Vol. II

p.105: Dr James Thacher, *The American Revolution: From the Commencement to the Disbanding of the American Army*, 1809

p.106: John Powell (ed.), *Great Lives from History: The 18th Century – Denis Diderot*, 2006

p.107: John Hawkins, *Life of Samuel Johnston*, 1787

p.108: Thomas Babington Macaulay, *Life of Frederick the Great*, 1870

p.109: Baron Ferdinand Rothschild, *Personal Characteristics from French History*, 1896

p.111: Friedrich Kerst, trans. Henry Edward Krehbiel, *Mozart: The Man and the Artist, as Revealed in his own Words*, 1906

p.112: C.S. Edgeworth, *Memoirs of the Abbé Edgeworth; containing the Narrative of the Last Hours of Louis XVI*, 1815 p.113: *Encyclopedia Britannica*, 11th edn, 1911

p.115: *Bartlett's Familiar Quotations*, 10th edn, 1919

p.117: Thomas Carlyle, *The French Revolution: A History*, 1837

p.118: Jean-Baptiste Delambre, *Notice sur la vie et les ouvrages de M. le Comte J.-L. Lagrange*, in J.A. Serret, *Oeuvres de Lagrande*, 1867

p.121: Allan Cunningham, *Life of Burns*, 1815

p.122: Anthony Lejeune, *The Concise History of Foreign Quotations*, 2001

p.124: Tobias Lear, *Journal Account of George Washington's Last Illness and Death*, 14–25 December 1799

p.127: Elizabeth Abbott, *Haiti: An Insider's History of the Rise and Fall of the Duvaliers*, 1988

p.129: H.C. Syrett and J.G. Cooke (eds), *Interview at Weehawken: the Burr-Hamilton Duel as Told in the Original Documents*, 1960

p.132: Lord John Russell, *Life and Times of C.J. Fox*, 1860

p.134: Roberto A. Scattolini, *Ethics and Warfare in the 1811 Peninsular War: a Story of Military Honour*, on the website napoleon-series.org/research

p.135: *The Weekly Register*, Baltimore, 10 July 1813

p.136: P.G. Tsouras, *The Book of Military Quotations*, 2005

p.137: James Edward Austen-Leigh, *A Memoir of Jane Austen to her Nephew*, 1869

p.138: *Notes and Queries*, 28 April 1855

p.140: Frank McLynn, *Napoleon*, 1998

p.141: Sir Archibald Alison, *Lives of Lord Castlereagh and Sir Charles Stewart, the second and third Marquesses of Londonderry*, 1861

p.142: 'History of Medicine after Missolonghi: Julius Millingen', *The Practitioner*, November 1978

p.142: Dr Julius Millingen, *Memoirs of the Affairs of Greece*, 1831, recorded in *Spurgeon's Sermon Notes*

p.146: Alexander Wheelock Thayer, *The Life of Ludwig van Beethoven*, 1921

p.147: Alexander Gilchrist, *Life of William Blake*. 1863

p.148: *Notes and Queries*, 28 April 1855

p.149: Elizabeth Dey Jenkinson Waugh, *Simón Bolívar: A Story of Courage*, 1941

p.150: F.R. Marvin, *The Last Words, Real and Traditional, of Distinguished Men and Women*, 1900

p.154: *Narrative of the Life of Davy Crockett, of the State of Tennessee*, 1834

p.156: Alexandre Dumas, *En Russie*, 1859

p.157: Anne Somerset, *The Life and Times of William IV*, 1980

p.160: Juliet Barker, *The Brontës*, 2001

p.162: James Heney-Skene, *With Lord Stratford in the Crimean War*, 1883

p.163: Elizabeth Gaskell *The Life of Charlotte Brontë*, 1857

p.167: Henry S. Salt, *Life of Henry David Thoreau*, 1896

p.168: J.E. Cooke, M.D. Hodge and J.W. Jones, *Stonewall Jackson: A Military Biography*, 1876

p.169: Earl J. Hess, *Pickett's Charge – The Last Attack at Gettysburg*, 2001, quoted in *Encyclopedia Virginia*

p.170: Marquis James, *The Raven: A Biography of Sam Houston*, 1929

p.172: J. Swanson, *Manhunt*, 2006

p.173: Gene Smith, *American Gothic: the story of America's legendary theatrical family, Junius, Edwin, and John Wilkes Booth*, 1992

p.175: Jasper Ridley, *Lord Palmerston*, 1970

p.178: *The New Grove Dictionary of Music and Musicians*, 2004

p.179: Mary. L. Williamson, *The Life of General Robert E. Lee*, 1895

p.180: John Roberts, *The Life and Explorations of David Livingstone LLD*, 1881

p.181: Rumer Godden, *Hans Christian Andersen*, 1955

p.181: Jackie Wullschlager, *Hans Christian Andersen: The Life of a Storyteller*, 2001

p.182: Charles Windolph, *I fought with Custer: the Story of Sergeant Windolph, last survivor of the Battle of the Little Big Horn, as told to Frazier and Robert Hunt*, 1947

p.185: Helen Langley (ed.), *Benjamin Disraeli, Scenes from an Extraordinary Life*, 2003

p.186: Michael Wallis, *Billy the Kid: The Endless Ride*

p.188: Peter Bushell, *London's Secret History*, 1983

p.190: Eugenia Kaledin, *The Education of Mrs Henry Adams*, 1981

p.191: David M. Jordan, *Winfield Scott Hancock: a Soldier's Life*, 1988

p.192: Martha Dickinson Bianchi, *The Life and Letters of Emily Dickinson*, 1924

p.193: Stuart N. Lake, *Wyatt Earp, Frontier Marshall*, 1931

p.193: Gary L. Roberts, *The Life and Legend of Doc Holliday*, 2006

p.196: John Peter Turner, *The North-West Mounted Police*, 1950

p.197: Jan Hulsker, *The Complete Van Gogh*, 1980

p.200: Vernon Duke, *Listen Here!*, 1963

p.201: Graham Balfour, *The Life of Robert Louis Stevenson*, 1906

p.202: Edwin Palmer Thompson, *William Morris: Romantic to Revolutionary*, 1955

p.202: Edwin Palmer Thompson, *William Morris: Romantic to Revolutionary*, 1955

p.203: Stuart Dodgson Collingwood, *The Life and Letters of Lewis Carroll*, 1899

p.204: Kenneth Baker, *The Faber Book of English History in Verse*, 1988

p.205: Barbara Belford, *Oscar Wilde: A Certain Genius*, 2000

p.206: Olga Knipper, *Memoir*, in Jean Benedetti (ed. and trans.), *Dear Writer, Dear Actress: The Love Letters of Olga Knipper and Anton Chekhov*, 1998 edn

p.207: J. Train, *True Remarkable Occurrences*, 1906

p.210: Mark Twain, *Notebooks*, 1935

p.211: *Oxford Dictionary of National Biography*, 2004

p.212: Professor Charles Alphonso Smith, *O. Henry Biography*, 1916

p.213: Vladimir Chertkov, trans. Benjamin Sher, *O Posledniakh Dniakh L.N. Tolstogo (The Last Days of Leo Tolsty)*, 27 December 1910

p.218: *The Suffragette*, 13 June 1913

p.219: Ambrose Bierce, S.T. Joshi and David E. Schultz, *A Much Misunderstood Man: Selected Letters of Ambrose Bierce*, 2003

p.220: Luigi Albertini, *Origins of the War of 1914*, Vol. II, 1953

p.222: I. Marcosson and D. Frohman, *Charles Frohman*, 1916

p.223: *Account by Reverend H. Stirling Gahan on the Execution of Edith Cavell*, recorded in Charles F. Horne (ed.), *Records of the Great War*, Vol. III, 1923

p.224: Howard Zinn, *A People's History of the United States*, 2001

p.227: A.J. Langguth, *Saki: A Life of Hector Hugh Munro*, 1981

p.228: Russell Warren Howe, *Mata Hari: The True Story*, 1986

p.231: Peter Cottrell, *The Irish Civil War 1922–23*, 2008

p.232: A. Boyle, *The Riddle of Erskine Childers*, 1977

p.234: *Life*, 27 January 1969

p.235: Publisher's note to Franz Kafka, *The Castle*, 1926 (Schocken Books)

p.236: *New York Times*, 18 March 1923

p.238: Steve Starr, 'Remembering Rudolph Valentino', article in

Entertainment Magazine, 31
December 1969
p.239: William Lindsay Gresham
Houdini, The Man Who Walked
Through Walls, 1959
p.241: Mary Desti ,Isadora Duncan's
End, 1929
p.242: Lord Beaverbrook, Men and
Power, 1956
p.243: Selwyn Raab, Five Families:
The Rise, Decline, and Resurgence of
America's Most Powerful Mafia
Empires, 2005
p.244 Tombstone Prospector,
16 August 1910
p.245: Francis Trevelyan Miller,
Thomas A. Edison, Benefactor of
Mankind: The Romantic Life Story of
the World's Greatest Inventor, 1931
p.246: Michael Holroyd, Lytton
Strachey, 1967–68
p.247: An image can be seen on
the eastmanhouse.org website
p.248: Robert Sobel, Coolidge: An
American Enigma, 1998
p.249: Dr Siriol Colley, Gareth
Jones: A Manchukuo Incident, 2001
p.250: T. Harry Williams, Huey
Long, 1969
p.251: Francis Watson, 'The Death
of George V', article in History
Today 36, 1986
p.252: Antonio Machado, Selected
Poems, trans. 1982
p.254: Ron Chernow, Titan: The
Life of John D. Rockefeller, Sr, 1998
p.255: Ric Gillespie, Finding
Amelia: The True Story of the
Earhart Disappearance, 2006
p.256: Newsweek, 15 July 1940
p.257: Elizabeth Nowell (ed.), The
Letters of Thomas Wolfe, 1956
p.258: Time, 23 November 1953
p.259: Peter Gay, Freud: A Life for
Our Time, 1988
p.260: Nathalie Babel Brown (ed.),
Peter Constantine (trans.), The
Complete Works of Isaac Babel, 2005
p.261: Natalia Sedova Trotsky, How
it Happened, 1941
p.262: Robert Self, Neville
Chamberlain: A Biography, 2006
p.264: Richard Ellman, James
Joyce, 1959
p.265: Phyllis Rose, Woman of
Letters: A Life of Virginia Woolf, 1986
p.266: Joe Reichler and Ben Olan,
Baseball's Unforgettable Games,
1960
p.270: Frederick W. Nolan, Lorenz
Hart: A Poet on Broadway, 1994
p.272: B.H. Liddell Hart, The
Rommel Papers, 1953
p.274: Eberhard Bethge, Dietrich
Bonhoeffer: A Biography, 2000
p.275: Conrad Black, Franklin
Delano Roosevelt: Champion of
Freedom, 2003
p.276: Ray Moseley, Mussolini: The

Last 600 Days of Il Duce, 2004
p.278: V.K. Vinogradov et al.,
Hitler's Death: Russia's Last Great
Secret from the Files of the KGB,
2005
p.279: Sara Mayfield, The Constant
Circle: H.L. Mencken and his
Friends, 1968
p.280: Gottfried Hasenkamp,
Heimkehr und Heimgang des
Kardinals, 1946; In memoriam
Clemens August Kardinal von Galen,
Adolf Donders, 1946
p.281: Roy Harrod, The Life of John
Maynard Keynes, 1951
p.282: Alice B. Toklas, What is
Remembered, 1963
p.285: Ed Wellner, The Damon
Runyon Story, 1948
p.286: Vanity Fair, June 1925
p.288: Time, 13 November 1950
p.289: Graham and Heather
Fisher, The Queen's Family, 1982
p.290: Alexandra Kathryn
Mosca, The Enduring Legacy of Eva
Perón, 2001
p.293: The Boston Globe, 5 July
2009
p.294: J.R. Cohen, L.M. Graver,
'The Ruptured Abdominal Aortic
Aneurysm of Albert Einstein',
article in Surgery, Gynaecology &
Obstetrics 170 (5), May 1990
p.295: Alec Guinness, Blessings in
Disguise, 1985
p.296: A.M. Sperber and Eric Lax,
Bogart, 1997
p.297: VH1's Behind the Music
'The Day the Music Died', interview
p.298: Florence Aadland and Tedd
Thomey, The Big Love, 1961
p.298: New York Times, 6 March
1955
p.299: The Spokesman Review,
22 November 1959
p.300: A.E. Hotchner, Papa
Hemingway, 1967
p.302: Guardian, 3 June 1963
p.304: New Yorker, 2 November
1963
p.305: Nellie Connally, From Love
Field: Our Final Hours with
President John F. Kennedy, 2003
p.306: Beatrice Behan, with Des
Hicket and Gus Smith, My Life
with Brendan, 1973
p.308: J. Grigg, Nancy Astor, 1980
p.308: Edward Renehan, 'Joseph
Kennedy and the Jews', History
News Network, 29 April 2002
p.309: New Statesman, 21 February
1964
p.310: New York Times magazine,
1 November 1964
p.312: Leonard Mosley, Disney's
World, 1985
p.314: Vanity Fair, June 1925
p.315: Jon Lee Anderson, Che
Guevara: A Revolutionary Life, 1997

p.317: Jules Witcover, 85 Days: The
Last Campaign of Robert Kennedy,
1969
p.319: Bhau Kalchuri, Meher
Prabhu: Lord Meher, The Biography
of the Avatar of the Age, Meher Baba,
1986
p.321: The Times, 23 September
1970
p.324: William D. Zabel, The Rich
Die Richer and You Can Too, 1996
p.326: Jack Benny and Joan Benny,
Sunday Nights At Seven: The Jack
Benny Story, 1990
p.327: Playboy, December 1975
p.328: Paul Robeson: A Biography,
2007
p.329: Interview with Lawrence
Buser, 19 August 1977,
ElvisPresley.com.au
p.330: Barry Norman, Movie Greats,
1981
p.331: Newsweek, 24 October 1977
p.332: Michael Löwy, The War of the
Gods, 1996
p.333: Robert Fontenot, about.com:
Oldies Music
p.337: Rolling Stone, 21 January
1982
p.340: The Times, 16 November
1983
p.342: Irvin Molotsky, New York
Times, 24 September 1987
p.344: 60 Minutes, 19 April 1958
p.345: Victoria Sun, 16 December
1989
p.346: Arthur Ashe, Days of Grace:
A Memoir, 1993
p.348: William Greider, 'The
McGovern Factor', article in Rolling
Stone, 10 November 1983
p.351: Daily Telegraph, October 1995
p.352: Christopher Andersen, The
Day Diana Died, 1998
p.355: The Times, 5 February 1997
p.359: Hutton Inquiry website
p.363: Rolling Stone, 8 September
2005
p.364: Daily Mail, 29 September
2008
p.366: The Times, 24 November
2006
p.367: CNN Entertainment News,
25 December 2006
p.368: The First Post, 6 September
2007
p.369: The Scotsman, 15 February
2007
p.370: Natasha Stoynoff, 'Show
Will Go On For Heath's Last
Movie', People, 28 January 2008
p.371: Daily Mail, 17 June 2008
p.373: Globe and Mail (Canada),
25 June 2009
p.374: Daily Express, 26 November
2009
p.376: The Times, 16 September
2009

Index

Quercus Publishing Plc
21 Bloomsbury Square
London
WC1A 2NS

First published in 2010

A catalogue record of this book is available from the British Library

UK and associated territories: ISBN 978 1 84916 478 8
USA and associated territories: ISBN 978 1 84866 085 4

All pictures in this book © Topfoto
Text by Terry Breverton
Typeset by Norman Tilley
Index by Patricia Hymans

Printed and bound in China

10 9 8 7 6 5 4 3 2 1